# Modern Caribbean Politics

# Modern Caribbean Politics

*Edited by*
*Anthony Payne and*
*Paul Sutton*

The Johns Hopkins University Press
Baltimore and London

© 1993 The Johns Hopkins University Press
All rights reserved. Published 1993
Printed in the United States of America on acid-free paper

05 04 03 02 01 00 99 98 97 96     6 5 4 3 2

The Johns Hopkins University Press
2715 North Charles Street
Baltimore, Maryland 21218-4319
The Johns Hopkins Press Ltd., London


Library of Congress Cataloging-in-Publication Data

Modern Caribbean politics / edited by Anthony Payne and Paul Sutton.
     p.     cm.
  Includes bibliographical references (p.     ).
  ISBN 0-8018-4434-7. — ISBN 0-8018-4435-5 (pbk.)
  1. Caribbean Area—Politics and government—1945–  I. Payne,
Anthony, 1952–  .  II. Sutton, Paul K.
F2183.M63   1993
320.9729—dc20                                           92-14475


A catalog record for this book is available from the British Library.

*To the memory of*
*Gordon K. Lewis*

# Contents

# Preface

In 1984 we published, under the auspices of Manchester University Press, a book entitled *Dependency under Challenge: The Political Economy of the Commonwealth Caribbean*. Composed of specially commissioned chapters by appropriate academic specialists, the volume reviewed political and economic developments in the Commonwealth Caribbean in the 1970s. It was well enough received, and we were emboldened to seek to produce a successor volume devoted to consideration of the 1980s.

*Modern Caribbean Politics* is the outcome. The formula adopted for this volume has been broadly the same: to cover all the major territories and themes, to organize the book from the standpoint of teaching needs, and to invite specialist scholars in the field of Caribbean studies to write original analyses in their particular areas of expertise. The one change was the decision to widen the scope of the book to cover not just the Commonwealth Caribbean but, rather, the whole of the Caribbean region, with all its intricacies and variations of history and culture. We were delighted by the ready acceptances of the many eminent scholars whom we asked to join us in this venture, and we hope that the final product will serve to introduce students and others to the politics of this fascinating region. We hope too that the arguments contained herein will also contribute something of value to the academic debate about the Caribbean.

A central figure and inspirational presence in much of this debate over a period of many years was Professor Gordon K. Lewis. We were saddened to hear, just before this book went to press, of his death. Gordon was one of the founding fathers of Caribbean studies. His many books on the history, politics, and ideas of the region are major statements of the condition of the Caribbean people.

Both of us date our commitment to the study of the Caribbean to our early reading of *Puerto Rico: Freedom and Power in the Caribbean* (1963) and *The Growth of the Modern West Indies* (1968). Along with his other books, notably *Main Currents in Caribbean Thought: The Historical Evolution of Caribbean Society in Its Ideological Aspects 1492–1900* (1983) and *Grenada: The Jewel Despoiled* (1987), they are landmarks of Caribbean scholarship and set standards that will long be admired. We are honored to dedicate this book to Gordon's memory.

# Abbreviations

| | |
|---|---|
| ACP | African, Caribbean, and Pacific countries |
| BLP | Barbados Labour Party |
| CAIC | Caribbean Association of Industry and Commerce |
| CARIBCAN | Canadian agreement with Commonwealth Caribbean countries |
| CARICOM | Caribbean Community and Common Market |
| CARIFTA | Caribbean Free Trade Association |
| CBI | Caribbean Basin Initiative |
| COMECON | Council for Mutual Economic Assistance |
| DAC | Democratic Action Congress (Trinidad and Tobago) |
| DLP | Democratic Labour Party (Barbados) |
| DOM | département d'outre-mer |
| FDO | Front for Democracy and Development (Suriname) |
| FMLN | Farabundo Marti Front for National Liberation (El Salvador) |
| FSLN | Frente Sandinista de Liberación Nacional (Nicaragua) |
| GATT | General Agreement on Tariffs and Trade |
| GNP | Grenada National Party |
| GULP | Grenada United Labour Party |
| IMF | International Monetary Fund |
| JLP | Jamaica Labour Party |
| KTPI | Indonesian Joint Peasants' Party (Suriname) |
| MBPM | Maurice Bishop Patriotic Movement (Grenada) |
| NAFTA | North American Free Trade Area |
| NAMUCAR | Caribbean Multinational Shipping Company |

| | |
|---|---|
| NAR | National Alliance for Reconstruction (Trinidad and Tobago) |
| NDC | National Democratic Congress (Grenada) |
| NDP | National Democratic Party (Barbados); National Democratic Party (Suriname) |
| NJM | New Jewel Movement; Jewel: Joint Endeavor for Welfare, Education, and Liberation (Grenada) |
| NNP | New National Party (Grenada) |
| NPP | New Progressive Party (Puerto Rico) |
| NPS | National Party of Suriname |
| OAS | Organization of American States |
| OECS | Organization of Eastern Caribbean States |
| OLADE | Latin American Energy Organization |
| ONR | Organization for National Reconstruction (Trinidad and Tobago) |
| OPEC | Organization of Petroleum Exporting Countries |
| PALU | Progressive Labourers and Farmers Union (Suriname) |
| PCC | Cuban Communist Party |
| PCD | Patriotic Coalition for Democracy (Guyana) |
| PDP | Popular Democratic Party (Puerto Rico) |
| PLD | Dominican Liberation Party |
| PNC | People's National Congress (Guyana) |
| PNM | People's National Movement (Trinidad and Tobago) |
| PNP | People's National Party (Jamaica) |
| PPP | People's Progressive Party (Guyana) |
| PR | Reformist Party (Dominican Republic) |
| PRD | Dominican Revolutionary Party |
| PRG | People's Revolutionary Government (Grenada) |
| PRSC | Social Christian Reformist Party (Dominican Republic) |
| RVP | Revolutionary People's Party (Suriname) |
| SCOPE | Standing Conference of Popular Democratic Parties of the Eastern Caribbean |
| TNP | The National Party (Grenada) |
| ULF | United Labour Front (Trinidad and Tobago) |
| UNC | United National Congress (Trinidad and Tobago) |
| UNHRC | United Nations Human Rights Commission |
| USAID | United States Agency for International Development |
| VFB | 25 February Movement (Suriname) |
| VHP | Progressive Reformational Party (Suriname) |
| WPA | Working People's Alliance (Guyana) |

**Modern Caribbean Politics**

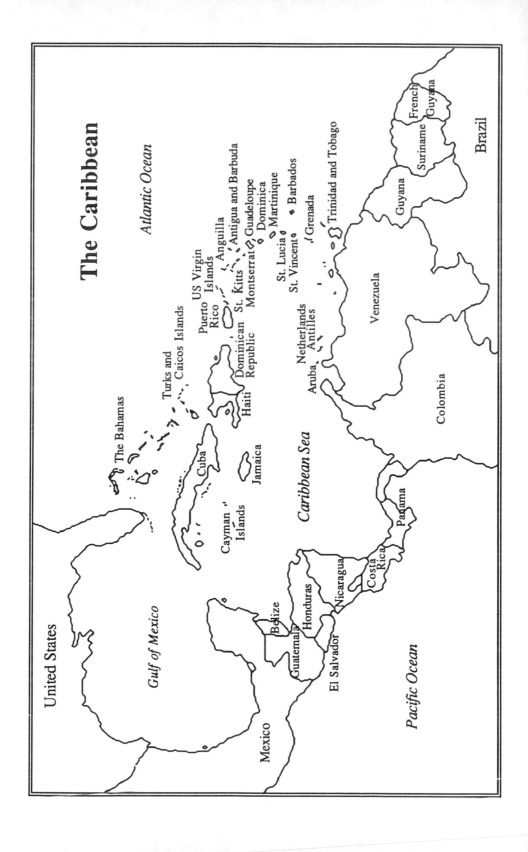

# The Caribbean

*Atlantic Ocean*

United States

*Gulf of Mexico*

The Bahamas

Turks and Caicos Islands

Cuba

Cayman Islands

Jamaica

*Caribbean Sea*

Mexico

Belize

Guatemala

Honduras

El Salvador

Nicaragua

Costa Rica

Panama

*Pacific Ocean*

Haiti

Dominican Republic

Puerto Rico

US Virgin Islands

Anguilla

St. Kitts

Montserrat

Antigua and Barbuda

Guadeloupe

Dominica

Martinique

St. Lucia

St. Vincent

Barbados

Grenada

Trinidad and Tobago

Netherlands Antilles

Aruba

Venezuela

Colombia

Guyana

Suriname

French Guyana

Brazil

# Introduction: The Contours of Modern Caribbean Politics

*Anthony Payne and Paul Sutton*

The Caribbean is defined, above all, by its geography and history. Although that is true, no doubt, of all societies, the point is particularly telling when applied to the Caribbean. In the first place, the physical geography of the region is highly distinctive: the Caribbean is a sea and not a continent. It consists of islands, each characteristically marked by a strong sense of psychological insularity. Water, on the whole, separates more effectively than land, thereby constraining the potential for effective collective action by the islands. At the same time, they are not separated by such great distances that a regional society, with attendant regular movement of peoples between the islands, does not exist. In the second place, the history of the region is also highly distinctive. The Caribbean does not possess cultural foundations dating back thousands of years. Its history is relatively young, 1992 marking only the 500th anniversary of the discovery of the islands by Europe. Yet what followed was searing in its impact, constituting nothing less than the elimination of an indigenous society and the creation of an artificial way of life in the Caribbean based upon the institution of the plantation and the forced importation of slave and indentured labor. These twin forces of geography and history thus shaped the modern Caribbean in the most compelling way.

These two considerations also establish the boundaries of the Caribbean although not in a straightforward or consensual fashion. They have to be blended to achieve that effect. From a simple geographical viewpoint, the Caribbean constitutes all the islands in the Caribbean Sea. They make up a huge archipelago, which runs some 2,500 miles from the southern tip of Florida in the north to the coast of Venezuela in the south, facing Central America to the west and the Atlantic Ocean to the east. The archipelago is

1

composed of two groups of islands, the Greater and Lesser Antilles. The Greater Antilles comprises the four relatively large islands of Cuba, Jamaica, Puerto Rico, and Hispaniola, which is now divided politically between the states of Haiti and the Dominican Republic. The Lesser Antilles curves from the Virgin Islands in the north to Barbados and Trinidad and Tobago in the south, and includes all the intervening Leeward and Windward Islands: namely, the English-speaking territories of St. Kitts–Nevis, Anguilla, Antigua-Barbuda, Montserrat, Dominica, St. Lucia, St. Vincent, and Grenada; the French possessions of Martinique and Guadeloupe; and three of the Dutch islands that partly make up the Netherlands Antilles—St. Eustatius, Saba, and St. Maarten. Also generally included within this geographical definition of the Caribbean are a few other very small islands: the Turks and Caicos Islands to the north of Hispaniola, the Cayman Islands to the west of Jamaica, and the remaining islands of the Netherlands Antilles—Aruba, Bonaire, and Curaçao—which lie off the Venezuelan coast.

From this point onward, however, problems of inclusion and exclusion begin to arise, even in geographical terms. By virtue of being a chain of islands adjacent to the main archipelago, the Bahamas is sometimes considered part of the Caribbean, but it is often treated only as a marginal member of the region.

The geographical approach is sometimes extended to include all those territories whose shores are washed by the Caribbean Sea: by this measure, the region would include the Yucatan province of Mexico, Belize, Honduras, Guatemala, Nicaragua, Costa Rica, Panama, Colombia, and Venezuela. This wider notion of the Caribbean basin, which does have its own geographical plausibility, has enjoyed considerable popularity in certain political circles, especially in the United States during the Reagan era. From this perspective, it captured the boundaries of a region deemed ripe for revolution and in which fundamental U.S. security interests were at stake. The notion of the Caribbean Basin cannot, therefore, be ignored: it shaped U.S. policy toward the islands for a number of years at a critical time. Overall, however, the effect is to lump together the Caribbean and Central America in a way that is artificial in anything other than geopolitical terms. This is made clear by the reintroduction of some historical considerations.

As already indicated, most of the islands of the Caribbean have been literally forged out of the mold of imperialism. They still bear many of the scars of their experience of slavery. This gives them a particular identity and separates them in important ways from many of their neighbors. The Central American countries have never had their entire societies reconstructed according to the demands of imperialism, even though, like the Dominican Republic and Cuba, they suffered the consequences of Spanish conquest. Historically, they have never looked toward a Caribbean destiny, and even now few of their centers of population lie on the Caribbean coast. The one notable exception to this is Belize, formerly British Honduras. In 1862, after the early exploitation of its forests by Spanish settlers, it became a British colony and, thereafter, had much in common with other British Crown Colonies in the Caribbean. These political and administrative links usually cause Belize to be considered a Caribbean country.

In a similar way, the question of historical experience also demands the inclusion of other countries not embraced by the geographical method. These are the territories of the three Guianas: the former British territory of Guyana, the former Dutch territory of Suriname, and the French territory of French Guiana, or Guyane. Their shoreline is the Atlantic, not the Caribbean, and they belong to the continent of South America. Yet their history is similar to that of the islands of the Caribbean; they have suffered the experience of plantation economy, and they too have long considered themselves Caribbean territories.

Thus geography and history provide the most satisfactory demarcation of the Caribbean, namely, the Greater and Lesser Antilles and other islands in the Caribbean Sea, with the addition of Belize and the three "enclave" territories of the Guianas.[1] Conceived in this way, the region possesses an intellectual coherence that makes it possible to analyze the modern politics of the Caribbean within a single framework, and that is the task to which this volume is devoted.

The remainder of this introduction seeks to establish the necessary background to the contributions of the many distinguished scholars of the Caribbean, which constitute the bulk of the text. First, it explores further some of the features of the imperial experience of the Caribbean, which continue to leave their mark on the political life of the region; second, it locates the beginnings of modern Caribbean politics in the post–Second World War era and describes the main contours of the politics of the 1950s and 1960s; third, it examines the "crisis years" of the 1970s, when new ideas and political forms seemed for a while as if they might radicalize and reshape much of the Caribbean; and, finally, it sets out the key themes of regional politics in the decade of the 1980s, the elaboration of which is the specific purpose of the book and the responsibility of the succeeding chapters.

## The Imperial Mold

The broad impact of imperialism upon the Caribbean was not only formative: it set in motion an important and enduring contradiction between a legacy of political fragmentation, on the one hand, and economic uniformity, on the other. From the outset, political conflicts were imposed on the region, conflicts that derived solely from the rivalry and competition for power of leading European states. Following its discovery by Columbus in 1492, the region was dominated for more than a century by Spain, a period of hegemony that shaped the character of countries such as Cuba, Puerto Rico, and the Dominican Republic. In the seventeenth century, Spanish power was challenged by British, French, and Dutch colonizers. Uninhabited islands were claimed for one or another of the European powers, and some inhabited ones, such as Jamaica, were seized from Spain. A period of intermittent warfare between the European powers followed throughout the eighteenth century, during which many of the smaller islands, such as Grenada and St. Lucia, changed hands several times in accordance with the ebb and flow of the fighting.

The conferences that brought wars to an end exacerbated the process, as Caribbean islands were again regularly swapped between the powers as the currency of victory or defeat. Indeed, for over half a century, from approximately 1760 to 1815, the Caribbean was one of the main areas of the world in which intra-European conflicts and power struggles were pursued. Moreover, by the end of the nineteenth century, the emerging power of the United States was beginning also to bear upon the region; in 1898, at the end of the Spanish-American War, when it acquired effective control of Cuba and Puerto Rico, the United States joined the ranks of those imperial powers that had a direct territorial stake in the Caribbean.

The consolidation of imperial rule following these struggles further entrenched the divisions established during the initial phase of conquest. Each territory was administered in accordance with the practice of its particular imperial master. Across the Caribbean, different legal and governmental systems were thus established in different languages within different cultures. The colonial tradition was mostly autocratic, with local legislative councils, where they existed, having only limited powers to shape policy.

Lines of communication and protest were conventionally directed toward the metropolitan capital rather than to other parts of the region. The European powers in general made little effort to bring about a sense of unity among their possessions in the area. British colonial administration, for example, was marked by occasional attempts to achieve a closer union between Britain's Caribbean possessions, chiefly for reasons of economy, but it never displayed a consistent concern for this question and certainly gave no thought to cooperation with other regional states beyond its imperial domain. As a result, all the territories of the region developed parochial political cultures beyond even the call of their natural insularity.

By contrast, the economic impact was broadly similar across the region. This uniformity resides in the fact, noted by sociologist Malcolm Cross, that all the countries of the region have either "had to, or still have to, come to terms with the uniquely New World experience of being dependent suppliers of tropical primary products for Western European or North American markets."[2] Their economies were formed, above all, as appendages of European metropoles in the era of mercantilist expansion. The metropole provided organization, decision making, capital, transport, supplies, markets, and even slaves transplanted from Africa, relegating the Caribbean to the mere locus of production. The local economy thus came to be composed predominantly of a plantation sector, exporting a single crop—sugar—in largely unprocessed form to European markets.

In the middle of the nineteenth century, the ending of slavery and the loss of preferences, particularly in the British market, seriously undermined the Caribbean plantation economy in the established sugar islands such as Barbados and Jamaica but did not cause its complete collapse. The plantation sector was rationalized everywhere, many estates and factories were consolidated, and inefficient ones fell into disuse. In Haiti, the system effectively came to an end. However, in other parts of the region, notably in the underpopulated territories of Trinidad and Guyana, the introduction of indentured labor from India, China, Portugal, and elsewhere shored up the plantation sector for another century or so. More important, though, was the emergence at this time of a new feature of the regional economy—a peasant class, consisting largely of former slaves growing food for themselves and their families as well as for the domestic market and, later in the century, pioneering the production of new export crops, like bananas, cocoa, coffee, and spices. The growth of this sector was given additional impetus in the last years of the nineteenth century by the long depression in sugar prices caused by the subsidization of beet growing in Europe.

The first half of the twentieth century witnessed further diversifications, but no major transformation, of the plantation inheritance. The economies of all Caribbean countries continued to remain dependent on their agriculture sectors, as means to both generate work and acquire foreign exchange. The plantations also tended to remain dominant within the agricultural sector, especially in the export sphere. Increasingly bought up by transnational corporations during the first decades of the century, they controlled the greatest proportion of land, and the best quality land at that, although still often remaining inefficient in production. For their part, peasants usually owned the majority of the farms in most Caribbean economies, but their holdings were typically small, often less than five acres. Nevertheless, the emergence of a peasantry did have the effect of firmly establishing as an essential part of the value system of the Caribbean the attraction of owning a piece of land. This turned out to be not the least important of the many legacies left behind by the imperial era.

## THE BEGINNINGS OF MODERN POLITICS

Modern politics in the Caribbean has been about nationalism. That is to say, it has been concerned with the achievement of political independence by the various colonies, with the pursuit of a measure of national economic independence consonant with that status, and with the necessity of coming to terms with the international system brought about by statehood. These have been the characteristic themes of the politics of the whole of the region ever since the end of the Second World War. It is important to note, however, that the nationalist movement has its roots in earlier times. Indeed, it was initiated in Haiti as long ago as the 1790s, when several slave leaders, most famously Toussaint L'Ouverture, took advantage of the turmoil generated by the French Revolution to launch a rebellion, which led to the declaration of Haitian independence from France in 1804. The Dominican Republic and Cuba also gained their independence (from Spain) in the nineteenth century—in 1844 and 1898, respectively—the latter struggle having been inspired by the nationalism of José Martí. Both countries, however, had to pass through long periods of effective U.S. control before independence came to have any meaning. In the English-speaking Caribbean, the advent of nationalist politics came much later, growing out of the depressed economic conditions of the 1930s. The first outbreak of popular violence occurred in 1935 in St. Kitts, from where the wave of protest spread over the next two years to Trinidad, Jamaica, St. Lucia, St. Vincent, British Guiana, and Barbados. In almost all of these territories, new nationalist parties subsequently emerged, committed to the enactment of a wider franchise and the eventual attainment of self-government.

The British government took the measure of the new tide of Caribbean nationalism and, from 1944 onward, began to guide its colonies toward greater self-government via a careful process of schooling, beginning with the grant of universal adult suffrage and followed by further constitutional concessions as and when Britain deemed each territory to be ready. Nevertheless, the process of decolonization was not as smooth as planned. In 1953, in British Guiana, the first popularly elected government was ejected from office after a mere 133 days on the unconvincing grounds that its leader, Dr. Cheddi Jagan, had embarked on the creation of a monolithic communist state. In 1962, in an even more damaging interruption of British plans, the West Indies Federation, which had brought together all the other British possessions in the region in an attempt to forge a unitary West Indian state, was dissolved after just four years of existence, crippled by bitter inter-island bickering. Virtually by default, British policy henceforth became one of granting political independence to its Caribbean colonies more or less when they asked for it. The four largest territories—Jamaica, Trinidad and Tobago, Barbados, and British Guiana—thus became independent between 1962 and 1966, the latter as Guyana. The concept of Associated Statehood (which granted internal self-government but preserved external and defense responsibilities in Britain's hands) was created in 1967 only because the islands of the Leewards and Windwards could not be persuaded to come together within an Eastern Caribbean federation and were still thought, at the time, to be too small to be viable as independent entities. The larger independent states all joined the British Commonwealth and, in a demonstration of their new postcolonial status, increasingly preferred to designate themselves members of the Commonwealth Caribbean.

In contrast with Britain, the other remaining imperial powers in the Caribbean—France, the Netherlands, and the United States—took different approaches to decolonization. In 1946, in keeping with the assimilationist philosophy that underlay French colonial administration, the French possessions in the Caribbean—Martinique, Guadeloupe, and Guyane—were incorporated into the metropolitan state as overseas departments (*départements d'outre-mer*, or DOMs), with their citizens having the same rights as any other French person. The Dutch reacted to the post–Second World War pressure to decolonize in a similar way, establishing in 1954 the so-called Tripartite Kingdom of the Netherlands, which linked Holland with the Netherlands Antilles and Suriname. For its part, the United States also sought to extend self-government to its two Caribbean colonies after the end of the Second World War. The Virgin Islands were granted a measure of internal autonomy in 1954 but still remained a U.S. external territory, with defense and external relations handled from Washington. Puerto Rico, on the other hand, was allowed to choose a novel constitutional arrangement by means of which, from 1952 onward, the territory was styled a commonwealth, or *estado libre asociado*—"a state which is free of superior authority in the management of its own local affairs,"[3] while remaining in association with the United States. This meant that Puerto Ricans could travel freely to and from the United States, enjoy the benefits of the U.S. social security system, participate in its currency and customs area, but could not take responsibility for their country's defense or foreign relations. On this basis, the U.S. government succeeded in persuading the United Nations General Assembly to remove Puerto Rico from its list of remaining colonies, at least for a time.

What emerged from the complex pattern of Caribbean decolonization was, of course, a political landscape still deeply marked by fragmentation. Each imperial power can be said to have done it its way. As a result, the region came to constitute the "crazy patchwork quilt" described by Gordon Lewis.[4] Different levels of constitutional advance and different external connections inevitably and repeatedly impeded collective action and even understanding. It also meant that several major external powers continued to have a constitutional foot in the region, which thus gave a measure of legitimacy to what might otherwise have been more widely condemned as outside intervention. Nor was that all: because of the nationalist character of political development in the region, divergent political traditions were maintained and, indeed, strengthened. Intellectuals and some more farsighted political leaders, such as C. L. R. James and Eric Williams of Trinidad and Tobago and Juan Bosch in the Dominican Republic, may have been able to identify a common political culture across the region, but it eluded most other participants in Caribbean politics at this time.[5]

The Westminster tradition of parliamentary government, inherited and substantially absorbed by most Commonwealth Caribbean countries, was sharply at odds with the more autocratic political mores passed on to Cuba and the Dominican Republic by Spain. The insertion into the French Caribbean of the major political parties and debates of metropolitan France was another strand serving to cut these territories off from their neighbors and, thus, rendering a figure such as Aimé Césaire of Martinique of perhaps greater significance to French politics than to Caribbean politics. Notwithstanding the genuine pan-Caribbean vision of its governor during much of the early postwar period (Muñoz Marín), Puerto Rico was similarly separated from the regional mainstream by its special status. And as for Haiti, the prevailing view, certainly in the Commonwealth Caribbean, was concerned in maintaining its isolation for fear that, somehow, the Haitian virus of authoritarianism would spread and infect healthier parts of the regional body politic. There was also, of course, the dramatic event of the revolution in Cuba in 1959, which introduced Marxist-Leninist ideas and practices into Caribbean political life and, in so doing, created a barrier around Cuba, which proved to be costly and difficult to dismantle. In other words, it is almost impossible to exaggerate the reality and the depth of the fractures entrenched in modern Caribbean politics during its formative nationalist phase.

These divisions were not much ameliorated, either, by the fact that nearly all Caribbean governments, in both the independent and nonindependent territories, faced similar economic problems at the end of the Second World War. Although these generally derived from the common legacy of the plantation economy, the responses of the governments were unavoidably conditioned by the fact of separate statehood. The achievement, even the prospect, of political independence served to create the further expectation on the part of the various peoples that economic improvements would follow. Governments everywhere were thus put under considerable pressure to deliver material benefits in the way of jobs, welfare, and advanced living standards. This was imperative if they were to win elections (as in the Commonwealth Caribbean) or to entrench the revolution (as in Cuba) but also if they were merely to maintain social order (as, say, in the Dominican Republic under the dictatorial Trujillo regime). The result was that, across the region, the response was broadly the same: to seek to develop by diversifying the national economy and by overcoming the traditional problems of dependence on monoculture.

In some Caribbean territories, the emergence of more modern export industries located in the mineral sector was the first sign of this new developmental thrust. Trinidad began to take advantage of its position as the only Caribbean country to possess significant reserves of oil and gas, and Aruba and Curaçao in the Netherlands Antilles, Puerto Rico, the Bahamas, and St. Croix in the U.S. Virgin Islands all became substantial refiners of imported oil in this period. Jamaica, Guyana, Suriname, Haiti, and the Dominican Republic produced bauxite, the ore from which aluminium is made, and ferronickel was mined in both Cuba and the Dominican Republic. However, these industries were all initially developed by foreign corporations, which limited their contribution to the economic development of the Caribbean. For example, as a consequence of foreign ownership, the lucrative processing of bauxite was undertaken only on a fairly limited scale. All these industries tended also to be highly capital intensive, the entire Caribbean bauxite industry being reckoned to employ no more than twenty-thousand people. Although these mineral industries often came to dominate a country's exports, they generally made little contribution to job formation. Indeed, their effect on employment was in one sense negative: the high wage rates paid in the new mineral sectors tended to raise the reserve price of labor and thus encourage people to leave low-paid agricultural employment in order to join the ranks of the urban unemployed.

In these circumstances, the panacea most widely adopted in the Caribbean in the postwar period as a means of providing the necessary new employment was the promotion of manufacturing. Puerto Rico was the pioneer, with its policy, labeled Operation Bootstrap, of attracting foreign companies to establish manufacturing plants on the island by offering tax and investment incentives. During the 1950s, this strategy of "industrialisation by invitation"[6] was copied by Jamaica and Trinidad and, subsequently, by nearly all the countries of the area. It worked to the extent that foreign capital responded and flowed into the Caribbean in substantial amounts, bringing in its wake a number of highly visible manufacturing industries. The contribution made to gross domestic product by manufacturing rose quickly to over 25 percent in Puerto Rico and some 15–20 percent in the larger Commonwealth Caribbean territories. However, the industries established were largely "final-touch" enterprises, based upon the assembly of imported inputs, which had relatively little value added and generally failed to penetrate export markets. They produced few jobs and were often itinerant in their commitment to the Caribbean, finding it profitable, once the incentive plan had expired, to move their operations to other locales offering a new package of inducements. Haiti, the Dominican Republic, and some of the smaller Commonwealth Caribbean islands benefited from firms moving on from Puerto Rico and even Jamaica, but the Caribbean economy as a whole lost.

The other new industry into which the Caribbean moved in a major way in the first part of the postwar era was tourism. In some territories, this was heralded, even more than manufacturing, as the road to prosperity, especially after the Cuban revolution took out of the market one hitherto favored tourist destination. Although tourism was developed most extensively in the larger and more northern Caribbean islands closest to the American market, such as Puerto Rico and Jamaica, it quickly also became critical to the economies of some of the smallest islands. Barbados, the Bahamas, the Netherlands Antilles, Antigua, and St. Lucia all moved into this category. However, the trouble with tourist development was that it was extremely vulnerable to recession in the developed economies and to bad publicity at any time. In the particular case of the Caribbean, where the industry was geared to a particularly affluent sector of North American and European society, it was able to compete only by maintaining the highest standards of accommodation and hospitality. This meant that foreign capital and foreign imports, especially of food, underwrote the tourist industry, producing the diseconomies of inflated import bills and extensive profit repatriation. To a considerable extent, therefore, the industry became an enclave within the Caribbean economy, having few linkages with, and contributing little to, the development of other sectors.

These various attempts to diversify the Caribbean economy were generally quite successful in the 1950s and 1960s in the single matter of engendering economic growth. Several territories, notably Puerto Rico, Jamaica, Trinidad, and the Bahamas, grew at an annual rate of about 5 percent during this period, which is, conventionally speaking, a good economic performance. These apparent successes should not, however, conceal either the fixed constraint upon long-term economic viability represented by the small size of most Caribbean territories or the many social problems of development that were not removed from the face of the regional economy by the growth of a few countries. Indeed, in the Commonwealth Caribbean it was officially admitted that, in many essential respects, the postwar era of fast growth represented only "a continuation of the centuries-old pattern of West Indian economy; growth without development; growth accompanied by imbalances and distortions; growth generated from outside rather than within."[7] The structure of postwar development strategy also served to exacerbate divisions within the region. Caribbean economies were unavoidably competitor economies: they produced broadly the same commodities, they wanted to attract the same foreign investors, and they appealed to the same would-be tourists. There were, then, from the outset clear limits to the potential complementarity of the national economic policies being followed across the region.

The same inclination to think nationally rather than regionally became apparent when Caribbean states turned to address the matter of international relations. Of course, for almost the first two decades after 1945, only Haiti, the Dominican Republic, and Cuba were able to pursue their own foreign policies. In opening relations with the Soviet Union in the aftermath of the revolution of 1959, the latter laid down the most fundamental challenge to the United States as the dominant regional power. The U.S. response, which included attempted diplomatic isolation, support for a disastrous invasion of the island by antirevolutionary exiles at the Bay of Pigs in 1961, and ultimately an economic boycott, left no part of the region in any doubt as to U.S. determination to prevent any more "Cubas." The point was again made clear in 1965, when the United States, fearing a communist takeover, sent U.S. marines to the Dominican Republic to prevent the return to power of a moderate nationalist government under Juan Bosch, who had briefly been president in 1963 in the confusing aftermath of Trujillo's assassination two years earlier. In other words, the geopolitical context in which the new independent states of the Commonwealth Caribbean emerged onto the international scene in the 1960s was one of unrelenting U.S. hegemony over the region, qualified only by the delegation of authority to the original European powers over territories for which they had either once been or were still responsible.

Cuba apart, the fact is that no Caribbean state made any sustained attempt to challenge this pattern of international relations in the 1950s and 1960s. Indeed, few sought to pursue an active foreign policy of any kind, the major exception being Guyana, which was motivated mainly by the need to make friends quickly in the face of a Venezuelan claim upon a substantial part of its land area. On achieving independence, the Jamaican government of Alexander Bustamante let it be known that it was "with the West,"[8] and the Trinidad and Tobago government swiftly backed away from an earlier challenge to the existence of the U.S. base on its territory at Chaguaramas. In the Commonwealth Caribbean as a whole, some steps were taken to recreate the basis for greater regional integration, and the Caribbean Free Trade Association (CARIFTA) was established in 1968. But no reference was made to foreign policy in the goals of the organization, so the initiative needs to be understood mainly as a device to overcome some of the constraints imposed by small size on the import-substitution industrialization being essayed across the region. In short, Caribbean states were generally hesitant to take up the external opportunities afforded by their acquisition of sovereignty.

## The "Crisis Years" of the 1970s

The 1970s marked a new phase in Caribbean politics; they have often been referred to as years of crisis, and with some justice. As the decade unfolded, several countries in the region began to search around for new strategies of development and new models of political organization. No clear pattern and no precise direction of change emerged, although the broad trend was to reject the traditional order. For example, in Guyana in 1970 the government of Forbes Burnham declared its commitment to "co-operative socialism"; in Jamaica in 1974, the Michael Manley administration announced its attachment to the principles of "democratic socialism"; while in the Eastern Caribbean the basic contradictions underpinning the notion of Associated Statehood were becoming increasingly unmanageable, and a renewed process of decolonization was initiated by the granting of independence to Grenada in 1974, Dominica in 1978, and St. Lucia and St. Vincent in 1979. Most dramatically of all, in March 1979 in Grenada, the corrupt regime of Eric Gairy was overthrown by force, and the People's Revolutionary Government was set up to popular acclaim. This constituted the first successful revolution in the history of the Commonwealth Caribbean. Cuba at last had a revolutionary partner in the Caribbean, and the region's new reputation for instability seemed to be fully justified.

What was happening? Contrary to the many oversimplistic interpretations immediately advanced in the United States and elsewhere, these changes did not all derive from the inspiration of ideology, and they certainly did not represent the victory, real or prospective, of communism, socialism, or any other variant of left-wing thinking. What actually characterized the Caribbean in the 1970s was a search, largely open-ended, for some better alternative to the traditional policies and practices of the past. New and radical ideas were abroad, and some governments were prepared to listen and be persuaded; new friends, both inside and outside the region, were also making their entreaties, and once more some governments were ready to open up new avenues along which trade, investment, and political cooperation could be pursued. The impression was thus given that Caribbean politics were in a ferment, whereas in the end rather less was changed than perhaps many had expected and some had hoped.

The emergence of more independent states onto the regional political scene was not of itself a point of departure. It is true that these latest members of the sovereign club were smaller (Grenada is just 133 square miles in area and had a population in 1974 of only some 110,000 inhabitants) and were long thought to have been unviable as independent units. Yet they were able to survive and operate in an international system in which several institutions had come into existence to sustain small, vulnerable states. This was something which, in fact, Eric Gairy grasped earlier than most when he observed that "independence will support Grenada, the people of Grenada do not have to support independence."[9] A non-English speaking territory also gained independence for the first time in the postwar era when, in 1975, Suriname parted company with the Netherlands. There was also some evidence of dissatisfaction with commonwealth status in Puerto Rico, where it was possible to detect the embryonic emergence of an *independentista* politics (although, paradoxically, there was also growing support for the option of statehood within the United States), and there were even a few signs of nationalist dissent in the French territories of Martinique and Guadeloupe. However, in none of these latter cases was there any real likelihood of a political crisis about status.

The argument in Caribbean politics in the 1970s was primarily focused upon the appropriate political economy of development to be pursued by the governments of the independent states. This debate was shaped by growing awareness of the structural deficiencies of the so-called Puerto Rican model, which had been so widely followed, but was given new urgency by the severe economic difficulties created across the region by the massive oil price rises of 1973–4. With the exception of Trinidad and Tobago, every other country was faced with hugely increased import bills, which they were unable to meet with their earnings from commodity exports and light manufacturing industries. In this situation, the validity of the orthodox model of free-enterprise development came increasingly under question, and in a number of countries, the state was pushed into a position of greater involvement in the management of the economy. The thinking generally was that the various countries of the region had to negotiate better terms for themselves in their dealings with the international economy and that the state, rather than the local bourgeoisie, had to assume responsibility for executing that task. In terms of political economy, the process was encapsulated in the title of the predecessor volume to this one: *Dependency under Challenge.*[10]

This shift of development strategy had no necessary implications for the political practice of the region. It was consistent in the Commonwealth Caribbean with the continuance of the Westminster model; indeed, it derived some of its inspiration from British and European social democracy and was specifically defended by Michael Manley in Jamaica as "a third path" for the region, signifying a rejection of both the Puerto Rican and Cuban models of development.[11] Nevertheless, it cannot be denied that the new radicalism in the region did also, in part, reflect the appeal of the impressive social gains made in Cuba since the revolution of 1959. Encouraged by what it saw as a shift to the left in Caribbean politics in the early 1970s, the Castro regime made itself available to governments, such as those in Guyana, Jamaica, and later Grenada, that were ready to establish close working relationships. Certainly, Castro and Maurice Bishop, the new Grenadian leader after 1979, built up a remarkable rapport, and Cuba in effect sustained the whole revolutionary process in that island . As it turned out, the Grenadian revolution was genuine in its endeavor to break with the capitalist liberal-democratic model, and it needs to be set alongside Cuba. For the rest, the "co-operative socialism" of the Burnham regime in Guyana sought only the entrenchment in power by ever more unpleasant means of the ruling party elite, and the "democratic socialism" of the Manley government in Jamaica stepped back when it reached the bounds of reformism. The challenge to dependency was seriously mounted only in Cuba and Grenada, and in the latter case, tentatively. In general, the much vaunted ideological pluralism of the Caribbean in the 1970s concealed only different techniques for "living with dependency."[12]

What was real, however, during the decade was the revival of the region's historical role as a cockpit of international competition. The various experiments in new forms of political economy occurred at a time when a measure of space had opened up in the international relations of the area. Following the traumas of Vietnam and Watergate, the Carter administration, which came into office in Washington at the beginning of 1977, sought to abandon the traditional U.S. hegemonic approach to the Caribbean in favor of a more tolerant, respectful, and supportive stance. As part of that new formula, neighboring middle powers, such as Mexico and Venezuela, themselves newly enriched by the rise in the price of oil, were encouraged by the United States to engage more in Caribbean affairs. Cuba was, of course, active diplomatically for its own reasons. On the other hand, Britain and the Netherlands were thought to be withdrawing from direct influence in the area, the European Community increasingly assuming some, at least, of their former responsibilities in matters of trade and aid. All of this added up to a geopolitical context of unprecedented fluidity in the postwar Caribbean.

In these circumstances, Caribbean states were drawn fully into international politics as independent actors for the first time in their history. Leaders like Manley, Burnham, Bishop, and par excellence, Castro marched the region into the Third World and the embrace of organizations like the Group of 77 and the Non-Aligned Movement. Clear positions of support were enunciated for the concept of a New International Economic Order, for the liberation of South Africa, and for the establishment of closer ties with the leading states of Latin America. This last matter was peculiarly problematic, for as much as they were all part of the Americas, most independent Caribbean countries (except, obviously, the two major Spanish-speaking states) were divorced by culture and language from mainland Latin America. The first attempts to overcome these barriers were thus fraught with difficulties, Venezuela finding itself denounced by the Trinidad government for its putative recolonization of the region in the mid-1970s, and Mexico drawing widespread critical comment for its vacillating policy.

Nevertheless, several Commonwealth Caribbean states did join Cuba, the Dominican Republic, and the other leading Latin American nations in such regional bodies as the Latin American Economic System, the Latin American Energy Organization (OLADE), and the Caribbean Multinational Shipping Company (NAMUCAR), all formed during the 1970s. Prompted largely by the need to negotiate new trade and aid agreements with the European Community following Britain's entry into that organization in 1973, Commonwealth Caribbean states also extended their own regional integration process in the same year. The new Caribbean Community and Common Market (CARICOM) did include foreign policy coordination as one of its goals, which was a significant advance on the format of CARIFTA. But apart from the relatively successful conclusion of talks about association with the European Community at Lomé in 1975, the instances of joint action being taken on major matters of international concern to Commonwealth Caribbean states were initially few, and certainly no priority was attached to the possibility of widening CARICOM to include the whole region.

## The New Themes of the 1980s

The 1980s were different again from the 1970s. Caribbean politics continued to focus upon the basic themes of the nationalist era: political development, economic development, and international relations. But what was new and intimidating about the 1980s was the extent to which the options open to Caribbean states in all these spheres were overlaid, almost overwhelmed, by the interests and actions of the United States. The context was not just the resumption of a "strong" U.S. foreign policy in the aftermath of the "weaknesses" deemed to have been displayed during the liberal phase of the Carter presidency; it was nothing less than the promotion by the United States of a worldview derived from trenchant ideological positions.

According to C. W. Kegley and E. R. Wittkopf, this "new right" view, as one might call it, embraced at heart three fundamental postulates.[13] The first was that the United States had to accept responsibility for the direction of international affairs and had, therefore, to be prepared to project U.S. power abroad more actively. The Caribbean was to constitute a secure base from which this could be done. The second component was the belief that communism was the principal danger facing the free world and had to be resisted by the United States with all the means at its disposal. For the Caribbean, as for other parts of the Third World, this meant that the causes of change lay less in the deprivations induced by underdevelopment and more in the subversive appeal of the communist ideology. The third element was the simple belief that, since the Soviet Union was the spearhead of the communist challenge, U.S. foreign policy must be dedicated, above all else, to containing the expansion of Soviet influence. In the context of the Caribbean, this drew attention to Cuba and Grenada and required that the model of political and economic development they represented be comprehensively undermined.

The Reagan administration, which held office in Washington between 1981 and 1989—virtually spanning the decade—was driven by precisely these ideas. What is more, the Caribbean and Central America, which the Reagan administration treated from the outset as constituent parts of the newly designated Caribbean Basin, were initially chosen to demonstrate the effectiveness of this new approach. In execution, the power of the policy stemmed in part from its simplicity but also from its capacity to integrate political, economic, and military activities within a single ideological framework. Indeed, it is not too much of an exaggeration to suggest that, under Reagan, the United States progressively succeeded in reshaping the agenda of Caribbean politics to the point where, in almost every arena, it was able to lay down the parameters of what could be done and even what could be thought. New themes thus came to dominate each of the main contours of political debate in the region in the 1980s, notably the emphasis attached to "democracy" as a political mechanism, the need for "structural adjustment" on the economic front, and the priority given to "security" in international relations.

The focus of political development in the Caribbean certainly shifted during the decade from the previous preoccupation with status to the actual substance of political life in the postindependence era. The Reagan administration laid down the principle of support for democracy as the moral basis of its anticommunist crusade in the region and thereby set a standard against which the entire region could be assessed. It was a clever device. It did not matter that the U.S. State Department was quite prepared to admit that support for democracy helpfully reconciled "the conflict that often arises between U.S. strategic interests and the need to give moral substance to whatever policy serves those interests,"[14] or that the official U.S. definition of democracy as the existence of free and fair elections was narrow and superficial. The theme of democracy was repeatedly highlighted by President Reagan himself and appeared ritualistically in every statement made about the region (and Latin America as a whole) by the Secretary of State, the Assistant Secretary of State for Inter-American Affairs, and other administration officials. All Caribbean states were therefore unavoidably hoist on the petard raised by Washington, regardless of their diverse political histories.

On the whole, the Commonwealth Caribbean states came through the test well enough. During the 1980s, there were transitions from one political party to another in Jamaica, Barbados, Trinidad and Tobago, and Belize, as well as several other fiercely but freely contested elections in the smaller Eastern Caribbean states. Grenada was forcefully returned to democracy following the extraordinary self-destruction of the revolution and the ensuing U.S. invasion of the island in October 1983, and Guyana was increasingly pressed to reform its corrupt political system following Burnham's death in 1985. However, by U.S. standards, the performance of the rest of the region was more mixed. The Dominican

Republic nearly succumbed to military intervention in 1978, when early election results showed the Dominican Revolutionary Party (PRD) in the lead, and the army had to be restrained by President Carter; but the Dominican Republic subsequently experienced open, competitive elections. Haiti also profited from the democratic impulse underlying U.S. policy when backing was at last withdrawn from Jean-Claude Duvalier at the height of extensive antiregime protests in 1986—although whether the United States subsequently did all that it could to support the fledgling pro-democratic forces in Haiti is highly questionable. Suriname, for its part, proceeded in the opposite direction of entrenched militarization following the initial coup of February 1980, the restoration of parliamentary politics after eight years scarcely weakening the real power of the military. This left, and still leaves, just Cuba, which was endlessly excoriated in Washington for its rejection of free elections, its alleged human rights abuses, and its reluctance even to countenance the type of democratic reforms being introduced in the Soviet Union itself.

Nevertheless, from the U.S. perspective, the trend was clear: the 1980s was "a period of deepening democratic experience and growth" in the Caribbean.[15] At a certain level, the claim can be sustained. Driven forward by U.S. pressure and active intervention, most Caribbean states saw the need to organize their politics on an open, electoral basis. Regardless of the intrinsic merits of such a system, which are of course considerable, this was the price of acceptability in Washington. Only Haiti was allowed special dispensation by the United States, the case for which in the future was clearly weakened by the army's overthrow of the elected government of the radical Roman Catholic priest, Jean-Bertrand Aristide, in September 1991. At a deeper level of analysis, however, awkward questions about the quality of Caribbean democracy still arose. The limits of democratic leadership were narrow indeed in a country like the Dominican Republic, ruled by a powerful economic elite. Even in the Commonwealth Caribbean, where the tradition of democracy was deeply rooted, the Westminster system was far from unblemished. It should have been a matter of concern that corruption came to have an insidious impact on public life in many of these states during the 1980s, that the military was being talked about more and more as a potential political actor, that racial divisions remained of political significance in some territories, that the old colonial taste for messianic leadership still existed, that the outcome of some national elections was influenced by the expenditure of outside money, and that business interests enjoyed almost a veto on the formation of public policy. In the context of democratic politics, these were all serious failings, and they needed to be addressed, not glossed over.

It is also worth referring here to the dog that did not bark in the debate about democracy in the 1980s: the cause of continuing colonialism in the region. British decolonization came to a halt with the grant of independence to Antigua-Barbuda and Belize in 1981 and St. Kitts–Nevis in 1983, leaving Britain in possession still of five Caribbean dependencies, namely, Anguilla, the British Virgin Islands, the Cayman Islands, Montserrat, and the Turks and Caicos Islands, none of which was keen to be independent. In the French case, the Mitterrand government instituted a greater degree of decentralization in the administration of its Caribbean departments in the early 1980s, thereby appeasing much of the previous demand for autonomy and ensuring the continuity of the DOM system into the foreseeable future. The Netherlands government was more inclined in recent years to divest itself of the Netherlands Antilles, but in 1989 it conceded to demands that the kingdom be restructured to give the Caribbean members both more autonomy and continued access to the mother country. The appeal of independence seemed, in other words, to have been widely replaced by a determination, substantially less heroic, to hang onto the tangible benefits of imperial protection. The next test of this new trend was due to come in the referendum on their future status, which the U.S. Congress initially granted to Puerto Ricans in 1991. According to local accounts, the choice of the people seemed likely to be between the continuation and enhancement of the commonwealth, on the one hand, or entry into the United States as the fifty-first state, on the other hand—not independence. (The bill authorizing the referendum was subsequently blocked in the Congress, and it is far from clear when or whether the vote will take place.)

The priority attached to democracy in U.S. policy toward the Caribbean during the 1980s was always linked in the mind of the Reagan administration with the need to promote associated changes in the economic life of the region. Its goal in this respect was to create a growing number of market-based economies capable of competing successfully in international export markets. This was deemed to require less reliance on statism, market intervention, and import substitution than had been the norm in the development strategies deployed in the Caribbean during the 1960s and 1970s. The tools to be deployed by the United States to bring about this economic revolution were the traditional ones of the carrot and the stick. The carrot was announced by President Reagan when he unveiled the Caribbean Basin Initiative (CBI) in a speech before the Organization of American Sates (OAS) in early 1982; the stick was wielded in the various structural adjustment packages imposed upon many Caribbean governments during the decade by the actions of the International Monetary Fund (IMF), the World Bank, and the U.S. Agency for International Development (USAID).

The two aspects of the policy might have worked if they had genuinely operated in tandem. In practice, the CBI was crippled from the start. As set out in Reagan's OAS speech, it offered considerable inducements to Caribbean Basin states, including one-way free trade for most exports, increased economic aid, tax incentives to encourage U.S. entrepreneurs to invest in the region, and technical assistance to the private sector. As eventually passed by Congress following intensive lobbying by special interests in the United States, it was described even by *Business Week* as "more a symbolic gesture than the ambitious program for economic stimulus" originally signaled.[16] In particular, a wide range of items, including textiles and garments, petroleum products, frozen citrus juices, and leather goods, were excluded from preferential treatment. Yet despite the fact that the U.S. market had not been opened up in a way likely to stimulate Caribbean production and exports, the IMF/World-Bank/USAID nexus still adhered rigidly to the need for structural adjustment. In essence, these institutions offered financial assistance to help with balance of payments difficulties, but insisted on the implementation of policies designed to adjust economies in such a way as to bring them back into financial balance. The favored measures were always the same: the liberalization of foreign exchange and import controls, the devaluation of the currency, and the deflation of domestic demand. After absorbing this medicine, the economy in question was then returned to the international marketplace supposedly ready and able to export its way back to solvency.

Caribbean states widely followed this prescription during the 1980s. Indeed, the CARICOM heads of government went so far at their summit in the Bahamas in 1984 as to issue the so-called Nassau Understanding, in which they endorsed structural adjustment as "a conscious shift to a new development path to accelerate development."[17] Why? The reality is that there was little alternative. The international recession of 1980–82 severely reduced demand for a number of regional exports—particularly bauxite, petroleum products, and sugar—and lowered the number of tourists visiting the islands. It created, in effect, three crises in one in nearly all Caribbean economies: a balance of payments crisis, a fiscal crisis, and a debt crisis.

Desperate for emergency financial support, governments of all political hues turned to the IMF and its associated bodies. They included not only conservative regimes, like that of Edward Seaga in Jamaica (1980–89), which espoused the ethic of structural adjustment with enthusiasm, but also reformist governments, such as that of Jorge Blanco in the Dominican Republic (1982–86). Even the People's Revolutionary Government in Grenada turned to the fund for support in its final months. In another case, that of Guyana, the successor regime following Burnham's death was forced to implement its own program of structural adjustment, having, as it were, to prove its credentials to the financial institutions before IMF funds were released. It is also highly significant that, on his reelection to office in Jamaica in February 1989, Michael Manley, renowned in the 1970s for his commitment to social democratic reform, endorsed and deepened the liberal market-oriented economic policies of the outgoing Seaga regime. To many observers, it was this shift of position on the part of Manley that most effectively symbolized the new consensus on economic issues (Cuba again excepted) that had emerged in the region during the decade.

In all these settings, the social costs of such market-friendly policies, measured in terms of unemployment, inflation, and sharply declining living standards generally, were immense, provoking riots in Jamaica and the Dominican Republic, underpinning widespread industrial action in Guyana, and generating a mood of popular indifference to the fate of the government in Trinidad when it was suddenly and unexpectedly faced with a coup in 1990. The likelihood of these consequences was always understood by the United States and other proponents of structural adjustment; the point was that the policies were supposed to engender economic growth, which would, in time, trickle down to the masses. At the end of the 1980s, it was far from obvious that this had been achieved anywhere. To take one example, the "showcase" of Seaga's Jamaica, average annual economic growth during his eight years in office was a mere 1.2 percent. It was still the case that the Caribbean economy as a whole faced fundamental structural problems associated with the character of its production base as well as with the distribution of its economic assets. As a study by Policy Alternatives for the Caribbean and Central America (PACCA) noted, "export diversification might reduce the degree of

Caribbean vulnerability to fluctuations in the international economy, but it can do little to foster a structure of production that can withstand the volatility of world markets, for decisions as to what is best to produce and at what price still remain external."[18] The observation is a telling one. It was true that, against the general gloomy trend, some Caribbean economies, usually the smallest ones, floated their way to prosperity during the 1980s by expanding tourism, trafficking in narcotics, and embracing the offshore economy generally, but the fact that they did so by these means serves only to reinforce PACCA's argument.

The final component of the new U.S. agenda for the Caribbean that was forged during the last decade was a preoccupation with the security of the states of the region. The United States had, of course, long concerned itself with exactly this question. It had sought to bring down the Castro regime in Cuba in the immediate aftermath of the revolution; it intervened to foment dissent against the Jagan government in British Guiana in 1963–64; it invaded the Dominican Republic in 1965; and according to some views, it tried to destabilize the Manley administration in Jamaica in the mid-1970s. In every case, the determination of the security interest at stake was made in Washington. In that sense, President Reagan was only following a well-worn path in bringing enormous external pressure to bear on tiny Grenada after the 1979 revolution. After all, he was able to declare without embarrassment in March 1983 that "it is not nutmeg that is at stake down there, it is the United States' national security."[19]

What was new, however, about the 1980s, especially after the eventual invasion of Grenada, was the extent to which Caribbean states themselves were forced to think about their own security. Many had never done this before, certainly not in the Commonwealth Caribbean. The leaders of many of the smaller Eastern Caribbean states were undoubtedly shaken by the ease with which 50 lightly armed men had been able to seize power in Grenada. Prompted in part by U.S. pressure but also drawing much of its impetus from local fears, there developed a novel debate about the threat of militarization in the Eastern Caribbean. In Grenada itself, the People's Revolutionary Army had expanded to over 800 persons by mid-1983, and its officers occupied senior positions in the revolutionary government. In response, in Barbados and other neighboring islands, military and paramilitary forces were recruited and their capabilities enhanced through intensified training and re-equipment, in which the United States was prominent. In the aftermath of the fall of the revolution and the subsequent invasion, plans were even advanced by "Tom" Adams in Barbados for the establishment of a sizable regional armed force.

In any event, this proved to be the turning point in the debate: the United States could not be persuaded to finance this force, and several political figures in the smaller islands began to have second thoughts on both its practicalities and its implications. Foremost in their minds, given the small size of states they governed, was the old question, Who guards the guards against unwarranted political interference? The other extraregional powers, such as Britain and Canada, also urged caution and a concentration on police and coast guard capabilities as more appropriate to the real security needs of the region. With the general acceptance of this definition of the situation and the election of Errol Barrow as prime minister of Barbados in 1986, the immediate threat of needless militarization receded.

The question that remained was whether the military forces possessed by Caribbean states, including the collaborative Regional Security System, which had come into being in the Eastern Caribbean as early as 1982, were appropriate to the security threats actually faced in the 1980s. By the middle of the decade, it had become clear that these were not so much the possibility of new "Grenadas" but rather the problems caused by drug traffickers and other criminals, who were often able, literally, to outgun the official defense forces of the smaller territories. The predominant need here was for an effective coast guard capability, rather than internal paramilitary bodies trained to snuff out radical political dissent. Paradoxically, the new importance of drug trafficking as a feature of modern Caribbean life also highlighted the fact that economic difficulties lay at the root of many of the region's security problems. This, in turn, raised the further question of the wisdom of devoting so much time and political energy to the security dimension of Caribbean international relations in the 1980s at the expense of deemphasizing and sometimes completely ignoring other pressing aspects of foreign policy and regional integration.

All of these new themes around which Caribbean politics was organized in the 1980s are highlighted and discussed in detail in the chapters that follow. There is, however, a further important general point that needs to be made here before proceeding: the states of the region substantially took on the issues the Reagan administration insisted they address. They worked at their democracy, tried out structural adjustment, and worried about their security. Yet to a significant degree, by the end of the 1980s and the beginning of the 1990s, the United States had again withdrawn its political interest from the region. The Caribbean was no longer "a circle of crisis" or "a sea of splashing dominoes," colorful phrases used by U.S. State Department personnel in the mid-to-late 1970s. Other priorities had emerged—in Eastern Europe, the Middle East and elsewhere—with the result that the Caribbean was downgraded. Perhaps in any case, the United States considered that its job in the Caribbean had been well done. After all, most states in the region could be said to have embraced Western economic and political norms, and the only significant exception, Cuba, was grappling with its own crisis of political identity, courtesy of the dramatic changes taking place in the Soviet Union. The administration of George Bush, which came into office early in 1989, preferred to take Latin America as a whole as its policy framework, initiating its Enterprise for the Americas project in mid-1990. The Caribbean was part of this design, but the region clearly no longer had its own profile within U.S. policy.

The continuing problem for the Caribbean, however, is represented by the contradictions underlying its new politics. At their root is the question of the role the region might play in the world economic order of the 1990s and beyond. Several trends that pose a danger to existing economic practices can be identified: the globalization of markets for goods, services, capital, and technology, which imperils the region's wage-cost and location advantages in relation to North American investment; the general dematerialization of industrial production, which bodes ill for all commodity producers; the strengthening of economic blocs in North America (via the 1989 U.S.-Canada free-trade agreement and its proposed extension to Mexico) and Western Europe (via the creation of a single European market by 1993), which threatens access to traditional markets for "uncompetitive" agricultural export staples, manufactured goods, and services; the emergence of the Pacific Rim as a pole of growth, which cannot but marginalize the Caribbean as a source of dynamic business opportunities; the transformation of Eastern Europe into a market economy, which seems likely to divert trade and aid in its direction; and the failure of the international community collectively to deal with the problem of Third World debt, which threatens Caribbean states, as others, with a continuation of debilitating service payments and consequent diminished growth.

The prospects are alarming, and on several counts. First, the economic viability of the region is at stake, with a real possibility of individually impoverished states being increasingly driven to function as mere offshore platforms of the United States. Second, the region's commitment to democracy is threatened, with ever more desperate attempts to find economic growth in the international marketplace inevitably bringing greater and perhaps ultimately intolerable pressure to bear on social stability. Third, the security of the Caribbean states themselves is at risk, with the temptations offered by collaboration with the powerful and wealthy drug barons presenting a constant invitation to corruption, lawlessness, and anarchy. A. N. R. Robinson, then prime minister of Trinidad and Tobago, warned his fellow CARICOM heads of government at their summit meeting in July 1989 that, unless something was done to address the situation, "the Caribbean could be in danger of becoming a backwater, separated from the main current of human advance into the twenty-first century."[20] As already indicated—and as Robinson himself was made aware when he was captured and held hostage during the coup attempt in Trinidad a year later—this is far from being the worst-case scenario.

The prospect of the Caribbean being left to fester on the edge of the world system is real. The CARICOM meeting at which Robinson delivered his warning also took the important decision to set up the West Indies Commission of wise men and women, headed by Sonny Ramphal, the Guyanese former secretary-general of the Commonwealth. The commission was charged with the task of presenting a report to the governments by 1992, the year of the anniversary of the arrival of Columbus, on the options facing the region in the future. In essence, two alternatives exist. The first constitutes a continuation of the trend of the 1980s toward ever closer integration, territory by territory, into the American system, thereby facilitating the continuation of the divide-and-rule policies of the 1980s. The major difference would be their pursuit in the even less attractive context of declining U.S. governmental interest in the Caribbean islands compared to Mexico and continental Latin America, generally. This option would amount virtually to a recolonization of the region and is not something the West Indies Commission, or any of the governments of the wider Caribbean, would be advised to endorse.

The second option is as yet uncharted, but it is based upon the notion of regional integration across the whole of the Caribbean. The framework of such a strategy was only just discernible at the beginning of the 1990s. The Windward Islands are continuing to explore the possibility of political union within an Eastern Caribbean state; Guyana is heading toward an election, which if freely and fairly conducted, as seems possible in the context of international supervision, would permit its full reentry into regional affairs; CARICOM is engaged in another attempt to revive its activities; Haiti and the Dominican Republic, by virtue of being admitted into the Lomé Convention, must coordinate positions vis-à-vis the European Community with the Commonwealth Caribbean; Puerto Rico retains commonwealth status, which implies a continuing, indeed developing, relationship with the rest of the Caribbean; and not least, Cuba may be looking for a greater presence in the region as a way of coping with major changes in its domestic and international position. This last observation begs, of course, a huge question: the future of the socialist experiment in Cuba. In response to the drastic curtailment of supplies from the former Soviet Union, Castro was forced to announce austerity measures, justified as a "special period in peace time." Greater openness to foreign investment is also apparent but, so far, little political movement on the part of the regime. What is new, and probably unstoppable, is the emergence of a debate both outside and (within bounds) inside Cuba about the country's future political and economic relationships; within that discussion, the prospect and problems of its reintegration into the Caribbean are central.

There is thus the basis of a second option built around the transcendence of national interest and the creation of a wider Caribbean project. The old antithesis in intra-CARICOM debates about "deepening" or "widening" the integration movement would need to be abandoned in favor of a recognition that the two processes have to proceed in simultaneous, complementary fashion. It would not eliminate the necessity for the Caribbean to settle upon a relationship with the United States in particular and Latin America in general, but it would enable the region to become a player of at least some significance within the negotiation of the new North American Free Trade Area (NAFTA) and the wider Enterprise for the Americas. Finally, it would require consistent and constructive political leadership of a genuinely pan-Caribbean nature. This is perhaps where Ramphal's West Indies Commission will play an important role. Certainly, no other body is so well placed to set out a post-1992 strategy for the region.

# 1 Liberal Economics versus Electoral Politics in Jamaica

*Anthony Payne*

Jamaican politics has been shaped since independence by the unsuccessful attempts of successive governments to find a form of economic development capable of satisfying the demands of a substantial cross section of the national society. The two political parties that have alternated in office, the Jamaica Labour Party (JLP) and the People's National Party (PNP), both emerged as rival multiclass, multiracial coalitions competing for the majority support of the Jamaican electorate. Each party has been financed by prominent members of the local capitalist class, serviced by trade unions run primarily as "vote-catching annexes," and defended in the ghettos of Kingston by political gangs drawn from the poor and unemployed. Within these boundaries, electoral competition has always been intense: free and generally fair, although often also violent. In other words, despite superficial similarities to the political norms of Western liberal democracy, what was built up in Jamaica after independence was a clientelist style of politics rooted in the management of the economy. Something of a tradition has also emerged whereby each party has been given two terms in office by the electorate but then punished by electoral defeat when it failed to deliver sufficient benefits to satisfy the particular network of voters that generated the initial victory.

Driven in this way by the demands of the political system, the country has been a veritable laboratory of economic modeling since independence. The policy of the 1962–72 JLP government was geared toward the orthodox import-substitution industrialization of the time; it offered foreign capitalists a protected market and relied upon the establishment, by the state, of incentives to attract them to set up industrial enterprises on the island. Local businessmen were encouraged to play a subordinate role as virtual junior partners to foreign investors. This strategy generated growth without development, delivering benefits to a narrow section of Jamaican society but failing to dispense the gains among the people as a whole.[1] The policy of the Michael Manley government, which came to power in 1972, envisaged a more assertive role for the state in winning greater independence for Jamaica within the world economy. Foreign capital was permitted to operate but, to an increasing extent, only on the state's terms, which included joint ownership. Local capital was equally encouraged but was required to distribute more of its profits to its workers in the form of higher wages and improved conditions. This populist model put the state in the driver's seat and temporarily won new welfare benefits for the poor and dispossessed. However, in the latter part of the 1970s it threatened to develop into a form of state socialism, which had the effect of frightening off capital and bringing the economy virtually to the point of collapse.[2]

The JLP was thus able to present itself in the 1980 election as nothing less than the bearer of "deliverance," as the party's campaign slogan so aptly put it. The key to this appeal was the reputation of its leader, Edward Seaga, as a manager and fixer. With his Harvard education and his smart business suits, he appeared as the experienced technocrat who understood the international economic system and had the necessary connections outside of the country to promote sustained economic growth. By contrast, Manley was presented in JLP propaganda as a dangerous ideologue who had unwisely allowed his personal political philosophy to dictate policy at the expense of pragmatic common sense. Certainly, the subsequent period of the JLP government that began in November 1980 and ended in February 1989 was characterized, as promised, by the complete rejection of the democratic socialist aspirations of the Manley era. Yet, somewhat unexpectedly in the light of these claims, Seaga's government itself quickly became associated with a model of economic development derived from ideological considerations.

The ideas that influenced the JLP's handling of the Jamaican economy during the 1980s were broadly those of neoliberalism, as refined over the course of the decade by leading international financial institutions such as the International Monetary Fund (IMF) and the World Bank. Indeed, the relationship the Seaga government established with the IMF was so central to its existence that the government's overall management of the economy and, indeed, its entire political record can best be analyzed by reference to the changing nature of this relationship. This chapter examines

the politics of the Seaga period and sets out in detail the phases of
policy through which the pursuit of economic revival and the
maintenance of political power passed. It starts by explaining
structural adjustment, which became the centerpiece of neoliberal
theories of economic management in the 1980s and was rhetorical-
ly embraced from the very outset by the Seaga government.

## STRUCTURAL ADJUSTMENT

The concept of structural adjustment can only be understood in
the context of the debate, which has gone on throughout the postwar period, about the working of the international economy and
the role of the IMF within it. Between 1945 and 1973, large U.S.
balance of payments deficits financed the whole international
trading system, which meant there existed no fundamental payments disequilibrium for developing countries as a group. During
these years it was generally accepted that those countries that did
get into balance of payments trouble, and consequently had to turn
to the IMF for help, did so because they had in some way mis-
managed their economic affairs, rather than because there was a
general lack of liquidity in the global economy. In a world of
growth, it was usually the case that the IMF remedy of a temporary
deflation of demand, combined with the provision of credit, quickly restored external balance and recreated the basis for economic
expansion. Relatively little controversy was attached to the IMF's
approach. After 1973, however, all that changed. Developing countries had to cope with major rises in the price of oil, a general
deterioration in their terms of trade, and sharp increases in the
rates of interest determining debt service repayments. Indeed, the
decline in their general balance of payments position was described by one political economist as "so continuous and so serious that there can be little doubt that it can only be described as
'structural' or 'fundamental' in its nature."[3]

In such conditions, IMF prescriptions were no longer capable of
generating an automatic economic recovery, and the harshness of
their terms attracted growing political opposition within the Third
World. Jamaica's experience with the fund under the Manley government in the late 1970s, although far from unique in its time,
was a key part of the emerging critique. The argument came to a
head in 1980 at a major conference on the international monetary
system jointly organized by Jamaica and Tanzania, another state
whose democratic socialist program of reform had been effectively

broken on the back of an IMF intervention. The conference drew
up the Arusha Initiative, which, inter alia, condemned IMF policies as "a form of political intervention" designed to subordinate
states to "the free play of national and international market
forces" to the advantage of the "traditional centres of power" in the
world.[4] It called, instead, for a major shift of resources from the
richer to the poorer parts of the world to enable deficit economies
to produce their way out of balance of payments problems. The
legitimacy of the fund was damaged by such criticism, and a response was soon forthcoming—the concept of structural adjustment.

The thinking underlying this new approach was well set out by
Manuel Guitian, one of the fund's theorists, in an IMF publication
in 1982. He accepted the argument that the payments imbalances
existing in the world economy in the 1980s were structural and
could therefore be dealt with only on the basis of longer adjustment periods than had been deployed in IMF programs in the past.
A new recognition was also given to the need for production—to be
achieved, it was said, by means of "foreign borrowing strategies
that directly enlarge the amount of resources to the member," thus
allowing "higher levels of expenditure . . . as well as higher growth
rates over the medium term."[5] Having incorporated this extra emphasis on the transfer of resources to developing countries, Guitian
then felt able to defend the IMF against the charge that its preoccupation with deflation served primarily to retard, rather than
promote, growth. Yet, as Brett has pointed out, this concession did
"not leave orthodoxy far behind."[6]

As it turned out, the domestic adjustment policies subsequently favored by the IMF were little changed from those of the
1970s. According to Guitian, they included "public sector policies
on prices, taxes, and subsidies that can contribute to eliminate
financial imbalances and to promote efficiency in public sector
activities; interest rate policies that foster the generation of domestic savings and improve inter-temporal resources allocation;
exchange rate policy that helps to control absorption and the external accounts but is also a powerful tool for development; and incomes policies that keep claims on resources from out-stepping
their availability."[7] The technicality of the language did not obscure the hostility toward state intervention in economic management, the attachment of merit to low wages, the rejection of protection as a trade policy, or the disregard for the impact the program
would have on domestic prices. Indeed, devaluation was recom-

mended as the best means to control the inflow of imports. In short, there was little real change in the IMF's approach—its new prescriptions were intended to be more sensitive to the timing and pace of the adjustment being demanded but were still firmly based in orthodox liberal economics.

The logic on which such neoliberal thinking depended was simple. If a country suffered from a balance of payments deficit, it meant that its currency (in effect, its externally traded commodities and products) was less in demand than the foreign currencies that it used to make purchases. The country should correct its payments deficit by allowing its currency to float until it found its correct level or by devaluing its currency sufficiently to eliminate the distortion. This would discourage imports and promote exports. It was also presumed that the country would attract enough extra foreign investment to generate more production in the medium-to-long run to offset short-run inflation. It did not need to impose any controls on imports or exports, as the market mechanism would do the job perfectly well. The market, in turn, would dictate all other required fiscal measures, such as the regulation of the money supply to control public expenditure, the removal of subsidies, and the privatization of state enterprises. In this way, the whole society would be returned to the environment of the free market, debts could be repaid, and the integrity of an open international trading system would be preserved.

Such an ideology was as crude as it was simple, which was one of the main reasons why Seaga, who had to operate within a competitive electoral system in Jamaica, never articulated it as clearly as the IMF technocrats. Nevertheless, in the period leading up to the 1980 election, he made no secret of his attachment to free enterprise, his awareness that Jamaica had to operate in an international marketplace, and his desire to shift the country's economy away from import substitution toward export promotion.[8] It was assumed in Washington that it was precisely a process of structural adjustment, as understood by the IMF, that the JLP government was seeking to effect after October 1980. Seaga, at the very least, did not deny it; indeed, it may have been an important part of his political strategy to give this impression. The debate about Edward Seaga's motivation and politics is considered later: it is necessary now to examine the performance and policies of his government.

IMF MANAGEMENT

**Phase I:.November 1980–October 1983**

The JLP administration set about its mission with style and confidence. Within months, Jamaica had emerged as probably the most committed client state of the U.S. government in the Caribbean area, a status neatly symbolized by Seaga's invitation to become the first foreign head of state to visit President Reagan in the White House after the latter took office at the beginning of 1981. Seaga played up to his host, extolling the virtues of capitalism and calling upon the United States and its allies to rescue the Caribbean Basin from left-wing influence by putting together a program along the lines of the Marshall Plan, prepared for Europe after 1945. Although the latter proposal took shape in much weaker form as the Caribbean Basin Initiative (CBI), the plea on behalf of Jamaica worked. Reagan instructed the State Department to set up a special office to coordinate U.S. governmental aid to Jamaica and asked David Rockefeller, the chairman of Chase Manhattan Bank, to mobilize the U.S. private sector to take an interest in the island. By March 1981, a U.S. business committee on Jamaica, composed of leading corporate executives, had been established and had begun meeting with a local counterpart, set up by Seaga, to find ways of promoting new inward investment in Jamaica.[9]

A commitment to begin negotiations with the IMF at the earliest opportunity had been given by the new Seaga government immediately on assuming office, and in the prevailing cordial atmosphere being signaled by Washington, the talks were quickly brought to a successful conclusion. An extended fund facility (EFF) agreement was signed in April 1981, providing for a loan of US$650 million over three years. In addition, the government received a further US$48 million from the compensatory financing facility, set up specifically to offset temporary shortfalls in traditional export earnings. The EFF agreement was also (in the language of the IMF) "front-loaded," which meant that 40 percent of the loan could be drawn in the first year of the agreement's term. To ensure payment of subsequent tranches, the government had to meet certain targets. Limits were set on the net amount of domestic bank credit distributed to the public sector and on the extent of the domestic and international reserves held by the Bank of Jamaica. The government further agreed not to introduce multiple currency practices (as the Manley regime had done) and not to place new restrictions on payments and transfers for current international

transactions. Finally, a ceiling was placed on new external borrowing by the government.[10]

What was interesting were the conditions the IMF did not see fit
to impose on the Seaga government compared to those it had demanded of the PNP government in the 1970s. Crucially, there was
no demand for a devaluation of the Jamaican currency, although
this was called for by the tenets of structural adjustment. Nor were
the restrictions on domestic public sector borrowing made to apply to the private sector. The ceiling on government borrowing
abroad excluded loans to refinance existing debts and loans from
foreign governments and their agencies or multilateral lending
organizations. Seaga certainly made a virtue of the absence of
"negative features" in the deal when he explained it to the Jamaican people,[11] and indeed, it does seem that he was able to negotiate
much more favorable terms with the IMF than did his predecessor.[12] He already had cleverly advertised his anticommunist,
pro-Western credentials in such moves as his expulsion of the
Cuban ambassador from Kingston immediately on assuming office, and they now won him due financial reward.

The whole episode also offered a textbook illustration of how a
loan from the IMF could put a stamp of financial respectability on a
country that had been effectively frozen out of the international
money markets for several years. Following the signing of the
agreement, the way was cleared for the Seaga government to
mount a massive borrowing and refinancing operation over the
next two years. Although the World Bank was the single most
important contributor, the sources of the loans on which it was
able to draw were so diverse that they implied nothing less than the
existence of a coordinated international rescue of the Jamaican
economy. The immediate gain was the ample provision of foreign
exchange with which to rehabilitate traditional industries and
stimulate new ones; the long-term price was a substantial rise in
foreign debt, which increased from an estimated US$1.2 billion at
the end of 1980 to US$3.1 billion by the end of 1983.[13]

On the basis of this financial support and the increased foreign
investment that the government expected to start flowing again
soon, ambitious growth and production targets were set in virtually all sectors, none more so than in the crucial bauxite and
alumina industry. Speaking in June 1981, Seaga revealed plans to
increase the annual production of bauxite from the 1980 figure of
12 million tons to 26 million tons within three years. Alumina
production was to be similarly expanded, from 2.4 million tons to
8.6 million tons, primarily through a proposed joint investment by

the government, several Norwegian firms, and the U.S. company Alcoa, which would double the size of the latter's refinery in Jamaica.[14] The trouble was that, just as the government was promoting this future expansion, Alcoa announced a cutback in existing production levels because of decreasing world demand for alumina. Despite warnings from local experts and opposition politicians, the government was unprepared for the recession that occurred in the bauxite market. The other companies operating in Jamaica followed Alcoa's lead, with the result that bauxite production, far from expanding hugely as anticipated, fell disastrously to only 7.3 million tons in 1983. Government revenue from the industry fell accordingly, from US$206 million in 1980 to US$137 million in 1982.[15]

This was a severe setback—and one against which the Seaga regime could not have protected itself other than by a more accurate prediction of market trends. It appealed for immediate assistance to its main overseas ally, the Reagan administration, which responded in December 1981 by ordering 1.6 million tons of Jamaican bauxite for its strategic defense stockpile. Although the purchase helped to maintain activity in the industry for a while, its contribution to the balance of payments was limited by U.S. insistence on paying for the bauxite, in part, in agricultural products. The emerging balance of payments problem caused by the reduction in bauxite production was further worsened by the poor performance of other traditional agricultural exports. Sugar production declined by 50,000 tons between 1980 and 1982 and banana production by 11,000 tons over the same period.[16] Only tourism offered consolation, the number of visitors increasing from 1980 levels in response to a vigorous publicity drive and the favorable impression that Seaga made on North American audiences. The difficulties experienced by these long-standing foreign exchange earners inevitably placed responsibility for the generation of economic growth on nontraditional exports at a much earlier stage in the process of structural adjustment than had been anticipated.

However, the fact was that, despite all the paraphernalia surrounding the establishment of joint U.S.-Jamaican business committees, foreign investors were slow and, ultimately, timid in their response to the new opportunities being offered. The reasons for this were several: apart from a general disinclination to invest in new activity at a time when international interest rates were at record levels, there was the residual legacy of Jamaica's reputation in the 1970s as a place of violence and extremism, the continuing problem of bureaucratic inefficiency, and new concern over the adequacy of the country's basic infrastructure. The Seaga team initially thought the Caribbean Basin Initiative to be a great source of future investment, but its delayed passage through Congress (it was not passed into law until mid-1983), the dropping of proposed tax credits on new U.S. investments in the Caribbean, and the exclusion of textiles, apparel, and a number of other categories of goods markedly reduced its impact on the Jamaican economy. As a result, although the government could point to the many inquiries handled by Jamaica National Investment Promotion Ltd. (JNIP), the new agency set up in 1981 to facilitate the inflow of foreign investment, the number of projects actually initiated in the first year or two was very few. Moreover, even when foreign business-men were persuaded to set up new operations, they often borrowed on the local market rather than bring in foreign funds. As for the response of the Jamaican capitalist sector, that was accurately en-capsulated in the Stephens's wry observation that it persisted in its "preference for quick and easy profits over entrepreneurial risk-taking, new investments and a search for new markets."[17] In con-sequence, the figures show that "non-traditional exports" grew from J$197 million in 1980 to J$235 million in 1982—not enough by any means to offset the poor performance of the traditional commodity sector.[18]

The Seaga government's development strategy was itself partly responsible for the unwillingness of Jamaican businessmen to take chances in export markets. To put it simply, they could make money more easily at home in conventional import-export ac-tivities. The policy of liberalizing the flow of imports fueled an enormous consumer boom during 1981 and 1982, as the rich and the middle class enjoyed imported luxury items forbidden to them during the foreign exchange squeeze at the end of the 1970s. There was launched what a local gibe referred to as the era of the three Vs—Volvos, videos, and venereal disease, the latter associated with the revival of the tourist industry. Although politically attrac-tive (and thus to some extent necessary) as a way of pleasing the government's more affluent supporters, the import boom created serious difficulties. In the first place, it raised popular expectations about improvements in the standard of living to new and unattain-able heights; second, it made it impossible for local manufacturers to preserve their hold on the domestic market, let alone launch themselves into the export battle; third, it put out of business many small farmers who could not compete with cheap food im-ports once restrictions had been lifted; and, last, it worsened the already shaky prospects for the balance of payments. The latter was especially critical.

By the middle of 1982, the Jamaican dollar, officially valued at J$1.78 to the U.S. dollar, was trading on the black or "parallel" market at nearly twice that figure. In what amounted to an offer of legitimacy to this system, the government initially tried to draw some of the parallel market dollars, many of which had been earned illegally from trading in marijuana (ganja), into specified imports intended to help local manufacturing. It issued so-called "no-funds licenses," which permitted businessmen to pay for certain goods without recourse to the Bank of Jamaica. By January 1983, however, it was forced to go a step further and openly institute a two-tier exchange rate. Seaga's aim was to encourage exports by making imported materials for manufactured goods less expensive than imported goods for consumption. The former would continue to be costed at the official rate, the latter at a rate expected to level out around J$2.70.[19] The move was thus a hidden devaluation of the currency, an issue of particular political sensitivity because of the JLP's earlier attacks on the Manley government's policies in this area in the 1970s. The most immediate effect of the introduction of the dual exchange rate was, of course, on prices, thereby threatening the reduction in inflation that had accompanied the liberalization of imports and the capture of the local market by the cheapest available foreign goods.[20]

The deepening balance of payments crisis was bound to make its presence felt in the quarterly tests the economy had to undergo as part of the 1981 IMF agreement. The moment of failure came in March 1983, by which time the deficit had reached US$150 million. The fund promptly suspended further disbursements, and Seaga had no alternative but to plead for a waiver. To maintain IMF support, he introduced austerity measures, including new taxes, public spending cuts, reduced foreign exchange allocations for imports, and the shift of many more items to the more expensive parallel market rate. The idea was to curb the use of precious foreign exchange on nonessential imports by pricing them out of the reach of most people. As such, the move was an extension of the previous devaluation, having the same inflationary consequences over an even wider range of goods, including many items of basic utility like gasoline. Jamaicans felt the impact of the squeeze, but the reaction of Seaga's external backers was favorable. The IMF granted the waiver, the World Bank produced two more small loans, and the U.S. government offered US$25 million in emergency balance of payments assistance as well as agreeing to make a further purchase of bauxite for its strategic reserve. It was, to say the least, an impressive demonstration of continuing support for Seaga by the dominant forces of the international liberal economy.

What is striking is that it was to no avail. Production in the Jamaican economy had reached a depth that could not be corrected simply by devaluation. In October 1983, the IMF again suspended payments following a further protracted dispute with the government over figures relating to the failure of the September test.[21] It was announced that the agreement was to be terminated six months early, and negotiations were started on a new package of assistance, with Seaga and his colleagues in a much weaker bargaining position than in 1980–81.

## Phase II: November 1983–March 1985

The talks with the IMF took place in the context of deteriorating political support for the JLP government. Its initial honeymoon with the Jamaican electorate ended with the increases in inflation and unemployment and the renewal of hard times for the poor, especially after the liberal consumption of goods in the preceding couple of years by business people and the middle classes. The political consequences were charted in the regular opinion polls taken by Carl Stone. A commanding 28 percent lead in May 1981 fell to 7 percent a year later. Then, for the first time, in October 1982, the PNP pulled ahead of the JLP—by 43 percent to 38 percent—and maintained that ascendancy into 1983.[22] It was not so much that the PNP had been able to arouse a renewed faith in its capacity to govern so soon after the debacle of the late 1970s but, rather, that its traditional association with the poor, with public expenditure, and with the expansion of welfare policies regained it some support as the issue of economic weakness again took precedence in the public mind. Thus by the autumn of 1983, the prospect of being the first Jamaican government since independence to lose office after just one term loomed before the JLP.

The crisis was further exacerbated because pressure on the exchange rate built up as the new IMF talks got under way. The government had seriously miscalculated the balance of supply and demand for foreign exchange: the decision to push extra imports onto the parallel market caused a rapid bidding up of the price to over J$3 by the end of October. The fund focused on this as a sign of the continuing uncompetitiveness of Jamaican exports and made a unification (i.e., another devaluation) of the exchange rate its main demand in return for a new standby credit. The original intention was that this new arrangement would run for fifteen months from the beginning of January 1984, but it soon became evident that the IMF had other demands, too, and wanted to see them implemented before it agreed to the loan, not after it had been approved and disbursed. Its approach can be aptly described in sporting parlance as one of "getting your retaliation in first." In this connection, the key announcement came at the end of November 1983: the Jamaican dollar would henceforth be fixed at a single rate, initially set at J$3.15, but adjustable every two weeks by the Bank of Jamaica in a kind of managed float. This signified a devaluation of no less than 43 percent for any item hitherto traded at the former official rate and was the beginning of a series of harsh economic measures introduced at the insistence of the IMF.

Politically, it was highly significant that the announcement of the devaluation came only after the murderous self-destruction of the Grenadian revolution and the ensuing U.S. invasion, in which Jamaican troops were actively involved, albeit in a minor supporting role, had served to create a surge of domestic support for the JLP. In fact, the Stone poll taken immediately after the killings in Grenada, which showed the JLP converting a 3 percent deficit vis-à-vis the PNP into a 5 percent lead, altered the course of Jamaican politics. It revealed the extent of the latent suspicion of left-wing ideology in Jamaica and led Seaga "to deepen the Jamaicanisation of the Grenada issue"[23] by seeking to tarnish local PNP figures by association with Cuba, the Soviet Union, and the Grenadian revolutionaries.

Given the tenor of the talks that were simultaneously taking place with the IMF, the temptation to call a snap election before the effects of a devaluation worked through the economy and before the Grenada issue was forgotten was plainly compelling. The only obstacle was an agreement between the two major parties that an election would not be called until a new voters' list being worked on by the electoral commission was ready. This was, however, overridden by Seaga, who announced the date for an election just two days after revealing the government's austere new economic package. The PNP chose to boycott the poll on the grounds that the interparty agreement on electoral reform had been unilaterally abrogated by Seaga, and thus, by default, the JLP won all sixty seats when voting took place in mid-December 1983. The ploy was highly controversial, even among some JLP activists, but it bought the JLP five more years in office and in that sense cleared the decks politically for the austerity that was to come.[24]

The IMF thus achieved its goal of a substantial devaluation; its other major demand related to the size of the government's budget deficit, which it wanted to see reduced from 15.6 percent of gross domestic product to a single figure in the space of just one year. Yet even before the task of meeting this requirement could be properly confronted, its achievement was made considerably more difficult by another damaging development within the bauxite industry. In March 1984, apparently without any prior warning to the government, another of the major North American multinational companies, Reynolds, announced that it was shutting down its bauxite operation. It blamed the international recession, although some felt than an argument with the government, a year or so earlier, about the distribution of the U.S. stockpile contract between the companies operating in Jamaica was at least a partial cause. Seaga expressed anger that a company that had worked in Jamaica for over forty years should behave in such a way and admitted, in a state of some shock, that the loss to the fiscal budget being planned for 1984–85 could be as much as J$100 million and the shortfall in the foreign exchange budget some US$30 million.[25]

If, therefore, the IMF target was to be met, the level of deflation had to be even more severe than had been projected. For political reasons, Seaga took two bites at it: he raised taxes by J$138 million in a "mini-package" in April 1984 and then extended the process by a further J$45 million in the regular budget in May. In addition, public expenditure was reduced, and many civil servants and other public sector workers were laid off, adding to the already high unemployment rate. Food subsidies were also cut, although a minimum level of support for basic commodities was maintained. Other measures designed to appease the IMF included restrictions on domestic credit, the promise of accelerated divestment of state enterprises, and a more intensive policing of the leakage of foreign exchange from the tourist sector, which was notorious for the way it was able to siphon money to Miami. It should be noted, too, that, while these measures were being put into place in the first half of 1984, the Jamaican dollar continued to slide downward on the floating exchange, reaching J$4.15 by June. Eventually, enough was enough. Jamaica's second major IMF loan in the Seaga era came five months late in June 1984: it provided US$143 million—well below the US$180 million the government had been hoping for since the end of 1983—divided between standby credit and compensatory finance; it was scheduled to last only until the end of March 1985. With the loan in place, debt rescheduling was again possible, and shortly afterward the Paris Club of international creditors agreed to roll forward US$135 million of external debts due for repayment before March 1985.

The idea behind this loan was to give the Jamaican economy some breathing space in which the prescribed free-market remedy, as insisted upon more firmly by the IMF on this occasion, could at last begin to work. The fund itself issued a statement declaring optimistically that the various measures that had been introduced would "place fiscal and credit policies on a sounder footing in order to improve the balance of payments and restore conditions for the implementation of structural reform."[26] The reaction, both inside and outside the country, can be imagined, therefore, when the economy almost immediately failed the regular quarterly test at the end of September. Seaga had to travel to Washington in person to seek the familiar waiver. On this occasion the fund chose to accept his argument that the failure was more technical than real—foreign loans had not been paid on time—and the only price exacted for the continuation of the credit was the removal of any attempt to manage the Jamaican dollar and to allow it to float freely from the beginning of December. Yet by the time the end-of-year test came around, the position of the reserves was no better, and two loans from the U.S. government, which still loyally supported the Seaga regime, were hurried through. Despite government denials, it was obvious that another IMF agreement was coming to an ignominious end.

Seaga's problem was that not only did he have to satisfy the IMF's demands, but he had to manage the domestic political situation in Jamaica, which by the beginning of 1985 was becoming more and more tense. The economic boom of 1981 had long since disappeared; inflation stood at 30 percent, the currency had floated downward to J$5.00, and unemployment (notwithstanding the continuation under JLP auspices of a number of former PNP job training programs) was estimated at 25.6 percent of the labor force. Regarding this last, the unpalatable fact was that creation of 6,705 jobs, which the JNIP proudly announced in mid-1984 as the result of almost four years of trying to promote new investment in manufacturing industry, barely exceeded the 6,200 jobs the government itself had agreed to cut from the public sector to secure the second IMF loan.[27] In the circumstances, the two days of riots and protests that followed the announcement of gas price increases in January 1985 were not unexpected.[28] Even so, the government was shaken by the extent of the anger obviously felt by ordinary working-class Jamaicans at its economic policies, and it was further taken aback by the announcement shortly afterward that Alcoa was to follow in the footsteps of Reynolds and close its alumina refinery on the island, pending a revival of market conditions. The conclusion the government drew, however, was not that the adjustment program needed to be abandoned but that the people would have to be told more openly of the harsh choices facing the country as a result of the economy's plight—especially as the next round of IMF talks was about to begin.

## Phase III: April 1985–April 1986

The new policy of candor was initiated in a nationwide television address delivered by Seaga in April 1985. He spoke of the need to secure a further IMF deal but warned there would have to be sacrificcs, in the form of more public sector job losses, higher interest rates, and still heavier taxation. The sole ray of hope he could offer was the news that the Alcoa plant would open again in July under a leasing arrangement, whereby production and marketing would be undertaken by a new government company, Clarendon Alumina Production Ltd., although operational responsibility would be retained by Alcoa. Seaga claimed that buyers had already been found for virtually all of the plant's capacity, albeit initially at loss-making prices. The government's willingness to intervene in this way was highly revealing: it showed how desperate it had become to preserve the basis of the bauxite industry for the future and to prevent any further redundancies in the meantime. It also revealed that, despite its free-enterprise rhetoric, the Seaga administration was prepared to use the powers of the state to defend key national economic interests. In this sense, its approach to the bauxite industry—when really put to the test—was more in keeping with the interventionist policies of the Manley government of the 1970s than with the neoliberal theories of economic management, which it generally espoused.[29]

As promised, the next IMF agreement was soon announced. It represented a twenty-month extended fund facility of US$120 million, to run from August 1985 to March 1987, and was deemed to require a further reduction in the size of the government's budget deficit. Apart from threatening more jobs, this permitted a wage rise of only 10 percent for public employees at a time when inflation was more than three times higher. The political reaction was both swift and fierce: within two weeks of the announcement

Jamaica was immersed in the first general strike in its postindependence history. For several days at the end of June 1985, essential services all over the island were either closed down or maintained at only skeleton levels, and a call from Seaga for an immediate return to work was rejected. Yet the action stemmed from despair rather than calculated planning, and the initial solidarity of the strikers was fairly quickly undermined by the government's uncompromising insistence that there really was no more money available for pay if the lifeblood of IMF credit was to be kept flowing. For all that, the strike indicated in a more tangible way than opinion polls the extent to which Seaga's program had lost the support of the bulk of the country. The fact that the Bustamante Industrial Trade Union (BITU) took part was particularly damaging, not just because it was affiliated with the JLP but because it was the very organization from which the party had been born in the 1940s.

Although the strike's collapse undoubtedly weakened the union movement and generally was seen as a victory for Seaga, it had a significant impact on his political tactics. The period following the strike brought no sign that investment and enterprise were responding to the cheap labor economy created by the massive devaluation of the currency over the preceding two years. The Rockefeller committee had been disbanded a year earlier, and indeed, the economy in general continued to worsen. Alpart suspended production at its alumina refinery in August 1985, with more loss of jobs and revenue; official forecasts warned of a decline in gross domestic product of as much as 6 percent in the year; tourism declined in the aftermath of the gas price disturbances; and the exchange rate almost reached J$6 to the U.S. dollar at the end of September. There was nothing new in these further manifestations of economic difficulty, except for the evidence of growing political opposition—not just from the unions, but from a more active PNP, which had been revitalized by what was seen as the deceit underlying the 1983 election and was again well in the lead in the opinion polls. These political pressures seemed to persuade Seaga of the need to adopt a softer stance to improve his domestic political position. The IMF annual meeting in the South Korean capital of Seoul, which Seaga attended in October, was thus treated to a description of the "huge toll in human suffering" experienced as a result of the "over-hasty" reform program demanded by the fund in countries like Jamaica. It was not the substance of the program that he challenged, but its pace; seven years, rather than three, was advanced as a more appropriate adjustment period.[30]

The political thinking that lay behind this plea was quick to emerge. The economy had failed the September 1985 quarterly test, several loans had been delayed, and once again the government required a waiver. In the face of restiveness among leading figures in his own party and a further fall in the currency to J$6.40 (at which point the Bank of Jamaica did intervene financially to arrest what had become an almost uncontrollable slide), Seaga knew that he could mollify the fund only by, in effect, arguing the opposition's case—that the Jamaican people could not take any more deflation of the economy. Accordingly, he used his contacts in the Reagan administration to engineer a visit to Jamaica in the first few months of 1986 by a joint team from the IMF, the World Bank, and the U.S. Agency for International Development. The visit was designed to enable the mission to witness the progress that had already been made toward structural adjustment and to hear the arguments for easing future terms. In the meantime, as a token of good faith, the government took a step toward the further reduction of its budget deficit by introducing another emergency tax package in January 1986. The measures included an annual license fee for television satellite antennae, the "dishes," which had become symbols of prosperity during the 1981 import boom.

The fund, however, was unimpressed. Although a waiver was given to enable more credit to be drawn while negotiations continued, the visiting Tripartite Mission roundly criticized the Seaga government for failing to carry out its promised program of structural reforms, particularly the divestment of public enterprises and adequate currency devaluation. It noted that, five years after the JLP took office, "there remains substantial government involvement in, and control of, economic activity, and the structure of incentives is still complex and even haphazard."[31] Seaga, by all accounts, was furious and tried to suppress distribution in Jamaica of the critical parts of the report. At the same time, pay disputes with teachers, police, and junior doctors, as well as protests from students at the University of the West Indies about the introduction of tuition fees, kept up the domestic political pressure and virtually eliminated scope for concessions to the IMF orthodoxy being demanded by the Tripartite report. In short, an impasse had been reached.

### Phase IV: May 1986–March 1988

The first move to end the stalemate was made by Seaga when in May 1986, in an extraordinary reversal of the deflationary approach of the preceding two years, he introduced an expansionary budget designed to regenerate growth in the economy. Its main features were a reduction in interest rates, a pledge to peg the exchange rate at J$5.50, the use of temporary controls to reduce the price of basic foods, animal feed, and cement, and an increase in capital expenditure from J$1.4 billion in the previous fiscal year to J$2.1 billion in the forthcoming year. In contradiction of earlier warnings, there were no new taxes. The change of approach was evident, but what it meant was unclear. The budget had been delayed a week following arguments about strategy with the Tripartite Mission and, on the surface at least, appeared to reflect a decisive rejection of IMF policy. Seaga also observed enigmatically that the government had prepared, but would not disclose, "a contingency programme in the event that there is any insistence by the institutions on returning this time to further devaluations, budget cuts, reduction of services, redundancies and no growth"—for all of which he now disclaimed responsibility.[32] Against this, the government did accept orthodox IMF/World Bank/USAID policy to the extent that it also announced the divestment of the government-owned National Commercial Bank and significant reductions of import tariffs.

The most likely interpretation of Seaga's behavior is that he was, in effect, playing poker with the IMF and its allies. The crucial background factor was the fall in the international market price of oil in early 1986. Given the Jamaican economy's considerable dependence on oil imports, this gave the balance of payments an unexpected boost, thus providing the government with more room to maneuver economically than had been anticipated. It quickly took advantage of the situation by buying three years' supply of oil when the price was US$10 per barrel. The probability is, therefore, that Seaga saw the oil windfall as the best chance to bargain with the IMF for softening its terms, which he had asked for in Seoul. Certainly, the May budget did not indicate the adoption of a non-IMF strategy of any kind, although Seaga did endeavor to use the dispute with the fund to regenerate public support in Jamaica.

Local elections had originally been due to be held in June 1984; they had been postponed once by agreement between the parties to allow new voter registration to be completed and a second time as a result of a proposed reform of local government, subsequently withdrawn by the government. Eventually called for July 1986, elections were fought as a national campaign (thereby constituting the first major electoral assessment of the JLP record since 1980) and were resoundingly won by the PNP, which took 57 percent of the vote and 126 of the 187 available local authority seats. Although Michael Manley repeated the demand for an early general election, which he had made many times since the nonelection of 1983, Seaga was predictably unresponsive.[33] The rebuff the voters dealt him had at least revealed that the symbolism of conflict with the IMF was insufficient to impress ordinary Jamaicans: they wanted a tangible amelioration of their economic circumstances.

In September, Seaga went to Washington for more talks, having revealed that repayments to the IMF had been deliberately delayed as part of his tactics. These were high stakes, since the debt to the IMF (some US\$70 million by late 1986) unquestionably meant a moratorium on new loans or debt rescheduling agreements. Indeed, it was debt and the threat of default that Seaga was trying to bargain with. According to Timothy Ashby's account, Seaga's meeting with the U.S. Assistant Secretary of State for Inter-American Affairs, Elliott Abrams, was especially blunt. Abrams apparently told Seaga to initiate a proper privatization process and to devalue the Jamaican dollar still further to its true market level.[34] The latter was certainly the key issue in dispute with the IMF. Attempts to rescue the stalled third agreement, which technically ran until the end of March 1987, were abandoned in favor of discussion of a completely new three-year program. As a prerequisite for this, the fund wanted another devaluation to take the rate from J\$5.50 to J\$6.06; Seaga countered with a proposal to move to J\$5.91 in fiscal year 1987–88 and then to J\$6.43 a year later. He defended this position by claiming that it maintained the rate in real terms and was not, therefore, a means to further restructuring; yet this was precisely why the fund's officials were reluctant to accept it. As an alternative, Seaga proposed a wage freeze, only to find that as soon as that possibility emerged into the open all the major trade unions on the island, including the BITU, rejected it emphatically.

The bargaining between the government and the fund was undoubtedly genuine and very hard, and for a long while no accommodation could be reached. The warmth had also clearly gone out of U.S.-Jamaican relations in general. Seaga's former easy access to the Reagan administration had been considerably curtailed by this time, and toward the end of 1986 a substantial cut in U.S. aid to Jamaica and a reduction in the country's sugar import quota into the U.S. market were announced in Washington. Fearful that his main means of external support were disappearing, Seaga pressed ahead with some privatization measures, finally offering 51 percent of the shares in the National Commercial Bank for public sale in December. However, on his difference of opinion with the IMF, namely the currency, he had no political alternative but to stand firm. In the end, the fund relented, with the result that, in January 1987, the JLP government's fourth major agreement with the IMF was concluded. It was for a loan of US$132.8 million for fifteen months, running until 31 March 1988.

Seaga presented the deal as a major breakthrough. "The negotiations were long and tough," he declared, "but they were worth it. We were determined to avoid any up-front devaluation of the Jamaican dollar. We did so! But we must maintain this with a low inflation level."[35] This last was a reference to the main condition of the agreement, which was a government commitment to reduce inflation in 1987–88 to only 7 percent, about half the existing level. With this objective in mind, the list of price controls on basic foods imposed the previous May was retained and new controls instituted on fertilizers, animal feed, herbicides, pesticides, medicines, and educational textbooks. Pay guidelines were also announced limiting increases to 10 percent a year, compared with the previous year's average settlement of 12.5 percent. Import duties were to be further reduced, giving extraregional goods even easier access to the Jamaican market and acting as a downward pressure on prices, albeit to the disadvantage, as before, of local manufacturing interests embedded in traditional import-substitution enterprise. In fact, Douglas Vaz, who had been minister of industry and commerce until the previous October, resigned from the government on this issue, revealing something of the internal conflicts going on within the JLP.

It appeared Seaga's relief was justified. The IMF had retreated from its demand for an immediate devaluation and had given him more time—both economically and politically. Once more too, debt rescheduling within the framework of the Paris Club was made possible by the signing of the IMF deal. Even so, the new agreement also had its dangers for the government. Under questioning, Seaga was forced to admit that a devaluation was likely to take place at the end of the fifteen-month period if the inflation target was not met, and with the trade unions reacting angrily to the proposed pay guidelines, problems were only to be expected, especially with public sector workers such as nurses, doctors, teachers, civil servants, and the police. The reductions in import duties also threatened to set in motion another consumer boom led by those who were well-off; this was likely to widen the trade deficit and force the government into new borrowing as the only means of taking pressure off the exchange rate but could be expected to win back middle-class political support for the JLP, which was still a long way behind the PNP in the polls. In short, Seaga's claim that "we have now left behind us the bitter part of these programmes"[36] of structural adjustment was premature: his plea to the IMF had won him a temporary easing of terms but still left him and his government firmly tied to the dictates of the fund.

In any event, this fourth IMF agreement was the most successful of the Seaga era. Introducing the 1987–88 budget in April, Seaga was able to announce real GDP growth in the previous fiscal year of 3–4 percent, which he claimed was the best figure since 1972. The main factors responsible were the fall in the price of oil, a slight rise in bauxite production, the growth of exports of apparel to the United States under the terms of advantageous tariff concessions like the so-called 807 and Super 807 programs[37] and, above all, the substantial expansion in tourist earnings (to US$503 million in the year ending March 1987, an increase of 21 percent over the previous year). Although there was a tourist boom in many parts of the Caribbean in the 1980s, it was the one unequivocal economic achievement of the JLP period in government and was attributable largely to the restoration of Jamaica's image as an attractive holiday destination in the minds of the American public, following the bad publicity of the 1970s. Although the balance of trade deficit grew as the economy continued to expand throughout 1987, it was financed—and all the IMF's performance tests were satisfactorily passed. As regards wages, the unions had no stomach for a fight with the government after their defeat in the general strike of 1985, and inflation was successfully contained to around 8–9 percent at the end of March 1988. Although higher than the 7 percent ceiling set under the IMF agreement, it caused no difficulties and was obviously within the margin of error permitted in the unspoken part of the deal.

## Phase V: April 1988–February 1989

The final phase of the Seaga government's intricate dealings with the IMF was overlaid politically by the impending election, which was due, in the normal sense of a five-year parliamentary term, by December 1988. But the precise wording of the Jamaican constitution requires that parliament be dissolved within five years of its first sitting after an election and another poll be called within three months of this dissolution. Since the first sitting of the post-1983 parliament had been on 10 January 1984, technically, Seaga had until 10 April 1989 to go to the country—although most commentators assumed he would be reluctant to enter the period of grace for fear of being thought frightened to face the people's verdict. Either way, the April 1988 budget was manifestly the last before an election had to be held. Even a year earlier, the government had significantly increased public expenditure, especially on road building, a classic form of political patronage in Jamaica; on this occasion Seaga announced a "social well-being programme," designed to rebuild the country's social services over a five-year period. Spending on health and education was to be increased by 123 percent and 67 percent, respectively, over the forthcoming year. In addition, expenditure on relief of the poor, school meals, and food subsidies was also to be increased, and no new taxes were proposed. The political message was evident—the social costs of adjustment could now be tackled but only because the country's finances had been put in order by a disciplined and diligent administration.

On the financial side Seaga signaled in his budget speech that further assistance from the IMF was to be sought under a fifth program, which he expected to be negotiated without any problems by the end of the summer.[38] By this stage in the relationship, the IMF was as much tied to Seaga as he was to the fund. The election was the dominant consideration. Although the PNP, and Michael Manley in particular, had worked hard in the second half of the 1980s to convince the international financial community that the party's reelection would pose no threat to Jamaica's capitalist orientation, and although Seaga was regarded with nothing like the favor in Washington that he once enjoyed, the JLP remained much the safer prospect from the point of view of most external interests, certainly those of the IMF. Its officials were pleased to see further privatizations taking place in respect to the Caribbean Cement Company and Telecommunications of Jamaica, but they knew that Seaga was willing to use the state to defend what he saw as key national interests—as when in March 1988 the government resolved its long-running dispute with Alcoa over the Clarendon refinery by agreeing to buy a 50 percent equity share (up from 6 percent) in the company's operation in Jamaica. In short, by late 1988 Seaga was a familiar customer to the fund. In all these circumstances, the negotiation of another agreement was indeed unproblematic: access to US$114 million was offered over fourteen months from September 1988 on terms that did nothing to restrain the expansionary approach, which the JLP government had adopted over the preceding two years, to the management of the Jamaican economy.

These various reflationary measures did little, however, to improve the JLP's poll ratings. An election had still not been called when, on 12 September 1988, Hurricane Gilbert struck Jamaica with devastating force. Agricultural production was badly damaged. Even though mining, manufacturing, and tourism were quickly restored, substantial emergency financial assistance was required, and the JLP briefly gained in political support as it presided over the recovery of a traumatized population.[39] The IMF agreed to readjust some of the targets in the agreement that had just been signed, and the Paris Club agreed to rescheduling. However, disputes over the distribution of aid to give one party an advantage damaged the JLP, and it was not long before the PNP's lead in the polls reasserted itself. Seaga had in effect run out of time politically. The economy had been slowing down in 1988—even before Gilbert—largely because of a downturn in bauxite production after the brief rise in 1986–87. The abolition of the controversial bauxite levy (introduced by the PNP in 1974) and the reinstatement of conventional corporate taxation were negotiated with each of the multinationals from mid-1988 onward but came too late for the government to benefit from the expected stimulation to production. Elections were eventually called for February 1989 and, following a generally peaceful campaign by local standards, were triumphantly won by the PNP, which took forty-five of the sixty seats, with 57 percent of the popular vote.[40]

## CONCLUSION

What emerges, above all, from this account of the Seaga government's management of the economy of Jamaica during the 1980s are the twists and turns by which it sought to stay afloat, both economically and politically. One discussion of the preceding PNP administration drew attention to "the zig-zag politics" it followed;[41] the same can be said of the JLP regime. Conventionally, the two governments have been differentiated by commentators: the PNP era was associated with the pursuit of democratic socialism and the JLP era with the pursuit of orthodox liberal development. In the same way, Manley as a man of the left has been contrasted with Seaga as a man of the right. The analysis offered here suggests that this line of argument is misleading and that it is the structural constraints on the freedom of maneuver of both governments that ought to be emphasized rather than the differing ideological predispositions or styles of their leaders.

In a nutshell, these constraints are of two kinds. The first is represented by Jamaica's geopolitical and geoeconomic location in the U.S. sphere of influence. This gives substantial power over the Jamaican political directorate to a range of external forces, from U.S. political leadership in the White House and various U.S. departments of state, to the officials of the IMF, the World Bank, and other U.S.-dominated international financial agencies, to the managers of major multinational corporations with investments and interests in Jamaica. The second constraint is represented by Jamaica's commitment to its particular form of electoral democracy— in a broad sense, the legacy of British colonialism. This ethic has been substantially internalized by the Jamaican people over the last fifty years. In other words, Jamaican leaders have two sets of masters, two constituencies that they must please—one external, the other internal. Put like this, many of the shifts of policy of the Seaga government become more explicable. Seaga was endeavoring to find and follow a path between conflicting pressures: from without, the pressure of "liberal economics" imposed by the IMF and the Reagan administration, and from within, the pressure of "electoral politics" imposed by the exigencies of winning votes and holding onto office.

This interpretation of Jamaican politics makes discussion of the real Seaga somewhat redundant. Admittedly, an accurate reading of Seaga's political outlook is not easy to arrive at. He has not written books or published collections of his speeches or given many revealing interviews. The clues that litter his political career are also contradictory. Born of Syrian stock and by training a sociologist, he early acquired a radical reputation in Jamaica by making a speech in the old Legislative Council in 1961 contrasting the lot of the "haves" and the "have-nots" in local society.[42] When Jamaica achieved independence, he was elected to (and continued to represent) a constituency in one of the poorest parts of West Kingston, his majority built up over the years by deliberate patronage. He later emerged as one of the key modernizers in the 1962–72 JLP government, first as minister of development and welfare and later of finance and planning, acquiring in the latter post a new reputation for his toughness in collecting taxes from the business community. As leader of the opposition from 1974 onward, he cultivated an appeal based on rabid anticommunism and a close association with the private sector, locally, and big business, internationally. In government in the 1980s, as we have seen, he both pandered to the IMF and bitterly criticized the institution; fawned over the U.S. administration and let his dissatisfaction with its support be known; and followed policies that reduced state control of the economy in some areas and promoted it in others. This led some writers from the right to condemn him as "a Caribbean con man,"[43] who led a government that was every bit as statist, indeed socialist, as that of Manley in the 1970s, and others from the left to characterize his beliefs at the end of the day as "a combination of populism and state capitalism."[44]

In the circumstances, it is sensible to view Seaga simply as a pragmatist or, more pejoratively, an opportunist. He is not a politician for whom a package of guiding ideas is particularly important. He saw in 1980 that the global trend in economic management favored the return of neoliberal premises; he knew that the Jamaican economy could not manage without the financial support of the IMF and that the idea of structural adjustment was dominant in the fund's thinking; and above all, he saw an opportunity for Jamaica to cultivate a reputation in Washington for free-market beliefs. On this basis he won for the country massive amounts of U.S. assistance in the early years of his government (Jamaica becoming one of the five highest per capita U.S. aid recipients in the world), and he clearly expected that innovations like the Rockefeller Committee would lead to a much greater flow of new inward investment than actually occurred. He also knew that the Jamaican capitalist class was weak and, having been nurtured on import-substitution industrialization, lacked the capacity to initiate and sustain export-led growth as an indigenous bourgeoisie. The state thus had to be used to protect the Jamaican economy—especially in moments of crisis—for no better reason than that there was no alternative agency available. In fact, state intervention kept bauxite alive in the midst of a major recession in the world aluminium industry for which neither Seaga nor Jamaica could be held responsible.

In sum, Seaga is best understood as a political manager who tried to reconcile external economic pressures with domestic electoral imperatives. In this effort, he showed a cunning and resourcefulness typical of the Caribbean political tradition. As Carl Stone put it in one of his newspaper columns, "those critics who are trying to make out Mr Seaga is simply a clerk administering IMF policies are being mischievous. The international agency input is great in helping to define the overall framework. But the game plan, the tactics and the strategies are entirely Eddie's doing."[45]

In the final analysis, of course, Seaga failed in his balancing act. On the economic front, this can be seen in the average rate of economic growth generated over his eight years in office—1.2 percent per annum, scarcely the stuff of economic miracles; in the continuing high levels of unemployment in the country; in its deteriorating social and economic infrastructure; and in the accumulated external debt of US$4.5 billion by the end of his term. On the political front, it can be seen in the crushing defeat he suffered in the February 1989 election. He failed because he was never able to gain control of events and chart a coherent development strategy for the country. He was constantly forced to be reactive, rather than proactive; he was pulled and pushed in different directions by different pressures at different times. Notwithstanding his reputation for personal authoritarianism, Seaga's role in Jamaican politics in the 1980s highlights more than anything else the weak position of Caribbean leaders in the world system.

## 2 Democracy and Disillusionment in the Dominican Republic

*Jan Knippers Black*

The Dominican Republic is both typical and atypical in the context of the modern Caribbean. Like so many other Caribbean states, it is a paradise plundered. Economically appended and politically subordinated to one external power or another throughout its history, despite the achievement of Dominican independence in 1844, the national territory, occupying the eastern two-thirds of the island of Hispaniola, has seen its luxuriant forests and fertile soils, equable climate and alluring beaches, and generous and industrious people perennially exploited for the benefit of foreigners. Dominicans have been left with the dubious blessings of entanglement in the contemporary world economy: dependency, drugs, and debt. At the same time, however, and unlike the majority of the Caribbean states, the Dominican Republic has had to live in the shadow of the United States for almost a century. This point is critical. Since falling under U.S. suzerainty at the turn of the twentieth century, the republic has found its independence repeatedly qualified by its dependence on U.S. markets and suppliers, U.S. foreign assistance, and loans and investments from U.S.-based banks and industries. The country's latitude for political decision making has also been circumscribed by the need of U.S. leaders to feel that they were in control—or at the very least, in a position to exercise a veto power over the choice of policies and policy makers. The modern political history of the Dominican Republic has, therefore, been less like that of the English, French, or Dutch-speaking Caribbean and more like that of Cuba and mainland Latin America.

During the 1980s, certainly, the Dominican Republic was in the vanguard of trends increasingly manifest throughout the whole of the Western Hemisphere. These included the withdrawal of the

military; the rise of democratic reformism; increasing indebtedness and surrender of economic sovereignty to the International
Monetary Fund (IMF); the discrediting of reformist parties and
leaders; and a return to economic conservatism buffered by the
rituals and institutions of formal democracy. This chapter examines these themes but begins by looking back to the formative era
of General Trujillo.

## THE LEGACY OF TRUJILLO

The seemingly endless dictatorship of General Rafael Leonidas
Trujillo (1930–61), who rose to power through command of the
constabulary established in the early years of the U.S. occupation
from 1916–24, left no aspect of national life untouched: no political institution had any domestic base independent of Trujillo and
his thugs. The military became the strongest institution in the
country. Politicians such as Joaquín Balaguer, who had associated
themselves with the regime, were widely discredited, especially
among the educated in urban areas. Those like Juan Bosch, who
had fled into exile, remained untainted but also unschooled in the
grisly reality of Dominican politics. Thus, albeit in different ways,
both Bosch and Balaguer, the towering caudillos of the post-
Trujillo era, were rendered less effective as national leaders by the
legacy of that awful tyranny.

Following Trujillo's assassination in 1961, Balaguer, who was
serving as puppet president, yielded to pressures from the Kennedy
administration and from the Dominican population and stepped
down. Power was transferred to a council of state, which scheduled
elections in 1962. The elections resulted in a solid victory for Juan
Bosch and his center-left Dominican Revolutionary Party (PRD).
Yet, after only six months in office, Bosch was overthrown in a
military coup backed by the country's traditional reactionary
forces—in particular, the oligarchy and the Catholic church. Collectively, they then sought to preserve their privileges through the
so-called triumvirate government. In effect a military-civilian junta, this regime was itself toppled in April 1965 by an uprising led by
pro-Bosch, or constitutionalist, forces. A civil war, centered upon
the capital, Santo Domingo, ensued, as reactionary elements within the military, encouraged by their U.S. advisers, launched an
attack against the constitutionalists and their PRD civilian supporters. Facing the prospect of a victory by the reformist, pro-Bosch
forces, U.S. President Lyndon Johnson sent in the marines.

Johnson first claimed that the intervention, which ultimately involved some 23,000 troops, was to save American lives but, later, asserted that it was to counter a communist conspiracy. (In fact, he had considerable difficulty finding, for the record, an American who would claim to have felt his life threatened or a quorum of live communists.) U.S. marines, supplemented by an Organization of American States peacekeeping force effectively under U.S. command, remained in the country for more than a year, eventually supervising elections in 1966.[1] In these, Balaguer and his personalist Reformist Party (PR) soundly defeated Bosch and the PRD. This outcome was just what the Johnson administration desired. Seeking to prop up the new government, demonstrate that the intervention had been beneficial to Dominicans, and smooth the way for more direct U.S. investment, it increased both military and economic assistance to unprecedented levels. With this support, Balaguer was reelected in 1970 and again in 1974 in elections that were boycotted by the PRD and most other parties.

During the long tenure of Balaguer, virtually all political activists, including some aligned with him, suffered death threats, narrow escapes, detention, and deportation. They learned both to accept risk and to exercise caution. Thus it was a moderated and subdued PRD that contested and won the elections of 1978. Even so, military officers sought to block its accession to power, backing down only after the Carter administration interceded in support of the democratic process. Carter himself issued a public warning that future U.S. support for the Dominican government would depend on respect for the integrity of the elections.[2] As Bosch had defected in 1973 to form another, more leftist, party, called the Dominican Liberation Party (PLD), the PRD's candidate was a wealthy rancher by the name of Antonio Guzmán, who thus became president.

## DEMOCRACY ON A LEASH 1978–86

Even those senior military officers who had been hesitant to participate in the abortive election-day coup were prepared to give Guzmán no more than a six-month probationary period. Furthermore, legislation passed during the PR's lame duck session placed Guzmán on a short leash. It raised military pay; directed the Department of National Investigation, a secret police and intelligence unit often used by Balaguer to repress the PRD, to report to the secretary of the armed forces rather than to the president; stipulated that the armed forces secretary must have been a major-general for at least five years; and provided that officers could not be transferred by civilian authorities before they had served two years in a given post. (Balaguer then reshuffled and promoted his loyalists to ensure them the full two years in place.)

Guzmán, nevertheless, managed to turn the tables. Strengthened by an intensely antimilitary popular mood at home and by continued support from Washington, Guzmán disregarded the tainted legislation and moved quickly to rid the government of those officers who most clearly threatened it. More than 240 potentially disloyal officers were replaced by more reliable ones. The armed forces did not necessarily accept such initiatives with good grace. A coup was plotted in 1979, but Guzmán was able to crush it before it unfolded. In the meantime, his promotions of junior and middle-ranking officers who had been sidelined by Balaguer boosted morale among that long disgruntled set and attenuated their hostility to the PRD.[3] In general, Guzmán opened up the system, eliminating restraints on civil liberties and urging respect for human rights. He also pledged to rein in runaway corruption, promote economic growth and modernization, and provide long-neglected social services.

Guzmán's political position always remained weak, however, as he encountered fierce opposition from within his own party as well as from Balaguer's Reformist party. Moreover, his assumption of power coincided with the beginnings of a steep economic decline. The sugar market went limp, most other exports were in low demand, and petroleum, all of which had to be imported, was scarce and expensive. To make matters worse, a devastating hurricane struck in 1979.

Social services, therefore, continued to be neglected, and development programs were sustained only at the expense of a sharply mounting foreign debt, which even by 1976 had reached some US$700 million. Corruption scarcely abated. In fact, it is generally believed that it was embarrassment over his own daughter's involvement in shady deals that drove Guzmán to suicide shortly before the end of his term.[4] Partly because of such alleged corruption and partly because Guzmán had been seen as too accommodating to U.S. interests, party leaders selected one of his archrivals within the PRD to succeed him. Senator Salvador Jorge Blanco, who had been serving also as party president, was elected to the presidency for the term beginning in August 1982.

Jorge Blanco had no significant popular following of his own, but he brought to the presidency the reputation of a serious and honest politician and human rights lawyer with a constructive program. He pledged to maintain and strengthen the social and political liberalism introduced by his predecessor; stem the tide of corruption, to which the PRD itself had fallen prey; trim the size of the bureaucracy, which had mushroomed under Guzmán; and expand services and legal protection to the disadvantaged majority. But it was not to be: economic and political circumstances largely beyond his control combined with the weaknesses of his own administration to discredit his government, his party, and perhaps even "reformism" in general.

The government inherited by Jorge Blanco was deeply in debt and virtually bankrupt. It also confronted weak markets and sinking prices for the country's major exports, which worsened the balance of payments deficit.[5] The resourcefulness and statesmanship demanded by the seriousness of the economic crisis were not forthcoming from either the government or its congressional opposition. While the poorest Dominicans had no choice but to accept greater sacrifice, the affluent made the usual choice. Jorge Blanco's proposals for new taxes were blocked in congress, not only by the Reformist Party, but by the PLD and the Jacob Majluta faction of the PRD as well.

In the absence of new resources, the most obvious means of reducing the budget deficit—as demanded by the International Monetary Fund—was a pruning of public employees. This was directly contrary to Guzmán's approach. His policy had been to expand the government payroll as a way of lowering unemployment and consolidating the base of the PRD. Far from dismissing the *reformistas* in government service, he had added another layer of employees loyal to the PRD, increasing the number of public servants by some 50–60 percent. Jorge Blanco had pledged to prune the bureaucracy, but he, too, found early on that such a move was not politically feasible. On the contrary, he found it necessary to expand the bureaucracy by another 40 percent or so. If anything, however, more bureaucrats seemed to mean less service. Public agencies were not able to acquire enough revenue to pay salaries and fulfill mandates as well. Most of them merely stumbled along, seriously undercapitalized, performing their duties only sporadically.[6] Moreover, more bureaucrats meant more hands illicitly in the till. It appeared that many of the PRD appointees, previously poor, had been in a hurry to get rich; if the PRD government had been unable to significantly expand services, it had at least been able to "democratize," or expand the base of, corruption!

The deepening crisis also aggravated antagonisms among classes and sectors and seemed to leave the civilian authorities more vulnerable to the machinations of the security forces. Among government agencies and programs, only the armed forces and police fared well—their budgets, for example, amounting to more than the combined budgets for health and education. It was because of the historic enmity between the PRD and the military, of course, rather than in spite of it, that military budgets, salaries, and perquisites were on the rise, while civilian programs faltered.[7]

Jorge Blanco was widely portrayed even by Guzmán and others of his own party as a leftist, mainly because as a lawyer he had frequently represented political dissidents and poor people whose rights had been violated. Thus he was even less acceptable to politically oriented officers than Guzmán had been. Having so much to overcome, Jorge Blanco essentially tried to bribe the armed forces to stay in their barracks and leave his government alone. Military housing facilities and commissary offerings were expanded. A new social security institute, including a hospital, was established exclusively for the armed forces and the police. Jet planes and modern patrol boats were purchased, and extralegal enterprises were overlooked (or perhaps even assisted). Nevertheless, Jorge Blanco never achieved the levels of control over, and respect from, the officers corps that Guzmán had enjoyed.[8]

With government coffers virtually empty of foreign exchange and facing the specter of default on foreign debts and interruption of imports, Jorge Blanco caved in to the demands of the IMF for the imposition of austerity measures, including frozen wages, higher prices and interest rates, and longer working hours, that severely penalized his own constituency and deepened the factionalism within the PRD. The fund's recommendations also included the abandonment of vestiges of protection of domestic industry and regulation of foreign investment and increased credit and infrastructural support for export production in general, particularly agro-industry, mining, and *maquila*-type light industry in duty-free zones. U.S. and IMF advisers also pressured the Dominican government to trim the domestic budget in ways that generally implied cutting social services. The peso, too, began to be steadily devalued. The devaluation of April 1984, in particular, resulted in sharp price increases for a number of essential commodities and ignited riots in Santo Domingo that went on for three days; they were put down eventually by a U.S.-trained elite force, leaving more than a hundred dead.[9] Jorge Blanco's government never recovered from this episode, and it sank ever deeper into unpopularity as charges of corruption mounted during its final months.

The PRD thus faced the elections of 1986 with a severely divided party, a reputation besmirched by corruption, and an economy in shambles. It was little wonder that many voters looked back through rose-colored glasses upon the "good old days" of Balaguer's rule in the late 1960s and early 1970s. Running at the head of a newly constituted Social Christian Reformist Party (PRSC), Balaguer took a plurality of some 41 percent of the vote, leaving the PRD's Jacobo Majluta with 39 percent, and Bosch, heading the Dominican Liberation Party, with 18 percent.[10] For Jorge Blanco, disgrace followed electoral defeat. Under indictment because he allegedly tried to take over and orchestrate military and other rackets, he took refuge in April 1987 in the Venezuelan embassy in Santo Domingo and later fled to the United States for an indefinite period of "medical observation."[11] He returned to the Dominican Republic in the spring of 1989 to stand trial, but the case was suspended later in the year after his wife suffered a minor accident. (Some observers believed that, for Balaguer, the indictment had already served its purpose, and that he had lost the will to prosecute.)

## BACK TO BALAGUER

The fact that so many voters misremembered the era of Balaguer as one of general, rather than highly selective, prosperity owed much to Balaguer's legendary political skills. Friends and enemies alike credit his intelligence and political acumen, and even those who know him best describe him as enigmatic. Under the tutelage of Trujillo, he learned to listen and not to speak unnecessarily; he also learned how to reward and discipline supporters, co-opt the uncommitted, and punish his enemies; and he learned finally how to profit from the dramatic gesture without subjecting himself to risk. When his early government was under assault in 1962, for example, he stood his ground, for media effect, saying, "Better a dead president than one in flight!" Only moments later he slipped easily over the wall from his own residence to refuge in the nunciature (residence of the papal nuncio)![12] Over the years, too, one of the most useful—and most cynical—devices used by Balaguer was the dual signature. One signature meant yes, that the measure had his approval or that the individual was cleared for housing, a job, or some other benefit; the other signaled to underlings that they were to stall and frustrate until the exasperated supplicant gave up the pursuit. In this way, the constituent (and potential voter) was led to believe that his misfortune was due to an obstinate bureaucracy's defiance of a generous president.

In short, Balaguer was adept at combining authoritarianism

with paternalism, but ever the pragmatist, he adapted with ease to operating in a more open and democratic system, building on his strengths in bargaining and conciliation as well as in dissembling. Campaigning for the elections of 1986, he promised hundreds of jobs; some people even left their homes in the provinces and moved to the capital on the strength of such promises. After his inauguration, however, Balaguer boasted that he had no commitments, that he "owed nothing to anyone except God."[13] His style of decision making remained as solitary under constitutional government as it had been in his earlier, more nearly authoritarian, regime.

Balaguer also profited, ironically, from his failure to establish a real party or any other civilian institution of consequence. No new generation of leaders was apparent in the PRSC or in any other party. Balaguer's early cabinet appointments were a veritable "Who's Who" of the center to right in Dominican politics, including many of his one-time enemies. The aristocracy, which was not always on good terms with Balaguer, was represented by Donald Reid Cabral, who had headed the very conservative triumvirate government of 1963–65; Reid Cabral served as minister of foreign affairs until he was replaced by Balaguer's nephew, Joaquín Ricardo. Foreign investors were reassured by the placement of Carlos A. Morales Troncoso in the vice presidency. Morales Troncoso, previously a local manager of Gulf and Western properties, had become a major stockholder in the properties of the Miami-based Funjul brothers, who in early 1985 had bought out Gulf and Western, a major U.S. corporation, which had hitherto controlled much of the country's economy. Since the vice president carries no significant duties, Morales Troncoso later took on the additional role of ambassador to the United States. For their part, the Christian Democrats, whose merger with the PRSC had provided Balaguer with valuable international ties and legitimacy, gained less from their bargain.[14] They still believe that they stand one day to inherit Balaguer's base in the peasantry. After 1986, however, Balaguer mainly used them to fill subcabinet positions, where it was important to have competent people who could be counted upon not to steal.

The need for trustworthy administrators has also been cited as one of Balaguer's reasons for appointing women to governorships of the provinces. Governors have little personal power, as they neither raise nor allocate funds; rather, they serve as personal representatives of the president to the provinces. During his first elective term (1966–70), Balaguer appointed only women to those positions. The second time around, women held only nine of the twenty-nine governorships. Nevertheless, this represented more recognition than women received from other leaders and parties. In general, women became better organized: there is an important nonpartisan organization of women voters as well as a number of partisan women's organizations. Towards the end of the decade, more women voted than men, and Balaguer's supporters claimed that he enjoyed an edge with female voters. Much of that loyalty is personal, however, rather than partisan.[15]

Balaguer's initial choice for secretary of the armed forces in 1986 was sure to displease some of the military's career officers but perhaps was designed more to reassure the Pentagon and the CIA. General Antonio Imbert Barrera was one of the two survivors from among those who, in 1961, at the behest of the CIA, assassinated Trujillo. The interior secretary, in charge of the police and responsible for public order, was General Elías Wessin y Wessin, who had masterminded the coup against the government of Juan Bosch in 1963 and, with the help of the U.S. marines, had put down the uprising of Bosch's constitutionalist forces in 1965. He had also conspired in the early 1970s against the government of Balaguer. At any rate, the military leaders in the new cabinet were essentially *gastado* (burned out), having little following of their own among younger officers. This left Balaguer free to mediate among services and factions whose loyalty was to him. Some speculated that Balaguer had drawn Imbert and Wessin into his cabinet in order, figuratively (he is almost blind), to keep an eye on them. It was certainly clear that confidence between the president and each of these officers was less than complete. In late 1987, Balaguer vetoed and pushed into early retirement Imbert's nominees for chiefs of the three services, and in June 1988, following rumors of a coup attempt, he dismissed Imbert, replacing him with Wessin as secretary of the armed forces.

As before, however, Balaguer was careful not to impede institutional (as opposed to PRD-based) military rackets. He had found during previous presidential terms that most officers were willing to surrender considerable political power and give him total loyalty in exchange for the opportunity to enrich themselves at the public's expense. Meanwhile, Balaguer himself maintained an ascetic life-style and was universally acclaimed for his "personal" integrity. Even Bosch and other political opponents gave full credence to Balaguer's assertion that the corruption stopped at the door to his office.[16]

Given the country's dire economic straits, particularly the

steady decline, at least since the collapse of the sugar market in the early 1980s, in the standard of living of the poor majority, the ambience that prevailed in the Dominican Republic until early 1988 was remarkably calm and stable. There were few manifestations of civil unrest. A general strike in July 1987 generated no disorder (due in part to the curiously passive role played by PLD-dominated student and labor groups), and the police did not fire a single shot, a restraint duly noticed and publicly praised by human rights monitors. Apparently, the riots of 1984 and the violent response of the security forces had had a sobering effect on both right and left. The left, at any rate, had good reason to fear military intervention if demonstrations got out of hand, while the right, in turn, were concerned that violent repression might lead to serious insurgency.

The record of the born-again-democratic Balaguer in this regard stood in stark contrast to that of previous Balaguer governments as well as the government of Jorge Blanco, though the rights of the poor were feebly protected even at the best of times, and Haitians in the Dominican Republic remained particularly vulnerable to scapegoating, or worse. Until 1988, however, even Balaguer's political enemies conceded that, relatively speaking, his government had shown sensitivity to human rights concerns and restraint in maintaining order. Furthermore, most of the country's economic ills were blamed on Balaguer's predecessor.

That climate changed suddenly and dramatically during the third week of February 1988. The protests that began at that time over low wages, the soaring costs of basic goods and services, and the scarcity of such amenities as electricity and potable water were remarkably widespread. At least eleven of the provinces were crippled by general strikes, and incidents of violence were reported throughout the country, particularly in the capital and several northern cities. By early March, casualties included ten dead and some twenty wounded, and several thousand protesters had been detained. In response, Balaguer offered a substantial wage hike to public employees, which, along with the massive show of military force, may have brought about the lull later in March. However, violence erupted once again at the beginning of April as thousands took part in street demonstrations throughout the country. Dozens were injured in bomb explosions and confrontations with riot squad police in Santo Domingo and Santiago, the country's second-largest city. A national strike committee, composed of labor confederations and civic neighborhood organizations, called for a forty-eight hour general strike. Negotiations between labor and business leaders mediated by the Catholic hierarchy served to quell the unrest in the short term. Even so, strikes continued throughout 1989, and riots erupted from time to time.

Balaguer's approach to this unrest and to the nation's very severe economic problems—which was to print pesos to cover public works programs and stimulate agricultural production—generated new jobs but also resulted in devaluation and accelerated inflation. Meanwhile, foreign reserves, accumulated partly from remittances from Dominican emigrants, partly from tourism, and to an unknown degree from drug deals, could not be expected to service adequately a foreign debt of some US$4 billion. A new class of financiers, however, had learned during the 1980s how to profit from the country's economic prostration: through currency exchange deals and speculation in scarce commodities. This group competed for influence with another newly rich sector, the *narcotrafficantes,* some of whom ply their trade in the Dominican Republic, while others merely launder their money there. In the face of such developments, the bargaining and conciliation that had served Balaguer well in the past in mitigating conflict among the elites appeared more and more to be an inadequate response to mounting economic difficulties and widespread frustration and deprivation. With Balaguer's refusal to change economic policy, a change of government began to present itself as a distinct possibility.

## Issues and Actors in the 1990 Elections

Dominicans went to the polls again for general elections in May 1990. Never one to play his cards prematurely, Balaguer spent several months aggressively touting the accomplishments of his administration, particularly in the area of public works, and acting in all respects like a candidate for reelection. He would not commit himself to candidacy, however, until very nearly the last moment for declaration, so that he might appear to be swept in by draft. Meanwhile, Fernando Alvarez Bogaert, frustrated in previous efforts to inherit the mantle of the PRSC leadership, had proceeded to declare his candidacy. Alvarez Bogaert commanded the loyalty of much of the party's midlevel management, such as it was; but Balaguer had a firm grip on the base of a party essentially lacking organization and characterized, instead, by a kind of amorphous populism. Alvarez Bogaert's slogan, and the only well-recognized plank of his platform, was "time for a new generation." No doubt there were many who shared that view. On the whole, however, he was simply ignored by Balagueristas, other parties and candidates, the media, and the public.[17] When it finally became unmistakably clear that Balaguer was running, Alvarez Bogaert withdrew and embarked on an extended overseas trip.

Other familiar candidates or precandidates who were also ignored included Narciso Isa Conde of the Dominican Communist Party, General Wessin, leading his Dominican Quisqueyana Party, lawyer and agrarian reform advocate Mariano Vinicio ("Vincho") Castillo, with his relatively new National Progressive Front (FNP), and José Rafael Abinader, backed by the Social Democratic Alliance, a splinter of the PRD. Along with a president and vice president, voters were to select 30 senators, 120 deputies, 102 mayors, and hundreds of municipal councilmen. A new electoral law, permitting ticket splitting, was expected to work against small, personalist parties, as well as against lesser candidates sharing tickets with Balaguer and Bosch, and to be particularly helpful to candidates with strong provincial or local bases.[18] As it turned out, however, relatively few voters took advantage of the option of ticket splitting.

The most professional campaign mounted was that of Jacobo Majluta, backed by his breakaway faction of the PRD, known as the Revolutionary Independent Party. This professionalism suggested the influence of U.S.-style TV politics and U.S. sources of campaign funding. Majluta was able to position himself squarely in the center of the political spectrum, with possibilities for maneuver in either direction. If he failed to inspire middle-class voters, neither did he scare them. His supporters acclaimed his experience and competence, while his detractors regarded him as opportunistic and corrupt. He was believed to have a firm grip on the remains of the PRD machinery, or midlevel infrastructure, particularly in the provinces, but he lacked grass roots support.

As has been seen, the PRD had been deeply split since the mid-1980s between the faction of Majluta and that of José Francisco Peña Gómez, known as the Bloque Institucional. The base of the party, among the poor of Santo Domingo, belonged to Peña Gómez, and he continued to cultivate that base. Middle-class voters, however, were left uneasy by campaign advertisements that showed the candidate surrounded by poor blacks walking through city slums, and his enemies gained mileage by alluding to his Haitian antecedents. There were grounds, too, for wondering whether his populist inclinations would have been acceptable to the United States. Yet in late 1989, Peña Gómez initiated a party unity dialogue by proposing to Majluta that they launch a joint

candidacy with the intent of sharing the four-year presidential
term. Majluta would take the first two years and Peña Gómez the
last two. Majluta rejected that proposal but countered with one of
alternating four-year terms, the decision as to which of them
would run first to be made by the party assembly (which Majluta
controlled). The Jorge Blanco faction of the party, now headed by
Hatuey de Camps, chief of the presidential staff during the last
PRD government, appeared open to the proposal for alternation; de
Camps allegedly hoped to be the party's candidate himself after
four years (an unlikely proposition, given his many enemies and
lack of a popular base). Unity talks continued for several weeks, but
without resolution; ultimately, Peña Gómez and Majluta launched
separate candidacies.[19]

The major beneficiary of the disunity of the PRD was Bosch's
PLD. Despite its rapid growth, it was by far the best-run party. Its
organization was cellular. New members were carefully trained,
and older members met regularly for study and discussion of political issues. Discipline was such that even after large PLD rallies
there was virtually no litter left behind. Although there was as yet
no heir apparent to Bosch, there was a well-established echelon of
midlevel leadership. Bosch himself had come to be noted for his
incisive commentary on social inequality and U.S. imperialism,
even before audiences likely to react negatively to such themes.
This led some observers to believe that he did not really want to be
president, that he preferred the role of challenger and critic. During
the campaign season, however, he trimmed his sails somewhat.
Responding, perhaps, to the recent decapitalization and dismal
mismanagement of some public enterprises, he even joined the
chorus calling for privatization.[20]

The main issue in the 1990 campaign, apart from the age and
health of the two major contenders, was the Balaguer government—
or the lack of it. As during his earlier terms, Balaguer had done a
great deal of building, but he had not given much attention to what
should happen inside the buildings—to ensuring, for example, that
his new clinics and schools would have the necessary nurses and
teachers. Government employees, in general, had been sadly neglected by his administration, and while the tripartite agreement
(government-business-labor) reached in the aftermath of the 1988
riots had generally kept a lid on the widespread discontent, strikes
by public employees had continued to break out sporadically. Indeed, many Dominicans believed that Balaguer's attention was
now more focused on his place in history, to the neglect of his
contemporary compatriots. That place was to be ensured by a

project worthy of the pharaohs; Balaguer's "pyramid" is a mammoth lighthouse, in the form of a cross, designed to beam electric light deep into the Caribbean. Built to commemorate the quincentennial of Columbus's arrival in the New World, it was to be inaugurated with great fanfare on Columbus Day 1992, perhaps by Spain's King Juan Carlos or the pope. At that time, the remains of Columbus, now resting in Santo Domingo's cathedral, were to be moved to the lighthouse.

While Balaguer prepared to floodlight the Caribbean, Dominicans increasingly had to live in the dark as a consequence of daily electrical outages, or *apagones*. The broken-down state electricity enterprise also governs water pressure, so that power failures usually meant interruption of the supply of running water, as well. In late 1989 and early 1990, *apagones* occurred at irregular hours throughout the day, causing spoilage of food and making "business as usual" impossible. In fact, small businesses were folding at an alarming rate, and the resulting hardships increased tensions between Dominican communities and foreign companies, like the Central Romana Corporation, that had their own power supply. At the same time, a further assault on the Dominican standard of living was caused by a steep rate of inflation. It was pegged officially in 1988 and 1989 at about 60 percent, but it was generally believed to be much higher.[21] The poor had learned to survive economic austerity over the years, but with the double shock of *apagones* and inflation, the prospect of economic insecurity increasingly stalked the Dominican middle class as well.

Given this state of affairs, the wonder was that Balaguer retained such a reservoir of popularity. Throughout the campaign, public opinion polls showed Bosch and Balaguer far ahead of other potential or announced contenders. Bosch persistently held a solid lead, although many Dominicans fully expected Balaguer to pull something out of the hat before election day. For example, a Gallup poll conducted on behalf on the newspaper *El Siglo* at the end of March 1990 gave Bosch 36 percent of the vote to 26 percent for Balaguer, 15 percent for Peña Gómez, and 9 percent for Majluta. Of the fifteen other candidates, none received more than 1 percent, and together they received only 2 percent. Ten percent remained undecided, while 3 percent indicated that they did not intend to vote. Curiously, the poll indicated that Bosch, a socialist, enjoyed a strong lead among the upper and middle classes and the most highly educated; he also led among lower-class voters, but less decisively. For the more conservative Balaguer, support derived mainly from the very poorest and least educated, particularly in rural areas. As for Peña Gómez, his support remained a uniform 15 percent across social classes, rising to 19 percent in Santo Domingo, where he had previously served as mayor. Bosch also led decisively among the new voters, aged eighteen to twenty-four (who helped to account for the increase in registered voters from 3 million at the time of the 1986 election to 3.5 million in 1990), as well as among those aged twenty-five to thirty-nine. Voters over forty years old gave a slim lead to Balaguer, a lead that became much stronger among voters over fifty-five years of age. The poll even showed Bosch having a slim lead among women, who constituted 54 percent of the registered voters.[22]

As election day approached, the rhetoric of the campaign became more personal and more negative. Balaguer, for example, began to allude to the "threat of communism"; and Bosch charged that Balaguer was making use of state resources in his reelection campaign and that the PRSC had arranged to rig the elections. Some 65 percent of the registered voters turned out for the elections on 16 May. Early returns showed Bosch in the lead, but after two days, with 87 percent of the polling stations reporting, Bosch trailed with 558,979 to 570,459 votes for Balaguer. Peña Gómez received 373,058. No other candidate had made a significant showing. After PLD officials met with foreign election observers, the PRSC and the PLD agreed to a recount. The Central Electoral Board finally announced the outcome of the recount on 11 June. Balaguer had received 678,248 votes, or 35 percent of those cast, to 653,423 votes, or 34.4 percent, for Bosch.[23]

## CONCLUSION: THE BROKEN PROMISES OF DEMOCRATIC REFORM

The Dominican Republic is a rich country populated by poor people. The collapse of the world sugar market in the early 1980s, followed in short order by a massive cut in the Dominican quota of the U.S. sugar market, left the country economically destitute and seriously indebted. The tourist industry has since become the country's major foreign exchange earner. Nontraditional export crops grown on land formerly devoted to sugarcane and light industry in the proliferating duty-free zones have also contributed to a measure of economic recovery. Nevertheless, the country remains utterly dependent upon dollar remittances from the nearly one million emigrants now living in Puerto Rico or the United States and on hard currency loans contracted at great cost to national sovereignty and social peace. For all that, the republic has weathered remarkably well the economic crises of the 1980s, although the calm that prevailed as the country entered the 1990s was an uneasy calm, which should not be mistaken for stability. Considerable economic readjustment and diversification had taken place, but it is not clear that these changes, featuring disincentives to internal market expansion, will solve the long-term problems of the balance of payments and debt servicing; and they are not even addressed to the shorter-term problem of the economic insecurity of the majority of Dominicans.

The blessings of the return to formal democracy beginning in 1978 are also not to be underrated. Freedom of expression and association have normally been respected, and the four elections that have taken place over the last dozen years were generally free of fraud, if not of bizarre incidents. By the end of the 1980s, middle-class political activists were no longer in danger of being swept off the streets or dragged from their homes to be tortured and perhaps "disappeared." But the poor, always vulnerable, remained subject to abuse; and while the middle class lived with economic uncertainty, the poor majority lived with the certainty of hunger and disease. Key questions, therefore, arise in reflecting on this experience. What happened to the economic development and social justice—or at least marginal improvement in living standards—that Dominicans expected to accompany democratic reforms? How is it that the PRD, popular and reformist in its origins, so lowered its horizons once in power? Why would a party that had once been a source of such anxiety for economic elites acquiesce meekly while even the most modest of its promised welfare measures were thwarted by IMF-imposed austerity measures? Why would a reputedly reformist president like Jorge Blanco make concessions to the armed forces, creditors, and other foreign and domestic elite interests that even more conservative presidents might have resisted, while failing to resist the lure of corruption? Bosch, during his brief tenure in the presidency in the 1960s, resisted both concessions and corruption; but does that in large measure explain the brevity of his tenure?

Answers to such sweeping questions can only be partial and speculative, but it appears that they lie largely in the constraints on democratic reformism, especially in times of economic crisis, and in the contemporary concentration of power in the global economic system. Earlier generations of reformist leaders in the Caribbean, presiding during periods of economic growth or at least of easy credit terms, were able to reward lower-income political constituencies without seriously threatening the material interests of elites. For Dominican and other regional leaders in the 1980s, however, no such options existed. With economies shrinking and creditors foreclosing, the election of reformers did not offer the prospect of redistribution in favor of the previously deprived; it meant, instead, shifting the burden of debt repayment to those who benefited least—the poor and the powerless. For the elites, it had the twofold payoff of protecting their interests and prestige and discrediting reformists and reformism.

Elections may reconfirm the locus of political power in a national system, but they do not transfer power away from an economic elite, especially where that elite is partly foreign and is favored by a more or less autonomous military establishment and an attentive hegemonic power like the United States. The PRD, like reformist regimes elsewhere, thus lacked the full range of powers normally associated with government—most important, control over the armed forces and the police. Governments taking office under such circumstances, like that of Guzmán and, even more so, of Jorge Blanco, had to spend inordinately of their scarce resources to cajole or outmaneuver armed bodies predisposed to oust them. Such a priority distracted attention and diverted resources from endeavors that might have been developmental or at least ameliorative of the worst injustices. Thus, simply completing one's term without being overthrown became the overriding concern, a concern readily justifiable as the best means of promoting the consolidation of democracy and countering the threats posed by a renewal of militarism.

Similarly, if the economic situation is not grim or deteriorating to start with—and reformers are often elected precisely because the economy is in trouble—it generally gets worse as the property-owning class expresses its unease through disinvestment and capital flight and as financial institutions tighten credit terms. In the Dominican case, the economic crisis brought on in the late 1970s by rising prices for energy and falling prices for sugar was compounded by the deep cut in the Dominican quota of the U.S. sugar market. Unable to tax Dominican elites or withstand a credit freeze, the Jorge Blanco government saw no alternative to servicing debts in the manner prescribed by the IMF—that is, at the expense mainly of the poor. Lacking both the capital to promote productive employment and any other means of rewarding supporters, Jorge Blanco, like Guzmán before him, resorted to bloating his own bureaucracy.

Reformers generally have better prospects of expanding human rights and civil liberties than of rewarding their constituencies with economic gains and opportunities. Thus high expectations soon turn to frustration, which is likely to be vented in ways newly legitimated by the reformer, such as strikes and demonstrations. During Jorge Blanco's term, such street action got out of hand and led to rioting and looting. Far more than conservative regimes, reformist ones have to fear that riots will bring on a coup d'état. Thus Jorge Blanco's government repressed the rioting with extraordinary violence, and the president who came to power as a defender of human rights left the office with that aspect of his image tarnished, as well. The Dominican would-be reformers—or their relatives, friends, and appointees—fell prey also to other familiar weaknesses and temptations. While reformers may be less likely than business-as-usual politicians to engage in corrupt practices, they are more likely to be accused and, if guilty, almost certain to be caught.

It is therefore difficult to avoid the conclusion that by the mid-1980s the Dominican Republic had reached the limits of acceptable reform within the existing political system. The modern history of the country shows that anything but trifling change has had to be agreed upon by the established elites and the United States. The latter continues to set the parameters of Dominican politics, but what was distinctive about the 1980s, compared to the preceding two decades, was the way in which the United States distanced itself from direct involvement in the country. The U.S. presence was not diminished by this fact, but it was undoubtedly made less visible. The economic costs and political consequences of external adjustment accordingly bore an unmistakable Dominican stamp. This permitted some room for the growth and development of a more robust domestic politics but not one supplanting the constraints of the past.

The politics with which most Dominicans are familiar is primarily authoritarian and traditional, which has favored the oligarchy, the military, U.S. economic interests, and Balaguer and has reinforced the legacy of privilege and confirmed the power of the executive, especially the president. At the same time, the political reforms of the post-Trujillo governments are irreversible to the degree that they are supported by the majority of the Dominican people and the U.S. government. These reforms generated hope and imparted a certain vibrancy to political life, especially at election times. Indeed, the outcome of the 1990 election showed the PRD and the PLD to be very evenly matched, if not necessarily irreconcilable. The strength of Balaguer, in the end, was his co-optation of the democratic impulse in the service of the authoritarian. Whether democracy is consolidated in the future will not be a matter for the Dominicans to decide entirely alone: the role of the United States and developments in the international economic system will be crucial. Nevertheless, the 1980s provide a small measure of hope that the worst excesses of the past are over in the Dominican Republic and that an authentic accommodation between the traditional and the modern, the transnational and the national, can be effected in the political life of the country to the future betterment of the Dominican people.

# 3 The Duvalier Dictatorship and Its Legacy of Crisis in Haiti

*James Ferguson*

*Dèyè mòn gen mòn. (Behind the mountains, more mountains.)*

The resigned pessimism of the well-known Creole proverb is particularly apt as regards Haiti's political experience in the 1980s. The decade saw the gradual weakening of what had in the 1970s appeared to be a resilient dictatorship and its final, violent collapse. The downfall in February 1986 of Jean-Claude, or "Baby Doc," Duvalier seemed to herald new democratic possibilities after almost thirty years of underdevelopment and autocratic rule. Yet that promise was short lived, as the realization dawned that Duvalier had left in place many of the political and military structures that would perpetuate the system that bore his name. "Duvalierism without Duvalier" was the phrase frequently used by the end of the 1980s to describe the various military-civilian forces that succeeded the family dictatorship without changing many of its fundamental characteristics.

Ironically, the Duvalier dictatorship began, in 1957, with free elections, which brought François, or "Papa Doc," Duvalier to power. After two decades of elite government and political instability following the end of a nineteen-year period of U.S. occupation (1915–34), Papa Doc promised social progress and democratic rights to the majority of poor Haitians. By 1964, however, he had established himself as "president for life" in a fraudulent referendum and had crushed all opposition to his rule. In 1971, the dying Papa Doc handed over absolute power to his son, Baby Doc, whose rule throughout the 1970s, although perhaps less repressive than that of his father, was marked by enormous corruption and economic mismanagement.

Haiti entered the 1980s as the poorest country in the Western Hemisphere, with per capita gross domestic product estimated in 1980 at US$253. By 1988, the figure was put at US$209, having

declined for eight consecutive years,[1] and Haiti remained at the
bottom of the hemispheric economic league, competing only with
Guyana for the distinction of poorest state. Yet even these figures
do not fully reveal the extent of the problem: that less than 1
percent of the population accounts for 46 percent of the country's
wealth, that 60 percent of Haitians are unemployed, and that approximately 80 percent earn less than US$100 annually.[2] Haiti's
enduring poverty, its grim social indicators, and its environmental
degradation are partly a legacy of long-standing patterns of underdevelopment, which can be traced back to its violent struggle for
independence and the ensuing economic isolation. But they are
also a testimony to thirty years of dictatorship and the unstable
political structure that evolved from it.

## Duvalier's Decline

Spectacular as Baby Doc's collapse was, it was neither entirely
unexpected nor unannounced: the regime he inherited began to
show signs of strain in the late 1970s and early 1980s. Its growing weakness was in large part due to the fact that the son had
moved away from the political practices of the father. Whereas
Papa Doc had established an efficient network of cadres, activists,
and supporters—including the notorious Tontons Macoutes[3]—
throughout rural Haiti, Baby Doc relied more upon the support of
the urban economic elite of Port-au-Prince. This apparent alliance
with the fairer-skinned, or mulatto, minority was viewed with
suspicion by those portions of the black majority that had profited
from Papa Doc's militantly antimulatto policies. Papa Doc, formerly a rural doctor and amateur ethnologist, could claim to understand the complex sociological and cultural structures of a
predominantly peasant society. His constituency and power base
lay with the Creole-speaking, voodoo-practicing peasantry, which
makes up perhaps 80 percent of Haiti's population. His son,
brought up in the capital, was familiar only with the urban milieu,
which is so divorced from rural Haiti as to be known ironically as
"the republic of Port-au-Prince." A potentially explosive mixture
of racial and class factors was therefore likely at any moment to
threaten a regime that had gradually drifted away from the power
base that had originally ensured its stability.[4]

The perceived shift in power and patronage from a newly ascen-
dant black middle class, enriched by state corruption and clientelism, to the traditional urban elite fueled discontent among
formerly loyal Duvalierists. At the same time, Baby Doc had to

contend with external pressures brought about by his desire to consolidate U.S. support and investment. Papa Doc's relationship with the United States had been tense throughout the 1960s, the mutual distrust only partly salved by the dictatorship's outspoken anticommunism. (There was even a Kennedy-sponsored coup attempt in 1963.) Baby Doc and his advisers, however, were keen to attract substantial U.S. investment during the following decade, in an attempt to "Taiwanize" Haiti's underdeveloped economy. This meant acceding to the Carter administration's demands for political reforms and human rights, and periods of "liberalization" followed between 1976 and 1979, during which limited relaxations took place.

As a result, the regime found itself forced to make cosmetic concessions, which internal opponents seized upon as a sign of the government's weakness. Liberal phases were accordingly succeeded by periods of extreme repression, which in turn alienated U.S. policy makers and investors. Hardliners alternated with modernizers in Baby Doc's frequently purged cabinets, while former ministers from Papa Doc's government openly condemned the regime's alleged betrayal of authentic Duvalierist principles. The inherent contradiction of a dictatorship making limited reforms ultimately weakened the fabric of Duvalierism, which depended at root upon the absolute suppression of opposition.

To a large extent, therefore, Duvalierism in its original sense had changed significantly before the collapse of the regime itself. During the 1980s, the militant black nationalism, the mysticism, and the personality cult propagated by Papa Doc gave way to a much more pragmatic system of government, which depended more on support from the U.S. government and on compromise with the traditional economic elite than had Papa Doc's isolationist regime. Within four years of the son's succession, foreign aid to Haiti had increased tenfold: bilateral U.S. support alone rose from US$33.7 million in 1981 to US$45.5 million in 1984.[5]

Despite the economic backing of the Reagan administration, Baby Doc, politically and intellectually, was no match for his father, who through clientelism and terror had maintained tight personal control over ambitious competitors and potential opponents. Inheriting a highly personalized and centralized political system, he was unable to command the respect and loyalty that his father had enjoyed and that was needed to ensure the functioning of that system. Instead, Duvalierism became "Jean-Claudisme," a corrupt and inefficient version of the original dictatorship, and one that lacked any significant popular support.

Three unrelated phenomena served to undermine an already vulnerable regime. First, in May 1980 Jean-Claude married Michèle Bennett, the daughter of a disreputable mulatto businessman. The marriage confirmed the suspicions of those orthodox Duvalierists who had supported the dictatorship as a vehicle for the advancement of the black majority. It also provided the Bennett family and their allies with considerable political power and, in the process, eclipsed Simone Duvalier, Papa Doc's widow, who had been the principal influence over her malleable and unintelligent son since Papa Doc's death. The marriage was therefore partly symbolic, exposing the regime's abandonment of its original ideology of *noirisme*, or antimulatto racialism. Another consequence was the influence it gave to a coterie of businessmen and technocrats who attempted to turn the Haitian economy away from the rural isolationism of Papa Doc's regime toward export-led growth and foreign investment. The struggle between these so-called modernizers and the orthodox Duvalierist "dinosaurs" intensified as Baby Doc's hold on power weakened.

Second, the much-awaited visit of Pope John-Paul II to Haiti in March 1983 seemingly authorized the Catholic church's political mandate. "Things must change here," announced the pope, echoing the increasingly political activism of the church's radical wing. Although the church traditionally has been allied to the elite and conservative in outlook, a new generation of priests and lay workers, influenced by Latin American liberation theology, had since the 1970s been committed to radical social change. Working with poor peasant communities within the spreading urban shantytowns, the so-called *ti-legliz* (or people's church) activists saw in the pope's message the endorsement of a political posture normally frowned upon by Rome. The highly influential church-run radio station, Radio Soleil, was henceforth to be a major force in mobilizing anti-Duvalier sentiment.

Third, opposition to the regime was mounting in the countryside, caused to a great extent by deteriorating rural conditions. In particular, an epidemic of swine fever had been reported in 1981, leading to a U.S.-financed extermination program against the indigenous Creole pig. Promises to replace Haitian pigs with stock imported from the United States frequently went unhonored, while peasants who received replacements were displeased with the U.S. variety, which required expensive feed and veterinary treatments.

The decimation of peasant pig production had serious nutritional implications; it also caused immense economic hardship in already impoverished rural communities, for which the sale of livestock represented the main source of cash income. Resentment was directed against the Haitian government, which, it was widely believed, had diverted money intended for the pig repopulation scheme. Traditional Duvalier loyalists among key sectors of the rural population—*chefs de section* (local policemen and government officials), magistrates, *houngans* (voodoo priests), and larger landowners—all became disaffected with what was increasingly seen as a weak and inefficient government.

By the mid-1980s, too, a combination of internal and external economic factors had eroded Baby Doc's power base. Rising oil prices, chronic droughts, and the collapse of tourism due to the AIDS scare had created what Baby Doc himself described in 1981 as an "economic impasse." The AIDS panic destroyed Haiti's tourist industry, depriving the country of its share in the U.S. market and its share of foreign exchange. This followed the announcement in 1981 by the U.S. Center for Disease Control that Haitians constituted a "high-risk group." Tourist arrivals plummeted from 190,000 in 1980 to 40,000 in 1983, sharply reducing revenue.[6] The country's economic malaise was also exacerbated by the government's systematic pilfering of national resources: a Canadian government report in 1982 described the system as a "kleptocracy."[7]

The scandal of the Haitian boat people (desperate refugees from the poorest rural areas trying to reach Florida and, sometimes, dying in the attempt) also focused international attention on Duvalier's unsavory rule. Some 2,900 boat people were intercepted by the U.S. Coast Guard in 1984, alone, and were returned to an uncertain fate in Haiti. The U.S. authorities made a distinction between political refugees from Cuba and economic refugees from Haiti, giving the former sanctuary and deporting the latter. This policy remained in force throughout the 1980s, with interdictions of deportations totaling 4,614 in 1988 and 3,368 in 1989.[8]

On the political front, a program of intended cosmetic reforms weakened Baby Doc's position. U.S. pressure had forced the regime to promise constitutional changes, and in July 1985, a package of measures consolidating the president's executive power was passed by a bogus referendum giving Baby Doc a supposed 99.8 percent "yes" vote. The fraud was widely criticized, even by Haiti's heavily censored press, and contributed to the president's growing unpopularity. All these issues, combined with the longer-standing internal tensions within the regime, came to a climax at the end of that year.

## DUVALIER'S FALL

Trouble flared first in the desolate coastal town of Gonaïves in November 1985, when a student demonstration against the referendum was brutally repressed by the army, which shot into the crowd, killing four young people. More protests took place in other provincial towns, supported often by local priests. As the momentum grew, the regime responded by increasing censorship and repression and by unleashing the army as well as the feared Tontons Macoutes against suspected ringleaders.[9] Repression was accompanied by half-hearted attempts at reconciliation. Several purges of Baby Doc's cabinet of ministers were carried out between November 1985 and January 1986, and the government promised an investigation into the Gonaïves shooting.

Neither violence nor compromise, however, could stop the popular impetus against the dictatorship. After a brief respite around Christmas, the protests grew in size and frequency, gradually moving from the provincial towns into Port-au-Prince itself. The beginning of popular mobilization in the capital marked a crucial turning point in the rebellion and the terminal disintegration of the regime, as former henchmen of Papa Doc were called back to the cabinet in an attempt to restore the dictatorship's fortunes.

During the first month of 1986, key allies in Haiti and abroad, one by one, deserted the collapsing government. Elements of the economic and professional elite, such as the Chamber of Commerce, publicly condemned the regime's handling of the crisis. They were joined by Protestant denominations, which at last followed several Catholic bishops in outspoken criticism. In the countryside, prominent Duvalier supporters began to distance themselves from the dictatorship, worried by the mounting tide of militancy. Most important, the United States began to show signs of withdrawing its support of Baby Doc. After a series of clearly coded warnings, the United States announced on 30 January that it was withholding US$26 million of scheduled aid for Haiti. After reports that U.S. Secretary of State George Shultz had publicly called for a democratically elected government in Haiti, there followed the bizarre and premature announcement on 31 January by President Reagan's spokesman, Larry Speakes, that Duvalier had left Haiti. This was interpreted as a sign not only that the United States had urged this eventuality upon Duvalier but, also, that Washington's eagerness to defuse the political turmoil in Haiti was obstructing its communications.

There remained only one major group to abandon Duvalier: the army. From the beginning of the rebellion, the military had played an ambivalent role, sometimes repressing demonstrations, sometimes avoiding confrontation. To some extent, this ambivalence reflected the troubled relationship between the army and the Duvalier dictatorship. The military establishment had traditionally wielded ultimate power in Haitian politics and, since the armed independence struggle of the early nineteenth century, had provided presidents from its own ranks or had sanctioned other choices.[10] Papa Doc, however, had been careful to reduce the military's role and had established the Tontons Macoutes as a loyal paramilitary counterweight to the regular army. With its influence curtailed and its officers periodically purged, the Haitian army was effectively humiliated under Papa Doc. At the succession of Baby Doc in 1971, the United States encouraged the formation of an elite counterinsurgency battalion, the Léopards, designed as an alternative to the Tontons Macoutes. Leading officers were sent to the United States from the military academy; among high-ranking soldiers with known U.S. connections were Henri Namphy, Williams Régala, and Prosper Avril, all later to become key figures in the unfolding of the Haitian crisis.

Recognizing the inevitability of Duvalier's departure, the United States and the Haitian army arranged, with Baby Doc's cooperation, a smooth transition from the dictatorship to a provisional military regime. For the United States, such an arrangement provided a means of containing popular mobilization by removing the regime's figurehead and, hence, preventing what might evolve into a full-scale revolutionary movement. For the Duvalierist establishment, of which high-ranking military officers were necessarily a part, it guaranteed continuity and an opportunity to direct political developments from a position of executive authority.

The fact that demonstrations had called on the army to take power and unseat Baby Doc in a coup was a clear indication of the political power vacuum at the center of the anti-Duvalier rebellion. No single party or individual could claim to lead the movement, and moral authority lay rather with sections of the Catholic church rather than with any political group. Composed largely of young people with no experience other than thirty years of the Duvaliers, the movement had limited aims and slogans and was easily stopped short by the apparent victory of Baby Doc's departure. Its strengths—a nonvanguardist structure, spontaneity, mass involvement, and purely local leadership—were also its weaknesses when it came to formulating a political program beyond the obvious objective of ousting Baby Doc. Leaders emerged, often from the slum quarters of the capital and the principal towns, but lacked the political experience to channel popular pressure toward longer-term aims.

Duvalier's departure took place in the early hours of 7 February 1986, exactly a week after the Reagan administration announced it. The final week of the dictatorship had been confused and violent, with rumors of an impending coup and ruthless repression on the part of the Tontons Macoutes. As Baby Doc was flown away on a U.S. military aircraft destined for France, there was initial disbelief, followed by a mixture of euphoria and savage retribution. The first to be exposed to popular anger were well-known but minor members of the Tontons Macoutes, who were lynched by crowds and whose property was destroyed. Other symbols of the dictatorship were smashed, such as the Duvalier family mausoleum, while huge crowds cheered soldiers outside the presidential palace.

## THE MILITARY TAKES POWER

Only hours after Baby Doc's flight, the Conseil National de Gouvernement (CNG) announced that it was ruling Haiti. A five-man junta, comprising three military officers and two civilians, was to head the CNG, and the provisional president was Lieutenant-General Henri Namphy, chief of staff during the old regime. But for the inclusion of Gérard Gourgue, a veteran human rights campaigner, the junta had impeccable Duvalierist credentials: a former minister and three previously loyal army officers. This was hardly surprising, since when Baby Doc arrived into exile in France, he claimed to have nominated the government to replace him. More important, Namphy and his colleagues had the full support of the United States.

The CNG's first and most urgent task was to dampen popular aspirations and organization. Several cosmetic reforms were approved; street names were altered, the national flag was changed back to its pre-Duvalier colors, and ceremonies of thanksgiving were held. Meanwhile, spontaneous acts of retribution against the hated Tontons Macoutes continued. Some were murdered, but others of greater importance in the organization were taken into military custody. The process of erasing the vestiges of the dictatorship (known as *déchoukaj*, or uprooting) was under way, and it was precisely this process that threatened the CNG and the interests it protected. At first, the junta attempted to reduce tension by reconciliation. It reluctantly agreed to authorize legal proceedings against several notorious secret policemen and torturers (others had been allowed to slip out of the country), sacked several ministers and advisers, and promised to regain the estimated US$600 million that Baby Doc and his entourage had taken with them into exile.

More ominously, the military junta was prepared to use force against those demanding more radical change. A demonstration in April demanding the closure of the notorious Fort Dimanche prison ended in bloodshed, as troops opened fire on peaceful protesters. Other outbreaks of unrest drew a military response, and a series of curfews and other restrictions were introduced. At the end of March, in protest at what he saw as the CNG's open protection of prominent Duvalierists and its violent repression of demonstrations, Gérard Gourgue resigned from the junta. Gourgue's resignation ended any semblance of liberalism on the part of the CNG; from June 1986 onward, recorded instances of military killings and civilian disappearances escalated.

But despite growing political repression, certain advances were achieved in the first post-Duvalier months. The press and other media, for instance, enjoyed unprecedented freedom, while political parties, trade unions, and other groups were able to organize openly for the first time in thirty years. In the towns, neighborhood committees, born out of the anti-Duvalier rebellion, dealt with local issues, while peasant groups, supported by the Catholic church and development agencies, began to campaign for better prices for their crops and for the provision of health care and education. Attracted by the political power vacuum, many Haitian exiles returned to the country from their temporary homes in the United States, Canada, or France. Many had political ambitions and began to organize political parties in readiness for elections, which in June 1986 the CNG promised to hold by the following November. This promise, like many other concessions, was not given freely but came at the end of two weeks of strikes and violence, which prompted rumors of direct U.S. intervention.

The Reagan administration wholeheartedly supported the CNG, on the understanding that the interim junta would administer elections and then hand over power to a civilian government. This had been the agreed-upon "managed transition," reached in the week preceding Baby Doc's flight and was to be the basis of U.S. policy toward post-Duvalier Haiti.[11] Economic aid, suspended during the final collapse of the dictatorship, was resumed, and Assistant Secretary of State for Inter-American Affairs Elliott Abrams claimed in Port-au-Prince that the overthrow of Duvalier had "inspired the world" and that Namphy enjoyed Washington's "total support."[12] It is significant that this support did not waver publicly throughout the difficult months leading to the scheduled elections, despite a spectacular deterioration in democratic and human rights under the CNG. Indeed, the well-publicized supply of antiriot equipment from the United States suggests that the prohibition of popular protest was a higher priority for the United States than the encouragement of democratic self-expression.

U.S. concerns in Haiti were thus primarily centered upon the threat of political instability in a country whose geostrategic significance in the potentially volatile Caribbean far outweighs its economic importance. In this respect, the army, with its established links with Washington, offered U.S. policy makers the most obvious vehicle for stopping any revolutionary impetus. Related issues include the flow of refugees from Haiti to Florida, which the CNG promised to stem, and the role of Haiti as a transshipment point for cocaine en route from the Andean producer countries to the United States. Confronted by all these security concerns, the State Department opted unconditionally to support the Haitian army as the most feasible agent of gradual democratic change.

The United States, meanwhile, had longer-term economic ambitions for Haiti, which in the country itself became popularly known as the *plan meriken*, or "American plan."[13] Outlined in documents produced by the U.S. Agency for International Development and other agencies, the plan envisaged the gradual elimination of Haiti's archaic peasant economy in favor of dynamic, export-led, agribusinesses. The corollary of transforming the Haitian rural economy from smallholdings and subsistence agriculture to modern agroindustries lay in encouraging rural to urban migration, which would provide offshore assembly plants in Port-au-Prince and other towns with a vast reservoir of cheap labor.[14] To some extent, the project was a continuation of existing international aid policy toward Haiti, which had often consisted of "modernizing" the rural economy through infrastructural and technological development. This policy had frequently had the effect of driving Haitian peasants from their land, as smallholdings became attractive to agribusiness due to improved access or irrigation. The post-Duvalier plan, however, was more formulated, proposing Haiti as a source of coffee, exotic staples, and low-paid factory workers which would function as an offshore U.S. economic asset through its geographical proximity.

The CNG, however, was attempting its own economic experiment in Haiti. Its primary objective, led by its Chicago-trained finance minister, Leslie Delatour, was to deregulate the state sector, which had provided the Duvalier dictatorship with lucrative sources of revenue. It abolished state monopolies on commodities such as flour and cement and closed state-owned factories. It effectively opened up the vulnerable Haitian economy to a flood of cheap imports and contraband by removing the tight import controls imposed by the Duvalier regime. For the agricultural sector, this was disastrous, since cheap rice and sugar, imported from Miami and the neighboring Dominican Republic, undercut the prices asked by Haitian farmers. Small manufacturers, too, could not compete with inexpensive imports from the United States, and the arrival of tons of secondhand clothes destroyed the Haitian domestic textile industry.

The army, however, was able to impose informal customs payments on contraband goods arriving at Haitian ports and to take over the systematic syphoning of foreign aid, which the Duvaliers had previously operated. The influx of cheap food, although significantly worsening rural poverty by depressing prices, had the effect of dampening hunger-related discontent in urban areas. This led to violent confrontation between peasants and the urban distributors of smuggled food. Unemployment also soared, particularly with the closure of the Darbonne sugar refinery and the state-run vegetable oil factory. U.S.-owned offshore assembly plants also closed, worried by the prospect of continuing unrest, and some twenty thousand jobs in Port-au-Prince were lost.

## ELECTIONS: TRAGEDY AND FARCE

Under the terms of its promised "transition to democracy," the CNG grudgingly allowed the election of the Constituent Assembly in October 1986. The election was overwhelmingly boycotted due to popular suspicion that the junta would manipulate the new body and the reluctance of leading politicians to participate. Yet the following March, to the CNG's discomfort, the Constituent Assembly produced a constitution that was strongly liberal and progressive. It provided for the drastic reduction of the president's executive authority and increased power for the Chamber of Deputies and the Senate. It abolished the death penalty, guaranteed freedoms for political parties and trade unions, and introduced military service as a means of democratizing the armed forces.

The new constitution also contained two measures that struck directly at the power of the military and at the political prospects of those connected to the former regime. The first was the creation of a Conseil Electoral Provisoire (CEP), or independent electoral council, charged with organizing and administering free and fair elections. The second was the infamous Article 291, banning "notorious" Duvalierists from holding public office for a period of ten years. Both measures were unacceptable to the army and its Duvalierist allies, who hoped to control and ultimately win any eventual elections. Yet the constitution was conclusively approved by a popular referendum on 29 March 1987, in which more than 50 percent of Haitians voted, an estimated 99 percent of them in favor of the constitution.

Weeks after the nine-member CEP took office, the junta made its move, claiming that the draft electoral law was unconstitutional and attempting to close the independent council down. It also banned the Centrale Autonome des Travailleurs Haitiens (CATH), a trade union that had called for a general strike against the CNG. The move against the CEP was predictable. Junta member Williams Régala had already stated that only the army could guarantee fair elections, while Namphy had clearly alluded to the CEP in a menacing speech made to the armed forces:

> The Haitian nation does not acknowledge having any foreign enemies. . . . We would do better to take a close look at the warning signs of a threat to the integrity of the Haitian nation from within. . . . The greatest enemy right now is perhaps the excesses committed along the difficult path of learning how to be a democracy, the path that is now being trod so painfully by the Haitian people, a people who, in these circumstances, deserve to be understood, supported and sometimes protected, sometimes even against their will.[15]

This attack on the CEP met with a popular resistance, which threatened to restart the revolutionary impetus. For most of June and July 1987, Haiti was effectively ungovernable, paralyzed by strikes and rioting. The junta responded with increased violence, and approximately forty civilians died in the course of the repression. But eventually the CNG was forced to give way, lifting its ban on the CATH and reinstating the CEP in its electoral responsibilities. Not only had the junta underestimated the force of popular resistance, it received a pointed reminder from the U.S. State Department that continuing economic aid was dependent upon the successful transition to civilian rule.[16]

From that moment onward, the CNG became seriously concerned that the electoral process and its end result was slipping out of its control. A curious situation of dual power also evolved, in which the military junta remained the nominal government of

Haiti, whereas the CEP enjoyed the support of most Haitians in its attempt to ensure a genuine transition toward democracy. The CEP thus effectively became a rival source of governmental authority, at odds with and bitterly resented by the CNG, which saw its own plan for "managed elections" thwarted. The army now cemented its informal alliance with those Duvalierists who were banned from participating in the elections under Article 291 of the constitution. Duvalier loyalists, such as retired General Claude Raymond, exminister Clovis Désinor, and former mayor of Port-au-Prince Franck Romain, who had survived the *déchoukaj* and who hoped to revive their political careers in army-dominated elections, shared the junta's grievance against the CEP and the constitution. The coalition of the army and Duvalierist leaders meant that the antidemocratic elements held a monopoly of force.

The CNG's abortive attempt to take back control of the elections left it with no other option than to destabilize the very process the United States had entrusted it with. Human rights violations and attacks against the CEP began to increase dramatically. In July, an unknown number of peasants had been massacred in the isolated region of Jean-Rabel as they demanded the return of land illegally expropriated by Duvalierist landlords.[17] In August, Louis-Eugène Athis, a moderate presidential candidate, was murdered by armed men in the southern town of Léogâne. Later that month, Jean-Bertrand Aristide, the most prominent spokesman for the radical *ti-legliz*, narrowly escaped assassination, while in October, Yves Volel, another presidential candidate, was shot by plainclothes police in the presence of journalists.

Yet despite the mounting incidence of army-sanctioned terrorism, the United States refused to condemn the CNG openly.[18] The United States having insisted on the reinstatement of the CEP, it was all the more paradoxical that, on the very day that Yves Volel was murdered, Richard McCormack, the U.S. ambassador to the Organization of American States, should officially announce that "we [the U.S. government] congratulate the Haitian government and the Haitian people for their dramatic progress, and we look forward to celebrating the emergence of a democratically chosen, constitutional government in that country."[19]

The gradual political polarization between the ruling military establishment and opposition forces reached an extreme point in the summer of 1987, revealing the unresolved contradictions of post-Duvalier Haiti. The slogan of *déchoukaj* was superseded by that of *rache manyòk*, the metaphorical call to clear society of the old crop before planting fresh seeds. The *ti-legliz* wing of the

Catholic church was most vociferous in this campaign, which, to a large extent, took place outside Port-au-Prince and away from the electoral arena. Peasant organizations such as that attacked in Jean-Rabel were pressing for fundamental land reform and the return of property expropriated by supporters of the Duvalier regime. Other demands centered on the removal of known Duvalierists from public office, whether in local government, the army, or the judiciary. The fact that few such changes had occurred was a measure of the CNG's continuity with the previous regime and the state's open defense of the status quo. Local initiatives to mobilize anti-Duvalierist opinion were thus often met with violence, from either regular or irregular forces or, frequently, a combination of both.

Despite the climate of violence, the CEP managed to register the majority of Haitian electors, drawing up voting lists in remote parts of the country. The would-be political leaders, many of whom had returned from exile, launched their campaigns, and by August there were estimated to be at least thirty contenders for the presidency. The number of candidates and the highly personal character of their campaigns were further symptoms of the power vacuum after Duvalier and the absence of any organization with real popular support. Many politicians were merely contemporary exponents of the traditional *gwo nèg*, or caudillo, school of politics, which dealt only in personal charisma and promises of advancement for a small coterie.

Perhaps four candidates enjoyed real support, each because of a record of opposition to the Duvalier dictatorship. The conservative Marc Bazin, a former World Bank official, had been sacked from a ministerial post by Baby Doc because he had threatened to campaign against government corruption. Louis Déjoie, the son of the mulatto millionaire who had campaigned against Papa Doc in 1957, had spent most of his life in exile and operated now like an old-style populist. Sylvio Claude, a Baptist minister, had been tortured and imprisoned by the dictatorship for attempting to establish a political party and was popular among the urban poor for his charismatic rhetoric of martyrdom. Gérard Gourgue, fleetingly a member of the original CNG and a respected human rights activist, drew support from the middle class and represented a loose alliance of center-left organizations. Class, regional, and racial considerations prevented any of them from claiming support from all sectors of society. The patrician Déjoie's popularity among the southern mulatto constituency, for instance, was far removed from the support enjoyed by Sylvio Claude among the dispossessed slum dwellers of Port-au-Prince. In this sense, there was no single front-runner, although highly rudimentary opinion polls suggest that Claude or Gourgue might eventually have won a free election. Neither, of course, was acceptable to the military establishment and its Duvalierist allies.

Up until the eve of the elections, the U.S. embassy in Port-au-Prince continued to predict, optimistically, that polling would take place. In reality, however, the climate of terror created by Duvalierist death squads and encouraged by the army made this eventuality impossible. Vigilante groups, organized by neighborhood committees, tried to defend poor areas of the capital against night attacks by armed men in unmarked jeeps. In retaliation, military personnel carried out sweeping arrests and ignored death squad activity. The CNG, meanwhile, refused to cooperate with the CEP in its attempt to organize the polling, banning military transportation from distributing ballot papers in rural districts and denying the CEP access to the state-run media. The junta's aim was now simply to prevent an election it could not control.

In any event, the Haitian elections of 29 November 1987 disintegrated into a massacre, which attracted headlines around the world. Within three hours of the opening of the polls, bombings and shootings left more than thirty voters dead in Port-au-Prince, most of them in a particularly savage attack on a polling station. The CEP had no alternative but to cancel the voting, and this announcement was followed soon afterward by a government statement dissolving the CEP and accusing it of treason and subversion. The violence, according to journalists and foreign observers, had come from former Tontons Macoutes, often accompanied by regular troops. The troops of the Dessalines battalion, commanded by Colonel Jean-Claude Paul, were particularly involved in the atrocities, as were men in the pay of the banned Duvalierist candidate, Claude Raymond.

The prevention of elections amounted to nothing less than a military coup and a renewed attempt, this time successful, to stop the long-awaited transition to constitutional government. The CNG had deliberately aborted the democratic process, fearful that an independent civilian regime would attack its power and privileges and investigate its human rights record. Ironically, the junta blamed the CEP for the violence and presented itself as the only guarantor of free elections in Haiti. However, the United States, forced at last to confront the true nature of the regime it had supported since February 1986, showed its disapproval by immediately suspending some US$62 million in nonhumanitarian aid and with-

drawing personnel from Haiti. Total U.S. aid to the CNG for the
fiscal year had been set at US$110 million, several millions of
which had already gone toward paying for the elections that the
junta had deliberately destroyed.[20]

The initiative now lay with the CNG, which rapidly assembled
an electoral council of nonentities and proclaimed that elections
would be held on 17 January 1988. Unlike the previous CEP, the
army's handpicked electoral council made no attempt to provide
for meaningful polling. It recommended that candidates should
print and distribute their own ballots and that completed ballots
should be inspected by a presiding official at the polling station.
Understandably, the four leading contenders from the November
elections—Bazin, Déjoie, Gourgue, and Claude—boycotted the
military junta's new elections. Others eagerly took their place,
hoping that the army would select them for the presidency. Foremost was Leslie Manigat, an academic who had spent years of exile
in Paris, Trinidad, and Venezuela, and who led what he described as
a centrist and nationalist party.

If the response of Haiti's main politicians and electorate to the
army's plans was unequivocally negative, that of the United States
was more ambivalent. The Reagan administration ignored calls for
further sanctions and intervention from sections of Congress and
abroad. It also used its principal Caribbean ally, Edward Seaga
of Jamaica, to head off a concerted Commonwealth Caribbean
campaign to isolate Namphy and the junta. Instead, the State Department attempted to persuade the leading candidates to stand
again—but to no avail. At the same time, it was reported that
Williams Régala, the CNG's second in command, had visited the
State Department only hours before the election violence and had
met with Elliott Abrams and other officials. The subject of the
talks and the State Department's attitude toward the election violence was the subject of intense speculation.[21] It became clear,
however, that the election of Manigat was quite acceptable to the
United States, and on that basis the CNG continued with its own
stage-managed elections.

The election itself was a formality, marred by overwhelming
popular abstention and clumsy fraud, in which perhaps only 10
percent of the electorate voted.[22] Predictably, Manigat emerged
triumphant, claiming a popular mandate. In reality, however, he
had been chosen by a majority faction within the CNG, albeit
without Namphy's personal endorsement, on the implicit understanding that he would not interfere with the army's economic and
political power. Yet Manigat was not an ordinary puppet president

of the type favored in nineteenth-century Haiti. Although elected on the junta's terms, he believed that he could create a democratic space by gradual reform and by slowly weakening the army's grip.[23] Known as an astute politician, capable of working pragmatically with left and right alike, Manigat appealed to the boycotting candidates to join in a process of national reconciliation. Their refusal and the sheer indifference of ordinary Haitians underlined Manigat's isolation and vulnerability. Only the United States offered support—a series of statements emphasizing Manigat's democratic credentials in spite of his dubious election.

## COUP AND COUNTERCOUP

President Manigat lasted no longer than 130 days in office—from 7 February to 19 June 1988. In that time, his government achieved little, other than to express criticism of the free-market policies of the CNG, which had led to an epidemic of smuggling. He gathered around him a number of non-Duvalierist technocrats as ministers and advisers, yet, strikingly, the vital Ministry of the Interior was given to Williams Régala, the chief architect of the fraudulent election.

Manigat's inevitable downfall in mid-June was brought about by what appeared to be an attempt to exploit differences within the military hierarchy. General Namphy had transferred the notorious Colonel Jean-Claude Paul, indicted in the United States on drug-running charges, to an administrative position from his post as commander of the Dessalines battalion. Manigat countermanded the order and dismissed Namphy on 17 June, placing him under house arrest. Manigat also retired or transferred thirty other officers in what amounted to a purge of the higher echelons of the army. Within two days of his house arrest, however, Namphy was liberated by loyal troops from the Presidential Guard. A brief and almost bloodless coup then ensued, after which Manigat was flown out of Haiti into exile in the Dominican Republic. Curiously, Colonel Paul appeared alongside General Namphy as the new military government was proclaimed, fueling speculation that Manigat had been enticed into providing the army with a pretext for his removal.

The anti-Manigat coup was the third stage in a process that had started with the army-endorsed destruction of free elections and continued with a stage-managed election of a nominally civilian president. It suggested that the hardline military faction, represented by General Namphy, was unwilling to tolerate any diminu-

tion of its influence and, equally, that Manigat had drastically
overestimated his ability to divide and rule the Haitian army. It
was not to be the last coup, however, and marked only a temporary
triumph for General Namphy.

The second Namphy-led regime was in fact shorter lived than
Manigat's ephemeral presidency and marked the lowest point in
Haitian politics since the demise of Duvalier. Nominating a
military-dominated cabinet, Namphy suspended the 1987 constitution and refused to commit himself to eventual elections. He
also demoted his former CNG colleague, Williams Régala, allegedly because of Régala's involvement in the election of Manigat,
which Namphy had apparently opposed. Political violence escalated, including the murder of Lafontant Joseph, a well-known human rights campaigner and former senatorial candidate. The worst
incident occurred on 11 September 1988, when a gang attacked a
mass conducted at Port-au-Prince's St. Jean-Bosco Church by *ti-
legliz* spokesman Jean-Bertrand Aristide, killing eleven worshippers
and wounding seventy more.[24] In both cases, army personnel were
either directly involved or were seen as sanctioning the violence.

The latter incident, in particular, aroused widespread revulsion,
both inside Haiti and abroad, and turned elements of the army,
already divided into warring factions, against the excesses of General Namphy. Namphy, meanwhile, had no apparent political program for Haiti other than the continuation of a military dictatorship. His allies were largely drawn from traditional Duvalierist
circles, and influential supporters in rural areas were rewarded by
posts in what the government announced would be a US$3-million
state-run development program. Ultimately, Namphy's second
government was a pariah regime, facing hostility from every regional state and from the United States in particular.

Within a week of the St. Jean-Bosco massacre, Namphy was
overthrown, following Manigat into exile in the Dominican Republic. On this occasion, however, the impetus came not from the
top of the military hierarchy but from noncommissioned officers
and the lower ranks. The so-called sergeants' coup was inspired by
progressive junior officers tired of the military's open alliance with
the Duvalierists and its instinctive posture of repression. A com-
muniqué read by Sergeant Joseph Hébreux in the early hours of 18
September announced that the coup was intended to "restore the
prestige of the Haitian people, disgraced by so many deeds which
have revolted the conscience of the people and the whole world, as
well as the enlisted troops."[25]

Seemingly at odds with the noble aspirations of the NCOs, however, was their choice of provisional president: Lieutenant-General Prosper Avril. (Hébreux, it transpired, had refused the office, pleading lack of experience.) Avril appeared a curious choice, since he was closely identified with the Duvalierist regimes, having served under both Papa Doc and Baby Doc—acting as the latter's head of personal security and financial adviser.

In the early days of the CNG, Avril had been forced to resign due to public outcry at his inclusion but had remained a powerful figure within the military regime. Moreover, not only had he played a leading role in Baby Doc's smooth departure, but he had also featured prominently in all ensuing political developments: the November 1987 violence, the election of Manigat, and Namphy's coup. Now he had been brought to the presidency by another permutation within the political-military power structure. Yet what made his accession to the presidency logical was his good relationship with the United States and his ability to repair the damage done to U.S.-Haitian relations by the Namphy coup. This factor fitted well with the army reformers' desire to modernize and clean up the army—as always dependent on U.S. goodwill for arms, training, and pay. What was less obvious, however, was how Avril's Duvalierist past would affect his alliance with the anti-Duvalierist army reformers.

The paradox of Avril's truce with the *ti-soldats* (little soldiers) was further sharpened by the appointment of several known Duvalierists to government posts. Avril had initially been closely supervised by the *ti-soldats*, to the extent that he could meet nobody on official business without Sergeant Hébreux being present. Gradually, however, Avril found space to maneuver and was able to attack those radical elements within the army that had brought him to power. An alleged coup attempt in October gave him the pretext to dismiss or jail several prominent members of the army's reformist wing. The mysterious death in November of Colonel Paul further strengthened Avril's position, ridding him of a powerful military rival and allowing him to avoid the crisis that would have developed if the United States had insisted on extraditing Paul on drug charges. The inevitable tensions within the army then culminated in an attempted coup against Avril from the Léopards battalion in early April 1989, allegedly brought about by the dismissal of several officers for their role in drug smuggling. Having been saved by loyal troops of the Presidential Guard, Avril subsequently faced a rebellion from the Dessalines battalion, with open fighting between opposed factions of the military.

In all, approximately thirty soldiers and five civilians died in the army's internal power struggle. At the end, Avril emerged victorious, supported by a majority within the over one-thousand-strong Presidential Guard, whose pay and conditions he had been careful to improve. The Léopards and the Dessalines battalion, however, were disbanded, and the entire structure of the army was reorganized around centralized presidential control. By the end of 1989, then, President Avril seemed to have won control of the Haitian army. Yet the dismissal or transfer of hundreds of troops, many of whom were formerly Tontons Macoutes incorporated into the regular army as "attachés" under the Namphy government, created an unprecedented climate of violence, as armed gangs resorted to crime and political assassinations. At no point, moreover, could Avril claim any popular support outside the ruling military clique. His regime, therefore, existed without legitimacy, permanently threatened by the same forces that had ousted the Duvalier dictatorship.

### An Irreversible Democracy?

Like many Haitian military leaders before him, President Avril promised to oversee a transition to what he described as an "irreversible democracy" in Haiti. His democratic rhetoric during the first months of 1989 was in large part determined by the conditions attached to the projected resumption of U.S. economic aid, which Congress was due to debate in June. These included the restoration of the 1987 constitution, the establishment of an independent electoral commission, improvements in human rights, and reforms in military and judicial structures.[26] While some measures were quickly imposed, it was clear that they fell short of demands made by the democratic opposition inside Haiti. The constitution, for instance, was restored, but with at least thirty controversial articles concerning the military's rights suspended. A new CEP, meanwhile, was largely composed of government nominees rather than representatives of civic groups. Most tellingly, however, despite the much-publicized signing of several international human rights treaties, the Avril regime presided over a continuing high level of political violence, much of which was authoritatively linked to the highest echelons of the army.[27]

Several other factors created doubts as to the Avril regime's democratic intentions. Notorious Duvalierists such as Franck Romain were allowed to escape into exile, despite popular pressure for legal proceedings against them. The appointment of Colonel Acédius Saint Louis to the key post of interior and defense minister was

further evidence of Avril's accommodation of the powerful Duvalierist establishment, with whom he maintained an ambivalent
relationship. Nevertheless, the United States supported Avril, as it
had Duvalier, the CNG, and Manigat before him. U.S. advisers
reportedly assisted him in fending off the April 1989 coup,[28] while
statements from the U.S. State Department and Democratic congressional leaders praised Avril's commitment to democratizing
Haiti. Approval was finally translated into financial terms when,
on 21 June 1989, Congress approved US$20 million in aid, to be
followed by US$40 million for the following fiscal year.[29] An addi-
tional US$10 million in food aid was approved in August,
prompted by news that a fresh electoral plan was shortly to be
announced by the Avril regime. This occurred in September 1989,
with a complex timetable for communal and legislative elections
stretching over a year, culminating with presidential elections in
November 1990.

The prospect of elections revived Port-au-Prince's political
class, which had been marginalized since the November 1987 election debacle, and a number of alliances and realignments were
announced in late 1989. Most important was the alliance between
the U.S.-supported Marc Bazin and the democratic socialist, Serge
Gilles, creating a credible centrist bloc. Others involved a three-
party conservative coalition led by Louis Déjoie, while seasoned
Duvalierists such as Claude Raymond expressed their intention to
contest the elections. Yet among most Haitians there was little
enthusiasm about the prospect of more army-dominated elections
and, instead, a depressing sense of déjà vu. President Avril's past,
his connections with the Duvalierist forces, and the army's apparent reluctance to relinquish unconditional power were all perceived as reminiscent of the CNG. The brutal treatment of three
prominent left-wing activists, accused of plotting Avril's assassination in November 1989, added to doubts about the army's
democratic commitment. As in late 1985, popular protest, and not
electioneering, was what moved the democratic process forward.

Prosper Avril's departure on 12 March 1990 marked the end of
another short-lived military regime. Forced out by a combination
of popular unrest and U.S. disapproval, Avril handed over power to
General Hérard Abraham, the chief of staff, who in turn appointed
Ertha Pascal-Trouillot as interim president. A Supreme Court
judge, Pascal-Trouillot was the first woman president in Haitian
history. Governing with the assistance of the nineteen-member
Council of State, she proclaimed her intention to oversee fair and
free elections within the existing timetable. Six months later,

however, such a prospect again seemed remote. Elections were postponed until December 1990, and many believed that they could not take place without a repetition of the bloodshed of the November 1987 election. The Council of State accused Pascal-Trouillot of conniving with the Duvalierist sector and allowing known terrorists—such as Baby Doc's former Interior Minister Roger Lafontant—to organize political activity with impunity. As before, lack of resources and political divisions between the government and the CEP seemed likely to put elections in jeopardy or to discourage many electors from participating.

It was something of a surprise, therefore, when polling took place, chaotically but generally peacefully, on 16 December 1990. In the presence of hundreds of foreign observers, led by former U.S. President Jimmy Carter, the army leaned heavily on leaders of the Tontons Macoutes not to disrupt the voting. The result expressed the suppressed desire of the Haitian people to see real change take place at last. They gave more than 60 percent of the vote to Father Jean-Bertrand Aristide, a radical and youthful Catholic priest, enabling him to easily defeat the other main candidate, Marc Bazin. Aristide dubbed his campaign Operation Lavalas, referring to the local term for the torrents of water that periodically wash the streets of Port-au-Prince after a heavy rainfall, and promised to govern in the interests of the impoverished majority. For its part, the U.S. government welcomed the poll and congratulated Aristide on his victory. However, the sense of hope generated by Aristide proved to be tragically short-lived. In September 1991 his government was overthrown by the army in yet another coup. This intervention unleashed an appalling period of killing and conflict, which rendered the prospect of democracy almost unimaginable.

## An Uncertain Future

The 1980s set in motion a complex and unpredictable process in Haiti, which clearly remains unresolved at the beginning of the 1990s. The Duvalier dictatorship was overthrown, to be succeeded by four military or military-dominated governments, none of which enjoyed any popular support or legitimacy. Rather, the four regimes were all unsuccessful attempts by the Haitian army to stem the tide of democratic reform and to fill the vacuum left by the dictatorship. In this respect, with the exception of the short-lived Manigat and Aristide administrations, the post-Duvalier governments replicated many of the essential characteristics of the dictatorship: a centralized, bureaucratic government structure, institutionalized corruption, absolute neglect of popular needs, and frequent recourse to violent repression.

The Haitian military, admitted Leslie Manigat, is "an inevitable fact of life."[30] Its return to the center of the country's political life after thirty years of comparative marginalization was perhaps the most significant feature of the 1980s and the post-Duvalier power struggle. This return was by no means unproblematic, however, and was achieved at the cost of factional fighting and the disbanding of both the Léopards and the Dessalines battalion. Several key military leaders—Henri Namphy, Williams Régala, and later Prosper Avril—were disgraced, while the lower ranks were torn between institutionalized crime and a more professional role for the army. In the final analysis, the army was unable to define its role in Haitian politics, remaining uncertain whether to act in alliance with the still powerful Duvalierist forces (as it did in the election debacle of November 1987) or pursue the U.S.-sponsored course of "managed transition" to civilian rule. Nonetheless, the military filled the political power vacuum as no other entity could and is bound to play a determining role in the 1990s.

By contrast, the Catholic church, the other significant national actor in Haitian politics, lost its radical direction and much of its popular support during the latter part of the decade. The successful and progressive literacy campaign, Misyon Alfa, was ended in April 1988, and the conservative hierarchy reestablished its dominance by changing the personnel and political content of Radio Soleil. In December 1988, Aristide was expelled from the Salesian order, thereby depriving him of his parish but not, of course, of his platform among the poor of Port-au-Prince. The campaign against the *ti-legliz* was led by Archbishop François-Wolff Ligondé (a cousin of Michèle Duvalier) and the papal nuncio in Haiti, Paolo Romeo.[31] Their desire to depoliticize the Haitian Catholic church weakened the single most influential focus for protest and popular mobilization. At the same time, the radical political and trade union organizations that emerged in the aftermath of Duvalier's fall, while surviving intermittent repression, initially found it difficult to organize an alternative national leadership to that of the church. Torn between the elusive "democratic space" offered by participating in elections and a well-founded distrust of the army, Haiti's political opposition was all too easily divided and rendered vulnerable, Aristide himself ultimately falling victim to this weakness.

For the United States, the principal challenge of the 1980s was the preservation of stability in an unstable situation. Having defused the immediate crisis in February 1986 by assisting in the departure of Duvalier, the State Department found itself committed to supporting a Haitian military establishment that never seemed likely to deliver the promised transition to civilian rule. After the election disaster of November 1987 and the brief Manigat interregnum, the United States became more cautious than it had been with the CNG, applying important and ultimately fatal pressure on Avril. What had often appeared as mere lip service to democratic change during the Reagan administration became more meaningful during the early part of George Bush's presidency. The tying of economic aid to demonstrable political reform was a vital element in preventing Avril from consolidating a new dictatorship. The United States also tried to work with Aristide.

In concrete terms, then, little of what was hoped for in February 1986 materialized in the ensuing four years. While Duvalier enjoyed a gilded retirement in the Côte d'Azur, political power remained in the hands of the army. The shadowy Duvalierist establishment, composed of former ministers, businessmen, landowners, and soldiers, also maintained power and influence, not least through its hired gunmen. Every experiment in democratic elections ended in bloodshed, and warring factions in a resurgent military junta struggled for political power and its attendant economic benefits. In the countryside, the barons of the ancien régime—larger landowners, coffee traders, and chefs de section—continued to oppress the poverty-stricken peasantry, as they always had. Environmental degradation proceeded relentlessly, the felling of trees for charcoal creating a vicious cycle of drought and soil erosion. Meanwhile, still more Haitian boat people attempted to flee to the United States, only to be turned away by the thousands. Finally, the economy continued its inevitable downward slide, with the sugar and tourist industries destroyed, manufacturing in decline, and peasant agriculture increasingly unable to provide a livelihood for the rural population.

Yet, uncertain and depressing as the picture seemed at the beginning of the 1990s, the preceding decade had at least revealed the possibility of real change in Haiti, a possibility strongly reinforced by the overthrow of Prosper Avril and the subsequent election of Aristide. Certain limited advances were made; political, press, and trade union freedoms were gained at least temporarily, allowing an unprecedented degree of debate and self-expression, which was curiously at odds with regular periods of repression. The organized peasant movement also gained a new impetus, and experiments in rural cooperatives, literacy, and political education survived the retreat of the Catholic church's radical wing.[32] Above all, the experience of overthrowing Duvalier and the slogans of *déchoukaj* and *rache manyòk* provided Haitians with a sense, however tenuous, of their political power. This understanding gives at least some grounds for hope in a country all too often depicted as beyond salvation.

# 4    Race, Politics, and Succession in Trinidad and Guyana

*Ralph R. Premdas*

During the 1980s both Trinidad and Guyana lost the charismatic leaders around whom political life had revolved throughout the postindependence period. Deep alienation during the last days of each leader's rule invited predictions of cataclysmic changes. Surprisingly, neither country experienced any major trauma in the succession of new leaders and regimes to power and governance. On the other hand, both states confronted major economic crises, which placed their survival on a daily brink. While the oil-propelled, once-vibrant Trinidadian economy nearly collapsed from plummeting petroleum prices, the Guyanese economy did collapse but continued breathing, receiving emergency attention in its unending coma.

In this weary, depressed state, both Guyana and Trinidad charted a pro-Western, pro-American foreign policy. No new fundamental solutions were offered; piecemeal reforms seemed to guarantee ongoing dependence. In their economic struggle, both countries continued with their old communal politics born of their multiethnic structure and nurtured by ambitious ethnic, chauvinistic leaders. Ethnically polarized politics, marked by deep-seated intersectional distrust, failed to yield the unifying collective consciousness needed to overcome economic disaster. In economic agony, racism persisted, each community refusing to surrender the old communal predispositions, which have over the years contributed so much to their poverty and plight.

It could be said, then, that after the first generation of leaders passed on, the new generation, after momentarily and bravely tinkering with the inherited system, soon fell into old habits and patterns. They used a new vocabulary and a high voice to be sure—but the more things changed, the more they remained the same.

When Eric Williams died, his successors were soon called PNMites after the People's National Movement, Williams's party and the founding organ of Trinidadian nationalism. Similarly, after Forbes Burnham passed on, the Desmond Hoyte–Hamilton Green administration was accused of retaining its Burnhamite texture. In many ways, these cutting commentaries were meant to express disappointment in not taking new departures. At another level, the failure to radically reorient the old system stemmed less from lack of imagination or will than from constraints imposed by powerful external actors, and the latter no longer offered a convincing argument for poor performance: the local populace knows that much of its underachievement comes from its own hands—from corruption, waste, lack of discipline, and intercommunal hatred.

There are, of course, many major differences as well as similarities between Trinidad and Guyana. Both dimensions can be elucidated by looking, separately but briefly, at each country to identify the underlying structures, which so much account for recent and contemporary failures.

## TRINIDAD AND TOBAGO

### People, Society, and the Economy

The colonial legacy of social structure and economic dependence haunts the present, imparting a stable underlying reality to Trinidad's politics. From Columbus's arrival in 1498, through to Arawak and African slavery, and on to Indian indenture, stretching across nearly five hundred years of history and traversing two oceans, came a multicolored immigrant people to populate Trinidad. Color differentiation and its correlative economic privileges thus tinged all aspects of politics, past and present.

Whites, near whites, and more recently, Chinese, even though only 1.5 percent of the population, enjoy considerable social and economic influence and, indirectly, disproportionate political leverage. Coloreds, or mixed races, who constitute about 16 percent of the population, tend to occupy intermediate positions in the class system. Creoles (or Afro-Trinidadians), who comprise about 41 percent of the population, are distributed along the economic ladder, half occupying the lowest economic rung, while the remainder enjoy middle-class status. From the combined colored and middle-class Creole sections have emerged technocrats and professionals who provide the political and administrative decision makers in the Trinidad polity. East Indians, descended from indentured laborers recruited from India between 1845 and 1915, also constitute about 41 percent of the population. Fifteen percent are Moslems, the majority are Hindus. They are mainly rural residents, and many can be classified as middle income.

Ethnic consciousness among these separate groups has emerged from the cleavages of color, religion, place of residence, and occupation. Whites (often called French Creoles, collectively) are concentrated in managerial posts in the private sector and tend to live in their own neighborhoods. In a highly urbanized and densely populated island, many Creoles, coloreds, and Indians live at close quarters in mixed townships, but most of the Creole population is concentrated in Port of Spain and in the towns of the east-west corridor. Similarly, most Indians are rural dwellers, with a strong core found in the plains of the sugar belt.[1] An all-pervasive and fundamental cleavage, therefore, dominates Trinidadian society: the Creole-cum-colored portion versus the Indian portion. Notwithstanding this, over the past century and a half, Indians and Creoles have shared a common language, a small island, an administrative system, and schools. Their food, clothes, tongue, and public utilities unite them daily, so that a shared identity—a common Trinidadianness—has emerged alongside a split personality based on politics and culture.[2]

Over several centuries of evolution, a primary product export processing economy evolved in Trinidad by the 1960s, based on sugar, oil, and cocoa. Sugar was linked to the Indians, oil to the Creoles, and cocoa to an ethnically mixed group of producers. The dependent structure of the export economy was reinforced by externally determined price structures. Throughout the 1960s and early 1970s, prices were low, and Trinidad drifted along in an economic malaise bordering on bankruptcy and endured persistent industrial disputes. The new governing nationalists in the PNM led by Dr. Williams relied on a strategy of "industrialization by invitation," modeled on the Puerto Rican example, to transform Trinidad into a prosperous country. The strategy failed to attract enough foreign investors, and the country was plagued by a 15–20 percent unemployment rate.

In 1969 and 1970, the collective and cumulative impact of a deteriorating economy, the near bankruptcy of government, industrial strife, and an inflexible political strategy triggered the black power revolt.[3] This event nearly toppled the Williams regime but, above all, forced the PNM to reexamine its development strategy and to begin to intervene more directly in the productive process, with a view to at least ameliorating the unemployment situation. New plans were formulated and new directions taken. In the end, the solutions proved ineffective; it took an event outside of Trinidad, the Arab-Israeli conflict and its attendant oil boycotts, to drive petroleum prices dramatically upward and to lift Trinidad out of its economic suffering.

The oil boom years saw the quadrupling of oil prices and, with it, the transformation of the Trinidad economy. Real output grew 7 percent annually, unemployment fell to 8.8 percent by 1980, and per capita income exploded to US$3,390 by 1978, catapulting Trinidad to among the ranks of the developed countries. Imports, especially of food, grew from TT$860 million in 1973 to TT$1,348 million in 1980, resulting in the practical destruction of the agricultural sector. Wages escalated, especially in the oil sector, causing workers in the other industries and the government to demand and obtain substantial increases. The overall impact was the creation of a bloated consumer society.

Government economic strategy during the boom years, from mid-1973 to 1981, saw the enactment of the old PNM strategy of import substitution and industrial export promotion.[4] Local firms, such as Neal and Massey, McEarneny and Alstons, Geddes Grant, and Kirpalanis, supplied the needs of the new internal consumer society by importing consumer goods and producing a few others. Most of their manufacturing effort was of the assembly plant type, lacking domestic depth, so that the import-substitution strategy failed to generate long-lasting secondary industries. The industrial export promotion thrust of the strategy involved the government in partnership with several multinational corporations to produce oil, gas, fertilizers, ammonia, methanol, petrochemicals, and steel for export. State participation in these enterprises reached TT$3 billion by 1980, or 21 percent of gross national product.

The vast revenues received by the government also allowed it to launch a number of public enterprises: school meals, road repair, and hospital administration. This strategy of launching wholly owned public enterprises or partnership arrangements with foreign firms resulted in the creation of sixty-five enterprises, thirty-five owned outright by the government, fourteen with majority government shares, and the rest with minority ownership. The public service expanded dramatically to sixty-five thousand civil servants. To prepare for the day when petroleum would be depleted in Trinidad, the government launched a massive industrial project at Point Lisas to build a complex of factories, all related to the shift in reliance to gas production.[5] Signs of falling oil prices were evident in 1980, but in 1981, before the turnaround became entrenched and the spiral of decline reached the level of recession, Williams died. The legacy of the economic boom was left to his successors.

## Constitutional and Political Change

After about three centuries of Spanish control (1498–1797) and about one and a half centuries of British Crown Colony rule (1797–1962), effective decolonization can be said to have begun with the introduction of universal adult suffrage in 1946. It took almost a decade for a relatively stable party system to evolve from this event and to effectively organize and mobilize the newly enfranchised voters behind alternative policies and programs.

The 1956 elections established the pattern of politics for some three decades: ethnic affiliation determined party preference, and a bifurcated Creole-Indian polity thus emerged, lacking unity and surviving on sectional legitimacy.[6] National politics stimulated this ethnic bloc formation as a defense mechanism against ethnic domination. The PNM was dominated by Creoles and coloreds, and after the 1961 elections it also won over the bloc of white, near white, and Chinese plus many Moslems. The Indian-based Democratic Labour party became mainly a Hindu party. Successive PNM governments reflected in their cabinet appointments a preponderance of Creoles and the near total exclusion of Hindus. Indeed, PNM multiracial rhetoric was belied by minimal Indian presence in the highest decision-making councils and in the upper echelons of the public bureaucracy of the government for virtually thirty years. In PNM rule, the politics of ethnic preference steadily hardened into the politics of ethnic dominance.[7]

The PNM became the acknowledged ruling party from 1960 to 1986, and Trinidad became for all practical purposes a one-party state. Notwithstanding the Creole middle-class ascendancy (expressed occupationally in the upper echelons of a broad government bureaucracy), the middle classes of other ethnic groups shared the prosperity in the private sector and professions. Many Indians, including Hindus—who prospered from PNM rule, especially during the boom years—openly offered their electoral support to the PNM. It would, however, be incorrect to argue that the PNM ever became transformed from a preponderantly uni-ethnic electoral base to a cross-communal, middle-class party. A cross-communal socioeconomic synthesis capable of integrating Creoles and Indians into a class with a common consciousness did not evolve. Wealth, after all, makes strange and often insincere bedfellows.

## Polity and Economy in the Post-Williams Period

In only a few significant ways had the actors in the political arena changed during the 1970s. With the passing of such as Bhadese Maraj and Rudrunath Capildeo, a new rising star, Basdeo Panday, appeared as the Indian leader. Starting as a lawyer representing and leading the All Trinidad Sugar Estates and Factory Workers Union (ATSEFWU), the main sugar union, Panday emerged as the leader of the United Labour Front (ULF). Initially, in 1976, the ULF was an apex trade union unit formed by a multiracial group of trade union leaders, among whom were oil workers' leader, George Weekes, and Panday, on behalf of the sugar workers. Here, on a single momentous occasion, oil and sugar did mix, as the ULF brought sugar and oil workers to joint industrial action against their employers in 1975. In less than a year, however, as the ULF transformed itself from an economic interest group into a political party under Panday's leadership, it quickly lost its Creole following. The ULF then became predominantly uni-ethnic in composition, like its antecedent Indian parties.

In the 1976 general elections, with ethnically based parties facing each other once again, Williams and the PNM romped home to an easy win. Throughout the latter part of the 1970s, Williams himself came more and more to distrust public servants, and he relied less on the PNM and the Creole technocrats in the public service to advise him in policy making. While the Creole community still solidly supported him electorally, he depended on a small group of trusted lieutenants to carry out his will. His habit was to personalize decision making by distributing these confidantes in multiple and interlocking appointments on a number of boards and ministries.[8]

Dr. Williams died in March 1981. Among his inner circle of ministers were three deputy leaders, Errol Mahabir, Kamaluddin Mohammed, and George Chambers. Of them, Chambers, the Creole, was least known—but in less than twelve hours, the party passed over the two Indians for Chambers. Events such as this show that just below the veneer of profuse rhetorical commitment to multiracialism lurks a powerful ethnicity. Elections were postponed as Chambers took control of the PNM and effectively gave it a new image in preparation for elections, which were rescheduled for the latter part of 1981.

The 1981 elections occurred just about the time the oil boom was turning sour. If rising prices fueled the expansion, then clearly the decline in prices, which had already begun in 1980, would puncture the balloon of prosperity. Williams had foreseen the trauma that would attend the end of the consumer period. Since, constitutionally, elections had to be called in 1981, he had planned for elections for early in the year rather than later, when the situation would be worse. The prospective problems were daunting: the virtual destruction of the agricultural sector; incredibly high import bills, especially for food; spiraling wages and salaries coexisting with the erosion of the work ethic; a bloated, inefficient public bureaucracy hitched to a proliferation of public enterprises, nearly all of which accumulated losses; the pervasive use of public office for corrupt private gains; and a hedonistic and undisciplined population galloping wildly from one modern supermarket to the next, oblivious of tomorrow. All of this descended on Trinidad as oil prices plummeted in a free fall. A poll in early 1981 showed that 50 percent of the population wanted Williams to step down, including 54 percent of the Indians and 45 percent of the Creoles.[9] Labor disputes were already multiplying, and perhaps Williams did not want to be around to witness the chaos. At any rate, refusing to see doctors or take medicine, the tired diabetic recluse died, leaving the PNM to fend for itself.

The new PNM prime minister reshuffled his cabinet, terminated a few extravagant projects such as the horse racing complex, settled a number of important industrial disputes, made himself accessible to the press, visited and held consultations with the people, and promised, in a persuasive slogan, that "what's wrong must be put right." This public relations assault created the illusion of a new PNM, with new hope. The party knew, however, that its showmanship was a camouflage concealing the tidal wave of problems that would soon deluge the population. Its leaders wanted desperately to win in order to spend the following four or five years in salvaging the economy and averting the popular wrath that was otherwise bound to bury them in future elections.

By this stage in Trinidad's political history, especially after the prolonged period of prosperity conferred by the oil boom, a cross-communal class structure had emerged, shaped rather like a diamond. In effect, in terms of the standard of living in Trinidad, a society of middle-income persons had become the majority of the population. To be sure, a large and disproportionate number of Creoles remained economically poor and marginalized, but even among these, a semiwelfare program of make-work jobs was initiated and made easily available to anyone willing simply to sign up and show up for a job. The overall impact was the creation of a relatively wealthy electorate, in Caribbean terms. They had come to expect prosperity and were prepared to evict from office any party in power during a fall in living standards.

At a certain level of consciousness, then, a cross-communal middle-class stratum had evolved ready to support capitalist and conservative parties. But this class factor operated in a multiethnic society marked by interethnic suspicions and fear of communal domination. Partisan choice is always governed by the interplay of these two factors. In the context of the PNM and the oil crisis, Creole middle-class citizens were willing to vote their economic interest in concert with the Indian middle class only when this party was led by a Creole. Ethnic interest and ethnic identification thus still constituted the most powerful and irrational force shaping partisan choice in Trinidad. Class interests were nevertheless powerful motivators in the service of overarching ethnic communal claims.

Chambers's honeymoon with the public notwithstanding, the death of Williams saw the blossoming of forces once suppressed by his awesome personality. New parties were formed and old parties revitalized. Foremost among the new parties was the Organization for National Reconstruction (ONR), led by former PNM stalwart K. Hudson-Phillips. The ONR attacked the Williams legacy of dependence and corruption and attracted large multiracial crowds. Another group that emerged was called the National Alliance and was composed of a loose alignment of the old Tobago-based Democratic Action Congress (DAC), led by A. N. R. Robinson, another former PNM stalwart, and the ULF, led by Panday. Yet the PNM minus Williams won the 1981 elections in what superficially was a resounding victory, winning twenty-six of thirty-six seats. However, voter turnout was only 54.7 percent. The opposition parties fared well. Although the ONR did not win a seat, it gathered an astounding 22.1 percent of votes cast. The National Alliance won ten seats, eight in the sugar belt and two in Tobago, taking 21 percent of the votes. In effect, while the PNM continued to control the Parliament, its popular victory represented only 29.8 percent support from the entire electorate. Together, the 45 percent absentee vote and the votes won by the ONR and the National Alliance pointed to a radical decline in the PNM's popular standing.

Chambers was no Williams. Not only did he lack charisma and the respect that Williams commanded, he now faced two towering former PNM leaders in Hudson-Phillips and Robinson, both from the same ethnic population. The Indian bogeyman in Panday was submerged by the new array of opposition leaders. In addition, Chambers had to face the full meaning of the decline in oil prices. Politically, what severely restricted his capacity to restructure the economy was the fact that he faced new county council elections in 1983. The PNM decided not to rein in the economy because of the distractions and demands of these elections, which were interpreted as an indicator of the party's popular acceptance. In place of the austerity—which was needed—the Chambers regime, wanting desperately to win, conceded a 76–104 percent wage and salary increase to the sixty-five thousand public servants. The government deficit escalated to TT$2,355 million.

The results of the council elections, conducted in the shadow of economic decline, rising unemployment, increasing retrenchment, and the growth in industrial strife, stunned the PNM. In a historic arrangement, the ONR and National Alliance coordinated their efforts against the PNM. In its first defeat since the federal elections of 1958, the PNM obtained a total of fifty-four council seats to the opposition's sixty-six. The Chambers regime was now mortally wounded. An increasingly powerful opposition and a decline in the economy, combined with a weakening PNM, signaled a major disjuncture in Trinidad's history and, before long, brought to an end thirty years of PNM rule. The ONR–National Alliance collaboration spilled over from the council elections into a new political formation, which in addition to Tapia House, a small radical grouping, called itself the National Alliance for Reconstruction (NAR). The NAR was a formidable alignment of races, classes, and regions in Trinidad and Tobago; it was that elusive multiethnic formation that had until now failed to appear in Trinidad's politics: a "rainbow party" based on "one love." Without too much difficulty, Robinson was chosen to lead it into battle against the PNM.

In 1986, oil prices collapsed to US$15 per barrel. While government revenues had grown at the phenomenal rate of 44 percent annually from 1974 to 1980, creating annual surpluses, in 1985 the deficit was TT$2,765 million. The government's industrial scheme at Point Lisas, which had been designed to capitalize on the country's ample gas reserves and fill the gap when petroleum production declined, in fact became a revenue liability. ISCOTT, the steel company that was 100 percent owned by the government and had been built at a price of US$485 million, lost TT$1.5 billion from 1980 to 1986. In 1986 alone, it lost TT$234 million. Retrenchment followed the collapse of oil prices, so that, by 1986, some ten thousand oil workers, 21 percent of them, lost their jobs. The balance of payments deficit increased from 1.3 percent of gross domestic product to 13.6 percent in the same year. Unemployment also increased, from 7 percent in 1981 to 17 percent in 1986, and the Trinidad dollar was devalued by about 33 percent.

It was in this economic morass that the PNM sought to confront its electoral adversaries at the end of 1986. An opinion poll just prior to the election showed that 41 percent of Creoles, 82 percent of Indians, and 47 percent of mixed races supported the NAR. It was also known that the French Creole elite had shifted its support to the new alliance and provided much of its financing and public relations propaganda. Unsurprisingly in the end, in elections held on 15 December, a tired, old, and frustrated PNM lost resoundingly to the NAR, which obtained 67.3 percent of the votes and won all but three seats in the thirty-six-seat House of Representatives. In the critical east-west corridor, which was the foundation of previous PNM victories, about 45 percent of Creoles shifted to the NAR, giving the corridor, except for Laventille and East Port of Spain, to the NAR. A new political era was thus inaugurated in Trinidad.

## The NAR in Power: Internal Disintegration

Although formally it was a unitary party, the NAR was in fact an uncemented combination of its four parts. When Robinson was appointed leader, no concession was made to his superiority over his coleaders, Panday, Hudson-Phillips, and Tapia leader Lloyd Best. He was chosen because, electorally, he was most likely to maximize votes for the NAR. In holding out the hope of victory, NAR never in its wildest moments anticipated winning as many as thirty-three seats to the PNM's three. Although Best had mentioned the need for it, no formula for sharing power in the event of victory was devised. A spirit of common purpose welded by the ardor of the campaign made a power-sharing formula appear clumsy and unnecessary. It was anticipated that the spirit of "one love" and consultation that held prior to the election would continue afterward. As time would tell, this was not true, and it was a damaging mistake not to have designed a formula for power sharing.

Almost as soon as victory was obtained, internal strife entered through the ethnic back door. As prime minister, Robinson took it upon himself to name his cabinet without consulting his partners in victory. Strictly speaking, he was following the protocol of the Westminster parliamentary system. But NAR was not a unitary party under the undisputed command of a Napoleon. The "one love" slogan notwithstanding, cabinet making in a plural society was bound to be perceived through the ethnic prism. The ethnic structure of the cabinet shocked Indians, who had voted overwhelmingly for the NAR. Of nineteen cabinet posts, only five were allocated to Indians, two to whites, one to a mixed-race person, and eleven to Creoles. Although NAR's overwhelming victory was a "combinational" event, each ethnic group interpreted its cabinet share by reference to its imagined input in the victory. Creoles, for instance, could argue that their proportionate allocation of cabinet posts was justified from the standpoint that it was they, through their 45 percent vote for the NAR, who broke the PNM's stranglehold over the strategic east-west corridor. Indians could counterargue that their population numbers equaled those of the Creoles, but while only 45 percent of Creoles supported the NAR, about 82 percent of Indians did. By this ethnic arithmetic, Indians were grievously shortchanged in cabinet posts. But Creoles noted that Indians were also appointed to the presidency of the republic and the speakership of the House of Representatives. Panday, deputy leader of the NAR, was appointed foreign minister in the new regime. He and his old ULF faction in the NAR decided against challenging Robinson, mainly because they could muster at best about ten of the thirty-three seats.

The NAR was therefore kept together, but a wedge of distrust had been sunk into the very heart of the NAR leadership. Robinson continued to separate himself from his erstwhile electoral co-leaders, retreating behind a cadre of personal staff and technocrats from the public service. Indeed, what especially irked the ULF faction was the fact that many of Robinson's key advisers were the same old Creole PNM-entrenched technocrats. Perhaps at this early stage Robinson had no choice in selecting his advisers, but the appearance was nonetheless given that he was trapped and had been co-opted by these PNM technocrats.

The ULF Indian ministers claimed that they were deliberately excluded from Robinson's inner circle by these people and privately talked about a racist conspiracy. Panday reminded the public that he had not dedicated his life to destroy what he called PNM-ism (that is, the institutional practices allegedly discriminating against Indians) only to see it slip back into power through the back door. "Three hundred and sixty thousand persons had voted for NAR and one hundred and eighty thousand for the PNM," he said, "but to many people the PNM is still in power." Panday went so far as to compare Robinson's formal commitment to multi-racialism to the rhetoric of Williams, who "used to make similar speeches and then went on to set up the most racist society that we ever had."[10]

Faced with county council elections in September 1987, the NAR temporarily closed ranks, put aside its internal squabbles, and won again. Yet its margin of victory was less than in the 1986 general elections: the NAR lost three of the eleven councils to the PNM. The internal ethnic struggle had restimulated ethnic polarization, so that many Creoles returned to the PNM.

The internal schism that the NAR experienced was matched in magnitude by the external economic situation that the party faced in assuming office. Looking at a deficit of TT$2.8 billion left by the PNM, an empty treasury, a debt service obligation that required TT$1.7 billion annually (39 percent of all anticipated revenues), and the exhaustion of the legal limits of public borrowing, Robinson remarked that "it was as though the PNM was determined to sink the country before being voted out."[11] Certainly, the NAR had underestimated the depth of the economic crisis. During its election campaign, it had optimistically promised to "roll back the recession." Lacking a plan or strategy to cope with the crisis, it fought desperately to rescue Trinidad, in Robinson's words, "from the jaws of three financial dragons—an unbridgeable budget deficit, a continuing balance of payments crisis, and the debt trap."[12] In other words, to survive, the NAR had to administer bitter medicine to the supporters who voted it into power.

In its first budget, the many and varied forms of subsidies the PNM had built into the economy were swiftly eliminated. The annual cost of living adjustment (COLA) was unceremoniously dropped. The two-tier currency exchange system, which subsidized food and drug imports to the tune of TT$700 million, was scrapped. Taxes were attached to gasoline, airline tickets, and other items, while old taxes were increased. A national recovery levy was imposed on all persons with annual incomes above TT$70,000. These measures and many others had the desired effect of substantially reducing the annual deficit. Yet the problem remained formidable, for oil prices continued to fall and unemployment passed the 20 percent mark. Eventually, the IMF was approached, with the result that more and new drastic measures had to be imposed in 1988.

After barely one year in office, then, the NAR was buffeted by external and internal crises that threatened to tear the new multiethnic party apart. The strains of facing two fronts simultaneously took their toll on Robinson's health and on the NAR's popular image. The internal fissure was resolved first. The continued public criticisms by Panday's faction about Robinson's leadership style, the alleged lack of consultation, and the existence of "an invisible government" of Creole technocrats and big business finally reached a climax on 26 November 1987, when Robinson asked the entire cabinet to submit its resignation. The country was deeply shocked. For forty-eight hours Robinson agonized and finally dismissed John Humphrey, the Pandayite minister of housing. Panday's own ministry of external affairs was shrunk by the removal from it of immigration and citizenship. Kelvin Ramnath, who had vocally criticized the PNM technocrats around Robinson, was transferred from the powerful energy ministry to public utilities, which, in turn, was shorn of several crucial utilities. Emmanuel Hosein, the minister of health, lost the welfare and women's affairs portfolios.

The Pandayite faction was not expelled but found itself with reduced responsibilities and power. At the same time, Robinson added three new ministries, all assigned to Creoles. The Hudson-Phillips ONR faction improved its standing from three to five ministries. Robinson's message to the NAR was that he was the prime minister and the intraparty complaints must be handled through established procedures. But the Panday group was not about to be silenced or intimidated. In turn, it was accused, in one famous *Sunday Express* news story ("ULF Grab for Power"), of wanting more power to secure Indian domination.[13]

The internal crisis reached a head when Panday proceeded to negotiate for the building of the Indian Cultural Centre, a gift from the Indian government to Trinidad, only to be thwarted by a racially divided cabinet. When Panday and his faction spoke out again, on 8 February 1988, they were expelled from Robinson's cabinet. The core of the ULF contingent—Panday, Trevor Sudama (who had been a minister at finance), Ramnath, and Humphrey—were now all out of the government. The internal bickering in the NAR had been resolved but at the expense of dividing Trinidad's population once more along Creole-Indian lines. To put it another way, national unity had been sacrificed to preserve cabinet solidarity.

Robinson now had to face the worsening economic crisis—increasing unemployment and decreasing oil prices—without the moral power that came with the unified NAR landslide victory. For all practical purposes, the NAR had become a minority party. An opinion poll taken in the wake of the Panday expulsion showed that the NAR could not win a single seat anywhere in the country except in Tobago. The new party configuration consisted of the NAR, which was now a composite of the ONR and the DAC, plus a few ULF Indians who refused to follow Panday's instruction to withdraw from the government. The opposition parties were the PNM, which under Patrick Manning was slowly regaining its strength, and the United National Congress (UNC), the name given to Panday's new Indian-based party. In a test of popularity in the Guaico-Cumuto by-election in mid-1989, the NAR ran third after the UNC and the PNM. This ominous performance was slightly reversed a few months later when a poll showed that the NAR had regained some support, receiving about 30 percent of popular approval, while the PNM obtained 20 percent, and the UNC 18 percent.

The various austerity measures successfully arrested the decline in the economy, but it was not clear whether it had really been turned around. An appeal to the IMF for US$115 million was necessary in November 1988. The IMF option was widely and intensely debated and even led to a countrywide one-day strike called by the public service unions. This was accompanied by two devaluations and a voluntary retrenchment of public service programs. The economy had partly stabilized, with a remarkable revival in agricultural production and an increase in oil prices to US$19 per barrel. However, another trip to the IMF was necessary in early 1990 to cope with the cost of servicing Trinidad's huge external debt. On this occasion, US$111 million was secured over eleven months. The social costs of adjustment also began to be felt, most immediately in an unemployment figure of 23 percent (41 percent in the 15-to-19-year age group). Law and order became tenuous, and drugs were increasingly used in all levels of society. Migration continued to North America, but fewer Indians claimed refugee status in Canada based on discrimination. In December 1989, one researcher revealed that only 29 percent of public service employees were Indian.[14] Of these, 24.6 percent were in the police service, 5.7 percent in the armed forces, and 16 percent in the coast guard. These figures are very suggestive of systematic discrimination in the public service, even if one were to concede that many Indians preferred nonpublic service occupations. When Panday gave the keynote address on 3 December 1989 at the first convention of the UNC, he made the call for an Equal Opportunities

Commission the centerpiece of his speech.[15] The small percentage
of Indians in the army and rising racial tensions continued to pro-
voke discussion in Trinidad of the local relevance of the coup in Fiji
in May 1987.[16]

This debate was prophetic. On 27 July 1990, a coup against the
government was mounted by a black fundamentalist Muslim
group, the Jamaat al Muslimeen, led by an expoliceman, Abu Bakr.
For nearly a week, Robinson and most of his cabinet were held
hostage in the parliament building, while Abu Bakr, in charge of
the television station, broadcast his demands for the resignation of
the government and for immediate steps to ameliorate the hardships imposed on the people by the IMF programs. Crucially, the
army remained loyal to the government and was deployed in force.
Abu Bakr and 113 of his followers were surrounded and eventually
were persuaded to release Robinson and the other hostages. They
then surrendered and were taken into custody. The costs were 23
Trinidadians killed, some 250 injured (including the prime minister), and 102 business premises destroyed or damaged by fire and
looting in the first hours of the coup attempt.

Although the NAR government survived the coup, Robinson's
reputation lay in tatters. The people of Trinidad supported his
government in taking decisive action to preserve democracy but
blamed him for creating the conditions that allowed it to happen. It
highlighted serious deficiencies in the security services and raised
the question of leadership and strategy within the NAR. It also fed
into ongoing concerns about race. In late 1989, Robinson, in an
attempt to refurbish the NAR's tarnished multiethnic image after
Panday's sacking, had elevated Winston Dookeran as his Indian
deputy party leader. Dookeran, as minister for planning and development, thus had the responsibility for improving the country's
economic fortunes, given the windfall of the Gulf crisis, which saw
oil prices rise briefly to as much as US$40 per barrel. It was clear
that the NAR hoped to use this extra revenue to reduce the austerity measures as new elections got closer. These hopes were,
however, to no avail. In elections in December 1991 the NAR was
swept aside, retaining only the two Tobago seats. The UNC won
thirteen seats, but the PNM returned to government, taking
twenty-one of the thirty-six seats in the House of Representatives.
The NAR thus failed to break the stranglehold of racially based
electoral politics and Creole domination of the government,
which has been the hallmark of politics in Trinidad since independence.

GUYANA

## People, Society, and the Economy

For most of Guyana's history, starting from the first settlement in the seventeenth century to the present—a period of almost three hundred years—the country was a colony. As in Trinidad, slavery and indenture were the twin pillars of labor supply, on which a viable plantation colony was established. As the indigenous population dwindled and disappeared, the African continent was tapped for a new source of cheap labor. Following emancipation in 1834, labor shortages saw the recruitment of Irish, German, Maltese, Chinese, Portuguese, and Asian Indians. The Indians proved the most adaptable, so that, between 1840 and 1917, approximately 238,960 indentured Indians arrived. At the expiration of their indentures, about two-thirds opted to stay and became permanent residents.

Thus, out of labor importation, a multiethnic society was created in Guyana. Again, as in Trinidad, the pattern of life of each of the ethnic communities separated them into virtual cultural, residential, and occupational islands. The Europeans, who lived in guarded enclaves on sugar estates and in urban areas, were managers and planters and benefited from a color-class status system, in which things English and white were highly prized. One difference between the settlement patterns of Trinidad and Guyana is the greater space that separates rural and urban areas in Guyana compared to Trinidad, where rural and urban areas are closer and where more urbanization has occurred.

After emancipation, as in Trinidad, former slaves gravitated from free villages to urban areas, where they acquired literacy, English ways, and skills. The impact of this opportunity subsequently resulted in recruitment for the public services, which by 1950 were dominated by Creoles. By 1960 the Creole portion of the plantation population was only 6.8 percent, while Indians still remained in and around the sugar estates. Most of them were allocated lands contiguous to the estates to ensure their availability as plantation laborers. By the 1960s, 25.5 percent of the Indian population was living on sugar estates, 13.4 percent in urban areas, with the remaining 61.1 percent in villages.[17] Guyanese Indians therefore became predominantly rural residents. The other ethnic elements in the population were small, and they too established their own peculiar and residential niches. Amerindians were consigned to reservations, while the Chinese and Portuguese who came initially as experimental indentured laborers gravitated to urban areas and entered the professions and service industries.

Economic activity in Guyana has been less diverse over the years than in Trinidad. Guyana evolved as a veritable sugar colony, dominated almost entirely throughout most of its history by plantation production of sugar. The main sugar multinational, which owned about 80 percent of Guyana's sugar estates, was Bookers Sugar Estates Ltd., a subsidiary of Booker McConnell Ltd. of London. Although three other much smaller foreign companies cultivated sugar in Guyana, the colony was widely known as Booker's Guiana. As in Trinidad, Indians succeeded Africans as sugar workers and became identified with sugar. Diversification of the sugar-dominated economy did occur to a limited extent when Indians who gave up their right to repatriation to India were offered lands contiguous to the plantations on which to live and cultivate crops. From this arose a viable rice industry, the second largest agricultural activity in Guyana, providing rice self-sufficiency to the country as well as export revenues. As for industry, Guyana's major activity focused on bauxite produced by two multinationals, Alcan Aluminium of Canada and Reynolds Ltd. of the United States.

There thus emerged an economy built around sugar, bauxite, and rice. In a typical year (1975), they accounted for 47 percent of gross domestic product. Bauxite's contribution to total exports ranged from 40 to 50 percent, sugar from 30 to 35 percent. Each industry relied on mainly one ethnic group for its workers, sugar and rice on Indians and bauxite on Africans. Sugar in particular occupied a strategic place in the economy, providing employment directly for twenty-thousand persons and using most of the cultivable coastal land for production. It was said that sugar ran through Guyana's society and polity like blood in the human body. The only real counterweight to commodity production was the public sector, which came to consume about 50 percent of the budget for wages and salaries and was the country's major employer. Along with the Guyana Defence Force and the Police Constabulary, the public service was staffed at all levels preponderantly by Afro-Guyanese. As for the indigenous private sector of businesses and factories, this was mainly the preserve of Portuguese, Chinese, and Indian entrepreneurs. Workers were organized around these various units of production, inevitably bringing on trade unions, which tended to be predominantly uniethnic.

whole period from 1961 to 1963 was marked by demonstrations, strikes, civil war, and external interference.[20] Elections under a new electoral system were called in 1964. Jagan lost to a coalition headed by Burnham and supported by the United Force, a small capitalist-oriented party, under whose auspices independence was achieved.[21]

The 1968 elections were a watershed in Guyanese history, for they represented the first of many rigged ballots subsequently effected by the PNC as the means of perpetuating its power. When Burnham seized power in 1968, he realized that the economy was essentially controlled by his political opponents. Gradually, he abandoned the capitalist structure of the economy, which favored businessmen, big property owners, and land cultivators. Toward the end of 1969, the PNC regime adopted a socialist framework for Guyana's reconstruction and in 1970 declared Guyana a "Cooperative Republic."[22] Instead of private enterprise, the economy was to be founded on cooperatives as the main instrument of production, distribution, and consumption. The regime thereafter floundered from crisis to crisis, periodically lost the support of the United States, and suffered from persistent boycotts by the non-African population, particularly Indian sugar and rice farmers. It was besieged by high unemployment (20–30 percent), double-digit inflation (25 percent), prohibitive fuel costs, demonstrations, boycotts, and strikes. A vicious cycle of poverty was created by a pattern of polarized and unstable ethnic politics intermixed with socialist ideological and programmatic justifications.[23]

Between 1971 and 1976, the government nationalized nearly all foreign firms, bringing 80 percent of the economy under state control. It then ran five banks, three bauxite companies, and all the sugar corporations. The bulging public bureaucracy was not, however, transformed into a socialist organization.[24] As in Trinidad, a middle-class African group of technocrats and managers was appointed to run the country's public service. What is more, Jay Mandle points out that the rulers were racist rather than socialist in composition: "The older colonial ruling class and its business firms have been banished and decision-making power now rests with a local elite of state and cooperative-based managers. In the Guyana context, this assumes the form of the emergence of an urban Afro-Guyanese leadership under the auspices of the People's National Congress."[25]

Western boycotts, along with the OPEC oil crisis, wrought havoc with the Guyanese economy. By 1978, the government was forced to curtail expenditures, retrenching even Afro-Guyanese

## Constitutional and Political Change

The policies the British practiced in colonial Guyana and Trinida were distinguished by the lack of political representation in Crow. Colony government. The only way residents could influence col lective decisions was mass action and violence—or "representa· tion by riot." Strikes and demonstrations in Guyana and Trinidad in the 1930s culminated in the appointment of the Moyne Com- mission, often regarded as the most penetrating study of the Brit- ish West Indies. However, the commission's recommendations for remedying the social and economic conditions were gradualist. In Guyana the denial of adequate reforms invited the emergence of an anticolonial movement with radical demands. In 1946, a Political Affairs Committee (PAC) was formed, led by Cheddi Jagan and others; it espoused the theory of scientific socialism.[18]

In January 1950, the PAC launched its own party, called the People's Progressive Party (PPP). Its ideological aim was to build "a just socialist society in which the industries of the country shall be socially and democratically owned for the common good."[19] Es- sential to the party's electoral success was the unity of at least a substantial number of Indians and Africans, who together con- stituted nearly 82 percent of the population. The PPP's program called for cooperation between racial groups. To ensure this end, Dr. Jagan and Forbes Burnham, an Indian and an African respec- tively, were installed as leaders of the party.

When the first general elections under universal adult suffrage were concluded on 27 April 1953, the PPP won overwhelmingly, gaining eighteen out of twenty-four seats in the unicameral legisla- ture. The PPP assumed office, with Jagan as leader and Burnham as president of the party. The "dual charisma" of these two sectional leaders legitimized control of the government in the eyes of most members of Guyana's multiethnic society. Within five months of PPP rule, however, the British government arbitrarily suspended the constitution and evicted the party from power. In 1957, new general elections were planned, but the two leaders of the indepen- dence movement disagreed over tactics, parted company, and formed their own parties. After 1957, therefore, a new pattern was set: a divided African and Indian leadership, each at the helm of a separate party, elicited and exploited sectional fears and prejudices in order to obtain votes. In particular, Burnham's predominantly African-based People's National Congress (PNC) viewed a Jagan victory as a threat of perpetual Indian domination. Jagan won the 1961 general elections in an ethnically inflamed contest, and the workers in the process. Supplies of basic commodities, electricity, and even water became sporadic, the national debt increased from G$250 million in 1970 to G$1.8 billion, and unemployment soared to 30 percent. From this crisis rose a predominantly African but, to some extent, a multiracial party, the Working People's Alliance (WPA), led by the eminent Guyanese scholar, Walter Rodney. Burnham, however, engineered the murder of Rodney and ruthlessly suppressed striking workers, Indians and Africans alike. His power by this stage had come to rest overwhelmingly on the coercive forces and a small group of middle-class technocrats.[26]

## Polity and Economy in the Post-Burnham Period

A new presidential-style constitution was promulgated in 1980, conferring imperial powers on Burnham. He was not only president of the government but, as leader of the party, was also able to convert the government apparatus into an executive extension of the PNC in accordance with the doctrine of "party paramountcy." This doctrine was first adumbrated in 1968, when the PNC acquired sole control of the government. It was taken to mean not only that policy direction emanated from the governing party but that, in practice, the public bureaucracy served in all its detailed activities the political will of the PNC party apparatus. Even the judiciary was politicized and made into an instrument of party rule and the personalistic predilection of an imperial president.

To counter his opponents, Burnham again swung foreign policy toward the West in the early 1980s. In effect, to placate the United States and in order to obtain aid as well as favorable treatment by the IMF, he opportunistically offered a noncommunist alternative to the WPA and the PPP.[27] Elections were held again in 1980, and again rigged, giving the PNC 77 percent of the votes. U.S. aid and IMF loans came but with strict rules of execution, at a time when the economy was collapsing from the continuing crisis. At the time of the invasion of Grenada, Burnham condemned the U.S. role, which drew attention to the fact that he had once again started to shift his foreign policy back to the East, Guyana having failed to join other Third World countries in condemning the Soviet Union's shooting down of a Korean passenger airliner in 1983.

The Reagan administration responded by turning its wrath on Guyana: the USAID branch in Guyana was closed down, and Guyanese applications for loans from multilateral agencies were blocked. In sum, Guyana not only faced an intense internal economic crisis, exacerbated by high oil prices compared to the low prices fetched by its exports, but externally it was on a collision course with its hegemonic neighbor.

Just as Williams had died in the midst of a downturn in the Trinidad economy, Burnham died in 1985 when his internal and external enemies had him cornered. It was left to their successors to try to restore the health of their shattered economies, the dire state of which also threatened to throw the political order in turmoil. Desmond Hoyte, who succeeded Burnham, had the much more difficult problem: the Guyanese economy had in effect collapsed; the government was bankrupt, and the IMF had declared Guyana ineligible to receive further loans because of failure to meet its performance criteria. A thriving black market developed in the face of ongoing government restrictions on imports and shortages in supplies of basic foods; indeed, a virtual parallel economy emerged, in which the American dollar was the main currency.

The cost of living also spiraled upward—to the point where public servants and teachers were forced to become part-time peddlers to make a living. Continued emigration drained the society of skills and stability, forcing it into becoming a remittance economy, which depended on small monetary gifts and barrels of assorted goods from overseas Guyanese to relatives and friends still in Guyana. The irony was that, in a country where some 80 percent of all production facilities were nationalized, a private underground economy met most of the needs of citizens.

The political legacy left to Hoyte was also difficult. Within the PNC itself, several factions existed, each with its own political program. President Hoyte represented the middle-class moderate African segment; Hamilton Green, the prime minister, commanded the allegiance of a hard core of supporters in the army and police, as well as many lower-income Afro-Guyanese; and Viola Burnham, a vice-president and the former president's widow, had strong support among the militant women's wing of the PNC, as well as among some lower-income Afro-Guyanese. To prevent the opposition from creating disorder in the political vacuum caused by Burnham's death, all the factions in the PNC had quickly united to appoint Hoyte as president and Green as prime minister. As in Trinidad, within a couple of days the succession was effected and stability guaranteed. The struggle for power would come later, but for the time being, internal political problems were suppressed.

It was widely felt that no one within the PNC was capable of solving Guyana's many problems and that a new political order would soon descend on Guyana. But Hoyte, like Chambers in Trinidad, surprised the unbelievers.[28] In a series of swift actions, he transformed the terror of Burnham's repressive rule, restoring some measure of law and order. He ordered the prosecution of the Rabbi Washington for murder; Washington was the leader of the thug group the House of Israel, which was notorious for its violence against Burnham's enemies. Political surveillance was dramatically reduced, and several political freedoms were restored. Newsprint was made available to the opposition press, and a new independent newspaper, *Stabroek News*, sprang up. The slogan "Give Hoyte a Chance" was designed to persuade the PPP and the WPA not to attack the new president until he had had an opportunity to establish his imprint on the new regime.

Hoyte also made changes on the economic front. In particular, he permitted the import of flour, which had been banned by Burnham. Flour meant bread and *roti*. The move directly addressed food shortages but was symbolic, too, of a political renaissance. In addition to domestic political liberalization, Hoyte sought to reverse Guyana's antagonistic relations with the United States, partly to obtain economic advantages. At Washington's behest, he dropped restrictions on foreign investment. A new procapitalist outlook was projected, and the target was clearly that of obtaining U.S. backing for a new IMF package and, with it, an assortment of loans for Guyana's economic recovery.

But while Hoyte succeeded in freeing Guyana from the grip of the Burnhamite repressive machine and was responsible for an optimism not experienced since the 1950s, one area above all had to be tackled before this new era of freedom would be authentic: free and fair elections. In the electoral area, as in no other, an uncompromising disagreement existed between government and opposition. Six months after he assumed power, Hoyte was required to hold new elections. Since 1968, a succession of rigged elections had kept the PNC in power. Through the decade and a half of Burnhamism, it had become clear that the party could not muster much support outside the African population. Repeatedly, using its rigged election results, the PNC had attempted to convince the world that it had persuaded large numbers of Indians to vote for the PNC. If this had been true, free and fair elections could have been held. But ethnicity was the key determinant of party preference, and few doubted that, in a straight electoral battle and given racial voting patterns, Jagan's PPP would be able to count on the Indian population, now estimated at 55 percent of the population, to put him into power.

In 1986, new elections were held. Hoyte made a few concessions to electoral reform, such as the abolition of overseas voting and restrictions in the use of proxy voting. But the most significant demand by the opposition, which was to have the ballots counted at the polling booths under international supervision, was not conceded. The transfer of ballots from polling stations to central locations had been identified as the critical juncture when the rigging took place. Again, and in the presence of many neutral local and international observers, electoral fraud was perpetrated in Guyana; with it, Hoyte's honeymoon came to an end. The PNC gave itself 78.5 percent of the votes, taking forty-two of the fifty-three seats in Parliament. The PPP was given eight seats, the United Force two seats, and the WPA only one seat.

On 9 January 1986, all the "defeated" parties except one joined together and formed the Patriotic Coalition for Democracy (PCD) to combat the PNC. The constituent elements in the PCD were: (1) the PPP under Jagan, (2) the WPA under Eusi Kwayana, (3) the Democratic Labour Movement under Paul Tannasee, (4) the People's Democratic Movement, and (5) the National Democratic Front. Revealing just how skin-deep and opportunistic its liberalization program had been, the PNC retaliated against the PCD and the churches, which criticized the election results, by mounting police searches of the homes of their leaders. This included the homes of the Roman Catholic bishop, the head of the Guyanese Council of Churches, and the chairman of the Protestant Presbytery of Guyana. One Catholic priest was deported. While all of this transpired, the U.S. State Department's annual review of human rights gave the Hoyte regime a positive rating. The Guyana Human Rights Commission was much more cautious, indicating that the situation was ambiguous but that a number of "hopeful signs" had emerged. At the same time, it pointed to the persistence of police brutality, attacks on organized religion, the reintroduction of the death penalty, and the shortages of basic foodstuffs and medicine.

The new PNC regime, then, was fundamentally oriented to the Burnham system of government: fraudulent elections followed by efforts to mobilize the entire population for economic recovery and growth. Put differently, both past and present PNC regimes were unable to see that their political dishonesty at election time led to failures in economic mobilization. President Hoyte, therefore, followed an old pattern: holding elections, rigging them, and then planning economic recovery schemes, oblivious to the fact that the lack of economic cooperation stemmed from the prior act of electoral fraudulence. Thus, while the "reelected" government endlessly reiterated the need for private investment (foreign and local) and drew up attractive conditions, incorporated in its Investment Agreement of 1987, the opposition PCD ignored it all, demanding electoral reform first.

The PNC's immediate objective, as indicated, was to satisfy IMF requirements for a package of recovery that would also involve financing from other bilateral and multilateral financial institutions. Accordingly, in September 1987, a consultation mission from the IMF and the World Bank arrived in Guyana, and by early 1988, negotiations had advanced to the point where Guyana knew precisely what it had to do domestically to obtain IMF funds. With the PNC's acceptance of IMF conditions, a new dark era of disruption descended upon Guyana.

While a number of anticipatory measures were taken in the 1987 budget, including a devaluation of the Guyana dollar from the official rate of G$4.40 to US$1 to G$10 to US$1, the full measure of the IMF medicine was not administered until the 1989 budget. When it came, it provoked unprecedented political protest, which has come to be called the April Rebellion. The central feature of the economic restructuring program was a 230 percent devaluation of the Guyana dollar. From G$10, it became G$32 to US$1. In part, this measure was intended to bring the official rate of the Guyana dollar into alignment with the price of the parallel market. Yet, on "Wall Street," Georgetown's popular open-currency market, the unofficial street rate went to G$64, then settled at G$50.

With devaluation came the removal of all subsidies on consumer goods, including fuel and food. The immediate impact was a 200–300 percent increase in the prices of basic food products and transportation. Interest rates moved upward, too, from 10 percent to 35 percent. To cushion the shock, the government offered a 20 percent wage increase.

The public response was dramatic and for a while seemed revolutionary. Guyana's major trade unions, ignoring the government-controlled Trade Union Congress, had united within a new formation called the Federation of Independent Trade Unions of Guyana (FITUG). It described the government's wage rate as "obscene," noting that it meant that the minimum wage (increased from G$25 to G$30 a day) was barely enough to buy a pound of chicken, a gallon of rice, or a pint of cooking oil. Strike action by FITUG was immediate, bringing African and Indian workers from the bauxite and sugar industries to join in an unprecedented common front against a besieged government. The Guyana Council of Churches, the Caribbean Council of Churches, and various international groups attempted to persuade the Hoyte administration to negotiate with FITUG as the legitimate representative of the workers.

Instead, in April, when the strikes commenced, seven FITUG leaders were arrested by the government. Demonstrations, strikes, and boycotts by a wide cross-section of the population lasted some forty-two days. Repression by the government was accompanied by open charges of communist infiltration and covert attempts to appeal to race to get African workers to return to their jobs. The damage done to the economy during the strike certainly wrecked the government's attempt to meet the IMF requirements. Sugar production plummeted, for instance, so that even Guyana's sugar quota for the European Community could not be met. The strikes, in fact, ended only because of worker exhaustion and internal disagreements within FITUG.

The April Rebellion of 1989 imprinted a number of important features on Guyana's politics. The PNC regime survived partly because of its willingness to use its coercive machinery to contain the activities of the strike leaders and partly because of the international support coming from the United States, Canada, and other Western countries, which constituted a virtual consortium of aid donors prescribing economic medicine for the Guyanese economy. The Hoyte regime thus demonstrated its capacity to outlast the combined action of the opposition, even when the protests reached the stronghold of the government's own ethnic constituency. To be sure, the damage inflicted suggested a complete victory for neither FITUG nor the government. At the political level, the Patriotic Coalition for Democracy, which included both the PPP and WPA along with moral support from FITUG, emerged as a powerful bloc, which could bring the government to a halt. However, dissension within FITUG and the PCD followed the April Rebellion, and the regime was thereby allowed to proceed with the administration of the IMF medicine.

Toward the end of 1989, a survey by a Commonwealth team of experts reported that the Guyanese economy had sunk to its lowest level ever, so that Guyana stood as the poorest country in the Western Hemisphere, a position traditionally held by Haiti. Emigration of skilled and educated persons from Guyana accelerated to 3 percent annually. Economic deterioration continued. The PNC had presided over a 6 percent decline in gross national product annually since 1980 (in global terms, only Mozambique, Libya, and Qatar registered steeper declines in the period 1980–87).

These considerations became more charged as elections, constitutionally due by the end of March 1991, drew nearer. Hoyte faced intense pressure to ensure that they were free and fair. A campaign mounted by the Guyana Human Rights Association and the PCD bore fruit in October 1990, when former U.S. President Jimmy Carter, in a visit to Guyana, extracted a commitment from Hoyte to permit a preliminary count of votes at the polling stations and the drawing up of a new voters' list. Earlier in the year, Hoyte had conceded to U.S. pressures for an open electoral process, with the implication that foreign observers would be present during the elections. The PCD, however, failed to reach agreement on a joint list of candidates to run against the PNC, and it came to look as if the four partners would contest the eventual elections individually, as would several other small parties. The PNC still believed in the paramountcy of the party, and its support still came from the African population. The main opposition was still the Indian-based PPP. The WPA and other nonracially-based parties remained an unknown factor, but their support was likely to be small. Periodic cross-communal efforts to bring about solidarity have been quickly forgotten since they were thought of as no more than temporary alliances of convenience. In Guyana, the ethnic monster is safe in its lair and shows every sign of perpetuating its rule.

## CONCLUSION

In many respects, the Guyanese and Trinidadian polities in the Caribbean belong to a universal category of ethnically bipolar states, which includes Fiji, Malaysia, and Sri Lanka, among others. The prototype of these polities describes institutional politics as being built around ethnic identity. At all levels, ethnic consciousness pervades social, cultural, economic, and political life, conferring on it at the individual level a pathological siege mentality and at the collective level persistent poverty and violence. Somewhere in the political history of these societies, an incorrect turn was taken whereby collective ethnic sentiments were mobilized competitively to obtain economic gains and avoid communal domination. Once this ethnic formation in politics was crystallized, these societies moved inexorably along a path of self-reinforcing descent, which had as its ultimate point self-destruction.

In Guyana and Trinidad, that fateful turn occurred about the time of self-government, when the major ethnic communities were mobilized around separate parties to win power. The parliamentary institutional system of zero-sum competition facilitated both group organization and communal conflict. Educated nationalists in pursuit of private ambition and office consistently nurtured ethnic consciousness at the grass roots level for electoral purposes, with the resulting emergence of deeply divided societies and developmental decay. In Guyana, all the stages toward total misery have been fulfilled; in Trinidad, only some aspects of that condition have been met. The passage from Burnham to Hoyte does not alter the fact that the basis of Guyana's polity is still ethnic dominance. The Trinidad case, by contrast, does at least show that, even after ethnic strife existed for many years, such confrontation could be supplanted by interethnic collaboration. In Guyana, this happened only briefly—from 1950 to 1954.

In sum, ethnic rivalry built around communal blocs destroys productive life and is the surest prescription for national disaster. The many brave attempts to design appropriate strategies for development—seeking funds from East or West, from the IMF and the World Bank—all add up to nought in an environment of illegitimacy and repression in ethnically bipolar states. New leaders succeed old leaders; they learn very little. In Guyana and Trinidad, new regimes made all the old mistakes again, still putting the cart before the horse. Both countries must first seek the political kingdom of cross-communal unity before they can expect prosperity and development to follow.

# 5 The March of Militarization in Suriname

*Peter Meel*

In 1975 Suriname followed Guyana to become the second "new" postcolonial state on the South American mainland. Despite its geographic position, it was, like Guyana, a typical Caribbean country. Its history was that of sugar and slavery, plantation agriculture and indenture, which resulted over the years in an ethnically divided population, in which no less than eight distinctive groups could readily be identified: East Indians (Hindustans), comprising some 35 percent of the population; Creoles (coloreds and blacks), 32 percent; Indonesians (Javanese), 15 percent; bush Negroes, 10 percent; Amerindians, 2.5 percent; Chinese, 2 percent; Europeans, 1.5 percent; and others (chiefly Brazilian Jews and Syrians), 2 percent. Suriname's economy was also characteristically Caribbean, being open and undiversified, overwhelmingly dependent on the exploitation of one commodity—first sugar and then bauxite—the mining, production, and marketing of which lay in foreign hands.

The dependent economy was further echoed in a dependent psychology, also typically Caribbean. The orientation of Surinamers is toward the Netherlands and not their neighbors. The Dutch provided example and model since 1667, when Suriname first became a colony; upward of one-third of the Surinamese people now reside in the Netherlands. Feelings of nationalism, in consequence, are much attenuated and certainly of less significance than ethnic identity, which for many years served as a focus for political allegiance and competition. As independence dawned, Suriname therefore faced problems similar to those of many other ethnically plural and economically underdeveloped Caribbean states. The question was whether these formidable legacies could be overcome to realize a peaceful and prosperous future.

The short answer is that they could not. The high hopes of the first year quickly gave way to dissatisfaction as the ineffective policies of the Henck Arron government led to mounting unemployment and increasing social malaise. It also became evident that the government lacked the will to maintain the democratic and social ideals that had underpinned the parliamentary system established in the country in 1948. The policies pursued by Arron and his cabinet in no way served the interests of the population at large, and both migration to the Netherlands and political alienation at home increased dramatically. The problems were felt particularly by the working classes, which waited in vain for promised reforms. Another dissatisfied group was the army. By 1978 the military already felt neglected by, if not isolated from, their superiors and the government. In 1980, unable to realize any improvement in their position, a group of sixteen noncommissioned officers executed a coup d'état, bringing to an end the old political order and introducing a period of political instability, the end of which was not in sight a decade later.

The 1980s, in fact, was a period of immense political complexity. Politics dominated all other concerns, and the twists and turns of successive governments were exceedingly difficult to follow. Nevertheless, four stages, characteristic of Surinamese domestic politics during the decade, can be discerned. They are the intervention stage (1980–81), the revolution stage (1981–84), the democratic revolution stage (1984–88), and the parliamentary democracy stage (1988–90). Although of great importance in themselves, basically all stages are derivative of one and the same phenomenon: the militarization of the country's political system. In this regard, the coup d'état in Suriname initiated a new phenomenon in the nation's political life but one very familiar to neighboring Latin American countries.

## PREINDEPENDENCE HISTORY

During the Second World War it became apparent that colonialism was doomed in Suriname. As a result of agreements between the Dutch and American governments, U.S. troops occupied the colony in 1941 in order to protect the supply of bauxite, which ranked as the most important raw material for the aircraft industry. By exporting it to the United States, Suriname actively supported the cause of the allied forces. Between 1942 and 1945, bauxite production brought in such profits that Suriname enjoyed a surplus in its budget for the first time since the early nineteenth century. Since the ties between colony and mother country had by this time been largely cut, politicians in Suriname became convinced that the country could stand on its own feet financially. This belief contributed to an awareness that Suriname no longer needed the Netherlands politically; on the contrary, the development of the colony would be restrained if Suriname maintained its ties with the Netherlands.

This expanding sense of nationalism was also stimulated by several other factors. There were, for instance, the self-willed and authoritarian policies of the then governor, which met with aversion and resistance and lent impetus to anti-Dutch feelings. In addition, the radio speeches of Queen Wilhelmina, particularly in her address of December 1942, held out the prospect of an autonomous status for all Dutch colonies. Moreover, the presence of U.S. troops acquainted Surinamese intellectuals with ideas recorded in the Atlantic Charter, a document signed by the Americans and the British championing the right of all people to choose their own government.[1]

After the Second World War, these developments resulted in a great number of meetings between representatives of the Netherlands, Suriname, and the Netherlands Antilles. It took no less than three round table conferences before a new legal order came into existence in 1954. The charter for the Kingdom of the Netherlands—intended to pave the way for Surinamese and Antillean independence—stated that from then on the Kingdom of the Netherlands consisted of three equal partners: the Netherlands, Suriname, and the Netherlands Antilles. While each would attend to its own affairs, a few matters were to be arranged through the efforts of the three dominions: foreign affairs, defense, nationality, and the guarantee of human rights and liberties, legal security, and proper administration.

The internal political structure of Suriname had displayed some of the characteristics of a democracy since 1950. There was a parliament called the Staten, whose members were elected on the basis of universal suffrage. All relevant powers were allotted to this body. The governor and a Council of Ministers shared the executive office: the governor held the prerogative, the Council of Ministers was accountable to the Staten. Politicians became members of the Staten as deputies of political parties, which were usually organized on an ethnic basis. The most prominent were the National Party of Suriname (NPS), which represented the interests of Creole society; the Progressive Reformational Party (VHP), whose rank and file was largely Hindustani; and the Indonesian Joint Peasants'

Party (KTPI), whose supporters were recruited from the Javanese portion of the population.[2]

The charter for the Kingdom of the Netherlands—commonly abbreviated as the Statuut—existed until 1975. On November 25 of that year, following two years of deliberations, Suriname became an independent republic. There could be no doubt, though, that this independence was mainly constitutional. Two of the areas in which the hand of the Netherlands remained clearly visible were defense and economy. These were precisely the areas in which spectacular developments were soon to take place, processes hardly imaginable at the time of independence but ultimately having an enormous impact on the country's polity and financial position.

Although The Hague initially had expressed a wish to leave Suriname with an extended police force rather than a standing army, the Surinamese government chose the latter option, believing it needed professional military forces at its disposal. Border disputes with Guyana and French Guiana were its rationale for needing an army. To steer the republic's defense into the proper channels, both countries agreed that a Dutch military mission, attached to the Dutch embassy, would be stationed in Paramaribo. It was expected to stay in Suriname for a maximum of five years. The mission was to assist the newly founded Surinamese Army (SKM) with organization, logistics, technicalities, and administration. It was also responsible for the repair and substitution of the materials that had been handed on by the former Dutch army. Surinamese regular soldiers who had gone from the Dutch army to the Surinamese army were paid a complementary salary by the Dutch government in order to prevent their income from decreasing.

The Dutch influence on the Surinamese economy remained immense. Prior to 1975, the Netherlands had granted Suriname millions of guilders of development aid. Following independence, a separate development treaty came into operation, providing for a total budget of 3.5 billion guilders. The biggest part of it—2.7 billion guilders—was to be spent within ten to fifteen years on the basis of a so-called multiannual development plan (MOP). According to the MOP, 25 percent of the funds would be invested in infrastructural projects, 25 percent in socioeducational projects, and 50 percent in directly productive projects. The four main goals of the MOP were to increase the economic viability of Suriname, to increase employment, to improve the standard of living of the entire population, and to promote the regional distribution of prosperity.[3] This, then, was the context in which independence was achieved.

## THE INTERVENTION

Almost from the outset, it was clear that independence did not mark the beginning of a new era of construction and solidarity. Despite the fine promises of the Arron administration, political and socioeconomic reforms were not enforced. The racial disposition of the NPS, the VHP, and the KTPI proved to be unsupportive of sound and well-balanced developments. Mostly, group interests prevailed over national interests, with the result that the government's policies were ad hoc, leaving little chance for timely management. On various levels, legal security was supplanted by patronage and corruption.

The lack of favorable future perspectives affected particularly the poor and underprivileged, who felt they had no share in the development cooperation with the Netherlands, nor did they expect anything from their representatives in parliament. With respect to the first, they knew that the principles of the MOP were violated and that the profits connected with the various development projects went to the Surinamese political elite and Dutch industries. They demonstrated their contempt for the Staten by labeling it "circus stupido" and by cultivating an attitude of indifference toward politics. With regret, The Hague watched the continuous migration of Surinamers to the former mother country, a process so extensive that by around 1980 the number of Surinamers living in the Netherlands was approximately 200,000, one-third of the total population.[4]

The government—although the country's major employer—did not offer any inspiration, and an atmosphere of apathy was created, providing a breeding ground for disaffection in the ranks of the Surinamese army. Before coming to these matters, the place of the army in Surinamese society needs to be noted, since the specific nature of its position was the main cause of the political bombshell that would follow. As Fernandes Mendes has pointed out, in the years following independence the government did not display much interest in the army. In fact, politicians seemed hardly aware of its existence, considering it a rather insignificant institution, politically neutral, and in an obvious stage of construction. Commanded by a megalomaniacal nonentity, the army was never the object of genuine study or subject to a concept of security that could serve as a basis for its functioning. As a result, many abuses occurred, and complaints became rife.

In the absence of any rational planning, the army became agitated. Feeling frustrated and demoralized, if not humiliated, it collectively thought of ways to let its voice be heard. A number of noncommissioned officers (NCOs) had been trained in the Netherlands, where they had gained some experience with democratic structures, notably the military unions. Seeing the merits of such structures in their particular circumstances, a group of Surinamese NCOs founded a union themselves. However, both the government and their immediate superiors refused to acknowledge their platform. The Arron administration, in particular, took pleasure in pretending that the grievances of the military were not its concern, and consequently, from January 1979 onward, the NCOs frequently went on strike. Apart from prosecuting board members of the union and using police officers to preserve order, the authorities took no firm action,[5] thereby precipitating a further move by the military. On 25 February 1980—a few hours before three board members of the military union were due to be court-martialed and one month before advanced elections were to be held—sixteen NCOs executed a coup d'état. Although six dead and twenty-five wounded were reported, the takeover of power was effected smoothly.

The group of sixteen—as the *putchists* were called—formed a tight company. While the coup was still in the stage of preparation, its members swore allegiance to each other, promising to assist each other in any situation and subordinate personal interests to those of the group. All of them were relatively young, their ages ranging from twenty-three to thirty-seven years. Most of them were Creoles, some of them lower middle class, the others of working-class origin. They shared a life-style closely related to the commando background from which they derived their status. Clearly, none of them possessed any knowledge or experience in the running of state affairs. After all, they had been raised with the logic of tanks and uzis, not with that of law books and policy documents. Indeed, with the exception of their later leader, their familiarity with the latter would hardly improve in the course of the years.[6]

The coup d'état was welcomed enthusiastically in Suriname— the people had been waiting for an alternative for quite some time. Although the nature of this alternative—and at this point the view of the people coincided with that of the army—was not yet filled in ideologically, anything but the Arron regime seemed to them a change for the better. So when the Arron cabinet was forced to resign and power was transferred to a National Military Council (NMR), no protests were made. The NMR allowed President Johan Ferrier to remain in office, declared the constitution and all treaties concluded by Suriname still in force, and promised that a civilian government would be installed as quickly as possible. The NMR tried hard to act reasonably in the first few weeks following the coup, in order not to spread panic.

In March, a civilian government was indeed appointed, presided over by the moderate and nationalistic politician, Henk Chin A Sen. Various criteria were used in selecting him and his colleagues: that candidates for ministers should have a clean past and be well qualified for their jobs, that identification with administrations in power prior to 1980 should not be allowed, and that as a team the new cabinet should represent all interest groups in society. Thus the Chin A Sen government was expressly presented as a national event. In the words of the prime minister, the ideal of national reconciliation, unity, and construction would have to be given shape through "a policy of production directed at a new Suriname." Shortly after the installation of the new government, the Surinamese parliament legitimated the coup d'état by discharging the group of sixteen and labeling their performance an intervention.[7]

In his declaration of policy issued on 1 May 1980, Chin A Sen announced the necessity of modernization in four areas: the political order, the social order, the socioeconomic order, and the educational order. A so-called urgency program covered the more concrete goals the government wanted to realize within two years. Following this period, according to Chin A Sen, new elections were to be held according to a new constitution. Certainly it seems that the intentions of the new administration were inspired by reformism and humanity. Politically speaking, the cabinet was relatively independent and technocratic. However, in reality the administration's plans lacked any clear basis; attempting to meet the desires of the entire community, they were the end product of a series of compromises and, as a result, difficult to translate into practical policy. It is typical of the naivety of those days that the Chin A Sen administration thought two years were enough to reconstruct Suriname from an ethnically determined society into a social democracy. Nevertheless, although the government relied too much on the lowest common denominator of agreement, it did try to bring about the rehabilitation of democracy.

Meanwhile, a number of political shifts attracted attention. Two weeks after Chin A Sen's declaration of policy, parliament had its last meeting and, under pressure, accepted a law abolishing itself. On 12 July, Desi Bouterse, the most prominent member of the group of sixteen, walked out of the NMR. Together with two other army officers—one of whom, Roy Horb, was a major *putchist*— he formed the Military Authority and proclaimed it to be the executive of the National Army. Bouterse scored his next hit on 13 August, when he announced that a coup d'état had been thwarted. He had arrested as its main instigators three leftist NMR members (not coincidentally, those who in 1979–80 had made conspiracy plans against Arron) and several representatives of the Revolutionary People's Party (RVP). In this way, Bouterse disposed of the most progressive trend in the center of power. However, reputations on the right wing of the political spectrum were also tarnished. The most prominent among these individuals was President Ferrier, who, unhappy with the growing irrelevance of parliament, resigned and left for the Netherlands.

All these events implied a redistribution of power. During the state of emergency that had been declared, Chin A Sen was appointed as Ferrier's successor. In addition to becoming president, he also began a second term as prime minister. In the new cabinet, his political ally, André Haakmat, was selected vice premier and minister of foreign affairs, justice, the army and the police. The constitution—which had served as a framework for the actions of the government so far—was suspended, and parliament and the Council of Advice dissolved. Ivan Graanoogst, a relative of Bouterse, took over the leadership of the standardized NMR. This meant that, whereas the executive functions of the government were previously exercised by the president and the government in close consultation with the military, the situation now changed to one in which the president, the government, *and* the army, collectively, were responsible for this task. It was concluded that a so-called Policy Center, consisting of Chin A Sen, Haakmat, Bouterse, and Graanoogst, would spell out the chief lines of policy and ensure that the ministers put them into effect. Thus six months after the coup d'état, the military had managed to obtain a full share of the country's administration. What is more, with the NMR robbed of its most zealous members, Bouterse was now the indisputable supreme commander of the National Army.[8]

## THE REVOLUTION

If the coup d'état was at first euphemistically termed an intervention, at the beginning of 1981 the military and their advisers renamed it a revolution. This change to what was defined as a socialist course was accompanied by several important events. First, "super minister" Haakmat—having manifested himself as an industrious but self-willed issuer of decrees—was discharged and replaced by Harvey Naarendorp, an intellectual with more leftist sympathies. Second, Bouterse released the NMR members and their associates who had been arrested in August and placed a few of them in important posts. Third, he decided to cooperate closely with representatives of the Progressive Labourers and Farmers Union (PALU) and the RVP.

These two organizations thus emerged as significant forces in the reshaping of Surinamese politics. The PALU—at the time resting on the prestige of Iwan Krolis, Errol Alibux, and Winston Caldeira—had its origins in a group of friends that in the 1960s had studied at the Agricultural University of Wageningen in the Netherlands. Their nationalism displayed some Marxist characteristics but was primarily fed by ideas on the economic future of their native country. In their view, small-scale projects should be the essence of any development policy. Only in this way could the economy provide the population with a standard of living appropriate for a newly independent country. Strongly opposed to the Netherlands as the colonial power par excellence, the PALU considered Brazil the ally most able to offer political and economic benefits to Suriname.

The RVP was another group of progressive intellectuals. Major members of the party were former students of the universities of Leiden and Groningen in the Netherlands. Largely basing their program on Marxist conceptions, they advocated the complete destruction of all colonial structures in society. Only when the remnants of capitalism—represented by the United States at its worst—had disappeared did they believe that a real people's democracy could be established. Whereas the PALU's nationalism revealed itself in a vehemently anti-Dutch stand, the RVP's internationalism induced the organization to make overtures to Marxist regimes abroad. The party thus felt especially attracted to the political experiments in Cuba, Grenada, and Nicaragua.

Despite these differences, both parties clearly had a good deal in common. They both relied on a small and devoted group of followers, used an academic and radical vocabulary, and appealed particularly to the younger generation, the very group to which the rebellious NCOs belonged. Obviously, their views contradicted parliamentary democracy, religious tolerance, and the Western spending pattern—considered the blessed trinity by the majority of Surinamers. Instead, they declared that Surinamese politics had to be determined by anticolonial and antiimperialist principles. The group of sixteen quickly became convinced that this approach fitted in well with the needs of the population.[9]

The new course manifested itself in different ways. Toward the Netherlands, an attitude of energy and firmness was adopted. First, the government denounced the treaty that provided for the presence of the Dutch military mission. Military cooperation with the Netherlands was not terminated altogether, but it was clear that Paramaribo believed that the mission clashed with the concept of a sovereign socialist state. This belief was boosted as it became known that members of the mission had been involved in the preparations for the coup d'état of 25 February 1980. The impact of this participation should not be underestimated: not only did the Dutch participation in the overthrow imply that the PALU and the RVP had entered the center of power thanks to their supposed enemy, it also implied that the revolution had not been a wholly Surinamese affair. By dismissing the Dutch military mission, both parties hoped to limit the damage already done to this idealized picture.[10]

Second, Surinamese authorities presented a reallocation plan that required a much higher percentage of development aid be invested in the production sector than in the infrastructure. Moreover, they persuaded their Dutch counterparts to stop reserving money for large-scale projects, which in their opinion were contrary to the interests of Suriname. Both the request for the withdrawal of the military mission and the reallocation proposal were received favorably in The Hague. The reasons were obvious: the maneuvers of the first, although officially denied, had after all been a violation of Surinamese independence, whereas the aims of the latter were definitely more in line with the principles of the MOP.

As for domestic affairs, the socialist course intensified tensions. The army, prompted by their PALU and RVP advisers, and the civilian government gradually went their separate ways. Whereas the army tried to unite in a Revolutionary Front all people willing to dedicate themselves to the "new order," Chin A Sen drafted a new constitution to clear the way for free elections. In June 1981, a specially appointed commission published a constitutional draft, which provided for a semipresidential system, in which the army was represented through a revolutionary council with extensive powers. However, the army—playing for all or nothing—rejected the proposal as insufficient to guarantee their preponderant position. The proclamation of their Revolutionary Front occurred in November of that same year and was attended by delegations from Nicaragua (FSLN), Grenada (New Jewel Movement), Guyana (PPP and WPA), and Cuba (Partido Comunista). Bouterse and Horb were nominated heads of the organization, which was supposed to embrace the army, trade unions, and political parties.[11]

As the months went by, it appeared that the army would finally decide the issue. In February 1982, Chin A Sen—having concluded that his democratic mission was not attainable—handed in his resignation and delegated his powers to the military authority. In restructuring the power of the state, Bouterse once more claimed a bigger share for the military. It was decided that the government of Suriname, henceforth, would consist of a Council of Ministers and a Policy Center. The Policy Center included the entire military authority, thus enabling the military to command a majority in this body. It was also no longer the president, but Bouterse himself, who acted as its chairman. Moreover, it was agreed that the Policy Center would function as the policy initiating organ and the Council of Ministers as the policy executing organ. In short, the new cabinet, led by Henry Neyhorst, was made completely subordinate to the Policy Center, which in effect meant the military authority. The same applied to the new (acting) president, Fred Ramdat Misier. He was made a direct subsidiary of the military authority and was entitled to perform only ceremonial tasks. As for politics, his contribution was nil.[12]

These political developments greatly concerned the Netherlands government. The departure of Chin A Sen, on whom government and parliament had set their hopes, the restricted freedom of the press, and the disappearance or deaths of people under baffling circumstances brought The Hague to the conclusion that a countermeasure was perfectly justified. On 19 February, Paramaribo was officially informed that the Netherlands had suspended all deliberations concerning development aid. Projects in progress would be completed according to plan, but the Netherlands would not enter into new obligations. Despite this strong signal, the Surinamese authorities determined to face the pressure head-on. All efforts were focused on the radicalization of the revolution. On the initiative of the RVP, the so-called people's militia and people's committees were strengthened, closer relations were established with Cuba and Grenada, the university, public enterprises, and the judiciary were standardized, and the militant Henk Herrenberg was appointed ambassador to The Hague. The most important result of this policy was an increased polarization between democrats and revolutionaries.

One week after Chin A Sen's resignation, and on the occasion of the funeral of a prominent member of the NPS, supporters of this party, the VHP, and Chin A Sen himself collectively demanded the restoration of democracy in Suriname. This mass meeting—a spontaneous outburst of dissatisfaction—was the first demonstration against the army since the expulsion of the Arron regime. Then in March, a coup d'état aimed at dislodging Bouterse failed at the last moment. The unsuccessful overthrow was in fact the fourth such attempt. But unlike earlier military plots—in May and August 1980 and March 1981—which seemed to have been chiefly inspired by personal rancor or a mere lust for power, the coup d'état staged by army officer Surendre Rambocus was believed to originate from a different motivation. Although Rambocus had a private grudge against Bouterse—in 1979–80 he too had worked out plans to oust Arron—nevertheless he was thought to be driven by a genuine desire to restore the democratic polity, an aim that won him the sympathy of large sections of the population. Moreover, the quashing of the Rambocus coup was attended by the summary shooting of one of its participants, an act generally met with fear and abhorrence. Afraid of possible repetitions and recognizing his narrow escape, Bouterse established the Echo Company, a corps d'elite composed entirely of military trustees. This well-trained and well-equipped company, whose backbone was formed by the group of sixteen, did indeed subsequently prevent other sections of the army from challenging Bouterse's authority.[13]

As yet, however, the Echo Company was unable to silence the civilian opposition. For them, the Rambocus coup constituted a turning point in that it had demonstrated Bouterse's all but total command of power. Opponents of the regime became aware that if something was to be done it had to be done quickly. This was particularly understood within the largest Surinamese trade union federation, the Moederbond, which in the autumn of 1982 decided to take action. Under the inspiring leadership of Cyril Daal, the federation began a campaign for the restoration of a democratic legal order. Utterly dissatisfied with what they considered to be ideological betrayal by the military, various organizations of journalists, scholars, lawyers, women, medical doctors, employers, and churches joined the Moederbond. These groups became united in the Association for Democracy, providing the opposition with the broad base that, until then, it had lacked.

Amid the chaos, representatives of government and the opposition held secret meetings and drew up political scenarios that were never officially published. One was concluded by Bouterse, Haakmat, and Horb and involved a blueprint for a gradual return to democratic practices. Another plan provided for the return to power of Chin A Sen, by this time a Pittsburgh resident. This option was supported by U.S. authorities as well as by Horb. Evidently Horb, in this period, was playing a double role, but he was not the only one. Haakmat, for instance, simultaneously acted as Daal's adviser, thus intriguing against Bouterse; whereas Bouterse himself publicly confessed his admiration for the Grenadian revolution, exhibiting accordingly his disregard for the democratic opposition. In fact, in October 1982, at Bouterse's request, Maurice Bishop, the Grenadian leader, visited Suriname. A rally specially organized in the guest's honor was supposed to produce a demonstration of loyalty for both revolutionaries but attracted only a small audience. For Bouterse, this meant a considerable loss of face, since Daal had organized a mass meeting at the same time, which was reported to have had ten times as many participants. The opposition exploited the situation with great skill, placing the growing controversy between Bouterse and Daal in a Goliath-David perspective.

Although the bankruptcy of the revolution was by now evident, Bouterse was still not prepared to give in. To muzzle the opposition for a considerable length of time, an operation was carried out in the night of 8 December that, in scale and precision, exceeded all previous human rights violations. Fifteen carefully selected opponents of the army—among them Rambocus and Daal—were assembled and transferred to the headquarters of the National Army, where they were tortured and subsequently killed. The offices of two radio stations, a newspaper, and the Moederbond were burned to the ground. Five dailies and weeklies were suppressed and two press agencies closed. The Surinamese population was horror-struck by these events. The unscrupulous methods used by the military aroused anger, fear, and dismay. Bouterse's explanation that the army had managed to thwart a coup d'état was not accepted. Most people assumed that the victims had been murdered purposely and not that—as the authorities alleged—they had been shot trying to escape. Military officers, police officers, students, intellectuals, and businessmen went underground or fled the country for fear of their lives. The Neyhorst cabinet resigned its office. On 10 December, the Netherlands suspended development cooperation with Suriname. The Hague announced that it would be possible to resume the cooperation only if guarantees were offered that fundamental human rights in Suriname were secured and substantial action was taken in the direction of democratization. Shortly afterward, the United States reacted similarly.[14]

Nevertheless, the army was determined not to let itself be intimidated by these sanctions. At the instigation of their advisers, the radicalization of the revolution continued on the same path. The people's militia and committees were further strengthened, the university was given a revolutionary image, and in November 1983, the unity movement Stanvaste was officially proclaimed. This organization—better known as the 25 February Movement (VFB)—was in fact the successor to the Revolutionary Front, which had foundered because of internal dissension. In order to prevent an early dissolution of the VFB, membership in this organization was available only on an individual basis. In other words, the movement—presided over personally by Bouterse—was not accessible to political parties or trade union federations as such.

With respect to foreign affairs, Suriname strengthened contacts with Cuba, Grenada, and Brazil and entered into relations with Libya. The decision to set up a Cuban embassy in Paramaribo originated from a visit Bouterse paid to Fidel Castro in May 1982. On the advice of his minister of foreign affairs, Edward Naarendorp—who was not affiliated with the RVP or the PALU but unmistakably shared the range of thoughts of the former—Bouterse privately asked Castro to accredit a Cuban ambassador in the Surinamese capital. Castro agreed, and in the autumn of that same year Osvaldo Cardénas Junquera, an old hand in the Cuban diplomatic service, paid his respects to the strongman of Suriname. It was obvious that in sending Cardénas to Paramaribo, Castro hoped to further export the Cuban revolution. Having a foothold in Grenada, he saw Suriname as the bridge to the Latin American mainland. Suriname itself considered the Cuban connection as a means to sever its relations with the Netherlands and to diversify its relations with representatives of the Non-Aligned Movement. Although the RVP sincerely wished to copy the Cuban model of political development, most government officials focused on the material benefits that could be derived from an understanding with Havana.

The Cuban connection, however, primarily produced moral and ideological support for Suriname. Practically, this meant that

Havana defended the Surinamese revolution abroad and used its influence to arrange introductions for Surinamers in nations allied to the socialist bloc. In line with this approach, Cuba provided education possibilities for Surinamese soldiers, students, and journalists. Clearly, their training was not only geared to their future professions but implied serious attempts to familiarize them with the principles of Marxism-Leninism. Finally, in Paramaribo itself, Cardénas and his staff—preferably using RVP channels—worked with a view to keeping the Surinamese revolution on a par with developments generated by similar revolutionary regimes. Their interventions in Surinamese state affairs were widely perceived as intimidating and frequently infuriated Surinamese ministers and civil servants.

Not surprisingly, the machinations of the Cubans in Suriname aroused the attention of the United States and Brazil. At three crucial moments, Suriname was given to understand that their political maneuvers were viewed as undesirable by both major powers. In April 1983, a Brazilian mission led by General Demilo Venturini unexpectedly arrived by plane in Suriname. Speaking on behalf of President Figuereido, he informed Bouterse that Brazil would not tolerate a Cuban stronghold on its northern borders. Bouterse grasped the warning and promised to act on it. In return, Brazil agreed to strengthen economic ties with Suriname and to begin military cooperation. In June, William O. Clark, a member of the U.S. National Security Council, met the Surinamese ambassador in Washington. Clark agreed to a normalization of Surinamese-U.S. relations on the condition that the Cuban presence in Suriname be considerably reduced. Finally, when four months later, in October 1983, Maurice Bishop was murdered in Grenada and the island was invaded by U.S.-led troops, many in Suriname dared not exclude the possibility that such an invasion could happen to their country as well. Fear over the close friendship with Cuba culminated in the conviction that Suriname's foreign policy would have to be adjusted drastically.

The PALU seized these three events in their power struggle with the RVP. The PALU aimed to cut off relations with Cuba, and in October 1983 they had their way. Cardénas was expelled from Suriname, and the year-long Cuban connection was traded for a Brazilian link. In his memoirs, Cardénas would recall his unfortunate departure from Suriname in bitter terms. Not surprisingly, the object of his ill feeling concerned the PALU, which he accused of selfish, authoritarian, and fascist behavior. But although the PALU had been victorious with respect to foreign affairs, the party experienced a severe blow in January 1984 when the Alibux cabinet was forced to resign as a result of strikes in opposition to government plans to raise taxes and nationalize industries. The dismissal of the Alibux administration, the most leftist government that Suriname ever had, marked the end of an unsuccessful socialist experiment.[15]

## THE DEMOCRATIC REVOLUTION

In explaining Bouterse's political motivation, it is probably not worth searching for philosophical conceptions or ideological views. It is generally believed that in this respect he was a tabula rasa, not unlike Surinamese politicians of the older generation. To get an insight into his conduct on the administrative level, it seems more fruitful to consider his social and professional background. With reference to the first, observers have called Bouterse a *wakaman*. A *wakaman* can be described as male, Creole, and lower class and who utilizes a network of relations and a variety of strategies to survive. At best, he is charming, smart, and flexible; at worst, he is unreliable and opportunistic. Exemplifying this type of drifter in mythical personification is Anansi, the trickster spider, a well-known figure in African and Afro-Caribbean literature.

Yet identifying Bouterse with Anansi is valid only if one connects this notion with another main feature of the Surinamese leader: his military education. Taking this into consideration, one realizes that the Bouterse version of Anansi wears a uniform, carries an uzi, and walks around in jackboots. The main elements of these phenomena complement and strengthen each other. After all, both the *wakaman* and the army share a sense of tactics and strategy, and thus the armed Anansi may be said to possess these qualities beyond measure. Since both also have one common goal— survival—the green spider that is Bouterse can be characterized above all else as keen on saving his own position.

This dimension of Bouterse's political personality has been amply demonstrated in the zigzag course that became the trademark of Surinamese politics. The fact that the country experienced four different political trends in a ten-year period offers the best illustration of this. However, these various stages often carefully hide the only constant in Surinamese politics since 1980: Bouterse's anxiety to maintain power. In order to secure his position, he gave top priority to the militarization of society; and since the most potent symbol of that process has always been the uzi, one may speak of a process of *uzinization*.[16]

Certainly, following the departure of the RVP and the PALU from the government in early 1984, it was difficult for Bouterse to maintain himself in power. Politically, he had been weak since early 1982, but during 1983 he was also confronted with an alarming economic situation. A few factors were responsible for this: the world economic crisis in general, which affected the demand for aluminium, thus affecting Suriname's chief source of economic growth; the suspension of development cooperation with the Netherlands; and the government's inability or unwillingness to design a sound economic policy.

The deterioration of the economy became apparent in several ways. One of its most serious consequences was the drawdown of reserves of gold and foreign currency, which the government tried to meet by import limitation and trading. However, these were not sufficient to make any significant improvement. Instead, inflation increased, unemployment grew, and many products became available for sale only at exorbitant black market prices. The lack of any favorable economic perspective expanded discontent over the army and increasingly expressed itself in opposition to Bouterse and in migration to the Netherlands and the United States.

Bouterse, in need of political and economic support, had no other choice at this stage but to compromise. He therefore developed a course that he labeled a democratic revolution. In this way, he aimed on the one hand at the acknowledgement of his regime and on the other at the consolidation of his power. At first he invited representatives of trade unions and employers to take the places that the RVP and the PALU had vacated. In January 1984, deputies of both interest groups entered the country's administration and also occupied seats in a think tank. In this council of advice they paved the way, together with the army, for a National Assembly, which was officially installed one year later. The National Assembly, consisting of appointed members of the three aforementioned groups, was given twenty-seven months to prepare a new constitution. Then in November 1985, a so-called Supreme Council was created to be the highest political institution in Suriname. Apart from the groups represented in the assembly and the government, the Supreme Council included deputies of the NPS, the VHP, and the KTPI. In July 1986, these three traditional parties also selected candidates for the government.

Still, the duality of the democratic revolution ultimately did more damage to the country than presumably was anticipated. Although the talks over a new democratic polity proceeded steadily, the positive effects it was supposed to generate were often counterbalanced by dubious army actions. This was true for example of the appointment of Henk Herrenberg as Suriname's minister of foreign affairs. Toward the Netherlands as well as toward the United States, this intimate of Bouterse adopted a line of action seemingly contrary to a policy of appeasement and constructivism. The Etienne Boerenveen affair also had a negative effect and was commented upon extensively in the national press. Boerenveen, number two in the military hierarchy in Suriname, had been arrested in Miami by the FBI and charged with involvement in cocaine smuggling. Although it was officially denied, there was evidence that he was acting on behalf of Bouterse and also that Herrenberg had a part in it. Boerenveen was finally sentenced to twelve years in prison. Subsequently, it has been said that the National Army had built an impressive expertise in the field of drug dealing.

The guerrilla warfare in east Suriname further complicated the process of democratization. On the one hand, one can argue that the war helped to hasten the process, on the other, that it proved the army to be essentially uninterested in democracy. At first the war was no more than a personal conflict between Bouterse and one of his former bodyguards, Ronnie Brunswijk. Brunswijk, of bush Negro origin, was sent to Cuba in the "revolutionary" years to receive commando training. He was dismissed from the army by Bouterse on the grounds of intolerable behavior. Feeling himself to have been treated unjustly, Brunswijk robbed banks and raided military posts in his native district, gaining the reputation of a modern Robin Hood by distributing money and goods among his people. In the summer of 1986 this rebellion degenerated into a guerrilla war when Brunswijk announced that he had formed a jungle commando committed to the overthrow of Bouterse, the restoration of democracy, and the emancipation of the bush Negroes, who were generally considered to be discriminated against in Surinamese society.

Brunswijk's ideals particularly appealed to members of the Surinamese opposition in the Netherlands, among them Chin A Sen, Haakmat, and representatives of the old Moederbond. For three and a half years, however, members of the opposition had not managed to do anything that could be interpreted as a threat to Bouterse. They had tried both violent and nonviolent resistance, but in the eyes of Bouterse they had only made themselves ridiculous, spending more time fighting each other than harming him. As a result, anti-Bouterse organizations lacked money, inspiration, and moral support—small wonder that they regarded Ronnie

Brunswijk as heaven-sent. Together, with Brunswijk, these members of the Surinamese opposition founded the National Surinamese Liberation Army, which, although small and minimally equipped, rapidly conquered the eastern part of the country. Psychologically, their actions certainly put Bouterse under pressure to keep his promise to move toward democratization.

Nevertheless, in the military sense, both parties maneuvered themselves into a stalemate early on, since neither could possibly control the entire Surinamese territory. In the long run, this frustrated the ranks of both armies and led to an increase in human rights violations. The National Army in particular was reported to be responsible for attacking the civilian population. As a result of the cruelties committed against them, thousands of people fled the interior and moved to Paramaribo, French Guiana, and the Netherlands, turning the Brunswijk guerrilla campaign into an issue attracting worldwide attention.[17]

In spite of these developments, which showed Bouterse as a military *pur sang*, an agreement was reached within the Supreme Council in March 1987 with respect to a draft constitution. Following a half year of uncertainty, in September of that year this constitution was accepted by the Surinamese population in a referendum, and two months later elections brought about a victory for the Front for Democracy and Development (FDO), in which the NPS, the VHP, and the KTPI cooperated. The army—organized in the National Democratic Party (NDP)—obtained only three seats, against forty for the FDO, four for the PALU, and four for the Pendawa Lima, a small Javanese political party.[18]

## THE PARLIAMENTARY DEMOCRACY

Although the elections showed that the military had lost the confidence of the population, this did not imply the immediate return of Bouterse to the barracks. Officially, parliamentary democracy was restored when, in January 1988, Ramsewak Shankar of the VHP was installed as president of Suriname, NPS leader Henck Arron, who had been removed from office in 1980, was sworn in as vice president and prime minister of an FDO government, and VHP leader Jagernath Lachmon was appointed speaker of the National Assembly. Nevertheless, the army remained constitutionally influential on the administrative level.

The new Surinamese constitution contained two articles (177 and 178) that defined the role of the army. According to these articles, the National Army was supposed to fulfill three tasks:

first, defend the country's sovereignty and autonomy; second, promote the development and liberation of the nation; and third, guarantee the peaceful transition to a democratic and socially minded society. Whereas the first task did not deviate from the demand made of almost every military force in the world and the second task pointed in the direction of an army with special development obligations, the third task could be regarded as the time bomb under the renewed democracy. In fact, this task gave the army carte blanche to intervene in the Surinamese polity at any time, since Article 178 did not specify the contours of a democratic and socially minded state. Thus the army had a perfect alibi to defend its own interests and reject proposals that were to its disadvantage.

Attempts to modify the constitution were fraught with difficulty, since changes contradicted the so-called Leonsberg Agreement. This agreement—secretly concluded between Bouterse and the three FDO leaders prior to the 1987 referendum—laid down that the constitution could not be altered. In this way the army safeguarded its prominent position, leaving the government and the National Assembly in a dependent position. The Leonsberg Agreement—basically a supraconstitutional document—was thus a main obstacle in the way of the Arron government's attempt to give real meaning to parliamentary democracy in Suriname. Finally, however, the army hedged against an erosion of its power through participation in the Privy Council. Although it shared Privy Council seats with representatives of the political parties and other interest groups, its position in this supervisory body enabled it to co-control all important state affairs.

The broken back of the government was personified by President Shankar. Although holding an impressive number of offices—head of the government, chairman of the Privy Council, and supreme commander of the military forces—not long after his installation people had already distorted his name to "Ram is *Zwak*" ("Ram is weak") Shankar. In every respect the president appeared unable to resist the interests of Bouterse and Lachmon, the most fervent advocates of the new democracy. Other considerations that influenced the actions of the FDO administration were interparty and intraparty rivalry as well as the fact that the selection of its members was in marked contrast with the composition of the first Chin A Sen government. Not all ministers, for instance, had a clean past (a few of them were members of governments in the period prior to 1980), while as a team, the Arron administration definitely did not reflect a nationalist ideal. Following their victory in the 1987 elections, the FDO parties started to apply the strategies of patronage and corruption with the same indulgence as in the pre-Bouterse era.

The results achieved by the Arron administration were thus meager. It succeeded in transferring or discharging many civil servants appointed between 1980 and 1988 but was clearly afraid of making a clean sweep. Many violators of the law were still awaiting prosecution at the end of the decade. In early 1990 Bouterse almost succeeded in eliminating Brunswijk in Paramaribo; however, following diplomatic intervention, he was forced to release his most resolute opponent. Later in the year, after an army offensive, the jungle commando lost a considerable portion of its territory. Ever since, Bouterse and Brunswijk have expressed a wish to conclude a peace treaty, but negotiations have not been opened. As for migration, the Surinamese population seems focused more than ever on the hope of residence in the Netherlands, particularly when the Arron government appeared to have no answer to the disastrous economic situation facing the country. Although the Netherlands resumed development cooperation with Suriname in early 1988, procedural difficulties prevented the cooperation from bearing fruit.[19]

CONCLUSION

Examination of Surinamese politics in the 1980s and into the 1990s has disclosed four stages aimed at the establishment, respectively, of a social democracy, a socialist people's republic, a military-led democracy, and a parliamentary democracy. None of these models, however, functioned adequately. They were each the result of arbitrary decisions and did not have the consent of the population; they thus served primarily as cosmetics, hiding rampant militarization. Indeed, there has been no evidence that the National Army was ever willing to retreat from the political role it took up in 1980.

Although the original group of sixteen is depleted appreciably—four blood brothers died and four others left the active service—and a lack of officers and NCOs has become manifest, Bouterse and the NDP remain determined to pursue their politics. Indeed, on running into conflict with the Arron administration, the army took over the reins of government once more in a bloodless coup on 24 December 1990. The Dutch government again suspended all development aid.

All in all, the Surinamese population feels misled, betrayed, and deserted, blaming both its civilian representatives and, more directly, the army. Faced with the disintegration of the state, the society, and the economy, most people tended to turn inward upon themselves, fostering an individualism that focuses on mere survival. The Guyanese standards, which Suriname proudly managed to avert in the 1970s, became a living reality in the 1980s.

# 6 Revolution, Democracy, and Regional Integration in the Eastern Caribbean

*Tony Thorndike*

On 13 March 1990, a date loaded with political significance for the people of Grenada, voting took place in what was the
second general election in the island since the collapse of the
Marxist-Leninist revolutionary regime some six and a half years
earlier. Although the turnout was a disappointing 66 percent, due
mainly to a reluctance to vote on the part of some of the young,
nobody in the Commonwealth Caribbean, least of all the hundred
thousand or so Grenadians, thought the election an exceptional
event; indeed, the only question was its timing. Neither was there
undue consternation at the five days of intensive negotiations that
followed, made necessary because no one party achieved a working
majority. A series of individual shifts of party allegiance, partially
encouraged by offers of ministerial office, eventually led to a government dominated by the National Democratic Congress (NDC)
and headed by NDC leader, Nicholas Braithwaite.[1]

Ten weeks later, on 28 May, another general election took place,
this one in Dominica. The ruling Dominica Freedom Party, led by
the Caribbean's "iron lady," Eugenia Charles, scraped home to its
third election victory, its majority reduced from thirteen seats to
only one as a result of a challenge by a newly established party, the
United Workers' Party.[2] Still further north, in Antigua, another
political drama was being played out, although of a fundamentally
different nature. Antigua has over two decades acquired the re-
grettable image of being the most corrupt society in the Commonwealth Caribbean, hosting a notorious amorality from top to bottom. Even so, most Antiguans were shocked at revelations that
their island home had been an important staging post for Israeli
weapons destined for Colombian drug barons. The scandal involved a senior government minister, Vere Bird, Jr., the elder son of

the prime minister and contender for the succession, whose reputation was already tainted by rumors of gross corruption involving
public works contracts. Pressure within the cabinet, led particularly by his sibling rival, Lester Bird—and from Antigua's main ally,
the United States—forced an inquiry by the eminent British lawyer Louis Blom-Cooper. Blom-Cooper found against Vere Bird and
recommended he never again hold public office.[3] Although the
government might not fall as a result of the scandal—if only because of the splintered opposition of the entrenched ruling Antigua Labour Party—political accountability of a sort was enforced
by the establishment of the official enquiry.

The point of these observations is that the liberal-democratic
multiparty model remains firmly established in the Eastern Caribbean. The case of Grenada notwithstanding, governments change
through electoral processes and not, generally speaking, through
the barrels of guns or by palace coups.

This chapter examines the postindependence political model
adopted by the small, economically dependent, polities of the Eastern Caribbean in terms of legitimacy and popular acceptability.
Does there exist an identifiably separate "small state" model? And
if so, how does it cope with the particular problems of these islands
and island groups, notably their need for development and security? Aiding the analysis is a comparative study of Barbados,
perhaps the clearest example of the pluralist, liberal democratic
model in action, and of revolutionary Grenada, the only institutionalized alternative to multiparty democracy to emerge within
the Eastern Caribbean. The culture of constitutionalism that un-
derpins the Barbados political process is described and then contrasted with the theoretical and philosophical foundations of the
Grenadian revolutionary experiment. This lasted from 13 March
1979, when power was seized by armed insurrection, to 25 October
1983, when U.S. paratroopers invaded to administer the coup de
grace to what was by then a discredited regime. The circumstances
of its failure are analyzed, the main question addressed being
whether the revolution collapsed because of external pressures and
destabilization policies, orchestrated by the United States, or as a
result of the contradictions experienced by the revolutionaries
when they tried to apply a Marxist-Leninist model to the Eastern
Caribbean environment.[4] The chapter concludes by exploring the
potential for economic and political unity among the territories
and speculates on the future of pluralist democracy in the Eastern
Caribbean.

## THE EASTERN CARIBBEAN CONTEXT

It may be presumptuous, even preposterous, to claim the existence of an Eastern Caribbean political model. Yet there is prima facie justification: there is a tradition there based on the Westminster system, which is a structure of political and legal institutions and mores based upon adversarial principles, where opposition is both legitimate and a duty, the whole informing a political decision-making process conducted within the principles and boundaries of the rule of law. Critical to its operation is a popular respect for human and civil rights, which no politician can ignore for long. Other major principles include the presumption of the neutral state, where the state is not representative of a particular class but rather is theorized in the "classic pluralist fashion as a neutral broker to which contending interests can make representation and from which some enunciation of an overarching collective or national interest can be expected."[5] The church and judiciary are formally separate from the state, and there is a presumption of political neutrality by the civil service elite. Lastly, there is the principle of civilian supremacy over the military.

That much, and more, is in common with the larger Commonwealth Caribbean territories, Guyana excepted. What is noteworthy about the structure and process of politics in the smaller islands—and some, like Anguilla, are *very* small—is that respect for democratic values and institutions and for human rights (which took several centuries and much violence to evolve in Britain) has developed in a different society in a different hemisphere. Of course, it is not *the* Westminster model; it has been adapted to local circumstances, especially those of smallness, and it does not work (in practice) as well as it might. But the main point is that these values, rights, and institutions have been developed, promoted, and maintained and that this has been done despite the myriad consequences of smallness: the tendency toward personalist political leadership and centralized decision making; the lack of political space in "goldfish bowl" societies, where little is private; and the problem of control and management of open, limited-resource and highly dependent economies, a problem that latterly also has encompassed the activities of drug traffickers and other criminals attracted to the islands.[6]

In addition, some characteristics of smallness are specific to Caribbean territories. One is the massive disparity in size between Caribbean states and the United States, which constrains their freedom of political action—a situation summed up by Eugenia

Charles as "not so much that we are in America's backyard but rather that America is in our frontyard."[7] Another characteristic is intense political partisanship, supported by a press often vitriolic in tone and content, notwithstanding often very limited ideological differences. Here it may be argued that the adversarial Westminster system is a weakness, since such partisanship is inimical to national unity. Yet it is not only accepted but expected by the electorates. Last, there is the phenomenon of insularity. This can, of course, be a natural consequence of smallness if small territories are geographically isolated; it can also be a function of scarce resources, when political power is bound up with the politically selective allocation of those resources—in short, with patronage, which political leaders are loathe to share, let alone lose. While no Eastern Caribbean territory is geographically isolated, all to varying degrees suffer from scarce natural resources. For this reason and, most important, because of the particular colonial legacy bequeathed by the British, insular attitudes in the Eastern Caribbean are particularly powerful. In sharp contrast to the French policy of centralization, the British insisted that each colonial administration be responsible for its own finances, exercise a wide measure of discretion within vague but well-understood rules, and trade directly with Britain.

The result was a tradition of individual territorial responsibility and separate, free-standing, governments—each governor, and later the elected political leader, being lord of his domain. There was little scope for the islands and territories of the British West Indies to work together, laying the groundwork for their later disunity. Insular attitudes were strengthened by the political role of public administration and public works, always an important source of employment in small, less developed, territories. In such an environment, successive proposals for regional cooperation and unity fell on stony ground. Yet, from the point of view of the development of the democratic model, insularity also had a positive effect: each island had to observe all the constitutional rules and the conventions of diplomatic etiquette in its numerous dealings with the metropolitan authorities.

These, then, are the justifications for arguing for the political distinctiveness of the Eastern Caribbean islands, which encompass seven independent states—Antigua-Barbuda, Barbados, Dominica, Grenada, St. Kitts–Nevis, St. Lucia, and St. Vincent and the Grenadines—and three British dependencies—Anguilla, the British Virgin Islands (BVI), and Montserrat. Together accounting for less than a million people, their populations range from 264,000 in

Barbados to a bare 7,000 in Anguilla (Barbados has one of the highest population densities in the world). As indicated, their resource bases are very narrow—although the sun, sea, and sand are free. Their greatest asset is their human resources, which, if literacy is the criterion, make them the envy of many an African or Latin American state.

Their peculiarity is that, despite their small size, most are relatively prosperous compared to their larger Commonwealth Caribbean partners, a few very much so if income per capita is relevant. Because of this, the international institutions have categorized them as middle-income countries, and they no longer qualify for concessionary aid to less developed countries. Intense lobbying led to a postponement of their "graduation" in the mid-1980s out of the so-called soft loan window of the World Bank, but that was still expected to take place in the early 1990s.[8] Although the islands may collectively be deemed to possess "developing" economies and many of their peoples see themselves as poor, they are in reality simply deprived, relative to the United States, which is only three hours away by air and is a magnet for the ambitious and the mobile among the population. Economic expectations are, therefore, uncommonly high. It may be harsh to describe them as "a scattering of small countries which could . . . have joined the first world, but ended up languishing in the third," but the observation has a grain of truth in it.[9] Their populations certainly have First World attitudes and aspirations, and the political leaderships know full well that failure to reasonably distribute wealth will ensure defeat at the polls.

## THE EMERGENCE OF A DEMOCRATIC TRADITION

The roots of the culture of constitutionalism in the Eastern Caribbean go deep. The most fundamental factor is, of course, the colonial heritage, which in some cases, for instance Barbados and St. Kitts–Nevis, stretches back some 350 years. Indeed, Caribbean constitutionalism owes as much to this longevity of colonialism as to colonialism itself. Another critical factor is the bequeathing of a world language by the British, albeit imposed upon peoples who were, for the most part, forcibly dispossessed of their African culture through slavery and gross exploitation. Values cannot be divorced from the language that gives them expression, and political institutions in turn reflect values. The result of this indoctrination is an ingrained respect for Westminster-style democratic practice. Political pluralism based on the concept of loyal opposition became the bedrock of political stability and the guarantor of civil liberties.

The role of history in this process of political enculturation is therefore critical. Since slavery led to the loss of much of the African culture, it was no wonder that the sugar planters' language and notions of social organization became firmly established. Despite the narrow base of the old representative system, where government was in the hands of the plantocracy and operated in the interests of that class alone, British parliamentary procedures were followed. They came naturally to the expatriate British and their descendants and, over time, became the accepted norm for those excluded from the political system and, certainly, for those with any aspirations to power. When from the mid-nineteenth century onward these regimes progressively gave way to the Crown Colony system, or direct executive rule by the British governor, correct procedure (and good table manners) were even more essential for those advising him. The middle-class representative associations, which emerged in response, fulfilled these requirements to the letter.[10]

Slavery also placed a premium on freedom, a quality expressed most clearly in the importance attached to property ownership and freedom of worship and speech, aspects of the Westminster system as important as elections and constitutional procedure. Indeed, procedure ruled popular institutions such as the churches, the homespun benevolent societies, and later, the trade unions. The latter's legalization in the early 1940s, following the recommendations of the Moyne Commission, was an important milestone in the development of democratic institutions. They marked the politicization of the working classes, acting as pressure groups and friendly societies. To be effective (and legal), they had to be efficiently administered and their leaders answerable, a task made easier by the educational system, which transmitted British values and produced at least functional literacy even for the common laborer.[11] When the trade unions spawned political parties modeled on British counterparts, the democratic political process was further institutionalized and formalized. Furthermore, despite the appalling social conditions that lay at the root of the labor disturbances of the 1930s, loyalty to the British Crown remained largely unquestioned.

The trade unions and political parties had as their priority the alleviation of this distress. But their campaigns proceeded for the most part on the basis of negotiation and constitutional action, using the newly legalized strike weapon to great effect. There was, in other words, no thought, let alone attempt, at revolution. Whether this was the inevitable consequence of hierarchical and authoritarian systems that bred inferiority is debatable. What was clear was a general belief that governments, societies, and economies could be reformed and that better times would come: in other words, that politics *mattered*.

Decolonization, which began in the Eastern Caribbean with the grant of universal franchise in 1951, was a much more drawn out affair than in other parts of Britain's colonial empire, thanks to the diversion of federalism. Promoted by the British, the Byzantine complexities of the Federation of the West Indies could not contain political rivalries and deeply ingrained insularism. Yet its formal demise in May 1962, after less than four years of life, was mourned by a number of Eastern Caribbean politicians to whom, at that time, the federation represented the only possibility of constitutional advancement for their territories. Notwithstanding their sentiments, a further attempt at federation in 1963–65 involving only Barbados and the Leewards and Windwards suffered the same fate.[12]

But this period did ensure the effective political socialization of the new political and bureaucratic elite. To them and their followers, political pluralism and the "neutral" state was an unquestioned part of the natural political order, where political rivalries were institutionalized through parliamentary democracy. This culture of constitutionalism rested on the fundamental principle that governments were to be defeated only through the ballot box. The result is impressive, for the electoral history of the Commonwealth Caribbean as a whole has been characterized by a relatively high rate of government defeats at elections, often involving large swings of voter choice and high turnouts. Between 1966, the year Barbados achieved independence, and 1990, there were fifty-four general elections in the Eastern Caribbean, all basically fair albeit ferociously fought; they led to twenty-three changes of government. During this period, political parties almost wholly replaced independents as the medium of political activity and articulation. Nevertheless, compared to practice in larger Caribbean polities, party discipline in the smaller islands is not tight. "Floor crossing" and the formation of breakaway parties are not unusual: indeed, in St. Lucia, Montserrat, Grenada, and Barbados, breakaway parties have won power. Admittedly, one-party parliaments have emerged in Antigua-Barbuda and St. Vincent, although not as a result of the Westminster first-past-the-post system, which has the tendency to favor winners and give little to minority parties and groups. In both cases, government parties won against poorly organized opposition parties, which, nonetheless, had access to most of the media.

## THE LIBERAL DEMOCRATIC MODEL AND BARBADOS

The use of Barbados as a case study of Caribbean democracy does not imply that other Eastern Caribbean territories are less democratic. The justification for focusing on Barbados is the longevity of its democratic traditions, the nature of its social structure, and its consequent well-deserved image of stability.

Claimed for the British Crown in 1624, the hitherto uninhabited island remained under continuous British sovereignty until political independence in 1966, thus earning itself the soubriquet "Little England." The first settlers were British smallholders, who grew tobacco using the labor of indentured English and Irish servants. The life of these servants was little different from the African slaves who gradually supplanted them following the introduction of sugar in the 1640s. As sugar production demanded considerable labor and capital, large plantation owners replaced the smallholders, many of whom left for Britain's American colonies. Those who stayed became overseers, merchants, or "poor whites," and their descendants account for the relatively large proportion (in Commonwealth Caribbean terms) of whites (or near whites) in the Barbadian population.

The House of Assembly established by the smallholders in 1639 to represent their interests was, of course, soon taken over by the emergent plantation owners. Rapidly acquiring a reputation for obstructiveness and factionalism, the House of Assembly exercised de facto power through its control of the public purse. Any attempt at reform was stifled if it threatened the planters' interest. Although this system was replaced in the 1860s by Crown Colony administration under strict British executive control, Barbados retained its House of Assembly. The reason was that, in 1876, the planters finally agreed to reforms. There was established the principle of responsible government inaugurating an Executive Council (later the Executive Committee) and, in 1884, widening the franchise. Ironically, the planters' hands were forced by the black population, who enthusiastically answered the governor's call for civil disobedience in his campaign against the landed establishment.[13] Yet even the reforms excluded the bulk of blacks from the franchise; further political advance had to wait until the rise of the labor movement in the 1930s.

The poor economic climate and the impoverished condition of

most Barbadians were the main causes of the labor disturbances that broke out in Bridgetown in July 1937, when the British deported a working-class activist, Clement Payne, to his native Trinidad. Riots spread all over the island. A Commission of Enquiry expressed no surprise at the disturbances once the inexcusable inequalities in Barbadian society were laid bare. In the aftermath, the Barbados Progressive League was founded, its leaders including Grantley Adams. It gained five seats in the House of Assembly in 1940 and was strengthened considerably by an alliance with the Barbados Workers Union (BWU), which was founded and led by Adams and Hugh Springer.

In 1943 the league successfully campaigned for an extension of the franchise, which helped it obtain a majority in the assembly in the 1944 election. Adams and other elected members subsequently joined a reformed and more important executive committee, and a stream of proworker legislation flowed. The league was renamed the Barbados Labour Party (BLP) for the 1946 poll. Its main opposition was the increasingly ineffectual Electors' Association, established by the landowning and merchant elite. The BLP allied with the like-minded proworker West Indian National Congress Party and, after that alliance broke up in 1947 largely over personality differences, managed to cling to power by divide and rule tactics. The achievement of unqualified universal adult suffrage undoubtedly helped the BLP in the 1951 election, when it won sixteen seats, making it inevitable that when ministerial government came in 1954 Adams would be appointed premier.

By 1955, schisms were evident in the party. Relations between the BLP and the BWU grew acrimonious. Further, a group favoring a more socialist approach, led by Errol Barrow, a charismatic and plain-speaking ex-RAF navigator who had entered the House of Assembly in 1951, opposed Adams and his supporters, who favored a gradualist policy.[14] Eventually, the former group, later named the Democratic Labour Party (DLP), broke away from the BLP. Barrow was elected its chairman in 1959, and in the election held in the wake of the grant of full internal self-government in October 1961, the DLP won a stunning victory, with fourteen seats to the BLP's five.

One reason for the Barbados Labour Party's defeat was that Adams was also the prime minister of the unpopular Federation of the West Indies throughout its life (1958–62). In poor health, he was also not able to fully employ his undoubted talents in Barbadian politics. Barrow was a convinced Caribbean regionalist, who worked strenuously for an association of Barbados and the neighboring Leeward and Windward Islands after the collapse of the federation. Ultimately, in the face of unresolvable arguments, he led Barbados to independence in November 1966 and became its first prime minister after an election in which, for the first time, the DLP commanded a plurality of votes.

After 1961, a two-party system based on the two labor parties established itself. The party as an institution was confirmed as the prime symbol of electoral mobilization, and popular support for the system as a whole was reflected in consistently high electoral participation. In addition, there was a measure of ideological and policy difference between the more conservative party (the BLP) and the more socialistic party (the DLP). But whereas the former fit easily into the island's deep-seated sense of constitutional propriety, the latter had to consciously conform. The result has been consistent tension within the DLP, by turns creative or destructive, with social democratic conformists coexisting with more radically minded activists. The tension never threatened the country's constitutional system or its values and mores; rather, it tended to express itself in the wider society as a tendency to challenge deep and long-standing class and race cleavages.

The 1976 election saw the end of fifteen years of DLP rule. Over time, internal divisions over matters of both substance and style weakened the party. The party now faced two questions. Could, indeed should, more and deeper socialistic reform be pursued, and how? And to what extent ought the grass roots of the party be involved in policy making in the framework of cabinet government? The intensity of this debate was such that, after the DLP's defeat, Barrow refused to be named leader of the opposition. For the BLP, of course, it was a wonderful opportunity. The general malaise in the DLP, together with allegations of corruption, were seized upon by the new BLP leader, lawyer "Tom" Adams, son of Sir Grantley, to build up a powerful position in his country's politics.

Adams again led the BLP to victory in 1981, after calling the election some months early when he realized that the economic situation was precarious. The fear was real: during the 1980s unemployment grew and factory closures became common as the Barbadian economy felt the loss of the Trinidadian market following the collapse of the oil price, the continued decline of the sugar industry, and the relatively poor performance of the tourist industry. The BLP's political fortunes plunged, although there was consistent and widespread support for Adams's firm policy of containing revolutionary Grenada and for his leading role in garnering regional and international support for the ousting of the military revolutionaries responsible for the killing of Maurice Bishop in October 1983. Adams died suddenly in 1985, and the BLP went on to be heavily defeated by the DLP in the May 1986 election, following the biggest swing of opinion in Barbados's electoral history—over 11 percent. Errol Barrow thus once again became prime minister, some two decades after first assuming that office.

While allegations of corruption, poor leadership, and economic stagnation had not helped the BLP cause, the underlying reason for the party's defeat lay in the island's history. The issue of racism and white power had never been far from the surface of political debate over the preceding five or so years, the BLP having become increasingly identified in many eyes with the white and near-white business elite, from which it received substantial funds. The issue came to a head dramatically just four days before the election with the defection to the DLP of one of the BLP's most popular ministers, former university lecturer Don Blackman. Blackman charged that the BLP "masqueraded" as a "so-called" people's party, allowing all the important decisions to be made by the prime minister and a handful of white businessmen, decisions that were then rubber-stamped by the cabinet; he cited examples of such decisions taken by the "white shadows." Large and enthusiastic crowds attended his every meeting. By contrast, Barrow made impassioned appeals to the black working class, proposing tax reform in its favor if he were reelected.

Nationalist sensibilities were also offended by the BLP's strong identification with U.S. security policy in the region following the collapse of the Grenadian revolution, when Washington's militarization program had appeared not only to be intolerant of legitimate constitutional opposition but to undermine the autonomy of regional decision making. Never a man to avoid controversy, Barrow's stand on this and other regional issues made him an imposing political force, and his sudden death in June 1987, after only a brief resumption of office, was a considerable shock. He was succeeded by his deputy, Erskine Sandiford.

Sandiford's first political test was provided by the renewal of intraparty tension, which characterized the DLP from its inception. Minister of Finance Ritchie Haynes resigned in September 1987, charging that the new prime minister had ignored party policy, that the government's handling of the economy had broken important electoral promises favorable to workers, and that anti-worker ordinances were being unfairly applied in industrial disputes. In February 1989 Haynes announced the foundation of the National Democratic Party (NDP). As three other DLP members joined him, he displaced BLP leader Henry Forde as the official leader of the opposition. However, the NDP did not long survive the logic of the "first past the post" Westminster system and the two-party culture of Barbados. In elections in January 1991 it lost all its four seats. Although the BLP recovered considerably from its poor showing in the 1986 poll, it was unable to prevent Sandiford from retaining office, albeit with a reduced majority.

The conclusion that can be drawn from the experience of Barbados is that, despite the great injustices suffered by the majority at the hands of the small planter minority, the institutions and procedures that this minority established and nurtured were effectively transmitted and became embedded in the social psyche. So was their conservative outlook. The idea of revolution in Barbados is, frankly, inconceivable. Nor would any political leadership be likely to refuse to play by the rules; it would receive short shrift from the electorate if it did. The Barbados experience, therefore, stands in sharp contrast to that of Grenada. Not surprisingly, therefore, Barbados was in the forefront of those critical of the self-styled People's Revolutionary Government, although generally more out of concern for the disregard for human rights and constitutionalism than from anticommunism, per se.

## THE CHALLENGE OF THE GRENADIAN REVOLUTION

In the light of the democratic traditions of the Eastern Caribbean, it is something of a paradox that this part of the region has been the locale of the only armed insurrection, the only successful military coup, and the only attempt to forge a political critique of the Westminster system in the modern history of the Commonwealth Caribbean. The Grenadian revolutionary experiment, in both theoretical and practical terms, was far removed from the values that informed the traditional Eastern Caribbean model, and indeed, a greater contrast with Barbados could hardly be imagined. Yet its fundamental contradictions made ultimate failure inevitable: if the U.S. troops who delivered the coup de grace had not been given the opportunity to intervene by the implosion of the regime, the experiment would have had to have undergone considerable reform to survive, especially in the post-Reagan era of superpower détente and Eastern European democratization.

A prominent Caribbean Marxist, Richard Hart, described the experiment as "the improbable revolution," and certainly the setting was unpropitious.[15] The Grenadian economy was heavily dependent on preferential markets, and resources were limited and poorly managed. Socially, the emergence after emancipation in 1834 of an independent peasantry based primarily on share crop-ping cocoa, spices, and bananas was another obvious constraint. As for politics, the revolution was more than improbable; it was unique and highly specific to authoritarian developments in Gre-nada during the decade before the armed takeover by some fifty youthful members of the New Jewel Movement (NJM) in 1979. Far from portending a swing to the left in the region, elections in other Commonwealth Caribbean countries from 1980 onward showed the opposite trend, and it is highly unlikely that the NJM or a successor similarly informed by Marxism-Leninism will again emerge as a ruling force in Grenada or, indeed, in any of the Eastern Caribbean territories, unless the unusual circumstances that gave rise to its birth and sustenance unexpectedly return.

The revolution followed a long period of political repression and economic stagnation under the dictatorial regime of Sir Eric Gairy, a one-time trade union leader, who first assumed power in the 1951 election after leading a spectacularly successful strike. Grenada had not experienced the typical labor disturbances of the late 1930s, because the peasantry and small farmers, besides being able to feed themselves, did not share the same grievances as their equals elsewhere in the region. Dubbed "Hurricane Gairy," the dashing young leader became the hero of the working classes, who became increasingly politicized as a result of his activities on their behalf. Calling himself "a little black boy," he was determined to be respected by members of the generally lighter-skinned mercan-tile and professional middle class, who loathed him. In his pursuit of social recognition, his life-style became extravagant, and he was deposed in 1962 by the British colonial administration for corrup-tion and "squandermania."[16] Yet in the 1967 elections, Gairy bounced back, and he and his Grenada United Labour Party (GULP) were restored to power. However, opposition to his increasingly authoritarian (and occasionally bizarre) rule deepened after he took Grenada into independence in February 1974, amid widespread disturbances and strikes. His opponents mourned the removal of whatever restraint on his rule was provided by Britain; for their pains, they suffered the violence of Gairy's secret police, the so-called Mongoose Gang. His manipulation of appointments and blatant corruption appeared to consolidate his position, for which, as a mystic, he also claimed divine protection.

The traditional opposition to GULP rule was the middle-class Grenada National Party (GNP), led by Herbert Blaize, who repre-sented Grenada's major offshore island, Carriacou. However, by

1970, a new force had emerged, spearheaded by returning young intellectuals, newly graduated from universities in Britain and North America and radicalized by the issues of the day, such as Vietnam and black power. They were also influenced by such values as agricultural self-sufficiency, associated with the Rastafarians. They formed various groups, which eventually came together in March 1973 as the New Jewel Movement (Jewel stood for Joint Endeavour for Welfare, Education, and Liberation), with a charismatic and highly articulate young lawyer and activist, Maurice Bishop, at its head. The independence crisis (during the course of which Bishop's father, Rupert, was murdered) saw the NJM effectively supplant the GNP as the main opposition in the eyes of many Grenadians, especially its youth, a position confirmed when the new party became the senior partner in a People's Alliance that captured six of the fifteen seats in the House of Assembly in the 1976 election. Gairy denounced the NJM as communist and stepped up the persecution. The NJM responded by forming an armed clandestine wing, which was later to form the nucleus of the People's Revolutionary Army (PRA). Taking advantage of Gairy's absence from the island (he was at the United Nations pleading for the establishment of a UN institution to study extraterrestrial phenomena), the NJM seized power (with very few casualties) early on the morning of 13 March 1979. The People's Revolutionary Government (PRG), with Maurice Bishop as prime minister, was subsequently legitimized by popular acclaim.

Regional reaction was at first ambiguous; leaders were outraged at the illegal takeover yet thankful that Gairy, a political embarrassment, had been deposed. After all, some reasoned, Gairy had not respected the Westminster "rules of the game," with his bribes and intimidating tactics. Furthermore, none could ignore the clear endorsement of the insurrection by the great majority of Grenadians. Adams voiced the demands of those who wanted to reestablish constitutionalism, advancing a complicated and unreal formula whereby Bishop would be appointed a minister in the outgoing GULP administration before emerging as the new prime minister.[17] Such schemes were dropped only after Bishop allegedly promised elections in a reasonably short time. The problem for the region's constitutionalists was that the NJM had no such intention. By 1978 it had evolved into an elitist Leninist party, having secretly embraced Marxism in 1974. From that time onward, the party structure began to take on orthodox elitist Leninist forms. Significantly, membership criteria became increasingly strict, and secrecy was firmly enforced. The theoretical shift of the party had also received a boost with the return to Grenada in September 1976 of former university lecturer Bernard Coard and his wife, Phyllis, both dedicated Marxists and disciplined Leninists. He took charge of political education and worked hard to bring about the establishment of institutions in the NJM modeled on those of the Communist party of the Soviet Union.

## NONCAPITALIST DEVELOPMENT IN GRENADA

Important to the redefinition of the NJM was its adoption of the theory of noncapitalist development as constructed by Soviet theoreticians in the 1960s.[18] Alternatively called the theory of socialist orientation, it was a strategy of revolution designed for preindustrialized, less developed economies. It assumed that less developed countries had not entered the era of developed capitalism (as opposed to petty capitalism). This stage in the Marxist progression had to be bypassed or poor countries would fall victim to the imperialist blandishments of exploitative international capital.

In other words, those countries guided by the theory would move directly from precapitalism to socialism, although the period of transition could be long. The process would be one of socialist orientation, the state increasingly taking a leading role in the economy by such means as the nationalization of multinational company investments (although not before a trained work force was in place) and the gradual communalization of agriculture, with the consequent undermining of traditional rural socioeconomic structures. Backed by a structured system of political education, these measures, the theoreticians predicted, would raise efficiency and ensure adequate and fairly distributed incomes and goods. As postcolonial economic ties weakened, the Soviet Union and other developed socialist countries would increasingly emerge as natural allies. At that stage the policy would be one of socialist construction aimed at deepening the whole process.

How was this to be realized in the absence of an industrialized proletariat? The key was the emergence and development of "national democracy" and the role of the national intelligentsia. Because of the limited proletarian strata and the expected reactionary attitudes of the peasantry, the educated class had to take the lead in shaping a multiclass alliance of antiimperial and nationalist forces. It would normally be expected that such an intelligentsia would be of middle-class origin. Identified as the "national democratic bourgeoisie," they had in particular to be distinguished from others of their social strata who had allied themselves with imperialism—in Marxist terminology, the *comprador bourgeoisie*. The progressive middle class was "national" in that it promoted national development with little reliance on international capital, and "democratic" in that it encouraged political organization by workers and peasants. Above all, "progressives" would work for the economic betterment and social transformation of the working masses—recognized as the great majority of the population—and facilitate the expression of working class and peasant interests.

Although superficially attractive, there were pitfalls in the theory. One risk was that the intelligentsia might see themselves as the only, and perpetual, vanguard. It was critically important that the vanguard did not become elitist, that the intelligentsia did not view their powers of foresight as justifying centralization and exclusivity of power, and that imperialist attacks on the process of noncapitalist development should not trigger paranoia and excessive secrecy. Another caveat was the necessity to guard against excessive zeal.[19] The masses would be alienated if the vanguard moved too fast and too far ahead of the people; it had to persuade, not force. The risk of overzealousness would also increase if the process of socialist orientation was a long one. Shortcuts to revolution would be counterproductive, and only the most careful analysis of objective, concrete, reality was acceptable.

Yet another risk was that, under the combined pressures of the "bourgeois environment," the material attractions of international imperialism, and in many cases, personal background and peer group identification, some of the "national intelligentsia" might be tempted not only to deviate but even to develop links with the *comprador bourgeoisie* and thus frustrate the revolutionary process. Life-styles were therefore important, as they would be expected to reflect commitment and discipline. In summary, the whole point of socialist orientation and socialist construction was the development of a revolutionary working class, nurtured but not dominated by the national democratic intelligentsia. The progression to socialism thus meant that the progressive middle strata had literally to work themselves out of history and at the appropriate time either give way completely to revolutionaries from lower social strata or at least relinquish their leadership role: tall orders indeed.

Not surprisingly, the secrecy that ruled the adoption of these theories led most Grenadians, let alone the outside world, to presume that the New Jewel Movement was a traditional, albeit radical, party. Admittedly, Bishop had in 1973 publicly announced that the NJM favored participatory democracy, whereby the Grenadian people would be much more part of the governmental policy-making process than hitherto. He certainly denounced the "two-seconds democracy" of the Westminster model: "the type of democracy where people walk into a voting booth and vote for two seconds every five years is not democracy at all."[20] What was favored were village assemblies on the Tanzanian *ujamaa* model. But although a parish and subparish zonal system of participatory democracy was established under the rubric of "people's power," there was little real popular involvement in policy making and implementation for the simple reason that such a development contradicted Leninist philosophy. Only the socialist vanguard party, and specifically its Central Committee, could make the decisions; only it had real power.[21] The consultation process was allowed to amend policy only at the margin, suggest tactics to be followed in a particular area or economic sector, or permit the occasional public questioning of ministers and civil servants. It was, in other words, largely confirmatory, the various assemblies functioning in the main as educative and mobilization mechanisms.

Despite the small party membership (72 full, 94 candidate, and 180 applicant members in October 1983),[22] contact with the "masses" was achieved through mass organizations, all headed by NJM activists, again on the Soviet model of the time. They included the National Women's Organization (headed by Phyllis Coard), the National Youth Organization, and the Productive Farmers Union. Relations with the trade unions were at times tense, but faced with the prospect of preventive detention, union leaders who were not party members were careful not to overstep the bounds. Within the party, a complex and time-consuming bureaucracy developed, with a number of subcommittees of the Central Committee covering such issues as security, economic development, women, and youth. At the apex was the Central Committee, established in September 1979, which over time tended to overshadow the earlier Political Bureau as the central organ of party policy making. Partly because of this bureaucratic complexity—and despite constant exhortations for more "discipline"— many important decisions were nevertheless taken in a relatively ad hoc manner at the highest levels, particularly by Bishop himself. Conversely, many other decisions were subjected to costly delays because of lack of coordination and accountability within the governmental system.[23]

To the outside world, especially the United States, the major manifestation of the four-and-a-half years of revolutionary rule was the PRG's close alliance with Cuba. This was most clearly exemplified by the construction of a new international airport at Point Salines, a project that became a major bone of contention with Washington. Of US$71 million budgeted for the airport, Cuban workers and supplies were worth US $40 million. Taking all Cuban assistance into account, it is hard to see how the revolution could have survived without Havana's support.[24] Not surprisingly, the Cuban link was nonnegotiable. Cuba also supplied liberal quantities of arms, as did the Soviet Union and North Korea. Other links were developed with East Germany, Hungary, Libya, and Iraq among nontraditional allies, all part and parcel of the PRG's insistence that Grenada was not in America's backyard. The United States was also concerned, as was the Commonwealth Caribbean as a whole, over the suspension of Parliament and habeas corpus. Preventive detention, or imprisonment without trial, was the normal fate of those who opposed the regime, and in general what were decried as "bourgeois" freedoms of expression and assembly were severely restricted. It is against such "revolutionary manners" that what social and educational advances the regime was able to achieve with diminishing resources—due as much to natural disaster and falling world commodity prices as destabilization by the United States—have ultimately to be weighed.

## THE COLLAPSE OF THE GRENADIAN REVOLUTION

The revolution collapsed primarily because of the contradictions in the application of Marxism-Leninism and the theory of non-capitalist development to Grenada. Or, to put the point another way, the NJM revolutionaries disregarded the pitfalls of the theory, as forewarned by its Soviet progenitors in Moscow.[25] U.S. pressure and world economic conditions were subsidiary factors exacerbating the contradictions.

An early sign of difficulties was increasing popular resentment about the lack of elections and the suspension of hard-fought-for human and civil rights, which showed by 1983 in the people's growing reluctance to attend rallies and become involved in voluntary work, both of which they were eager to do early in the revolution. Little could be done to change popular attitudes toward private property and commerce, toward religion, and toward American values in general. And even less could be achieved in terms of central economic planning and the construction of a command economy (not that it was ever seriously discussed). Some 30 percent of Grenada's gross national product derived from international trade, while the currency, the East Caribbean dollar, was not only shared with seven other territories but was also convertible. The export of bananas was dependent on preferential access to European countries under the auspices of the European Community's Lomé Convention, the Soviet bloc and Cuba offering low prices and very little in the way of consumer goods. A "new" tourism policy was proclaimed, concentrating on attracting Caribbean and Soviet bloc visitors, but the former spent little money and visits by the latter were impracticable: for example, although a tourist exchange agreement was signed with East Germany, the Berlin government permitted only two of its citizens to travel to Grenada each year, accommodation to be at the PRG's expense![26] No wonder there was little visitors could see, other than slogans, indicating the existence of a revolution. As for Grenadians, they increasingly felt the economic pinch, which added to their demoralization.

In short, the evidence was depressingly clear: the theory of noncapitalist development was not appropriate to Grenada. The island economy was already well into the capitalist stage, and socialist orientation would be an extremely long-drawn-out process. To the NJM Central Committee, there was but one answer: an intensification of effort. No thought was given by the zealous members to the possibility that the masses could be pushed too far or to the consequences if coercion and repression had to be applied to recalcitrants. Already highly exclusive, the Central Committee arrogantly saw itself as the sole source of political wisdom. After all, the masses "did not know the science"[27] and could not be trusted. Although a little more thought went into the problem of overseas relations, and Bishop was dispatched to the United States in June 1983 to attempt to begin a dialogue with the Reagan administration (in which he was singularly unsuccessful), policy in this area was dictated more by tactical considerations than any considered strategic thinking. The PRG's friends were few, especially after the Michael Manley government was voted out of office in Jamaica in 1980. Its sense of beleaguerment deepened steadily, and U.S. harassment and open intimidation became an ever sharper thorn in its side.

The revolution's response to external threats was to boost the strength of the PRA, and plans were made to create an 11,000-person force, an extraordinary total given that the island's population was barely 100,000. Although the full-time strength of the

PRA had reached only 2,000 by October 1983, its youthful and often arrogant members were not well regarded, adding to popular disaffection with the revolution. Within the regime, the demands put upon party members generally, and Central Committee members particularly, also increased to near intolerable levels under these pressures. The degree of secrecy imposed and practiced was extraordinary. Slowly, the atmosphere became one of paranoia. Whenever U.S. military exercises took place, its naval forces were literally on the horizon. In the end, when revolutionary progress slowed and public morale fell, the reason offered was not the theory but rather counterrevolutionary activity, which allegedly reached to the highest levels of the government and party. Indeed, by August 1983 recriminations within the Central Committee had begun to be focused on Maurice Bishop.

Bishop's easy going life-style and disregard of organizational procedures was fiercely criticized. By comparison, the dedication of Bernard Coard was legendary: he had little time for frivolity as he toiled for the revolution. He had been critical for some while of the declining state of party organization and political education. He had in fact resigned from the Central Committee in October 1982 because of what he saw as the lack of revolutionary direction. He wanted more rapid progress toward socialism, and he was not a lone voice in articulating his frustration. Matters came to a head in September 1983, when, after a series of tumultuous and emotional meetings, the Central Committee decided upon "dual leadership."[28] Bishop would remain prime minister, with responsibility for political mobilization; Coard would run the party. Bishop reluctantly agreed. Then, while he was away on an aid mission to Eastern Europe, Coard assumed the chair of the Central Committee. He rapidly held a number of meetings, which set an invigorated socialist agenda for the country.

However, while Bishop was in Hungary, he changed his mind about dual leadership, believing the scheme to be unworkable. He himself would be "marginalised," and the masses would be "confused." He realized that the Grenadian people would be left lagging behind the Central Committee and that nothing short of disaster would follow if the committee attempted to realize even some of its schemes. When he returned home, he was committed to house arrest. When this eventually became known, public reaction was swift.

The events of 19 October 1983 are well recorded.[29] Coard had never been a popular figure, and rumors that he had replaced Bishop intensified public anger. A large crowd freed both Bishop and another minister incarcerated with him and took them to a former colonial military fort overlooking the capital, St. George's, for medical treatment. Bishop planned to appeal to the people for their support in the intraparty struggle, but under Central Committee instructions, the PRA invaded the fort and restored it to the army. After a rain of gunfire had left some sixty dead and scores wounded, Bishop and some of his supporters, including other ministers, were executed. It was then announced that the Revolutionary Military Council (RMC) under PRA leader General Hudson Austin had assumed power and that a ninety-six-hour curfew would be applied under pain of death. The people were understandably stunned and fearful.

Within the RMC there was confusion. Austin had never been an ideological heavyweight; Coard had helped guide the RMC but had remained in the background. The RMC was taken aback at the hostile international reaction, particularly from Cuba. When it became clear that Coard could not obtain Cuban or Soviet aid and that he was a liability, a "coup within the coup" took place on 23 October. Coard was dropped, and the search began for a broad-based civilian government.[30] But the RMC's efforts were in vain, as nobody wished to be involved. In the meantime, the regional reaction at both official and popular levels became a determination to oust the regime. The regional Organization of Eastern Caribbean States was the chosen vehicle. Following private meetings with Edward Seaga, prime minister of Jamaica, and the White House, the then chairperson Eugenia Charles requested U.S. military assistance. (Military intervention was also considered to rescue Bishop, but that proposal lapsed with Bishop's death.) To the lasting embarrassment of many skeptics, the great majority of Grenadians welcomed the U.S. paratroopers as they fell from the sky in the early hours of 25 October; the invasion, labeled Urgent Fury in Washington, was the intervention that saved them from the hated military government. That was not all, for a majority of the Commonwealth Caribbean states, with the notable exceptions of Guyana, Trinidad and Tobago, Belize, and the Bahamas, enthusiastically joined what became the U.S.-led multinational Caribbean Peacekeeping Force, which was established once the island was secured. Barbados and Jamaica were prominent in the force, Tom Adams making Barbados available as a base for the action. The alien ideology of noncapitalist development had been truly purged.

## THE RESTORATION OF GRENADIAN DEMOCRACY

One of the many paradoxes of revolutionary Grenada was that it remained, in name, a monarchy, since Governor-General Sir Paul Scoon continued to fulfill his duties as the representative of Queen Elizabeth II, head of the Commonwealth. During the U.S. invasion, he was swiftly "rescued" by the U.S. forces and taken to a U.S. warship, from where he issued a predated appeal for assistance. By that dubious legal fiction, Grenada's sovereignty remained intact. Although U.S. authorities, diplomatic and military, clearly influenced the course of political events as they unfolded, Scoon formed an Advisory Council of nine prominent Grenadians under Nicholas Braithwaite's leadership. This council became known as the "interim government." Its first task was to restore the 1974 independence constitution but with some sections suspended pending an elected government.

The Advisory Council, however, was in no hurry to arrange elections. The trauma had been great and politics had a tarnished image; in any event, there were no established parties. Scoon's action was considered entirely legitimate, and economic reconstruction was the order of the day. In that respect, the interim government greatly benefited from a US$43-million aid package from Washington, which included US$19 million to complete the controversial airport. Another US$6 million was disbursed as compensation for war damage, and numerous technical experts arrived to replace the Cubans. Although the bulk of the U.S. army left in December 1983, some 300 troops remained until mid-1985, together with Caribbean police and military contingents.

It was not long before political groups emerged. There followed a confusing period of maneuvering, but by early 1984 it was clear who were the major contenders. Foremost were the remnants of the Grenada National Party, GNP leader Herbert Blaize insisting, despite his age and illness, that his party, as the traditional opposition to Gairy and thus representing stability, should take the lead. Not surprisingly, Blaize assiduously cultivated both the Reagan administration and regional leaders.[31] The centrist National Democratic Party led by George Brizan (who had been an early member of the NJM but had broken with the movement when it declared itself to be Marxist) and the right-wing Grenada Democratic Movement (formed in exile during PRG rule) under former academics Francis Alexis and Keith Mitchell were also active. The left was represented by the Maurice Bishop Patriotic Movement (MBPM), the NJM having faded away with the jailing of its leaders (who were later sentenced either to death or to long prison terms, subject to an exhaustive appeal process).

Exasperated by the squabbling and the failure to agree upon merger proposals, Adams, with the support of other Eastern Caribbean leaders, initiated a meeting of all the contending factions, except Gairy's GULP and the MBPM, on Union Island, one of the Vincentian Grenadines. The result was a forced merger under Blaize's leadership, and the newly christened New National Party (NNP) went on to win the December 1984 election, with fifteen seats against one for the GULP. In February 1985, a Constitutional Commission was sworn in to make recommendations for the reform of the independence constitution. It eventually recommended, inter alia, fixed-term parliaments, the power of recall by constituents of unsatisfactory members, and the restoration of local government. But very little was done to implement these changes, because by 1986 the facade of unity within the NNP government had been torn apart. Cabinet meetings became such charged affairs that it was impossible to continue them, particularly when austerity measures became necessary once U.S. aid was used up (much of it had been wasted on large imports of expensive consumer goods). There was also growing unease about Blaize's apparent paranoia over alleged security threats.

Eventually, in April 1987, both Alexis and Brizan resigned and, in July, linked up with other dissidents to create the National Democratic Congress. Braithwaite was invited to become its leader at its first congress in November 1988. Within the NNP, the situation went from bad to worse. Blaize consolidated his position by blatant patronage, large numbers of public sector workers being replaced by GNP supporters. He also broke with Mitchell, who went on to claim the NNP as his own while Blaize formed The National Party (TNP). Blaize died in December 1989, and Ben Jones, the deputy leader of the old GNP, took over. In the March 1990 elections, the NDC captured seven of the fifteen seats but was able to form a government only when Jones and the other TNP member agreed to support Braithwaite, as did two of the four elected GULP members. Mitchell and the erstwhile NNP was left isolated, with only two seats. There was a low turnout by young voters, which was worrying but not surprising given the unedifying picture presented by the restored democracy of Grenada since the "intervention."[32]

## The Westminster Model and the Lessons of Grenada

What conclusions can be drawn from the revolutionary experience of Grenada? One, above all, comes to mind: the Marxist-Leninist model, or that version of it deemed orthodox by the revolutionaries, was quite inappropriate for Eastern Caribbean society and political economy. It is a moot point whether a revolutionary experiment that did not so slavishly emulate the Soviet Union—or "the land of Lenin," as Bishop was wont to call it—might have had a greater chance of popular acceptability. Leninism, after all, is orthodox only because it was the sole doctrine of communist organization that was operationalized after Lenin and his Bolshevik supporters overcame their rivals either in prerevolutionary exile or after the February revolution in Russia. But given the history and the social and cultural environment of the Eastern Caribbean, it is to be doubted whether any socialist alternative that did not take account of traditional values would have succeeded. No matter how the Westminster model has been abused by unscrupulous and authoritarian politicians, it has come to be regarded by the great bulk of the Grenadian people as infinitely preferable to all other alternatives. Indeed, the revolutionary experiment served only to strengthen the classic Westminster system. Participatory democracy, at least as practiced by the NJM stalwarts, was deemed a second best to competitive elections, and socialist rights (to employment, health, housing, education) inferior to human and civil rights as traditionally understood.

However, the operational record of the Westminster system in Grenada both before and after the revolutionary interlude has a deeper significance in that it highlights its vulnerability to prime ministerial exploitation. No prime minister under the Westminster system is a mere first among equals in the cabinet; he or she can act in a manner more familiar to a colonial governor, especially if an efficient prime ministerial office exists. The problem is that the operation of the model depends a good deal on unwritten, often subtle, assumptions about the rules of the game—the conventions of fair play so beloved by the British—and of course, there are none of the formal checks and balances that characterize the American model.

In addition, the promise of ministerial office is a considerable disciplinary weapon in the Eastern Caribbean. In small legislatures of the Westminster type, the latter is always an important consideration, for no matter how small the territory, assuming it has its own government, the number of ministerial portfolios required does not vary too much from those in larger polities. Since legislatures in the Eastern Caribbean are inevitably small, the prospect of office is all the higher. In the end, the lessons of Grenada for the Westminster model in the Eastern Caribbean are double-edged: on the one hand, its appeal has been deepened by the collapse of one widely proclaimed alternative; on the other, its vulnerability to authoritarian abuse serves only to remind all observers of the Gairy era and the particular circumstances from which the whole revolutionary experiment emerged.[33]

## THE PROSPECT OF EASTERN CARIBBEAN UNITY

One further theme needs to be considered: the prospect of closer unity in the Eastern Caribbean. Note has already been made of the factors that have militated against the development of regionalism in the Commonwealth Caribbean as a whole. Yet the Eastern Caribbean territories have a history of economic and functional cooperation dating from 1966, and following the establishment of the Organization of Eastern Caribbean States (OECS) in June 1981, they have succeeded in institutionalizing political cooperation. In November 1986, Prime Minister James Mitchell of St. Vincent went still further, proposing political union of the Leewards and Windwards—or all the Eastern Caribbean islands except Barbados, Anguilla, and the BVI—in one unitary state. Objections based largely on insular or partisan self-interest, not dissimilar in their essentials to those that had sealed the fate of earlier constitutional plans for regional integration, were not long in being expressed. Indeed, for a while what momentum there was appeared almost lost. Nonetheless, the possibility remains of greater cooperative machinery, even if it falls short of political union as far as some of the territories are concerned.

There was no immediate and pressing reason prompting Mitchell's initiative; rather he appreciated the economic marginality of the island economies and saw only a bleak economic future as separate entities. Export prospects appeared poor due to high production and transport costs, and the plan for a unified European market threatened the privileged position the Windward banana producers enjoyed under the banana protocol of the Lomé Convention. Employment prospects were seen as equally discouraging because of the sharply rising population, which no longer could take advantage of the emigration safety valve. Conservative estimates suggest that growth in the labor force by the year 2000 could reach 54 percent, certainly no less than 23 percent. In St. Lucia's case alone, that would imply a population of over 200,000: at the OECS annual meeting in May 1987, Prime Minister John Compton pointed out that full employment under those circumstances would require an annual growth rate of 9 percent, an impossibility if St. Lucia stood alone.[34] Not surprisingly, Compton fully endorsed Mitchell's initiative.

In spite of these and other realities, reservations and outright opposition soon surfaced. Prime Minister Vere Bird, Sr., who did not attend the 1986 and 1987 OECS meetings, led the attack. Within days of a strong statement in favor of union issued by the OECS heads of government meeting in the British Virgin Islands in December 1987, he highlighted Antigua-Barbuda's main objection, which was the provision for freedom of movement. The proposed union was denigrated as "a kind of colonialism,"[35] and in any event, there was little economic incentive in the proposal for Antigua's booming (albeit heavily indebted) tourist- and casino-based economy: even most of its bananas and citrus came from Puerto Rico rather than from OECS producers. The leaders of St. Kitts–Nevis and Montserrat, which relied heavily on Antigua's transshipment facilities, took their cue from Bird. Grenada, preoccupied with its own political problems, was lukewarm, while Eugenia Charles was quite happy to endorse Puerto Rican investment in Dominica, which cut directly across existing cooperative production facilities in the case of banana packaging.

Surprisingly, neither Mitchell nor Compton made any attempt to query Bird or suggest a federal structure to preserve Antigua-Barbuda's autonomy. Another failure was the cavalier way in which the opposition parties were treated; this was surprising, since central to the Mitchell plan was a popular referendum (involving a two-thirds majority) on each island to test the principle, the success of which would have depended on cross-party support. The referendum was planned originally for mid-1988, but that was soon forgotten as political temperatures rose and the opposition parties formed into a single grouping, the Standing Conference of Popular Democratic Parties of the Eastern Caribbean (SCOPE), to coordinate and represent their views.

But Compton, as current OECS chairman, pointedly refused to respond to a request by SCOPE to meet the heads of government to discuss union. Furthermore, he imposed entry bans into St. Lucia upon several opposition leaders he deemed subversive. He was supported in his action by his fellow leaders, who strongly resisted the inclusion of nongovernmental representatives in discussions on administrative arrangements and constitutional forms. In fact, few of SCOPE's constituents favored union, most being far more concerned with national politics and electoral prospects. But the government leaders played into their hands, as the lack of consultation enabled them to oppose the process on this issue alone.

Undeterred, Compton and Mitchell and an enthusiastic OECS secretariat pushed ahead; a series of task forces was proposed to make detailed proposals. But little was achieved, and by late 1988 there was only the prospect of more functional cooperation (such as liberalized interisland travel arrangements), and then only among the Windward Islands. No clear course was set, no proper consultative machinery was established, and no serious discussion was conducted on constitutional forms. If a referendum had gone ahead, it would have been difficult to envisage what the electorates would have been asked to judge! A despairing commentator aptly remarked that, if a union was to be achieved, then "political parties in these states will have to overcome their intense aversion to talking with each other. They will have to learn that integral to the Westminster system of government is that on important issues of national concern, political leaders from all sides of the House must hold dialogue as representatives of the people to whom they are accountable. If they fail to do so, the national consensus, which is an absolute prerequisite for altering their constitutions and proceeding to a political union, will never be achieved."[36]

Perhaps regional politicians took this warning to heart, for in August 1990 unity plans were revived at a meeting held on Palm Island in St. Vincent of the leaders of the four Windward Islands. The Palm Island Statement committed the heads of government to full consultation "involving the populations of the Windward Islands . . . parliamentarians, political parties and special interest groups to discuss and make recommendations on the necessity for political union and on appropriate arrangements for bringing into effect unification."[37] A regional constituent assembly would be established, each island having a delegation of ten. Of these, three would be government members and two drawn from the opposition, the remainder being representatives from the private sector, trade unions, churches, youth groups, and farmers' groups. The assembly was to meet successively on each island for five days, commencing in St. Vincent in November 1990.

However, despite a meeting in October 1990, between Mitchell, representing the heads of government, and SCOPE, opposition leaders announced a boycott of the assembly. Their spokesman, Julian Hunte (leader of the St. Lucia Labour Party), charged that they were "being treated with disrespect by the four governments" and that "this whole initiative [was] being placed in a particular direction for the convenience of the governments in office."[38] Specific objections were that the proposed assembly lacked both legal status and a sense of direction and that it should have an independent chairman and secretariat. Notwithstanding advice from the OECS secretariat that the assembly was intended to be only an advisory body, not a legislative one, SCOPE's members were unmoved, promoting the observation that "it was clear that SCOPE viewed the whole exercise from partisan political perspectives."[39] The St. Vincent meeting was postponed to January 1991 to enable the OECS secretariat and SCOPE leaders to prepare a draft bill outlining the assembly's terms of reference. This would then be discussed by the assembly and sent to the four island legislatures for approval. This substantial concession was felt by the heads of government to be more than sufficient to find favor and restore confidence in union.

## CONCLUSIONS

The main threat to parliamentary democracy in the Eastern Caribbean is not revolution, unless the exceptional conditions that helped prompt the Grenadian insurrection recur, an unlikely but not impossible prospect. Rather, the main threat is two-fold. One is corruption stemming from the temptations of the narcotics trade, as the examples of the Turks and Caicos Islands and the Bahamas make clear. The other is economic dependency. Despite apparent prosperity in some sectors of their economies, notably tourism and offshore finance, Eastern Caribbean democratic structures unavoidably remain vulnerable to debt and poverty. While there is currently no reason to suppose that these islands will suffer breakdowns in the near future—although a financial collapse in Antigua under the burden of corruption and debt could spark unrest and should be noted—widening disparities in income and increasing unemployment cannot but undermine over time the national consensus so necessary for the working of the Westminster system throughout the Eastern Caribbean.

These, then, are the real threats. Nevertheless, the prospects for the 1990s seem more likely to be the continued support of a lively democracy. For the moment, there is no doubt of the legitimacy and acceptability of the Westminster system, as locally adapted. It will, of course, evolve, but it will probably do so in a conservative way and at a slow pace, because that is, above all, what the peoples of the Eastern Caribbean islands want.

# 7 The Grenadian Revolution in Retrospect

*Courtney Smith*

The Grenadian revolution undoubtedly shook to the core the liberal democratic model of development that had come to dominate the politics and economics of the Eastern Caribbean by the end of the 1970s. It constituted only the second revolution in the Caribbean's post-1945 history and was the first attempt to implement a radical program of economic, social, and political transformation in one of the smaller territories. Its significance in this respect and its ultimate failure to offer a convincing political alternative to the liberal democratic model is discussed in the previous chapter. But in addition to its relevance to the affairs of its immediate subregion, the 1979–83 revolutionary experience of Grenada was an episode of importance for the whole of the Caribbean.

This chapter addresses a vital but hitherto neglected dimension of these years: the efforts of the People's Revolutionary Government to transform the Grenadian economy. Lessons for the whole region of this particular strategy of development are drawn. The chapter also assesses the role of economics in the final derailment of the revolution.

## ECONOMIC BACKGROUND: POVERTY, DEPENDENCE, AND STAGNATION

On the eve of the March 1979 revolution, Grenada was an agrarian appendage of the international economy—fragile, dependent, and vulnerable to the prevailing economic conditions in metropolitan economies. Of course, this is not to deny the modicum of diversification the economy experienced during the 1960s and 1970s with the advent and growth of tourism, banking, insurance, commerce, construction, and light manufacturing. But the contribution of these sectors to the socioeconomic life of the country, especially in the critical areas of gross domestic product, employment generation, and foreign exchange earnings, lagged considerably behind the agricultural sector. For example, despite the setback that this sector experienced during the Gairy years, it still accounted for 30 percent of the island's gross domestic product in 1978, provided employment for some 40 percent of the work force, and consistently generated over 90 percent of total exports between 1971 and 1978.

Although constituting the backbone of the economy, agriculture was constrained by legacies of the plantation economy era, most pronounced in the pattern of land ownership. Of the 14,039 farm holdings existing in 1975, the vast majority (12,265, or 87.4 percent) were small farms of five acres or less, accounting for only 28 percent of the farm acreage. At the other end of the scale, 99 farms (0.7 percent of the total) accounted for approximately 33 percent of cultivable acreage.[1] Yet the contradiction went further. The best land was concentrated among the larger holdings, while the small farmers subsisted on the rugged and mountainous terrain left uncultivated by the plantocracy. Despite this severe land hunger, thousands of acres of arable land remained idle.

In keeping with tradition, the large estates were predominantly involved in commercial, export-orientated agriculture, comprising three primary crops—nutmeg (including its by-product, mace), cocoa, and bananas. These were exported in an unprocessed state, as in the days of plantation agriculture. Although small farmers were also involved in the production of these tree crops, their main output was geared for the domestic market. In 1975, for example, they provided 85 percent of all the food and vegetables produced on the island. But small uneconomic parcels of land, limited access to credit facilities and agricultural inputs, and ignorance about soil conservation, irrigation methods, and agronomical practices in general inevitably led to low yields and low incomes. In addition, small farmers had to contend with lack of a market infrastructure.[2] This factor did much to undermine domestic agriculture, since guaranteed markets were provided only for the three export crops. Given these deep-seated problems in the agricultural sector, it is not surprising that the economy was consistently beset by a net deficit in agricultural trade. In 1972, for instance, total foreign exchange earnings from agriculture amounted to EC$9.2 million, while imported food items stood at EC$13.3 million.[3]

The retention of features of the old plantation system could also be seen in the tourist industry, Grenada's second major source of foreign exchange. This sector expanded throughout the 1960s and 1970s on account of the steady and rising demand for holidays in this tropical Garden of Eden. Hotels were designed to meet the desire for ostentation of tourists from affluent backgrounds. The bulk of the trade was from North America, making the island vulnerable to developments in the U.S. economy and the foreign policies of the U.S. government. Although some of the hotels and guest houses were owned by local businessmen, the industry was dominated by foreign interests. For example, the Holiday Inn alone accounted for 60 percent of the total bed space in the sector. Typically, hotel owners were also involved in complementary services, such as transport and restaurants. In addition, foreigners also invested in holiday and retirement housing settlements, thereby reinforcing their hold on the island.

The growing investment in real estate also exerted inflationary pressure on land prices and further exacerbated the problems in the agricultural sector. A further constraint on this sector was inadequate infrastructure and air transportation. The limited interrelation between the tourism industry and other sectors, particularly agriculture and construction, also placed a severe strain on the country's balance of payments. The principal bottleneck was the lack of an international airport equipped with night landing and instrument landing facilities and capable of accommodating large, wide-bellied jets. The impossibility of night landing was a drain on the economy, since visitors often had to stay overnight in the neighboring islands of Barbados and Trinidad. According to one estimate, some 50 percent of the visitors to Grenada stayed overnight in other islands, at approximately US$85 per visitor, causing an annual loss of US$1.3 million to Grenada.[4]

A somewhat similar picture exists for the financial sector. The banking system was dominated by foreign ownership, mainly Canadian and British. The lending policies of these banks were instrumental in deepening the structural problems of the economy. Short-term borrowing, especially by merchants, was favored at the expense of long-term strategic loans. For example, of the EC$27 million loaned to the agricultural, tourism, manufacturing, and distribution sectors in 1977, 55 percent was allocated to the distributive trade, 22.2 percent to agriculture (mainly export agriculture), 14.8 percent to tourism, and 7.4 percent to manufacturing.[5] By financing merchandise activities, the banks were simultaneously securing the Grenadian market for foreign goods and services.

Dependence was also acute in the island's fledgling manufacturing sector. The contribution of this sector to the gross domestic product averaged a paltry 3 percent throughout the 1970s. Among the main manufacturing operations during the prerevolutionary period were food, drink, and tobacco processing, garment factories, and furniture making. These activities were based overwhelmingly on imported raw materials and capital equipment. In the case of the tobacco and beer brewing industries, all the inputs were imported. This dependence contributed to the uncompetitive nature of many of the goods, notably furniture. As one government source noted, "It is quite common to find cheaper imported products on shop shelves. In cases where some raw materials are obtained locally, these are so highly priced that the finished product is beyond the range of the ordinary consumer."[6] Finally, Grenada's manufacturing sector was distinguished by the lack of a functional, formal, and systematic organizational structure along company lines, largely a reflection of the size and ownership structure of these businesses. The majority were small, family-owned, cottage industries, typically employing fewer than five people. Manufacturing also operated with considerable excess capacity; capacity utilization in food and beverage processing, for example, averaged only 56 percent.

Given these problems, we can begin to understand why the economy performed so sluggishly under the Gairy regime. The period from 1960 to 1978 was one of uninterrupted and growing balance of trade deficits, reaching a record level of EC$50.5 million in 1978. Before 1974 the deficit was financed primarily by grants from Britain, but after independence this source of finance diminished in importance. Indeed, it proved increasingly difficult to procure external loans as a result of the government's poor debt-servicing records and its mounting corruption. For example, the tendency for money to disappear from the treasury led the Caribbean Development Bank in 1977 to refuse to grant further loans and aid to the country. For the same reason, some EC$19 million from other foreign sources was also withheld in 1977.[7] The drying up of all forms of foreign inflows, allied to the deteriorating foreign exchange situation of the country, produced a number of predictable consequences: an escalation of unemployment, the deterioration of social services (especially health care, education, and housing), a net depreciation in the island's capital stock (particularly its transportation infrastructure and other public utilities), and an acute reduction in the national savings ratio. There was also a marked decline in business confidence, as witnessed by the pattern of investment growth during the last years of the Gairy regime. In 1976 total domestic investment amounted to US$13.6 million, rising marginally to US$14.7 million in 1977, and falling to US$11.8 million in 1978.[8]

These developments had a particularly deleterious impact on Grenada's workers, small farmers, and the unemployed. Their lot was made worse by the exploitative pricing policies of Grenada's merchant class. According to figures published in the *Grenada Abstract of Statistics*, between 1964 and 1975 the price of basic foodstuffs escalated by 200 percent, clothing by 164 percent, and housing by 135 percent. It is believed that the markup on a bag of rice, for example, was in excess of 200 percent.[9] Assessing the state of the Grenadian economy on the eve of the revolution, the World Bank noted that "the country was plagued by a low standard of living, heavy unemployment and under-employment, inadequate production of basic foodstuffs, inflation and persistent deficits in the balance of payments."[10]

### THE PRG's DEVELOPMENT STRATEGY

When the People's Revolutionary Government (PRG) came to power in March 1979, the party had already diagnosed the causes of the legacies it had inherited from the Gairy era.[11] It had also worked out the general thrust of the development strategy it would pursue, the essence of which was articulated in the 1973 Manifesto of the New Jewel Movement.[12] Some of the tasks for transformation were dictated by the immediate problems afflicting the country: chronic maldistribution of income and means of production; mass unemployment and underemployment; a high and rising cost of living; an inadequate social and economic infrastructure; irrationalities in the utilization of resources, especially agricultural land; a disjuncture among the sectors of the economy; an excessive dependence on external powers; foreign ownership and domination of critical sectors of the economy; an inadequate motivation to work; and political apathy, aggravated by a backward, patronage-ridden political system that engendered a something-for-nothing mentality.

The analysis of the origins of these problems was more controversial. Drawing upon the insights into Caribbean underdevelopment provided by a radical group of university intellectuals from the larger Commonwealth Caribbean territories and known as the New World Group, the PRG attributed these problems to colonial domination, neocolonialism, and the ill-fated development policies of Grenada's traditional political leadership.[13] Contrary to conventional wisdom, the physical size of the country was regarded as a secondary constraint. Prime Minister Maurice Bishop summarized the party's thinking on this question in telling terms: "The real problem is not the question of smallness per se but [that] of imperialism. The real problem that small countries like ours face is that on a day-by-day basis we come up against an international system that is organised and geared towards ensuring the continuing exploitation, domination, and rape of our economies, our countries, and our people. That, to us, is the fundamental problem."[14]

Consequently, several far-reaching structural and institutional changes at the national, regional, and international level were called for. In the spirit of the economic strategy espoused by Clive Thomas (one of the New World Group), the manifesto articulated an economic program predicated on the resource endowment of the country.[15] To provide more houses it thus advocated a national low-cost housing plan, utilizing as much as possible indigenous materials such as wood, clay, and river sand. Similarly, to improve the problem of insufficient clothing, it called for a revitalization of the cotton industry in Carriacou to supply the raw material requirements for a textile and garment industry.

Emphasis was also placed on the establishment of linkages between the different sectors of the economy, particularly agriculture, agroindustry, and tourism. These three sectors were identified as the principal catalysts for growth and economic transformation. As an example of what was possible once the structural contradictions of the economy were eliminated, an impressive list of products that could be made from Grenadian raw materials was compiled, including jams, nutmeg oil, jellies, liqueurs, marmalade, juices, spice powder, pharmaceuticals, preserves, flour, baby foods, cereals, farine, animal feeds, baby foods, flour, chips, cake mixes, and, from Grenada's abundant fresh fruits, fruit juices, nectars, liqueurs, and wine.

The manifesto also emphasized the need for state control of essential sectors, agrarian reforms (including the establishment of cooperative farms), price controls, wage reforms, heavy investment in social and productive infrastructure, and the creation of a national importing board and a national exporting board empowered to handle Grenada's import and export trade. On the international plane, it made a plea for diversification of international relations to include the Third World and socialist states, a strong commitment to regional cooperation, a New International Economic Order, and respect for the sovereignty, legal equality, and territorial integrity of all states, however small. The party summarized its ideological orientation in the following words: "We stand firmly committed to a nationalist, anti-imperialist, anti-colonialist position."[16]

Sensitive to likely opposition to its program, members of the NJM were careful to avoid affixing a political label to the society they envisaged. However, once in power, sources close to them were quick to confirm that socialism, via a noncapitalist route, was uppermost in their minds from the outset. In their study of the Grenada revolution, Jacobs and Jacobs thus described the party as "displaying certain selected scientific socialist tendencies, especially in the area of democratic centralism."[17] This was further supported by public pronouncements made by prominent members of the PRG. In November 1979, Selwyn Strachan declared in an interview that Grenada was undergoing a process similar to Cuba's: "We believe that our course of development will be more or less the same as the Cuban revolution. There may be one or two minor differences, but nothing dramatic."[18] In an interview two years later, Bishop himself pointed out that the revolution was at the "national democratic stage, the antiimperialist stage of the process we are building."[19]

The main theses of the theory of noncapitalist development are generally well known. All that needs to be reemphasised here is that the economic corollary to the postulated class alliance is the mixed economy model, comprising a state sector, a private sector, and a cooperative sector.

## THE STRATEGY IN PRACTICE

The Grenadian economy during the period of the revolution was consciously developed along the mixed economy model, albeit with the state sector dominant. Some critics, most notably Fitzroy Ambursley and Hilbourne Watson, construed this pattern of ownership as evidence of the regime's commitment to the capitalist ethic.[20] However, this interpretation is erroneous, since it fails to realistically appraise the utter impracticality of a total state-sector model in the context of Grenada's objective conditions. As revealed by Bishop's "Line of March" address in 1982, the PRG opted for the mixed economy model in the hope that it could continue to draw on the skills, experience, material resources, and market connections of the private sector. In addition, it was recognized that "the capitalist prefers to deal with the capitalist and capitalist governments allow other capitalists to come in, even when their government is a socialist-oriented government like our government in Grenada."[21]

The alliance was therefore conceived in tactical terms. By assuming leadership of the development process, the state would be able to guide the pattern of economic and social development to ensure that capitalist relations did not dominate at the expense of socialist-collectivist forms. Simultaneously, it also sought to enlist the cooperation of private sector interests by granting them economic incentives and engaging them in constant dialogue as a means of assuring them of their continued role in the new society. The hope was that they would boost production and hence offset the constraints of the inexperienced and undercapitalized state sector.

However, much to the chagrin of the PRG, its relationship with the private sector did not develop in this way. Almost from the outset, it was characterized by conflict and mutual distrust, particularly after the first year of the revolution, when the contours of the government's development strategy began to crystallize. The most worrying problem for the private sector was the rapid growth and expansion of the state sector in productive activities. By mid-1983, the state had come to control approximately 15 percent of the country's agricultural land. Among its most notable initiatives in this pivotal area of the economy were the establishment of the Grenada Farms Corporation, Grenada Agro-Industries, the Marketing and National Importing Board, the National Fisheries Corporation, the Livestock Production and Genetic Centre, the Forestry Development Corporation, and the National Agricultural and Co-operative Development Agency. It also gained an important foothold in the tourist, financial, and marketing sectors with enterprises that included the Grenada Resorts Corporation; the Grenada National Institute of Handicrafts, together with Grencraft, its marketing arm; the Holiday Inn; the National Commercial Bank; and the Grenada Bank of Commerce. The dominance of the state in the banking sector placed it in a strong position to marry the resources mobilized by commercial banks to its developmental priorities. Additionally, the Grenada Development Bank, formerly the Grenada Agricultural and Industrial Development Corporation, was overhauled and empowered under People's Law 33 to play a more strategic role in the country's development program.

TOURISM

Despite its relatively strong foothold in the agricultural sector, the main emphasis of the PRG's economic policies centered initially on the development of tourism. This reliance on tourism was dictated by the need for scarce foreign exchange, especially in the short term. Bishop candidly set out the dilemma facing the PRG as follows: "In terms of the development of the economy . . . over the next 10–15 years, as we see it, the next 5 years—emphasis will undoubtedly be on tourism. That is not to say that we like tourism, that is because we have no choice. Tourism is the sector that has the greatest potential for giving us the profits to invest in the areas we really want to invest in—agriculture, agro-industries, fisheries and non-agro industrialization generally. That is really where we would like to go, but those cannot produce the money at this time, while tourism can."[22]

But before tourism could play this role satisfactorily, the principal constraints on this sector had to be removed. Estimated at a cost of US$71 million, the international airport project thus became the centerpiece of the PRG's economic strategy. It is not an exaggeration to say that members of the PRG regarded its completion as *the* decisive factor in the island's developmental fate. Bernard Coard, the deputy prime minister and minister of finance, predicted that the opening of the airport would mark "the beginning of a whole new economic era for our country."[23] In a similar vein, Bishop described the airport as "the gateway to our future. As we see it, it is what alone can give us the potential for economic take-off. . . . It can help us to develop our agro-industries more. It can help us to export our fresh vegetables better."[24] Tourist arrivals and receipts were thus projected to increase substantially. The influx of visitors was also expected to stimulate activities in related sectors, thereby boosting employment opportunities and government revenue.

To maximize these economic benefits and, at the same time, to alleviate the undesirable social, cultural, and environmental outcomes normally associated with tourism, the revolutionary government sought to promote a policy of "new tourism," conceived as the antithesis of traditional tourism prevalent in the Caribbean.[25] New tourism would seek to diversify Grenada's tourist base to include nonwhite visitors from the Caribbean and the wider Third World, establish intersectoral linkages with the rest of the economy, promote indigenous culture, and foster regional integration. Laws would also be passed to deal with prostitution, gam-

bling, drugs, and other socially deleterious tourist-related practices.

Apart from the PRG's modest efforts in the handicraft sector,
virtually nothing was done during its tenure in office to implement
the new tourism.[26] It was, perforce, a long-term goal, given the
contradiction between the immediate foreign exchange needs of
the economy and the decline in revenue that was bound to follow
from a shift toward nonaffluent, Third World visitors. The likely
magnitude of the decline can be gauged from the findings of a
survey conducted by the Caribbean Tourism and Research Centre
in 1982: visitors from traditional markets spent an average of 9
nights per visit, compared to 3.6 for visitors from the Caribbean;
traditional visitors typically stayed in hotels and guest houses,
while regional visitors stayed with friends and relatives; traditional visitors spent an average of US$901 per party trip (US$60 per
person per night), while the latter spent an average of US$329
(US$20) per person per night; and the average size of the visiting
party was 1.7–1.8 for traditional visitors and 1.32 for regional visitors.[27] These constraints forced the PRG to retreat, if only temporarily, from its pledge to implement the new tourism. It thus
contented itself with laying the infrastructural foundations for a
more viable tourist industry of the traditional sort.

Among the steps taken to boost tourist arrivals, the most notable were the restoration of Grenada's membership in regional and
extraregional tourism-promoting organizations; the establishment of a Ministry of Tourism; the appointment of a director of
tourism for the very first time in the island's history; the establishment of a Grenada interline desk at the Grantley Adams international airport in Barbados; the purchase of a Banderanti Commuter
Aircraft (at US$1.5 million) to mitigate the air access problem;
expansion of the tourism budget; and the establishment of tourism
offices overseas and the sponsoring of numerous promotional
tours.[28]

Despite these measures, the tourist sector performed dismally
under the PRG's administration. From 32,000 when the PRG assumed power, the number of overnight visitors fell to 30,100 in
1980, 25,000 in 1981, and 23,200 in 1982. The decline was particularly pronounced in the U.S. segment of the market. For example,
in 1979 there were 9,100 American overnight visitors, compared to
only 5,000 in 1982.[29] The plummeting tourist trade seemed to
come as a shock to the PRG, given the amount of scarce resources
it allocated to tourist development and the importance assigned to
this sector. The virtual dislocation of the industry, largely a prod-

uct of the "propaganda destabilization" campaign waged by the United States, exposed the fundamental flaw in the design of the PRG's development strategy. The new airport, no matter how well endowed, could not magically solve Grenada's development problems, since tourism itself was incompatible with the antiimperialist and overtly pro-Soviet stance of the government. Ironically, although Gairy did virtually nothing to promote tourism, Grenada experienced a more buoyant trade during his administration (except for 1974, when the number of visitors declined drastically due to the civil unrest on the island).

## AGRARIAN POLICIES

The arduous task of transforming the agricultural sector was also part of the revolutionary program. Bernard Coard described this sector as "the base, the bedrock of everything we do."[30] Symbolically, 1981 was officially declared the Year of Agricultural Production and Agro-Industry. This critical sector was to generate foreign exchange, provide inputs for industrial development, create employment, supply food, and increase the country's self-reliance by utilizing all agricultural land to its fullest.[31]

One of the government's first moves in this sector was the establishment of the Grenada Farms Corporation (GFC). Conceived as the leading vehicle for modernizing the island's agriculture, the GFC sought to manage and develop the thirty state farms (accounting for 9 percent of the land under cultivation) inherited from the Gairy regime. As a result of neglect, poor organization, corruption, ad hoc marketing, and inept management, these farms had consistently operated at a loss before the revolution. They were placed under new management teams and, it was hoped, would become profitable within the first five years of the revolution. Through various emulation and incentive schemes, workers on the farms were also encouraged to improve their productivity.[32]

To complement the efforts of the GFC, the government also instituted, in 1980, a National Cooperative Development Agency (NACDA), with a revolving loan of EC$1 million from the state-owned National Commercial Bank. The slogan of the organization—Idle Hands plus Idle Lands = End to Unemployment—clearly symbolized its intent. To provide land for the NACDA and the GFC, the Land Utilization Act was enacted in 1981, giving the government the power to acquire ten-year leases on any estate over 100 acres that was declared by the Land Development and Utilization Commission to be idle or underutilized. Plans were made to target estates under 100 acres at a later stage.

A number of measures were also introduced to modernize the already well-established private sector. The problems highlighted by the 1981 agricultural census (credit, infrastructure, underprovision of extension services, pests, diseases, praedial larceny, and labor shortage) constituted the basis of government policies in the countryside.[33] Established in 1980 with 1,200 small farmers, the Productive Farmers Union became the leading organization representing the interests of small farmers. Its functions were complementary to those of the NACDA. To improve farmers' incomes, feeder and farm roads were also constructed, some EC$6 million being raised through the Caribbean Development Bank for this purpose in 1981. Another twenty-five miles of roads were also constructed in 1982. The PRG also began the Eastern Main road project; the Eastern Main, over which some 40 percent of the island's export crops passed, was designed to connect St. George's to St. Andrew's. Other notable initiatives included the overhauling of the commodity boards to represent the interests of small farmers; the reestablishment of the Mirabeau Farm Training School, which was closed under the Gairy regime; the opening of four new agricultural schools at La Sagesse, Bocage, Boulogne, and on Carriacou; the provision of extension services and other technical assistance to farmers, especially in the area of disease management; and the provision of overseas scholarships to enable Grenadians to pursue studies in forestry, farm management, and agricultural science.

Plans were also formulated, and significant efforts made, to endow the countryside with services similar to those found in the urban areas, thus making it attractive to young people. Chief among these were the provision of electricity, pipe-borne water, transportation, health facilities, low-cost housing units, a national housing repair program, and a national insurance scheme to provide sickness, injury, and maternity benefits. As a result of these social advances and the PRG's deliberate policy of making them available in the countryside, the farming community was better able to raise agriculture output, if only because less time was spent on traveling to urban areas for these services.

To further rationalize the operations of the farming sector, efforts were made to establish close linkages with the Marketing and National Importing Board (MNIB) and Grenada Agro-Industries (GAI). Although the MNIB predated the PRG, it was not until 1979 that it began to play a major role in the economy. Under the PRG, it was to execute import-substitution policies, provide guaranteed markets and stable prices for produce, and oversee the importation of such basic commodities as rice, sugar, cement, and powdered milk. The MNIB also served as the principal distribution outlet for the output of the GAI, which operated a factory at True Blue and a food-processing laboratory at Tanteen, St. George's. The laboratory processed and packaged spices for both the local retail and export trade, processed fruits and vegetables into canned juices and nectars, and bottled jams, jellies, and chutneys. A state-owned fish-processing plant, specializing in the processing of frozen and salted fish products, was also established. To boost the demand for GAI's products, Grenadians were encouraged to "buy local and eat local," and efforts were made to market surplus output overseas.

Such technical and infrastructural assistance was certainly welcomed by the farming sector, particularly small farmers. However, this sector met the same fate as the tourist industry did under the PRG, largely due to natural disasters, market shortages, and declining prices. The depression was particularly noticeable in the performance of traditional exports: cocoa prices plummeted from US$1.88 per pound in 1979 to US$0.83 per pound in 1983; nutmeg prices fell from US$0.91 per pound to US$0.61. Total foreign exchange from bananas, cocoa, nutmeg, and mace fell from US$19.26 million in 1979 to US$11.31 million in 1983.[34] Under these circumstances, there was hardly any incentive for farmers to accede to the PRG's pleas and invest more resources in agriculture.

INDUSTRIAL POLICIES

In recognition of the untapped potential of the manufacturing sector, a number of policies were designed to develop this sector and integrate it into the national development program. The PRG's industrial strategy was based on the utilization of indigenous natural and human resources, the development of less energy intensive forms of product, the manufacture of products either not produced or underproduced in the Caribbean (in the hope that they could serve as marketing outlets), and the development of products for which there was a large local demand.[35]

Working on these principles, the government identified a range of products that could feasibly be produced in Grenada, hoping that foreign and local investors would cooperate with the state sector to exploit these opportunities. To this end, the PRG promulgated an investment code in 1983, which outlined government policy toward all forms of private capital and provided guidelines for processing investment proposals and applications for incentives. The major theme of the investment code was the emphasis it placed on the needs of the national economy. Investment proposals from foreigners were required to do one of the following: facilitate the transfer of appropriate technology, utilize domestic raw materials and labor, boost government revenue and foreign exchange earnings, provide new market outlets overseas, stabilize the cost of living, or augment the supply of capital in the domestic economy (rather than being financed from local resources). At the same time, foreign capital was forbidden from certain activities deemed by the state to be central to the national interest.[36]

In short, the PRG's investment code sought to depart from the so-called Lewis model of "industrialization by invitation," which was notorious for reinforcing dependency and underdevelopment in the region.[37] The principles embodied in the code were severely criticized by members of the private sector and their representatives. The UN Center on Transnational Corporations argued that the code was likely to scare foreign investors rather than attract them. It drily observed that, "if foreign investment is to be attracted, the policies in this regard will require careful consideration of the government."[38] In a similar vein, the World Bank insisted that the code was based on "very subjective principles,"[39] while the local private sector was scathing in its criticism. Indeed, it took eighteen months of intensive discussion between the government and the local private sector before the investment code could be published. Even then, the private sector as a whole refused to respond to the government's plea for increased investment; contrary to the wishes of the PRG, it did not ally itself with the revolutionary government. Unsurprisingly, the government's constant references to members of the private sector as "invoice technocrats," "percentage gatherers," and "parasites in the full-time service of capitalism" alienated them still further.[40]

## Economic Performance

In general, the PRG's program of reconstruction experienced mixed fortunes, as reflected in the variable performance of the economy under its stewardship. The economy certainly grew between 1979 and 1982, although there is some controversy surrounding the magnitude of the growth. According to the PRG's own figures, real gross domestic product increased 2.1 percent in 1979, 3.0 percent in 1980, 3.1 percent in 1981, and 5.5 percent in

1982.[41] The International Monetary Fund, on the other hand, reported a generally lower growth rate: 2.1 percent (1979), 1.8 percent (1980), 1.9 percent (1981), and 4.7 percent (1982).[42] Interestingly, the fund had misgivings about these figures. Its 1984 report thus noted: "The Statistical Office is in the process of revising statistics on national accounts and production. Its work is at the initial stage only, but preliminary indications are that previous estimates of Grenada's GDP, including those in this report, are inflated."[43] However, the revised figures by the statistical office failed to confirm this contention. On the contrary, it eventually reported higher real GDP growth of 2.1 percent for 1981 and 5.3 percent for 1982.[44]

The construction sector accounted for the bulk of this growth. Indeed, this sector recorded a growth rate of 20 percent between 1979 and 1983, caused mostly by infrastructural projects undertaken by the state. Although both traditional agriculture and tourism experienced sharp downturns, they were still regarded by the PRG as important generators of foreign exchange. In 1981, for example, the tourism sector—despite its sharp decline—contributed approximately 50 percent of Grenada's total foreign exchange earnings for that year.[45] The insignificant contribution of the manufacturing sector to the gross domestic product, coupled with its sluggish performance, reflected the failure of the PRG to change the historical antimanufacturing bias of Grenada's private sector. It was also indicative of the nonresponse of foreign capital to the government's investment code.[46]

In general, both the state and cooperative sectors performed dismally, with the exception of the National Commercial Bank. State enterprises failed to attain their targets and most of them recorded deficits. Their weaknesses were candidly admitted by the PRG in its 1982 report on the Grenadian economy.[47] Among the reasons noted were poor management, lack of organization, bad record keeping and accounting, low worker productivity, overstaffing, and the use of primitive technology. The cooperative sector also suffered from the same problems. The majority of these enterprises operated at a loss, rendering it impossible for the National Agricultural and Co-operative Development Agency to recover the loans it had made to them. The slow development of the cooperative sector meant that it was not able to contribute significantly to the gross domestic product or employment. As Coard noted, "our youth are more interested in working with government than in joining Co-ops."[48]

For the private sector and other opponents of the PRG, the deficits recorded by both the state and cooperative sectors were symbols of failure and evidence of the ill-founded premises of the government's development strategy. Their critique of the PRG's approach to economic and social development was articulated in a 1982 Chamber of Commerce conference paper entitled *Brief History of the Private Sector*. Its main theme was summarized as follows: "The commercial sector possesses the capacity to competently and competitively satisfy the needs of the society now and in the future."[49] The state enterprises were described as an "encroachment on the private sector." The principal sore spot was the MNIB, which had been given monopoly privilege in the importation of five basic commodities previously under private sector control. Supported by the IMF and the World Bank, the Chamber of Commerce also charged that the MNIB was operating under conditions of "unfair competition" and that it would ultimately marginalize the private sector "in the name of the people." The direction of the government's foreign policy was also scathingly criticized. Indeed, the decline in the tourist sector was attributed directly to this factor.[50]

As a result of this discontent, aggregate private sector investment fell dramatically, from US$5.4 million in 1980 to US$2.6 million in 1983.[51] Although the growth in public sector investment initially compensated for this decline, the situation became more precarious after 1981.[52] The government's investment program, which was almost exclusively dependent on foreign aid and concessionary loans, began to falter as a result of difficulties in mobilizing further external resources and of the poor performance of traditional exports. The airport was the only project that was kept going, given its highly symbolic nature and the PRG's determination to complete it in time for the fifth anniversary of the revolution. The liquidity problem eventually became so severe that dues and subscriptions to regional and international organizations went unpaid, a situation reminiscent of the Gairy era.

The social wage, which had increased dramatically during the first three years of the revolution, was also frozen in the face of the same budgetary pressures. In PRG parlance, the term was used to describe all the benefits that came with the revolution. Among those singled out by Coard in the *Report on the National Economy for 1982* were the provision of free secondary education, free school books, and free lunch and uniforms to impoverished children; the eradication of illiteracy; the provision of free or subsidized medicine to patients; the ruralization of social services (especially health facilities); the improvement of transportation services; and the institution of the house repair program and price controls.[53]

Largely as a result of the latter, the inflation rate fell to 7 percent in 1982, an achievement corroborated by the World Bank and the IMF, while the social gains represented by the former items in a poor society need no explanation.

The crisis in the economy further meant that the PRG was not able to sustain and consolidate the inroads it had made into the massive unemployment problem inherited from the Gairy regime. Estimated at 49 percent in 1979, the unemployment rate fell to 14 percent by April 1982, according to the PRG. However, this claim was rejected by both the IMF and the World Bank, largely on the grounds of data inadequacies.[54] Although both bodies were correct about inadequacies in labor force statistics, it does not follow that the PRG's claim was wholly inaccurate. Jobs were certainly generated during the government's tenure, if only because of the phenomenal capital expenditure undertaken in the public sector. What the PRG's *Report on the National Economy* (intended for public consumption) failed to point out was the seasonal nature of many of the jobs created and their overwhelming reliance on foreign resources. With the interruption of the public sector investment program (on account of cash flow problems), many of these workers were forced to rejoin the ranks of the unemployed, a development that led to much social discontent.

The situation was graphically summarized by a member of the Central Committee in the Extraordinary Meeting of mid-September 1983: "The honeymoon period of the revolution [is] over. In the past 4 ½ years progress was seen in many areas and the masses were on a high; now the work is becoming more difficult and complex. A striking feature in this period is the absence of the masses in the activities of the revolution because of the deep frustrations which exist. . . . The serious economic situation we face is affecting the people."[55]

In desperation, the PRG resorted to the IMF in August 1983, despite its awareness of the fund's notoriety in undermining and subverting the development strategy of progressive regimes.[56] The recourse to the IMF was a sure sign of the deteriorating state of the economy. In particular, it reflected the liquidity problem engulfing the economy and the PRG's inability to mobilize further resources from external and domestic sources on sufficiently congenial terms to continue to implement its various capital and social welfare programs. Claremont Kirton, a consultant on economic policy and economic planning to the PRG between 1980 and 1983, argued that the government had other motives for turning to the IMF at this juncture, including the belief that "once an IMF 'seal of approval' was granted to Grenada . . . a much more favourable economic climate would exist allowing for increased levels of participation of both domestic and foreign capital in the country's development efforts."[57] The government was also of the view, according to Kirton, that its bargaining power would be greater if it approached the IMF before the crisis manifested itself fully.

Whatever the true motive may have been, the 1983 IMF package was unprecedented by Grenadian standards. Unlike the previous standby arrangement in 1981, which involved only EC$9.25 million, a total of EC$39.7 million was negotiated on this occasion. The leverage of the IMF in dictating how these funds should be used was comparatively strong, given the crisis in the economy. The lion's share of the money was earmarked for what the IMF diagnosed as the main problems of the economy: the liquidity of the commercial banks, the growing indebtedness of the government, and the stifling of the private sector. Only EC$9.7 million was allocated to the government's investment program. A number of conditions stipulated by the IMF also ran counter to the government's development strategy. Among the most detrimental were the curtailment of the role of the state in foreign trade (particularly the activities of the MNIB), the imposition of ceilings on the contraction of further commercial loans, wage constraints for public sector workers, the trimming of government expenditure on social programs, and the introduction of new and increased tax measures to augment government revenue. These conditions, as they unfolded, would certainly have further alienated the social forces on which the PRG's development strategy relied.

## THE DEMISE OF THE REVOLUTION

It is clear from the captured documents that the crisis in the economy contributed in no small measure to the demise of the revolution. Issues relating to the economy surfaced on several occasions in the intense NJM debates after the party's Line of March meeting of September 1982. On this occasion, the economy inherited by the PRG was described as "backward" and "underdeveloped," with "a very low level . . . of technological and economic development [which] in turn resulted in very underdeveloped class formations."[58] The party was in effect conceding that the objective conditions in Grenada were not propitious for the construction of socialism.

By the time of the July plenary session of 1983, which lasted for a marathon fifty-four hours, the parlous state of the economy was being discussed at length. The difficulties in mobilizing external funds and procuring sums already promised were highlighted. The party was warned that "1983/1984 will be difficult years . . . requiring maximum efforts of the party on the economic front, hence the ideological work has to be stepped up to combat the consequent difficulties that these two years will pose for us."[59] Among the recommendations agreed to were the establishment of a Ministry of State Enterprises to generate badly needed efficiency in all public enterprises, the continuation of the government's land acquisition policy, the dispatch of a ministerial delegation to Libya to solicit funds, and the encouragement of the private sector to explore investment opportunities under the Caribbean Basin Initiative. The thinking underlying the last point was not made clear, given that it seemed to contradict other parts of the PRG's overall development strategy.

The problems on the economic front received further elaboration in the three-day Central Committee meeting of 14–16 September 1983. Significantly, the "comrades" at this meeting were of one accord—that the revolution was in crisis. The prevailing mood was summarized by Edward Layne's opening remarks: "The revolution now faces the greatest danger since 1979. There is great dispiritiveness and dissatisfaction among the people. . . . The state of the party at present is the lowest it has ever been. The international prestige of the party and revolution is compromised."[60]

So far as the economic dimensions of the crisis were concerned, Layne noted that "we are faced with the tasks of managing the state sector in great economic difficulties, to build the economy in the face of tremendous pressure from imperialism." In more telling terms, Tan Bartholomew added, "The economic problems are not explained to the people, and the church has grabbed a number of people in this situation." He described the 300 supporters who attended an indoor rally in Sauteurs as "a very weak turnout in the context of the amount of mobilisation done. Mobilisers were actually chased in some areas." Bishop also voiced concern about the state of the economy: "We have not paid sufficient regards to the material base of the country, changes in the economy, changes in social wages and the predominant petit bourgeois character of the masses and society as a whole. Our propaganda positions have consistently fed economism. . . . We have to take the blame for the over-economic expectation of the people."

Fitzroy Bain, George Louison, and Unison Whiteman, all noted for their strong allegiance to the prime minister, also remarked on the state of the economy and the party and the impact this crisis had had on the mood of the masses. In Bain's words, "the strongest supporters of the revolution are demoralised. . . . We had expected social benefits to do the work for us." Whiteman echoed the same sentiments. In his view, "the propaganda work [of the party] has been too idealistic on the economy. Too much time is spent on small issues instead of fundamental issues, e.g., the church. . . . We also need to think of how to build and sustain the mass organisations in the face of economic difficulties." The conclusions reached at this extraordinary meeting are instructive. It was concluded that "there is a state of deep crisis in the party and revolution. . . . The main reason for these weaknesses is the functioning of the Central Committee. . . . The crisis has also become a major contributing factor to the crisis in the country and revolution and the low mood of the masses. . . . The crisis has also been compounded by the weakness in the material base, electrical black outs, bad roads, retrenchments and jobs as an issue."

These remarks suggest that there was general consensus within the NJM, among both pro-Coard and pro-Bishop factions, that the revolution was in crisis and that the crisis had an important economic component. One cannot therefore accept the argument advanced by Gordon Lewis that the criticisms of the general progress of the revolution were exaggerated by the ultraleft faction within the party "to paint a dismal diagnosis of the patient in order that they, as the doctor, could move to undertake radical surgery." His claim that "the relationship between the public and private sectors remained buoyant, with both sectors enthusiastically working together, especially in tourism promotion" is also at variance with the facts.[61]

In sum, by 1983 the Grenadian economy was engulfed in a profound economic crisis. Although it cannot be claimed categorically that this was responsible for the parallel political crisis, it is clear that the former exacerbated the latter. In particular, adverse economic conditions did much to undermine the confidence of large segments of the population in the revolution. Significantly, in the intensive deliberation over solutions to the crisis, economics was completely subordinated to politics, as reflected by the party's firm insistence on Marxist-Leninist measures. Even if the proposed joint leadership model had been accepted by the prime minister, it is difficult to see how the economic crisis could have been averted. In all probability, the economy would have continued to bleed to death, forcing the regime to rethink its development strategy. The IMF would have also helped to ensure this outcome.

CONCLUSION

The disappointing performance of the Grenadian economy under the PRG should not be allowed to obscure the important gains made by the revolution. Among the most notable were the near completion of the international airport, which had been on the national agenda since 1955; the amelioration of price increases and, to a lesser extent, unemployment; the diversification of international economic relations and of foreign policy in general; the broadening of the country's export base (as witnessed by the development of new products—eggplants, various types of nectar, pepper sauce, mango chutney, nutmeg jelly, nutmeg jam, guava cheese, and a range of fruit juices); and the introduction of a number of initiatives in education, health care, housing, transportation, and culture. Indeed, so significant were these social advances in the first three years of the revolution that the World Bank was led to caution the regime that "the rate at which new social benefits such as those in education and health are introduced requires the attention of the government, as does the number of new public sector initiatives in areas which can be left to the private sector."[62]

Positive steps were also taken to marry the resources of the financial sector to the productive requirements of the national economy. The government's plans for the agricultural, tourism, and manufacturing sectors—with their emphasis on intersectoral linkages—were also laudable. Although the failure of the PRG to make substantial advances in the transformation of these sectors and the elimination of the other structural weaknesses of the economy (notably, dependence on foreign aid and borrowing) has not escaped the attention of critics, no leader (and no revolution, for that matter) could have reversed the intractable problems the government inherited in each of these sectors in a mere four and a half years.[63]

The PRG's main failure stemmed from the type of political organization it attempted to erect in Grenada. The slavish embrace of the Soviet-formulated theory of noncapitalist development was completely out of line with the realities at both the national and geopolitical levels. The refusal of the private sector to respond to the government's entreaties and the dislocation of the island's tourist industry almost overnight were clear manifestations of these objective realities. Ivar Oxaal captured the seriousness of this point for an earlier upheaval in Trinidad: "The intellectual's question, 'which models of the future are desirable?' becomes quickly transformed into the politician's question,

'which models of the future are possible?' "[64] In short, the real
failure of the PRG was political, rather than economic.

The PRG's experience has important lessons regarding developing a socialist project for Caribbean economies. One lesson is the
need to fashion a route to socialism congruent with local social,
cultural, and geopolitical conditions. This calls for innovation,
creativity, and adaptation rather than wholesale emulation of alien, authoritarian models that bear no relationship to the traditions or aspirations of Caribbean people. Since economic dyna-
mism, material advancement, and social justice inevitably
constitute the essence of the project, every effort should be made to
develop, at the very least, a modus vivendi with the United States
and other Western states, the natural partners of Caribbean economies, given their propinquity and resources. The economic benefits to be gained from maintaining some level of integration in the
international capitalist system should never be sacrificed in the
name of socialist purity, especially since the international socialist
system no longer offers a viable alternative.

Many of the reforms on the PRG's agenda could have been
achieved within a social democratic framework. Arguably, this
path would have had a greater chance of succeeding if it had been
pursued by the PRG. It would have certainly attracted a better
response from the tiny, but influential, private sector, whose cooperation was vital to the health of the economy. No doubt it would
have also reduced, although not eliminated, the hostility and suspicion of the United States and its allies. This, in turn, would have
abated the deterioration of the economy, thereby making it easier
for the regime to consolidate and extend its economic and social
achievements.

# 8 Political Economy and Foreign Policy in Puerto Rico

*Jorge Heine and Juan M. García-Passalacqua*

The ambivalence with which Puerto Rico's role in the Caribbean is regarded in the rest of the region was perhaps best expressed by the former prime minister of Barbados, Errol Barrow, while visiting Puerto Rico in May 1985. "Almost five hundred years after Columbus set foot in the Americas," he observed, "another Colón has discovered the Caribbean," the latter an allusion to Puerto Rican Governor Rafael Hernández Colón and his widely publicized Alliance for Prosperity, which had just been launched.[1] The mocking tone and undiplomatic nature of these and Barrow's ensuing remarks were, on the face of it, puzzling. As the economic powerhouse of the Caribbean, Puerto Rico could have done much to help the Eastern Caribbean economies, and although Barbados generally operated on a more solid footing than most of its neighbors in that subregion, to spurn Puerto Rico's offer to cooperate hardly seemed in keeping with Barbadian pragmatism and business sense. The question therefore arises, Was Barrow's skepticism justified, or will 1985 go down as a milestone in the region's evolution?

Taking as its point of departure the process of Caribbeanization that Puerto Rico underwent in the 1980s, this chapter examines the complex and ambiguous nature of Puerto Rico's ties with the region; it also aims to throw light on the changing nature of the island's political economy during the 1980s, as "the children of Bootstrap" struggled to come to terms with what some consider to be the Greek gift of Luis Muñoz Marín's legacy.

## SECTION 936 AND THE TWIN-PLANTS STRATEGY

As he started to chart the course of his incoming administration following his election victory in November 1984, Governor-elect Rafael Hernández Colón cannot have doubted that he faced extremely difficult circumstances. The island's economy was only starting to recover from its dismal performance in 1982 and 1983, the first two consecutive years of negative economic growth in half a century, during which the unemployment rate had reached an all-time high of 25 percent. The reelection of Ronald Reagan to a second term in the White House seemed to portend a second round of cuts in U.S. spending programs for Puerto Rico, perhaps even larger than the ones enacted in 1981 and 1982, which had wrought so much havoc in the island's economy.

Moreover, by allowing free entry into the U.S. market of a wide range of imports from the Caribbean and Central America, the Caribbean Basin Initiative which had become effective on 1 January 1984, in effect provided one of Puerto Rico's former economic advantages—unrestricted access to the U.S. market—to many of Puerto Rico's neighbors. Perhaps most ominous, however, was the movement to eliminate section 936 from the U.S. Tax Code, the provision that allowed the untaxed repatriation of the profits made by U.S.-registered corporations, thus making Puerto Rico attractive to U.S. manufacturing firms for setting up subsidiaries. These bleak economic perspectives were compounded by the unpromising nature of the political relationship that seemed likely to develop between a conservative, Republican administration in Washington and a Puerto Rican government headed by a liberal, autonomist governor widely identified as a "Kennedy Democrat."

Yet, over the next four years Puerto Rico's gross national product grew by 15.5 percent, to US$18.4 billion; per capita income reached US$5,157; unemployment declined to 15 percent, its lowest since 1974; and capital investment reached US$3.6 billion.[2] Not surprisingly under these circumstances, Governor Hernández Colón was reelected in the November 1988 elections; the ruling Popular Democratic Party (PDP) won such an overwhelming majority in the House and Senate that, for the first time since 1972, the rule whereby minority representatives were added to the House when the majority won more than two-thirds of the seats had to go into effect.[3]

There is little doubt that the political strategy developed by Hernández Colón to internationalize and Caribbeanize the key issues in the political economy of U.S.-Caribbean relations played a decisive role in this dramatic turnaround in the island's situation.[4] In an imaginative display of political craftsmanship, the seemingly unrelated issues of the Section 936 corporations and President Reagan's Caribbean Basin Initiative were linked. This effectively took the issue of U.S. policy toward Puerto Rico away from the accountants at the Treasury Department, concerned with the tax expenditures caused by Puerto Rico, to the makers of foreign policy in the State Department and the National Security Council.

Given the highly visible presidential commitment to the Caribbean Basin Initiative, and the difficulties the program was having in attracting U.S. investment to the region, the argument was made that Puerto Rico could play an important role in redressing that situation.[5] If Section 936 was kept intact, the government of Puerto Rico argued, up to US$700 million would be made available for investment in CBI-designated countries. The CBI itself had promised an increase of only US$350 million in U.S. assistance to the region. The sudden emergence of a program that might double that amount was a powerful incentive for the State Department and the National Security Council to deter the Treasury Department's efforts to eliminate Section 936.[6]

A carefully orchestrated campaign thus took place, in which Puerto Rico enlisted the support of Jamaica, Grenada, Dominica, Costa Rica, the Dominican Republic, and several other Caribbean countries to prevent the elimination of Section 936. Foreign leaders were urged to write to President Reagan requesting him to refrain from abolishing Section 936 and pointing out that the funds that would thus be made available from Puerto Rico would relieve the dire economic straits their countries were in.

Puerto Rico's emerging foreign policy, although triggered by the threat to Section 936 corporations, was a sophisticated response to a number of global changes of the 1980s. On the one hand, it used the high priority the Caribbean had acquired in the United States from the late 1970s to the mid-1980s as a bargaining chip with U.S. congressmen and members of the executive branch. On the other hand, it recognized the increased globalization of the world economy, as economic actors came to rely less on individual nation-states for their production and marketing operations, preferring to see the world as a single economic unit.[7] This latter element was vital for the "twin-plant" program subsequently set forth by Puerto Rico's Economic Development Administration.

The key tool to utilize the US$700 million in Section 936 funds deposited in the Government Development Bank would be the twin-plants mechanism. Since Puerto Rico's salary levels had made it uneconomical for many labor intensive industries to continue to base their operations on the island, manufacturers would split their operations between the initial, often more labor intensive, processing and the subsequent, more sophisticated and more capital intensive, completion of the product. The first phase of the production process would be moved from Puerto Rico to lower-cost locations in other parts of the Caribbean.

The twin plants strategy had existed for a long time, but only the government of Puerto Rico effectively made it the centerpiece of its Caribbean policy. By relying on the private sector, the program fit nicely with the ideological thrust of the Reagan administration's international economic policy and harnessed the increasingly global character of the manufacturing process of transnational corporations to Puerto Rico's best interests. The twin-plants financing scheme allowed Puerto Rico to take part in the U.S. governmental process through bargaining rather than special pleading. The fact that the major tax reform bill enacted by the U.S. Congress in late 1986—one of whose main features was the drastic cutback of a wide range of corporate tax exemptions—left Section 936 intact is the best evidence of the success of Governor Hernández Colón's overall strategy.

## BEYOND TWIN PLANTS

The Hernández Colón administration recognized that the internationalization of Puerto Rico's political economy had to go beyond the twin-plants program. It needed to develop a foreign policy that would allow the island to develop links to a number of countries, links that had not previously been possible due to Puerto Rico's relative isolation. This new foreign policy, in which Governor Hernández Colón for all practical purposes became his own foreign minister, had three concentric circles. The inside circle, and the most important, was formed by Puerto Rico's traditional friends, countries with which government and party links dated back to the 1950s: Venezuela, Costa Rica, and the Dominican Republic. The second circle included the Commonwealth Caribbean countries, particularly Jamaica, Grenada, and Dominica, all led by conservative governments close to the Reagan administration and all of which supported Puerto Rico in the battle to preserve Section 936. The third circle encompassed countries like Japan, the United Kingdom, West Germany, and Spain, advanced capitalist states and potential sources of new investment and capital.

Through a variety of means, therefore—whether by endorsing Venezuela's idea to set up a Caribbean Parliament with headquarters in San Juan, signing a treaty with Costa Rica, proposing a link between the electrical power systems of Puerto Rico and the Dominican Republic, inaugurating a program of visits abroad, or sponsoring the annual Caribbean Basin Conference—Governor Hernández Colón succeeded in making Puerto Rico a force to be reckoned with on the Caribbean scene.

In so doing, he was subjected to criticism in Puerto Rico. From the left, the president of the Partido Independentista Puertorriqueño, Rubén Berríos, violently denounced the increased use of Puerto Rico's national symbols and the fact that the governor was being received abroad with the honors and formalities normally accorded heads of state. For Berríos, all this was a pharisaic exercise in political manipulation, designed to take advantage of Puerto Rico's national pride. From the right, such a PDP stalwart as Salvador Tió argued that geography was but an accident, that Puerto Rico had nothing in common with its Commonwealth Caribbean neighbors, and that its Hispanic roots gave Puerto Rico its true identity. Paying obeisance to a long-standing idol of organizations such as the Institute of Puerto Rican Culture, Tió claimed that a revival of Hispanicism should be the primary goal of any effort to reassert Puerto Rico's international presence, rather than the forging of ties with the "black republics" of the West Indies. Puerto Rico's Caribbean policy thus resonated far beyond the economic sphere and brought to the fore issues of race and historical origins—issues of Puerto Rico's self-image and the possible Puerto Rican role in the Caribbean.

As for the rest of the Caribbean, the effects of Puerto Rico's policy were distinctly less than might have been expected. In a progress report to the Ways and Means Committee of the U.S. House of Representatives in September 1988, Fomento, Puerto Rico's Economic Development Administration, stated that it had promoted an investment of US$111.7 million in eleven CBI countries, creating as many as five thousand jobs. Even if taken at face value, this figure was at sharp variance with the US$700 million in investment funds Puerto Rico had originally offered and considerably less than the US$100 million a year cited later by Fomento in its scaled-down offer. As of December 1988, in fact, only three projects involving the use of Section 936 funds had been approved. One was a US$8.5 million loan to Jamaica for a housing project, one was a US$2 million loan for a cardboard factory in Dominica.

These facts were telling indictments of the extent of Puerto Rico's Caribbean program after three years.

Was Errol Barrow's skepticism therefore justified? What accounted for the seeming inability of Puerto Rico to translate its economic prowess into effective cooperation with other Caribbean countries? An answer to this question requires a broad historical assessment of the evolution of Puerto Rican–Caribbean relations.

## THE LEGACIES OF NONLINKAGE

Puerto Rico's failure to establish stronger economic, cultural, and political relations with the rest of the Caribbean and Latin America has been subjected to a number of interpretations.[8] The most widely known is the structural interpretation: given Puerto Rico's colonial condition as a territorial possession of the United States, it is simply unable to establish diplomatic relations with other nations.[9] Undoubtedly, the fact that the conduct of Puerto Rico's foreign relations is constitutionally entrusted to the U.S. State Department is a major obstacle to the development of an autonomous foreign policy. However, this dependence is not sufficient reason for Puerto Rico's relative isolation within the region. Other associated states in the Caribbean (the British Leeward and Windward Islands previous to independence and the Dutch Antilles) developed a more active international presence than Puerto Rico, and the Marshall Islands, another U.S. territorial possession, has more rights than Puerto Rico has to engage in international affairs. Moreover, the variety of international initiatives taken by the governments of Puerto Rico over the years demonstrate that, even under the restrictive legal framework of U.S.-Puerto Rican relations, Puerto Rico has a considerable measure of leeway in the international arena.[10]

A second interpretation is historical.[11] It argues that the dependency-incompetency syndrome affecting Puerto Rican foreign relations is due mainly to the absence of a national diplomatic tradition. In some measure associated with the structural interpretation in which it is rooted, this analysis suffers from the prescriptive conclusions derived from it as well as from a lack of predictive power. The only way to overcome the absence of a diplomatic tradition is to establish one. However, the efforts Puerto Rican governments have made in this arena have not led to continuity, consistency, and regularity. The many initiatives taken from the early 1950s to the mid-1960s were followed by almost twenty years of isolation, an isolation broken only in the early 1980s. The historical interpretation is also static: it is impossible to predict future changes on the basis of it, since the inner logic of the lack of a diplomatic tradition is self-perpetuation.

A third interpretation—ostensibly the most useful in terms of its explanatory power, though perhaps the least satisfying in scientific terms—is political.[12] It claims that the intensity of Puerto Rico's relations with the Caribbean depends essentially on the commitment to foreign relations of any given administration in Puerto Rico. Accordingly, it divides the evolution of these relations into five phases, which coincide with five Puerto Rican administrations.

Although useful as a way of understanding some variations in the policies followed by the governments of *different* parties (the statehood movement in Puerto Rico has been wary of ties with the Caribbean and Latin America, fearing they might interfere with the full integration of Puerto Rico into the United States as its fifty-first state, whereas the Popular Democratic Party has obviously not shared this fear), the political interpretation is of little help when it comes to explaining the significant differences in the conduct of foreign relations between governments of the *same* party. For example, it illuminates neither the progressive lack of interest in foreign relations of successive PDP administrations, ranging from the last term of Governor Luis Muñoz Marín (1961–65), through the government of Roberto Sánchez Vilella (1965–69), to the first term of Governor Rafael Hernández Colón (1973–77), nor the variations within any given administration. It is, of course, always possible to find contingent explanations for such fluctuations, but if our objective is to place Puerto Rico's relations with the Caribbean within a broader interpretative framework, we must necessarily go beyond the changing fortunes of any given administration.

The basic flaw of all three interpretations is that, in the best *insularista* tradition, they look at Puerto Rico in isolation, without taking into account the overall character of U.S. foreign policy and its particular impact on the Caribbean and Latin America. An examination of both sets of policies in conjunction—those followed by Washington and those followed by San Juan—might be of considerable help in explaining the fluctuations in the island's foreign relations. It might also explain the relative failure of Puerto Rico to establish economic, cultural, and political relations with its neighbors compatible with the enormous potential of Puerto Rico's contribution to Caribbean development and the benefits the island might derive from it. Both the explanatory and the predictive powers of this instrumental explanation are likely to be considerably greater than that of the alternative interpretations examined above. The evolution of Puerto Rico's foreign relations between 1948 and 1989 breaks into three phases. This new periodization lays the foundations for the instrumental interpretation.

## TOWARD A NEW PERIODIZATION

### Phase 1: From the Cold War to the Dominican Intervention

There is widespread consensus that the golden age of Puerto Rico's foreign relations took place in the Muñoz era. Starting with his election to the governorship in 1948, Muñoz played a key role in the creation of what has been called, with a certain degree of poetic license, the democratic left in the Caribbean.[13] Presidents José Figueres of Costa Rica and Rómulo Betancourt of Venezuela were the other important players in this movement, which fought dictatorships such as those of Rafael Leonidas Trujillo in the Dominican Republic and Marcos Pérez Jiménez in Venezuela, as well as revolutionary and socialist movements, such as that which triumphed in Cuba in what was perhaps the biggest defeat faced by the group. But, even beyond Muñoz's assistance to many Caribbean and Central American leaders in exile, for whom San Juan came to be a safe haven in a hostile world, it was also the case that Puerto Rico showed regional leadership in scientific and technical cooperation, in marked contrast to Puerto Rico's subsequent detachment.[14]

In short, Muñoz and Puerto Rico exercised a leadership in the Caribbean and Latin America that has remained unequaled by any of Muñoz's successors in La Fortaleza. Although the personality, ascendancy, and prestige of Muñoz played an important role in this, as did the talent of many of his collaborators, none of it would have been possible if his approach had not fit the needs and priorities of U.S. foreign policy for the Western Hemisphere and for the developing world in general. With the beginning of the Cold War, the United States had launched a program to win over "the hearts and minds" of Third World peoples, part of which was the so-called Point Four program, started by President Truman in 1949 to offer technical assistance to developing countries. As Morales Carrión put it, "Muñoz. . . . offered Puerto Rico as a training center, particularly for Latin Americans, and as a demonstration area for new techniques in matters like planning, education, public health and economic development. Truman . . . accepted and the program started under the Puerto Rico Planning Board."[15] This close linkage of Puerto Rico's Caribbean and Latin American policy with U.S. policy objectives was continued and expanded during the Eisenhower presidency and was reflected in the signing of a formal agreement between the island's government and the U.S. Agency for International Development (USAID).

The culmination of this collaboration took place with the Alliance for Progress, the ambitious and innovative development program launched during the presidency of John F. Kennedy in reaction to the Cuban revolution. Fomento administrator Teodoro Moscoso, the man behind Puerto Rico's Operation Bootstrap, was appointed as head of the alliance; Puerto Rico Undersecretary of State Arturo Morales Carrión was appointed Deputy Assistant Secretary for Inter-American Affairs in the State Department headed by Dean Rusk; and Arecibo, on Puerto Rico's north coast, was chosen as the training site for the Peace Corps volunteers going to Latin America. It is difficult, in other words, to conceive of a greater degree of overlap between U.S. policy and Puerto Rican toward the region.

Contrary to the conventional wisdom, however, Puerto Rico's interest in continuing its links with its Caribbean neighbors did not disappear once Muñoz left La Fortaleza and was replaced by Secretary of State Roberto Sánchez Vilella in 1964. In fact, during the first half of Sánchez's four-year term a number of important initiatives toward the region were undertaken. In 1965 Puerto Rico founded the Corporación de Desarrollo Económico del Caribe (CODECA), a government agency whose main objective was "to promote Caribbean regional integration" and "Puerto Rico's participation in the process."[16] Shortly afterward, the government also started to take an active role in the creation of the Caribbean Development Bank. By 1967, however, Puerto Rico had lost interest in regional developments, thus initiating the long period of isolation that lasted until 1982.

A number of reasons have been set forth for this unhinging of the island from its Caribbean environment, ranging from the departure of Secretary of State Carlos Lastra to the political difficulties that Sánchez faced within the PDP and that culminated in his loss of his party's nomination for the 1968 elections. Yet this shift of approach also clearly coincided with, and was not independent of, the growing lack of interest of the United States in the Caribbean and Latin America. The region had, after all, been a high priority area on the U.S. foreign policy agenda, thanks largely to the Cuban revolution and its ensuing crises (like the Bay of Pigs invasion in April 1961 and the missile crisis of October 1962). This preoccupation with the Caribbean reached its apex with the U.S. invasion of the Dominican Republic in April 1965; significantly, Sánchez's last bilateral international measure of any consequence was the creation of the Dominican–Puerto Rican Commission, made public with communiqués issued simultaneously in San Juan, Santo Domingo, and Washington, thus legitimizing the Balaguer regime set up by the United States after the invasion. After 1965, U.S. foreign policy concerns focused more and more on Southeast Asia, and the "Alliance that lost its way," as it was dubbed, died a natural death. Washington had lost interest in the Caribbean, and Puerto Rico followed suit.

## Phase 2: From Vietnam to the Grenadian Revolution

Puerto Rico's first elected pro-statehood government, headed by Luis A. Ferré (1969–73), discontinued the island's international activities, closing down CODECA and withdrawing from possible participation in the Caribbean Development Bank. With this last decision in particular, a precious opportunity for Puerto Rico to become a founding member of a regional organization that would subsequently help foster economic development and regional integration in the Commonwealth Caribbean had been missed.

However, more interesting from an analytic point of view was the continuing low international profile adopted by Puerto Rico after the PDP returned to power under Rafael Hernández Colón (1973–77). As Luis A. Passalacqua put it in 1979, "it starts with a strong expression of interest and statement of purpose, but its performance is so weak and pusillanimous that nowhere in the Caribbean is it understood."[17] The ideological and partisan explanation that underpinned the timid and weak-kneed policy of international withdrawal of Luis Ferré cannot be applied; so what does account for the fact that the rhetoric of commitment and interest in the Caribbean and Latin America, with which the government of Hernández Colón started out, was not followed up by action?

If the focus of analysis is shifted to Washington, the answer to the question becomes obvious. The 1973–77 period saw a critical transition in U.S. foreign policy, coinciding with Henry Kissinger's tenure as secretary of state. Having finally signed the Paris treaties that opened the doors for withdrawal from Vietnam, the United States began to deploy its diplomatic resources to resolve the Middle Eastern crisis, to reestablish relations with China, and to develop détente with the Soviet Union. In Kissinger's balance of power vision of world politics, the Third World was totally marginal and Latin America and the Caribbean were of little consequence.

Under these circumstances, there were no special programs for Latin America in the 1970s nor any high-profile presidential initiatives with which Puerto Rico could associate itself and thereby obtain economic and political benefits. In short, the incentives offered to Puerto Rico to become involved in the region and increase its international presence at either the bilateral or multilateral levels were minimal or simply nonexistent. Therefore, according to the instrumental framework, the first Hernández Colón administration behaved very rationally. After a series of initial statements aimed at marking the difference between its approach and the isolationist policies of Ferré, as well as at placating the Latin Americanists within the autonomist wing of the PDP, it worked on a redefinition of its association with the United States, with a view to increasing the already accelerating flow of federal funds to the island.

In fact, the degree of continuity in foreign relations between the first administration of Rafael Hernández Colón and the first of his successor and main political rival, Carlos Romero Barceló (1977–81), leader of the prostatehood New Progressive Party (NPP), is remarkable. Over and above certain semantic differences and some measures regarding possible membership in the Caribbean Development Bank, passivity and inaction continued to set the tone. Puerto Rico continued to see itself as an island closer to Manhattan than to Hispaniola. It was thus not until a radical change in U.S. foreign policy priorities took place in the early 1980s that the government of Carlos Romero Barceló, already in its second term (1981–85), came to "rediscover the Caribbean."

## Phase 3: From the Caribbean Basin Initiative to the Panama Invasion

During 1982, 1983, and (at a somewhat slower pace because of the electoral campaign) 1984, the government of Puerto Rico undertook a veritable pan-Caribbean offensive. This included the first visit of a Puerto Rican governor to Jamaica and the Dominican Republic, the active promotion of twin plants in the region to stop the outflow of labor intensive industry from Puerto Rico, the visit of Secretary of State Carlos Quirós to Jamaica, the Dominican Republic, and several states in the Eastern Caribbean, and a whole publicity campaign designed to sell Puerto Rico as the natural transportation, stock, and communications hub of the Caribbean. The same questions again arise: What triggered this sudden change in Puerto Rico's Caribbean policy from one four-year term to the other in a government headed by the same governor and inspired by the same political objective—to make Puerto Rico the fifty-first state of the Union? What made Governor Romero Barceló change his party's traditional hostility toward official links with the Caribbean? Once again, the answer has to be looked for in Washington rather than in San Juan.

In 1979 three events gave rise to a reevaluation of U.S. policy toward the Caribbean. The first was the Grenadian revolution in March, which brought to the fore a fear that many U.S. strategic analysts had been voicing in private: that the gradual withdrawal of Britain from the Eastern Caribbean (as more and more of its Associated States became independent) would lead to a power vacuum in the subregion and encourage revolutionary forces. The second was the Nicaraguan revolution in July, interpreted as proof that the hitherto stable and predictably pro-United States Central American dictatorships were undergoing a deep crisis. The third was the U.S. government's discovery in September of a Soviet brigade in Cuba. These developments led to a hardening of the Carter administration policy toward the Caribbean, a shift taken to its extreme by President Ronald Reagan, who both adopted a more militarized policy toward the region and launched the Caribbean Basin Initiative, perhaps the most significant and innovative policy initiative toward the region taken by any U.S. president since the Alliance for Progress.

Significantly, the role assigned to Puerto Rico in the CBI was minimal, in marked contrast to the precedent set in the 1960s with the Alliance for Progress. The Puerto Rican government was suddenly compelled to adjust to a new reality, in which it would have to compete with other Caribbean producers for a share of the U.S. market. Given the harm the CBI and its one-way free-trade zone threatened to cause Puerto Rico by granting to its neighbors one of its former exclusive advantages (i.e., unrestricted access to the U.S. market), Governor Carlos Romero Barceló tried to convince the U.S. government that in this new project Puerto Rico might be (and the expression is a revealing one) "the logical beachhead for the Caribbean Initiative."[18] In February 1982, only weeks before the long-awaited presidential speech that was to formally announce the CBI, the government of Romero Barceló launched its own "Caribbean offensive." He signed a special agreement with Jamaica, sought to increase trade with the Dominican Republic, and implemented Fomento measures to establish twin plants for industries already in Puerto Rico but considering leaving the island because of high labor costs.

Thus the long period of Puerto Rico's de facto isolation from the Caribbean, which began in the second half of the 1960s under a government ideologically committed to expanding Puerto Rico's Caribbean ties and served by many who had a proven record of engagement in regional affairs, was paradoxically broken by a government ideologically hostile to the establishment of ties with Puerto Rico's neighbors and whose leading officials looked upon the Latin American and Caribbean "republics" as potential opponents of Puerto Rico's incorporation into the United States as its fifty-first state. But the paradox was only apparent. From the late 1960s to the early 1980s, Latin America, and particularly the Caribbean and Central America, were relegated to the lowest of priorities for U.S. foreign policy. Given the rationale that guided the behavior of Puerto Rican governments in these affairs, Puerto Rico had little or nothing to gain from an involvement in regional affairs. The Grenadian revolution and the subsequent Central American crisis brought about a dramatic change in this situation, and the governments of both Romero Barceló (1981–85) and the second administration of Hernández Colón (1985–89) adjusted their behavior to these new realities. Both showed in their symbolic and material policies an interest in increasing Puerto Rico's involvement in the region and in making a contribution to Caribbean development that neither had shown during their first terms in office in the 1970s.

In general, then, this pattern of behavior is consistent with that which emerged in the late 1940s and continues: Puerto Rico is not so much a tool of U.S. policy as a user of U.S. policy to obtain its own ends.

CONCLUSION

It is in this context, then, that Puerto Rico's relations with the Caribbean has to be set. Its strategy is based not only on securing short-term economic benefits from the United States but on the notion that Puerto Rico, with its own emerging foreign policy, can make a contribution to U.S. strategic and military interests in the region. As Governor Hernández Colón observed in 1985, "the effort we are making raises the issue of Section 936 from a purely internal tax matter to the level of the fundamental issues in U.S. foreign policy."[19]

This rationale also helps explain the most apparent paradox of this Caribbean policy—why the very government that has done the most to strengthen ties between Puerto Rico and its neighbors is also the one that, abandoning the centrist and liberal tradition of the Popular Democratic Party, has endorsed the militaristic and interventionist policies of the Reagan and Bush administrations in the Caribbean and Central America.[20] Several sectors in Puerto Rico, including many members of the governor's own party, were surprised by the support given by candidate Hernández Colón to the Grenada invasion and by Governor Hernández Colón to the economic embargo against Nicaragua and the invasion of Panama. This surprise is misplaced.[21]

There is no contradiction between strengthening Puerto Rico's relations with the Caribbean and Latin America and support for U.S. military expansionism in the Caribbean Basin. The positions complement each other; they are in reality different faces of the same coin. To think otherwise would be to believe that Puerto Rico's Caribbean policy has been based on an attempt to bring Puerto Rico back into the fold of the Caribbean family of nations, something that would imply on the part of Puerto Rico a respect for the principles of nonintervention and self-determination. Any such reading of Puerto Rico's Caribbean policy is not compatible with the essential instrumentality of this policy. In the final analysis, Puerto Rico's ties with other Caribbean countries have no intrinsic value to Puerto Rico but are simply a means to obtain the benefits or to protect the privileges Puerto Rico gains through its relationship with the United States.

# 9 The Odyssey of Revolution in Cuba

*H. Michael Erisman*

*Two roads diverged in a wood, and I—*
*I took the one less traveled by,*
*And that has made all the difference.*
                    *—Robert Frost*

The Cuban revolution fits Frost's profile of both the trial and triumph of the pursuit of a unique identity, for Cuba has been engaged from the revolution on an odyssey that has taken it down paths unexplored by any other modern Caribbean nation. Such audacity has, as might be expected, met with mixed reactions and has generated intense controversy. In particular, questions emerged after the revolution with regard to Havana's status and role in Caribbean affairs. There was, of course, no question that the revolution fundamentally altered the region's political complexion. What remained to be seen was the extent to which the island would influence the rest of the Caribbean.

During the 1970s, Cuba's standing as a regional influence moved generally upward; for example, not only were diplomatic relations normalized with some of the area's important English-speaking nations, but the emergence of the Manley government in Jamaica and the New Jewel Revolution in Grenada meant that Havana had neighbors with ideological affinity. Furthermore, Grenada looked to Cuba for leadership in international affairs. By the late 1980s, however, Cuba's influence in the Caribbean, and elsewhere, was believed to have declined precipitously, and the Cuban model was seemingly no longer attractive. Some observers suggested that the revolution's decline was irreversible and could even lead to its demise.[1]

It is, of course, appropriate and important to analyze the larger implications of the Cuban model. What must be kept constantly in mind, however, is the fact that the revolution is an ongoing process rather than a finished event. This means that its leverage in the international arena has inevitably varied according to stage and circumstance (with some stages being more attractive to outsiders than others). As such, except for some very general long-term goals common to many contemporary Third World nations and some basic strategic principles entailing certain socialist mechanisms for development, there is not in the final sense of the term a "Cuban model" that other countries could emulate. Instead, what exists is a Cuban "experience" or "experiment," which can be seen as a dialectic whose dynamics have yet to be fully played out.

In addition, one must be careful not to focus too heavily upon the extremes; otherwise there will be a tendency to see the Cuban revolution in highly polarized terms: as a paradigm to be either embraced or repudiated; as either a complete success or an abject failure. Rather, attention should be directed at the synthesis of thesis and antithesis, examining its adequacy both as a response to the current environment and as a vehicle for making progress toward the revolution's long-term goals.

Adopting the latter approach, this chapter traces the evolution of the Cuban revolution as a regional influence in the Caribbean, with the larger Third World dimensions also receiving some attention. Special emphasis is placed upon developments in the island's domestic and international affairs during the 1980s. The basic argument of the chapter is that—while the dysfunctional interplay of these two dimensions, which characterized much of the 1980s, has since ameliorated somewhat—the situation in Cuba was too fluid as the revolution entered the 1990s for firm conclusions to be reached regarding Havana's influence in the Caribbean and other parts of the Third World.

## CUBA AND THE CARIBBEAN: A BRIEF HISTORICAL OVERVIEW

One aspect of socialist countries' approach to international affairs has been the dual nature of their foreign policies—they have conducted conventional state-to-state relations while simultaneously pursuing a distinct and sometimes even antithetical agenda at the party level. There have, for instance, been numerous examples of the Kremlin maintaining correct and even cordial ties with a particular government while at the same time supporting the efforts of indigenous communists to overthrow it. Havana has also been known to behave in like manner, particularly in the early years of the revolution. Consequently, when assessing Cuba's role as a regional influence in the Caribbean, such dualism must be taken into consideration, since the nature and extent of Havana's influence has always varied according to which dimension of its foreign policy is under scrutiny.

In general, Cuba has been much more stable in its role as a regional influence on the party side of the equation than on the state side. No sooner had the revolution triumphed than it developed a wide following among left-wing circles throughout the Caribbean and Latin America, a following that has remained strong throughout the years. Disputes have, to be sure, occasionally erupted, and in a few instances dissidents have become so dissatisfied with Havana's leadership that they have repudiated it.[2] Overall, however, Cuba's vanguard role among Latin American and Caribbean revolutionaries has not taken too many dramatic or unexpected turns. On the other hand, the island's state relations and their impact on its status as a regional influence has been much more volatile, with wide swings of the political pendulum. These dynamics demand special attention when tracing Cuba's Caribbean odyssey.

## Duality and Its Latent Tensions, 1959–1962

Once they have seized the reins of power, revolutionaries inevitably confront a paradox: some expect them to adhere to their principles (which implies an ongoing commitment to the radical restructuring of existing social orders), while others emphasize the need for moderation in wielding their newly acquired governmental authority, in order to establish their credentials as responsible members of the international community. Reconciling such cross-pressures is by no means an easy task, as the Fidelistas discovered.

The radical dimension of the new Cuban presence in the Caribbean quickly became apparent. In June 1959, for example, a rebel group sponsored by Havana landed in the Dominican Republic but was quickly wiped out by forces loyal to the government. In September 1959, another small insurgent band, which reportedly included Cubans and was said to have Che Guevara's enthusiastic backing, tried unsuccessfully to topple the Duvalier regime in Haiti.[3] Such swashbuckling was hardly new in the Caribbean; on the contrary, the practice of outsiders providing support and even leadership for attempts to overthrow such widely despised tyrants as the Duvaliers in Haiti, the Trujillos in the Dominican Republic, and the Somozas in Nicaragua was a well-established regional tradition.

Indeed, such highly respected leaders as José Figueres and

Rómulo Betancourt, who were hailed as the epitome of democratic moderation when they were elected president (of Costa Rica and Venezuela, respectively), were heavily involved during the late 1940s with the formation of the Caribbean Legion, a private multinational force patterned loosely after the international brigades of the Spanish Civil War and dedicated to overthrowing dictatorial regimes in the Caribbean and Central America.[4] In the early 1960s, however, there was little tolerance for such clearly subversive activities on Cuba's part, especially after Castro declared the revolution to be irrevocably Marxist-Leninist. At this point, the problem confronting the Fidelistas was not merely that a policy of revolutionary internationalism had the potential to generate a negative backlash but, more important, that Havana itself could be running serious security risks if it pursued a course that produced strained relations with nearby countries.

Cuba's main international concern throughout the whole of this early period was its deteriorating relations with the United States, which posed a growing danger to the revolution's very survival. Neither the Fidelistas' nationalism, expressed in stridently anti-American statements and in attempts to achieve full economic independence by expropriating foreign (mostly U.S.) businesses, nor their ideological leftism sat well with Washington, which was accustomed to Caribbean countries being docile client states. Consequently, the U.S. government launched a virulent anti-Cuban crusade, which included severing all diplomatic ties, organizing the Bay of Pigs invasion, instituting an economic blockade of the island, and attempting on several occasions to assassinate Castro.

As U.S. efforts to isolate Havana within the hemispheric international community escalated, so also did the tensions between the two components of Cuba's dualistic Caribbean policy. Specifically, pragmatism suggested that Cuba concentrate on maintaining solid government-to-government contacts with its neighbors to counteract the security threats implicit in Washington's campaign. In other words, the more isolated Cuba became, the greater its vulnerability to U.S. attempts to destabilize and destroy the revolution: as long as Havana remained committed to revolutionary internationalism, its prospects for cordial state relations in the Caribbean region were not promising.

## The Tumultuous Years of Fidelista Radicalism, 1962–1968

Given Havana's inability to implement its dual policy in the Caribbean and Washington's increasing success in isolating the island from the hemispheric community, Cuban foreign policy became increasingly radical, emphasizing close cooperation with Fidelista guerrilla movements committed to violent revolution. The clarion call for this new militancy was the Second Declaration of Havana, proclaimed by Castro on 4 February 1964. In an impassioned speech, Fidel eloquently pleaded the case for armed struggle, insisting that

> the duty of every revolutionary is to make the revolution. It is known that the revolution will triumph in America and throughout the world, but it is not for revolutionaries to sit in the doorways of their houses waiting for the corpse of imperialism to pass by.
> . . . From one end of the continent to the other they [the common people] are signaling with clarity that the hour has come—the hour of their redemption. Now the anonymous mass . . . is beginning to enter conclusively into its own history, is beginning to write it with its own blood, is beginning to suffer and die for it.[5]

As Castro made clear, Havana intended to plunge into the thick of the fray. While there would be some ebb and flow in Cuba's commitment to revolutionary violence, the Second Declaration generally set the overall tone for the era of Fidelista radicalism.[6] For those who embraced Havana's brand of Marxism, concrete support was forthcoming. In 1963, for example, the Colombian Army of National Liberation was organized by Cuban-trained leaders, with money sent from Cuba, while in Venezuela the authorities discovered a three-ton arms cache smuggled in by Havana for Venezuelan rebels. Such behavior naturally minimized the prospect of normal state relations, thus limiting Cuba's allies to small left-wing insurgent movements.

Although this somewhat puritanical radicalism was in part attributable to ideological zeal, security considerations also came into play. The Fidelistas' defense posture at this time was rather precarious. Washington persisted in its attempts to find an antidote to the "Castroite virus," managing to isolate Cuba by eventually persuading all the countries of the Western Hemisphere except Mexico to sever ties with the island. In partial response to this Yankee hostility, Havana established its Moscow connection and received economic and military assistance from the USSR. Yet Castro harbored serious doubts (which the Cuban missile crisis intensified) that Moscow would actually risk a military confrontation with the United States to defend Cuba.

The Fidelistas responded by extending aid to fraternal insurgent movements, the idea being to create diversions so that the United States could not devote its full attention to Cuba and possibly also to break the blockade by bringing to power new revolutionary allies. In the final analysis, however, Fidelista radicalism failed: the guerrilla offensive in Latin America was smashed; the associated ideological quarrel with Moscow left Cuba's Soviet connection in considerable disarray; Washington remained vehemently hostile; and the U.S. economic and diplomatic blockade continued to function effectively. Prudence—if not the revolution's very survival—seemed to demand some changes.

## Reconciliation and Regional Assertiveness, 1968–1980

One crucial shift made by the Cubans early in this period was to become more ecumenical in defining their friends. Rather than relying on the strict criteria that had in the past tended to limit its political partners to like-minded radicals, Havana became more flexible, giving higher priority to nationalist and antiimperialistic credentials than to philosophical orthodoxy. In the Western Hemisphere, for example, Cuba proclaimed its willingness to cooperate with noncommunist "progressive" regimes committed to socioeconomic reform and pursuing an independent foreign policy (which in Fidelista terms meant that the country could not be formally aligned with or consistently supportive of the United States). Thus, while not abandoning its pledge to support revolutionary movements, Havana did open the door to normalizing its relations with a broad spectrum of governments.

Operating within this new moderate framework, Cuba established diplomatic ties with the following Latin American and Caribbean countries during the early 1970s: Barbados, Guyana, Jamaica, Peru, and Trinidad and Tobago in 1972; Argentina in 1973; Venezuela in 1974; and Colombia in 1975. Chilean-Cuban relations were normalized in 1970 when Salvador Allende assumed the presidency in Santiago but were ruptured again when he was driven from power in 1973. Nevertheless, Cuba's new diplomatic respectability prompted the view that it was time to lift the sanctions imposed by the Organization of American States on Castro's government in 1964. Peru proposed this move in 1972, and it was approved in 1975.

The Caribbean nation with which Havana had the most cordial dealings during most of the 1970s was Jamaica, following Michael Manley's election as prime minister in 1972. Although a democratic socialist rather than a Marxist, Manley nevertheless displayed considerable admiration for the Cuban revolution (particularly following his reelection by a landslide in 1976); not only did his foreign policy take on a more radical, nonaligned coloration, but he exhibited growing interest in the Fidelista model of socio-economic development. Havana, as might be expected, responded enthusiastically; it extended substantial moral support (but rather less material support) to this new progressive Jamaican government. During his highly successful visit to Jamaica in October 1977, Castro seized every opportunity to stress his eagerness to extend developmental aid, promising Cuban-built schools, buses, tractors for sugar cooperatives, prefabricated housing for construction workers, and doctors, teachers, and technicians wherever they were needed. The attention lavished on Jamaica was symptomatic of Havana's desire to play an increasingly assertive role in the Caribbean. Developmental aid personnel were also dispatched to other countries, such as Guyana and Suriname.

Cuba's attempts to cultivate goodwill and influence in the Caribbean were not, however, limited to material rewards for those willing to maintain cordial ties with Havana. Symbolic gestures were also important. For example, in an attempt to improve their image and relations with the predominantly black, English-speaking nations of the Eastern Caribbean, the Fidelistas stressed their society's African heritage and their consequent cultural and historical affinity with the Lesser Antilles. To demonstrate the latter, they hosted—and gave immense publicity to—the Third Carifesta in July 1979.[7] Carifesta is a cultural celebration originating in the Commonwealth Caribbean and always previously held there. The Havana festivities marked the first time that a Hispanic state assumed a leading role in the event.

Although Cuba's efforts to establish itself as a regional influence in the Caribbean in the 1970s concentrated on conventional state-to-state relations, a major breakthrough in the radicalization of the area's politics (at least from Havana's perspective) occurred when a group of young leftists led by Maurice Bishop staged the Commonwealth Caribbean's first successful armed insurrection. They began to implement their brand of radical socialism in Grenada in March 1979. Although the Cubans played no direct role in Bishop's coup, they had over the years maintained strong fraternal relations at the party level with his New Jewel Movement and moved quickly to demonstrate their continuing solidarity by providing arms, security advisers, and various types of developmental assistance to the new revolutionary regime. The showcase project in this program was a new international airport, for which Havana would pay half the overall US$50-million cost, as well as doing most of the actual construction.

Ironically, just as it appeared that Cuba's increased Caribbean presence was beginning to pay major dividends, the political tide began to turn. Although the emergence of Bishop's regime in Grenada as well as the triumph of the Sandinistas in Nicaragua in July 1979 were obviously bright spots for Havana, elsewhere in the Caribbean moderate and often strongly anticommunist conservative parties scored a series of electoral victories over left-wing parties. The most important switch occurred in Jamaica in October 1980, when Edward Seaga defeated Michael Manley.[8] Shortly thereafter, following the lead of the new Reagan administration in Washington, Jamaica adopted a hard line anti-Cuban stance; diplomatic relations were severed in October 1981, and practically all Cubans were expelled from the island. As the 1970s ended, Havana's pursuit of regional influence once again became uncertain.

## The Uncertain Eighties: A Blurred Balance Sheet

During the 1970s, Cuba made considerable progress in pursuing its foreign policy agenda and increasing its influence on the international stage. In the 1980s, however, the Fidelistas had a somewhat stormier time, especially in their immediate Caribbean neighborhood, where developments in both the international and domestic realms combined to complicate Havana's efforts to consolidate and enhance its status as a regional influence.

The problems the Cubans faced were in some instances due to circumstances beyond their control. For example, Ronald Reagan entered the White House determined not only to implement the containment concept more vigorously than many of his predecessors but to incorporate into his foreign policy an idea dear to hard-line anti-Marxists in the United States—the rollback of communism. Accordingly, the Reagan doctrine, which committed Washington to providing strong material and logistical support for insurgent movements fighting to overthrow Marxist regimes in the Third World, began to be implemented, with the Caribbean–Central American region a major theater of operations. Such a policy, especially when combined with the 1983 U.S. invasion of Grenada, which demonstrated that the United States was willing to use its own troops to move against Caribbean governments it perceived as radical or aligned with Cuba, had a sobering effect in many quarters, causing some who might otherwise have been inclined toward cordial relations with Cuba to put some distance between themselves and Havana. Such tendencies were reinforced by the fact that Cuba did not always accord the Caribbean archipelago a prominent place on its international agenda during the 1980s. It gave higher priority to Central America and non-hemispheric Third World affairs. Ultimately, however, the extent to which Havana was still able to function as a regional Third World influence (especially over the long run) depended, as always, on the strength of the political foundations of the whole revolutionary experiment. In short, Cuba's stature rested heavily on its performance in both the domestic and international realms.

## The Domestic Dimension of the Influence Equation

While the list of variables that contributed to Havana's domestic performance is almost endless, three broad categories of activity receive special attention here: socioeconomic development; political efficacy (as it relates to maintaining systemic legitimacy); and human rights.

### Socioeconomic Performance

The broad developmental challenge confronting any society is essentially binary, demanding both increases in productivity and the establishment of structural safeguards to assure a roughly equitable distribution of the material benefits. Any serious modernization agenda must, therefore, not only concern itself with mastering the highly technical complexities of generating new wealth but must come to grips with the often explosive political issue of distributive justice. To the extent that the Cuban approach demonstrated a long-term capacity to do this, notwithstanding occasional setbacks and frustrations, Havana's stock in Third World circles appreciated. Chronic ineptness, on the other hand, implies an unraveling of the Cuban odyssey.

Evaluations of the revolution's economic productivity raise problems regarding data, especially in cross-national evaluations of Cuban productivity, since Havana uses accounting concepts rooted in Soviet-style economics that are not readily comparable to standard international criteria. For example, Cuba calculates its total productivity in terms of gross social product and gross material product, rather than the more commonly used gross national product and gross domestic product.[9] Unfortunately, since no consensus exists regarding appropriate conversion procedures, considerable controversy has raged over the revolution's performance, and various Cubanologists have applied their own particular formulas. The most vigorous debate occurred between what might be called the Zimbalist/Brundenius and the Mesa-Lago/Perez-Lopez camps.[10] The generalizations that follow draw primarily on the work of the former group.

During the 1970s, the Cuban economy, despite a shaky start attributable in part to the disruption caused by the unsuccessful campaign to bring in an unprecedented ten-million-ton sugar harvest in 1970, functioned quite well from a macroperspective. Although the specific figures for overall growth rates vary somewhat from one source to another, there is general agreement that trends in both the gross social product and gross material product were solidly upward throughout the decade. The most vigorous expansion, which was driven primarily by the high sugar prices being paid at the time on the international market, occurred during the 1970–75 period. The GSP and GMP rates contracted slightly in subsequent years but still remained healthy for the rest of the 1970s.[11]

The 1980s proved, however, to be another story, as Latin American and Caribbean economies were dealt a series of blows, which included dramatically reduced prices for many of their commodity exports, escalating costs for their petroleum and other imports, reduced markets for their goods due to recession in many developed Western countries, high inflation rates, and increasing unemployment. These factors combined to produce an overall gross national product growth rate of minus 2.8 percent for the period 1981–83.[12] Cuba, while not suffering as much as other states caught in this whirlwind, certainly did not escape unscathed.

Initially, it appeared that Havana, given its special (and privileged) relationship with the Soviet bloc, would be able to weather the storm. A striking example of the peculiar advantages Cuba acquired from its Moscow connection is in the dynamics of the sugar and oil trade. The USSR had for years, of course, been purchasing Cuban sugar at prices often markedly above the prevailing international rate. The rubles that the Fidelistas earned were then used to finance imports from the Soviet Union and Eastern Europe, chief among which was Russian petroleum.

A new dimension to these transactions in the early 1980s involved Moscow's agreement that Havana could reexport whatever Soviet oil it did not use. Thus with no reserves whatsoever of any significance, Cuba nevertheless became an oil exporter, earning US$1.9 billion in precious hard currency between 1981–1985.[13] Along with a solid performance by many other sectors of the

Cuban economy, this boost produced a very respectable average growth rate of approximately 8 percent a year from 1980 to 1984.[14] Even so, by the mid-1980s it became apparent that not only was it unreasonable to expect that such a pace could be sustained, but that the specter of economic retrenchment was looming. This possibility became reality during the rest of the decade, with foreign trade, debt, and unemployment emerging as the three areas exemplifying the revolution's productivity problems.

Cuba's foreign trade dependency has always been a key element in its economic health.[15] During the 1980s, however, its contribution was not very positive. For example, between 1980 and 1985 Havana ran up a negative trade balance of almost US$16 billion with the Soviet bloc and a little over US$2 billion with Western countries.[16] Conditions improved somewhat in the late 1980s, with Cuba transforming a 1986 deficit of US$199 million in convertible currency to a 1987 surplus of US$22.5 million. But as often happens, there was a price to be paid— in this case, drastic cuts in imports[17]—which meant greater austerity for both the domestic economy and the general populace.

Such negative trade balances have been an important, but not a unique, component of the difficulties Cuba has confronted in trying to satisfy its Western creditors. Havana has, of course, also run up large debts with the Soviet Union and various Eastern European countries, but it has not in practice had to worry about these obligations, since it has been standard practice to reschedule the payments whenever necessary. Western banks and governments, where the total amount owed by the Cubans increased from US$2.853 billion in 1981 to approximately US$6.77 billion in 1989, have not been as accommodating. As Cuba's deteriorating economic situation made it more difficult to service these debts, repeated efforts were made to renegotiate the terms of repayment. A series of agreements were concluded during the 1982–86 period, which did relieve some of the immediate pressure, but the debts were not forgiven and it was therefore necessary to take steps toward their eventual repayment. These included diversion of resources that otherwise could have been applied to broadening and strengthening the economy's productive capabilities, increased austerity for the Cuban public, and reduced employment.

Communist Cuba, like other socialist states, has prided itself on its commitment to providing everyone a full-time job. The data indicate that it has gone far toward achieving this target: its unemployment rates have consistently been far below those of pre-revolutionary Cuba and below the Latin American–Third World experience, in general.[18] The ranks of the island's unemployed have, however, expanded in the 1980s, official statistics indicating a 5–6 percent rate in the late 1980s.[19] Moreover, there have been increasing complaints, voiced most vehemently by Castro himself, that too many Cubans who do have jobs are not working very hard at them. Therefore, low unemployment does not necessarily imply higher productivity. Instead, the key to greater productivity in Cuba would seem to depend more on upgrading worker efficiency than generating new jobs.

Productivity provides a means to measure a society's economic muscle, but to fathom its heart, one must focus on its commitment to distributive justice. Ideally, maximum productivity will be combined with perfect distributive equity. Yet too often the latter is sacrificed to the former, one popular rationale being that to do otherwise would simply mean equal poverty for all. The Fidelistas, while perhaps recognizing that there is some truth to this proposition, insist that they have achieved an acceptable balance, pointing with particular pride to the advances they have made in promoting greater socioeconomic justice. Redistributing wealth has certainly been a major theme of the Cuban revolution; Castro embraced it early in the anti-Batista struggle, and for many it represents a litmus test of the revolution's success. As table 9.1 indicates, considerable progress has indeed been made in establishing more equitable income patterns.

Some may contend that the changes indicated in table 9.1 are not particularly dramatic, especially when one considers how far the lowest-paid decile was in 1978 from its fair share of 20 percent. According to Claes Brundenius, however, the critical statistic is the Gini coefficient. It indicates that there has indeed "been a radical redistribution of income in Cuba since the revolution, with the major transfer of income going to the bottom quintiles during the first years after 1959 and more moderate transfers during the latter part of the 1960s and the 1970s."[20] Therefore, Cuba has, in his opinion, definitely met the challenge of economic growth with equity.

In addition to their regular pay, nearly all Cubans receive a hidden income in the form of programs designed to meet their basic needs, programs operated and wholly financed by the state. Indeed, in these human services areas, especially education and health care, the revolution has made its greatest strides, as illustrated by table 9.2. Cuba's performance in relation to Latin America and the rest of the Third World can be measured by the physical quality of life index (PQLI). Admittedly, the PQLI, which is computed on the

*Table 9.1* Estimated Income Distribution, Cuba, 1953 and 1978 (percentage)

| Population Deciles | 1953 | 1978 |
|---|---|---|
| Lowest, 0–20 | 2.1 | 7.6 |
| Lower middle, 21–40 | 4.4 | 12.1 |
| Middle, 41–60 | 11.1 | 19.7 |
| Upper middle, 61–80 | 24.5 | 26.7 |
| Highest, 81–100 | 57.9 | 33.4 |
| Gini coefficient | 0.55 | 0.27 |

*Source:* Claes Brundenius, *Revolutionary Cuba: The Challenge of Economic Growth with Equity* (Boulder: Westview, 1984), 113, 116.

*Note:* The Gini coefficient is a measure of the degree of inequality. In the case of perfect equality, the coefficient is zero; in the opposite case, that of perfect inequality, the coefficient is 1.0.

*Table 9.2* Basic Needs Performance Data, Cuba, 1950s and 1980s

| Basic Need | 1950s | | 1980s | |
|---|---|---|---|---|
| Social security coverage in relation to total workers (percent) | 53.0 | (1958) | 100.0 | (1984) |
| Illiteracy rate (percent) | 23.6 | (1953) | 1.9 | (1981) |
| Life expectancy at birth (years) | 61.8 | (1955–60 average) | 73.0 | (1984) |
| Infant mortality rate (per 1,000 births) | 32.5 | (1958) | 15.0 | (1984) |
| Inhabitants per doctor | 1,067.0 | (1958) | 500.0 | (1984) |
| Per capita expenditures on public health (pesos) | 3.5 | (1958) | 72.6 | (1984) |
| Housing (percent) | | | | |
| In poor condition | 47.0 | (1953) | 31.0 | (1980) |
| In average condition | 40.0 | (1953) | 47.0 | (1980) |
| In good condition | 13.0 | (1953) | 22.0 | (1980) |

*Source:* José Luis Rodriguez, "Cubanology and the Provision of Basic Needs in the Cuban Revolution," in Andrew Zimbalist, ed., *Cuban Political Economy* (Boulder: Westview, 1988), 91–94.

basis of life expectancy, infant mortality, and literacy rates, has been criticized (and probably rightly so) as being too simplistic.[21] Nevertheless, it is one of the few mechanisms whereby human needs performance can be measured on a broad cross-national scale. It is therefore noteworthy that in 1984 Cuba had a PQLI score of 98 (out of a possible 100 points), the highest index for any Latin American country and, in fact, equal to that of the United States.[22]

What conclusions, then, can be reached as to how well Cuba fared during the 1980s in its two key developmental issues—

productivity and wealth and distributive justice? And what are the consequences for its regional and Third World influence? Certainly, the macroindicators suggest that Havana's attempts to expand its economic base suffered a series of setbacks during the 1980s: overall growth rates were down, the foreign debt was up, and little significant progress was made in moving beyond the island's traditional sugar monoculture to a more diversified economy. But these trends were hardly unique to Cuba, for almost every other country in Latin America and the Caribbean had similar experiences. Hence the revolution's prestige and the influence flowing from it should not be adversely affected in any major way by these productivity problems, especially when Havana did better than many other Third World governments in addressing them. Counterbalancing its negative economic growth was Cuba's continuing ability to maintain its commitment to distributive equity, unmatched by any other developing nation. Distributive justice rather than economic muscle has always been Cuba's trump card in the esoteric alchemy of transforming socioeconomic performance into political influence, and this equation did not change significantly during the 1980s.

*Political Efficacy Performance*

Most of the work involved in institutionalizing the Cuban revolution and in creating mechanisms to facilitate mass participation was undertaken in the 1970s. For example, extensive reforms implemented in 1973 almost totally revamped the judicial system, the Cuban Communist Party (PCC) held its first official congress in 1975, and a new constitution was adopted in 1976. Also, operating under the general rubric of "people's power" (*poder popular*), efforts were made to improve public administration through limited decentralization (entailing more grass roots control over local affairs) and to ensure more public input into governmental decision making (through the creation of the Cuban equivalent of an elected legislature, known as the National Assembly of People's Power).

Since there was little need for major initiatives in the 1980s, attention was focused on refining existing processes and structures, especially as they related to the party's role in society and to increased bureaucratic efficiency. The trends that emerged during the 1980s suggest that attempts were under way to decentralize and depersonalize power by grooming the PCC to serve as the organizational focal point of the revolution. Party membership grew from 202,807 in 1975 to 523,639 in 1986 (an increase of 156 percent).[23] Party congresses became a regular if relatively infrequent feature, with considerable fanfare accompanying both of those held during the decade (1980 and 1986). While such developments were consistent with the larger process of institutionalization launched in the 1970s, they also signaled the jettisoning of the charismatic brand of authority, which had characterized the revolution from its inception. However, it is probably still premature to expect major transformations along these lines, for Castro remains the epicenter of power and, indeed, has reaffirmed his commitment to a mobilizational style of politics, wherein his charismatic authority plays the central role.

To some degree, this resurrection of vintage Fidelismo can be attributed to Castro's concern about inefficiency, and even corruption, within the party as well as the government. In various diatribes both during and since the Third Party Congress, he indicated that those in positions of responsibility had sacrificed efficiency to bureaucratic manipulation and that abuse of status and power had become common. The Ochoa case in 1989, which revealed that some of Cuba's most respected military officers were deeply involved in the international drug trade, presented graphic evidence of the revolution's vulnerability to such scandals.[24]

Assessing the impact of these events on the average Cuban's sense of the revolution's political efficacy and legitimacy is extremely difficult. There are pessimists who believe that popular dissatisfaction is widespread and who point for support of their arguments to the Mariel exodus of April 1980: this dramatic boat lift clearly embarrassed the Cuban government, since most of the migrants were working class and could not be written off as neobourgeois elements. It also does not appear that significant gains were made in the 1980s in improving bureaucratic efficiency; nor, given Castro's skepticism about embracing *perestroika*-type reforms, can any major experimentation be expected in the near future. On the contrary, Havana has reverted to moral incentives to increase output and efficiency and to renew the dedication of the masses. Although this decision is usually explained in pragmatic instrumentalist terms, it may also suggest that there are some doubts about the depth of the people's commitment to building Cuban communism, especially among the youth, who have never endured the crucible of revolutionary struggle and may therefore lack collectivist ideals.

There is no doubt that the changes that swept Eastern Europe and the stunning defeat of the Sandinistas in Nicaragua's February

1990 elections contributed to a climate wherein Cuban dissidents, enboldened by what they perceived as a seminal shift in global political trends, became bolder in voicing their demands for Western-style pluralism and democracy. Such developments breathed new life into the anti-Castro activities of the exile community in the United States, whose claims that the revolution is on its last legs have received widespread publicity and whose convincing of Florida's governor to appoint a commission to plan for dealing with a noncommunist Cuba lent credence to speculation that Fidelismo is in its final death throes.

But despite the attention that such doomsday scenarios attract, little concrete evidence supports the contention that a legitimacy crisis is imminent in Cuba. Clearly, there is some discontent, part of which is likely the result of expectations lifted to unrealizable heights by the revolution's past successes in redistribution. Also, given the fact that the masses have been storming the revolutionary barricades for so long, it would not be surprising to find some political apathy rooted in psychological exhaustion, thereby creating the impression that the revolution is losing its vitality. What actually seems to have happened during the 1980s is that the revolution entered a retrenchment phase. Such phases have occurred before in Cuba, and obviously they do not enhance Cuba's position as an influence in the Caribbean or a major actor on the Third World stage.

## Human Rights Performance

The most controversial aspect of the Cuban revolution's domestic performance has always related to human rights. Beyond the fact that all governments consider such issues highly sensitive, the debate regarding Cuba is complicated by some basic conceptual discrepancies: the Western liberal democratic tradition tends to accord top priority to civil and procedural rights (e.g., freedom of speech and religion, due process, equality before the law), which protect the individual against the government; the Marxist-Leninist perspective emphasizes society's socioeconomic obligations to its members (e.g., housing, jobs, medical care). These philosophical differences produce opposite responses when these two sets of rights come into conflict. Communist countries like Cuba see nothing wrong with policies and practices that subordinate the interests of the individual to socioeconomic equality. This collectivist conception of rights was illustrated by Castro, when having been accused of violating human rights by refusing to allow those who did not embrace the government's Marxist ethos to express their views publicly, responded: "Within the Revolution—anything; outside the Revolution—nothing."

The United States has long tried to capitalize on such philosophical differences in order to undermine Cuba's prestige abroad. In particular, the Reagan administration launched a major campaign in the late 1980s to brand Havana as one of the world's most flagrant violators of human rights. Partially in response, Cuba permitted inspection visits in late 1988 by both the International Committee of the Red Cross and the UN Human Rights Commission (UNHRC). Neither group supported Washington's position, the most vigorous battle being waged at UNHRC's March 1989 meeting in Geneva, where the United States failed in its efforts to convince the commission to continue to monitor the human rights situation in Cuba. Instead, the view that prevailed seemed to suggest that UNHRC's members felt that, while some criticisms could perhaps be leveled, Havana's human rights performance was acceptable when measured against both the demands of its own ideological paradigm and contemporary international standards.

Despite such international victories, Cuba cannot claim to have won the war. The human rights issue is one of the weakest threads in the tapestry of international influence that Havana worked so hard to weave over the years. Although there is a crucial socioeconomic dimension to the human rights mosaic, in respect of which Cuba has performed in an exemplary fashion, and although very few Third World nations (and perhaps also some highly industrialized countries) can match the Cuban revolution's achievements in advancing egalitarian socioeconomic justice, uneasiness persists regarding Havana's human rights priorities and its apparent reluctance even to consider experimenting with multipartyism. Instead, say its critics, Cuba has opted to constrict its political space, going so far in August 1989 as to ban the circulation of two Soviet magazines—*Moscow News* and *Sputnik*—on the grounds that they were impugning Marxism-Leninism and promoting bourgeois democracy. No matter how logical or necessary such moves may be from a Fidelista perspective, they undermine Havana's prestige and leadership potential in areas like the English-speaking Caribbean, where the currents of civil libertarianism and political pluralism run deep.

## The International Dimension of the Influence Equation

As already indicated, during the latter part of the 1970s Cuba enjoyed an almost unprecedented string of successes in its Third World policies. Among the high points were the projection of its conventional military power into the Angolan and Ethiopian conflicts; its developmental aid programs, enabling it to show off its socioeconomic achievements; the expansion of diplomatic and trade relations in the Third World; and its assumption in 1979 of the chairmanship of the Non-Aligned Movement, establishing Cuba's acceptance into the inner circles of Third World leadership. However, the law of averages gradually caught up with Havana during the 1980s, as situations developed that lessened the revolution's international influence.

The most immediate problem was Afghanistan. The Soviets, by intervening militarily in late 1979 to ensure the emergence in Afghanistan of a pro-Moscow regime, created a worldwide wave of indignation. This reaction ultimately engulfed Havana and seriously undermined the prestige in the Third World that the Fidelistas had so carefully nurtured during the 1970s. The problem came to a head on 14 January 1980, when the UN General Assembly overwhelmingly passed a resolution condemning the Kremlin's invasion, with members of the Non-Aligned Movement voting fifty-six to nine (with twenty-six others abstaining or absent) in favor. Twenty-two developing nations not in the movement also backed the resolution, bringing the Third World total to seventy-eight for censure, nine against, and twenty-eight abstaining or absent.[25]

The General Assembly vote put the Cubans in an extremely uncomfortable position. On the one hand, they were grateful to Moscow for its aid and were under pressure to reciprocate. Conversely, there was strong sentiment within the Non-Aligned Movement, of which Afghanistan was a member and whose cause Havana (as the organization's head) was therefore expected to champion, that the Cubans were obligated—morally if not legally—to maintain solidarity with the Third World majority. Caught in the middle of a political tightrope, Havana desperately tried to decide which direction to go. It voted against the resolution and then tried to placate its nonaligned constituents by contending that it had done so, not because it approved of the Kremlin's invasion, but because it did not want to strengthen Washington's hand.

Few if any Third World nations were persuaded by this argument, as illustrated by the outcome of Cuba's bid for a seat on the UN Security Council. Even before the Afghanistan crisis, Cuba's battle with Colombia for the council's vacant Latin American slot was highly contested, with Washington strongly backing Bogotá as part of its campaign to undermine Cuba's international prestige. Although Cuba had led on most of the early ballots (usually by a substantial margin), neither country had been able to muster the necessary two-thirds majority. After the Afghanistan debacle, however, it became obvious that enough anti-Cuban sentiment had been generated to render a Fidelista victory impossible, and Havana therefore withdrew (with Mexico emerging as the compromise selection).

Cuba has always been susceptible to charges that it is too willing to sacrifice its Third World commitments to its ties with the USSR. This perspective became popularized in the 1970s as the "surrogate thesis," which held that Havana's international agenda was shaped and controlled by the Kremlin.[26] This analysis implied, of course, a negation of the whole concept of Cuba as a Caribbean or Third World influence, since the Fidelistas could not wield influence independently of the USSR. The Afghanistan crisis was thus a textbook illustration of the thesis. The Cubans, finding it impossible to finesse this contradiction, voted in a way that lent real credence to the accusation of surrogacy. As such, it was perhaps the best example during the 1980s of the havoc Havana's Moscow connection could wreak on its Caribbean–Third World odyssey.

Another factor complicating Cuba's efforts to maximize its Third World prestige in this period was its support of revolutionary elements in the Western Hemisphere and Africa. Such Fidelista radicalism had, of course, contributed to Havana's isolation in the 1960s, and this same response was again evident in the early 1980s. The source of discontent in this instance arose from Cuba's aid to radical left-wing regimes in Angola, Nicaragua, and Grenada. In addition, although there was considerable controversy over the extent of its material assistance, Havana was openly sympathetic toward the FMLN's (Farabundo Marti Front for National Liberation) armed struggle in El Salvador. This policy of proletarian internationalism, especially when it involved close military relationships with revolutionary regimes, immediately resurrected old fears about Cuba's commitment to subversion and to militant ideological expansionism.

Trepidation about these developments was probably most pronounced in the Commonwealth Caribbean, which at the time was experiencing something of a conservative renaissance, symbolized by Edward Seaga's victory in Jamaica. Such anticommunist proclivities were strongly encouraged by the Reagan administration, which was determined to cut the Cubans down to size. This environment was, to say the least, hardly conducive to enhancing or protecting Havana's Caribbean influence. The precariousness of Cuba's situation was driven home in Grenada, where in October 1983 the United States launched the invasion that destroyed Havana's efforts to utilize the New Jewel revolution as a showcase in the Eastern Caribbean for the Fidelista model of socioeconomic development.[27]

For all the heroism the Cubans displayed in fighting the American troops, Grenada was a major setback. Shortly afterward, the Fidelistas' previous close relations with Suriname also deteriorated, when the authorities in Paramaribo, apparently to placate Washington, expelled Cuba's ambassador and suspended all educational and cultural agreements with the island. Naturally, such a development undermined Havana's prospects for influencing Caribbean affairs. Certainly the fact that most of the English-speaking islands supported or acquiesced in the invasion (with Jamaica, Barbados, Antigua, Dominica, St. Lucia, and St. Vincent actually contributing troops to the operation) put them in a position of reinforcing the Reagan administration's virulent anti-Cubanism. Havana was thus confronted with even greater economic and political isolation in the Caribbean.

Even before the Grenada crisis, the Malvinas-Falklands war, which pitted Argentina against Britain, strained Havana's relations with the Commonwealth Caribbean nations. When fighting broke out in April 1982, the Fidelistas put aside their ideological quarrels with the military regime in Buenos Aires and rallied behind Argentina in a show of solidarity against what many Latin American governments felt was a reprehensible display of British (and U.S.) imperialism. Consequently, Havana's status within the hemisphere's Hispanic community improved considerably. The Commonwealth Caribbean reaction, however, was a different matter, for these countries were extremely critical of Buenos Aires for resorting to force in attempting to resolve its differences with London. This position was heavily influenced by the long-standing Guyana-Venezuela and Belize-Guatemala boundary disputes, in which a large chunk of each Commonwealth Caribbean country was being claimed by its powerful Hispanic neighbor. Guatemala, in fact, insisted that it owned all of Belize. The Commonwealth Caribbean states were, therefore, opposed to any action—

including the Argentine invasion of the Malvinas Islands—that might serve as a hemispheric precedent for a military solution to territorial controversies. Viewed from this perspective, Havana's stance was incompatible with continuing cordial ties with the Commonwealth Caribbean, since it had implications detrimental to the vital security interests of some of these countries.

The last major obstacle the Cuban odyssey confronted in the 1980s came from the same source as the first—the USSR. In this instance, rather than being ostracized for being too pro-Soviet (as happened in the Afghanistan case), Havana was criticized for its reluctance to embrace Gorbachev's call for "new thinking." The point was that Havana insisted, as it always had, on being stubbornly independent, and Castro made it clear that he saw neither a pragmatic need nor an ideological rationale for Cuba to set off along the same road that Gorbachev was traveling, especially when such a move might entail major unilateral concessions to Washington.[28]

This Cuban reaction to the Kremlin's initiatives was not received favorably in many Caribbean and Third World quarters. The complaint was that it was unnecessarily intransigent, locking Havana into a purely obstructionist role and thereby placing it on a collision course with the majority of nations, which hoped to capitalize on the remarkable opportunity to moderate international tensions presented by Gorbachev's flexible posture. In this context, Cuba could no longer be expected to exert significant influence on the international stage.

This analysis, while persuasive at first glance, overlooks the fact that Havana was not opposed to détente, per se. Rather, it has long contended that any process for ameliorating tensions and ending the Cold War must involve all countries, not just the superpowers and, perhaps, their European allies. Without such comprehensive involvement, Cuba argued, the more powerful nations (read the United States) believe they have carte blanche to pursue hegemonic policies in what they consider their natural spheres of influence. Such fears trace their roots to the fact that Moscow was never willing, despite repeated prodding by Havana, to guarantee that Soviet armed forces would defend Cuba if it was attacked by Washington. For the Cubans, then, Gorbachev's new thinking had ominous security overtones. Indeed, it portended the Kremlin's abdication from any commitment (even an informal one) to deter the United States from gunboat diplomacy in the Caribbean.

Havana's contention that East-West détente was unacceptable unless accompanied by a North-South counterpart may have become more palatable following the Bush administration's invasion of Panama in late 1989. While there was little sympathy in the Caribbean or Latin America for General Manuel Noriega's regime, the specter of resurgent unilateral Yankee interventionism raised the nationalist hackles of many hemispheric governments. Arguably, it may have engendered a climate in which Havana's caution about embracing any new international political order would be seen as constructive, rather than obstructive.

The positive connotations of Cuba's reaction to Gorbachev's agenda underscore the fact that Havana's international ledger during the 1980s was not written solely in red. The dynamics at work in the early 1990s in Cuban–Latin American and Commonwealth Caribbean–Latin American ties may well evolve into a triangular relationship, in which Havana would function as the fulcrum. In the 1980s, Havana's relations with Latin America improved significantly, particularly with such important countries as Argentina and Brazil. Buenos Aires announced in June 1984 that it was extending to Havana a three-year trade credit of US$200 million annually; Argentina received a contract in early 1986 to build eight hotels on Cuba's famed Varadero Beach in support of Havana's efforts to increase the island's tourist trade; later that year, arrangements were made to promote cooperation between Cuba and Argentina in the development of nuclear energy.[29] On the Brazilian front, diplomatic relations were restored in June 1986, followed by a flurry of activity to enhance bilateral trade. This general pattern—normalization and improvement of political ties as a prelude to expanded economic exchanges—was not uncommon. In a similar vein, the Commonwealth Caribbean countries, driven by the need to find new sources of trade and perhaps even aid, also displayed increased interest in strengthening linkages with Cuba.

Overall, then, a common denominator in the international agendas of most hemispheric nations during the 1980s was the desire to move beyond rhetoric to the reality of greater inter-American cooperation and integration. It is difficult to see how Cuba would not benefit from this process. At the least, the fact that Havana has been accepted into the family of Hispanic hemispheric nations increases the likelihood that any improvement in relations between the Commonwealth Caribbean and the Latin American mainland will also include détente with Cuba. Otherwise, the Commonwealth Caribbean countries would find themselves in the anomalous situation of trying to strengthen their Latin American connections while simultaneously ostracizing a country—Cuba—that has increasingly been accepted as part of that community. Moreover, Havana may be the natural candidate, given its status as both a major Caribbean power and a Latin American nation, to function as the broker between Caribbean countries and the Hispanic mainland. Such a role would obviously enhance considerably Havana's regional influence.

While the linkage scenario is admittedly speculative, hard evidence that Cuba's prestige has grown in Caribbean, Latin American, and Third World circles can be found in the fact that Havana received overwhelming support from these quarters in its 1989 bid for a seat on the UN Security Council. Cuba had, of course, sought this position in the early 1980s but had been frustrated by U.S. opposition and by recriminations deriving from the Afghanistan crisis. In this instance, however, even though Washington mounted yet another offensive, the Fidelistas prevailed with surprising ease. In May 1989, the Latin American–Caribbean caucus in the United Nations designated Cuba as its consensus nominee for the hemispheric seat being vacated by Brazil. When the formal General Assembly balloting occurred in October, Havana's candidacy received the largest number of votes ever recorded in such a Security Council election—146 countries, out of a possible 156, in favor. This triumph, along with other developments such as the OAS announcement that it would rescind the January 1962 suspension of Cuba's membership, suggests that Havana is again recognized as a major player in Caribbean and Latin American affairs.

Third World debt is another issue in which Cuba tried to assume a vanguard role.[30] In 1985 Havana began promoting a sweeping radical solution and calling for the creation of a cartel of Third World countries to pressure creditors to accept blanket cancellation of debt. Recognizing, however, that a straight write-off would be unacceptable because it could lead to chaos in Western financial circles, Castro also proposed that the governments of the developed countries guarantee repayment, arguing that the operation could easily be underwritten through a modest decrease (10–12 percent) in military spending. Finally, contending that the root causes of the debt problem could be traced to structural inequities in global economic relations, he insisted that the New International Economic Order, which Third World countries had long been demanding, had to be part of the package.

Havana obviously felt that the debt crisis was a cause that the hemisphere's diverse political and ideological elements could rally around. Accordingly, Cuba's initiatives were deliberately ecumenical. For instance, while supporting the efforts of the largest debtors to form the Cartegena Group as a forum for developing common debt renegotiation strategies, Havana also insisted that the concerns of smaller nations, such as those in the Commonwealth Caribbean, should not be ignored, noting that these countries often had per capita debts greater than the larger states and thus confronted situations proportionately more serious.

The two-stage strategy that Havana adopted to relate its debt campaign to the wider dynamics of Third World affairs was designed partly to enhance its overall international stature and influence. First, of course, the Cubans stressed that the crisis had to be viewed and handled as not only a Latin American but a global problem. The Western Hemisphere, they argued, simply happened to be the area where the situation was most acute and, therefore, where the major battles had to be fought. But the war affected practically all developing nations, and hence a comprehensive Third World solution was necessary. Second, to provide additional incentives for Third World countries to become involved in the debt question, Havana linked its debt cancellation scheme to two other issues, traditionally high priorities in Third World politics—a reversal of the U.S.-Soviet arms race and the establishment of a New International Economic Order.

Another consideration that probably enhanced Havana's international prestige in the late 1980s, especially in sub-Saharan Africa and the Commonwealth Caribbean, was the role Cuba played in helping Namibia free itself from the control of the white-minority regime in South Africa. Many Caribbean governments had not supported Havana's dispatching of combat forces in the mid-1970s to Angola to assist the Popular Movement for the Liberation of Angola consolidate its hold over the former Portuguese colony—the criticism generally being that Havana was serving as a surrogate for Soviet expansionism. Once involved, Cuba found it difficult to disengage, with the Cuban expeditionary force eventually reaching fifty thousand. Throughout, Havana insisted it would withdraw once there was no longer a direct South African threat to Angola's security, which realistically meant South Africa and its Angolan allies no longer using Namibia as a staging area for attacks on Angola.

In December 1988, after protracted negotiations, Cuba, Angola, and South Africa signed an agreement providing for Namibian independence in 1989 and a gradual, but ultimately total, withdrawal of Cuban combat troops from Angola. Whatever initial uneasiness there was about Havana's operations in Angola, these operations were undeniably pivotal in ending South Africa's control of Namibia.

Finally, the dramatic changes in superpower relations that began in the late 1980s have important ramifications concerning Havana's influence and standing. Specifically, as the perception of a Soviet menace recedes, the whole idea that Cuba represents a significant danger to other nations becomes much less credible. After all, such sentiment has always rested heavily on the conviction that the Fidelistas functioned primarily as the Kremlin's stalking horse in the international arena. Or as U.S. Senator Daniel Moynihan more colorfully put it, the Cubans have basically served as the modern Gurkhas of the Russian Empire. However, with the demise of the Soviet Union the most compelling reason for other countries to fear Cuba evaporated. Havana's status and role within the international community may instead be reconceptualized in more benign fashion to reflect Cuba as a Caribbean and Third World influence.

## Conclusion: Cuba's Prospects

In the early and mid-1980s, Cuba projected an aura of drift and indecision. By the decade's end, the picture was not necessarily any clearer. There were trends suggesting that the revolution had not lost its vitality and capacity to adapt. Whatever the twists and turns in its odyssey, Cuba still has many advantages in comparison to other developing countries, such as highly trained and motivated citizens, a good developmental infrastructure, strategic location, and strong leadership. It also displays many of the attributes and certainly the determination necessary to be a major player in Caribbean and Third World affairs.

Bringing uncertainty into this picture is the headlong rush toward a new political and economic order in Eastern Europe and the former Soviet Union. Cuba had previously pursued an ambitious international agenda through its privileged relationship with the COMECON (Council for Mutual Economic Assistance) community. Cuba's ability to extract trade and aid concessions meant that Eastern European resources could be drawn upon to stabilize the island's economy, thereby enabling the country to devote substantial attention to overseas initiatives (especially in the Third World). Indeed, Castro's effectiveness in orchestrating such arrangements while still maintaining policy autonomy stands as one of his most remarkable achievements.[31]

Developments in the early 1990s, however, raised serious questions as to whether such economic and political sustenance would continue. COMECON disintegrated, Germany was reunified, and the Soviet Union disintegrated. These changes foretell a somewhat bleak economic situation for Cuba. Adjustments will have to be made to accommodate new realities, which will almost certainly mean that Caribbean and Third World activism will be accorded a lower priority than before in order to allow Havana to deal with more pressing concerns. Castro has, however, shown a remarkable ability in the past to rebound from adversity, and no one should be surprised if he does so again.

# 10 Domestic Policy, the External Environment, and the Economic Crisis in the Caribbean

*Ramesh F. Ramsaran*

This chapter examines domestic policy and external factors, their interaction, and their impact on the economic conditions and performance of Commonwealth Caribbean countries during the 1980s and into the 1990s. In the period immediately following the attainment of political independence, either the significance of external factors for domestic planning was underrated, or it was assumed that the external environment would adjust to whatever domestic policies were adopted. The fact that the international situation was generally supportive of the development ethos in the 1960s encouraged this feeling. Despite progress in certain areas, persistent economic and social problems forced Commonwealth Caribbean countries to rethink the development paradigms that were once thought likely to lead to self-sustaining growth and greater economic independence. The experience of the 1970s and 1980s shattered the idealism and naivete associated with the economic nationalism of the early postindependence period. The preparation of development plans became less fashionable in the highly unstable and rapidly changing environment of the 1980s. Sensitivity to external developments and to the perceptions of aid donors increased significantly as Commonwealth Caribbean countries sought to refashion the framework of development against the background of their own and other experiences.

## THE ECONOMIC EXPERIENCE OF THE 1980s

Differences in economic performance among countries in the world economy have drawn increasing attention to issues of economic strategy. There is as a consequence an increasing perception that these strategies can be far more critical to growth than either a

238

country's size or its natural resources. In the Commonwealth Caribbean, postindependence economic strategy revolved largely around import substitution, the groundwork for which was, in certain cases—such as Jamaica and Trinidad and Tobago—laid even before independence. Whatever may have been the theoretical attractions of the import substitution model, its implementation was not properly thought out, and the process came to essentially involve local packaging or assembling of imported goods along with high import barriers. Efficiency and exporting received little attention, for job creation was the major objective. It was thought that import substitution would provide job opportunities for new entries into the labor market, and for the "excess" agricultural labor perceived to be associated with backwardness and underdevelopment. Modernization was synonymous with industry. The relative neglect of agriculture led to increasing dependence on foreign sources for food and raw materials, thus increasing the pressure on foreign exchange reserves.

To penetrate Commonwealth Caribbean markets, traditional suppliers simply entered into arrangements with local businessmen, arrangements that generally did not involve export development. With the import of machinery and intermediate inputs and the export of profits, dividends, and service payments, the export sector emerged as a net loser of foreign exchange. The incentives used favored capital intensive production processes, and so the employment creation potential was minimized. With the onset of the oil crisis in the 1970s and the emergence of adverse conditions in the traditional export sectors, the foreign exchange problem became more acute, particularly in the non-oil-producing countries of the region. External borrowing increased as governments sought to preserve both consumption and investment. Western banks, flushed as they were with liquidity, also encouraged commercial borrowing. Increased interest rates, reduced capital flows, and poor export performance thus resulted in a serious debt problem in the 1980s for countries such as Jamaica, Guyana, and, more recently, Trinidad and Tobago. Even for countries oriented toward tourism, like Barbados and Antigua, the external debt situation worsened in the 1980s.[1]

While the economic experience of the 1980s varied from country to country, the decade was a disastrous one for the Commonwealth Caribbean, generally. Indeed, it is widely viewed as a "lost decade of development" for the whole Latin American and Caribbean region.[2] For countries like Jamaica and Guyana, the economic setbacks of the 1970s persisted into the 1980s. For others, such as

Trinidad and Tobago, which managed to escape the impact of the oil shocks in the 1970s, other factors conspired to make the 1980s a period of decline or stagnation. In the case of Jamaica, though the economy grew by an average annual rate of 3.5 percent between 1986 and 1989, real gross domestic product in 1989 was still only about 5 percent above that of 1976. In 1977 the Guyanese economy entered a phase of such continuous decline that, by the early 1980s, real gross domestic product had fallen below the levels of the early 1970s. In the case of Trinidad and Tobago, the economy experienced seven consecutive years (1983–89) of negative growth. This followed an average growth rate of almost 7 percent in 1976–82. Following a period of buoyant growth between 1976 and 1980, the Barbadian economy also entered a period of stagnation. Real gross domestic product in 1988 is estimated to have been less than 10 percent above that of 1980. A combination of tourism, foreign aid, private capital, and in some cases, increased production of traditional crops enabled the smaller Eastern Caribbean countries to experience reasonable growth rates in the latter part of the 1970s and the 1980s. Antigua, St. Lucia, and St. Vincent experienced a growth rate of over 5 percent in real gross national product in 1980–87, while that for Dominica was about 4 percent.[3]

This poor economic performance was reflected in declining standards of living, balance of payments problems, deeper debt levels, and increased unemployment. In Trinidad and Tobago, real per capita gross national product declined by 6.4 percent between 1980 and 1987, in Jamaica by 2.5 percent, and in Guyana by 6.8 percent. Guyana's present per capita income dropped to less than that of Haiti, long regarded as the poorest country in the Western Hemisphere. Smaller islands such as St. Kitts and St. Lucia came to enjoy per capita incomes three to four times that of Guyana.[4] In a difficult period, the microeconomies generally performed more impressively than their larger, better-endowed neighbors, indicating the importance of foreign investment, monetary policy, and exchange control. Tourism seems to have been a crucial factor in helping the smaller islands deal with the foreign exchange problems that bedeviled the more developed countries. The pooling of reserves and the discipline inherent in a common central banking arrangement also helped the smaller islands maintain an atmosphere conducive to growth.

Poor economic performance was manifested in a wide range of other indexes. In many countries, foreign exchange reserves, government revenues, savings and investment, and nutritional standards fell to unsatisfactory levels. In addition, the problem of unemployment seemed endemic to the Commonwealth Caribbean. Even at the height of the oil boom, the economy of Trinidad and Tobago was not able to fully employ its labor force: in this wealthiest among the regional states, unemployment increased from 8.8 percent in 1980 to 22.4 percent in 1989. In Barbados, unemployment increased from 12.2 percent in 1981 to almost 20 percent late in the decade.[5] However, the stagnation of or decline in government revenue and the rapid growth in current expenditure were mainly responsible for the growth of the public debt, which, in turn, was the major reason for the reversal of certain policies in some countries.

Jamaica's outstanding external debt of US$4.5 billion, though not large compared to those of Brazil and Mexico, amounts to over 100 percent of gross domestic product and makes Jamaica one of the most highly indebted countries in the world. Like Jamaica, Guyana's external debt in absolute terms also does not seem large (about US$1 billion), but it amounts to over 200 percent of its gross domestic product. Barbados's official external public debt (including guaranteed debt), around US$500 million, increased by almost 700 percent between 1978 and 1988. With the drop in oil prices in the 1980s, Trinidad and Tobago's debt service ratio also increased sharply, though it is significantly below that of Jamaica, which is 40–50 percent. Because of its greatly reduced foreign exchange capacity, Guyana ceased servicing its foreign debt in the mid-1980s and temporarily lost access to new credit.[6] For that matter, Jamaica, Guyana, and Trinidad and Tobago all sought a rescheduling of their repayments of commercial and official loans and had to negotiate agreements with the IMF as necessary prior steps.[7]

To deal with the debt problem, Commonwealth Caribbean governments, either acting on their own initiatives or under pressure from external aid agencies, were forced to rationalize the pattern and growth of national expenditure. Cuts in wages and salaries, reductions in the public service work force, and the removal of subsidies even in the face of increasing prices worsened the social situation. In certain cases, capital expenditure suffered more significant cuts than current expenditure. Debt servicing unavoidably took high priority and in some countries became a major item of expenditure. The frequent and significant devaluations of key Caribbean currencies (e.g., Jamaican and Guyanese dollars) increased the pressure on servicing foreign debt. Between 1983 and mid-1990, for example, the Jamaican dollar was devalued by over 250 percent. In the same period, the Guyanese dollar's valuation against the U.S. dollar dropped from G$3 to G$45. Similarly, the

Trinidad and Tobago dollar stood at TT$4.25 to US$1 in October 1990, compared to TT$2.40 in December 1987.[8]

Although the Commonwealth Caribbean enjoys a standard of living higher than many other Third World regions, nutritional problems emerged in the 1980s. Furthermore, increasing unemployment and declining per capita incomes in some cases led to an increased crime rate. This deterioration in social conditions encouraged emigration in large numbers, particularly to Canada and the United States. The fact that some of the emigrants were highly skilled or trained people is bound to affect the prospects for recovery. In fact, their citizens' ability to migrate has long presented Caribbean governments with a dilemma: while emigration can cause a country to lose people trained at public expense, it nevertheless provides a safety valve, particularly when the unemployment rate is high and governments are unable to provide adequate social services. At the same time, the difference in the standard of living between Canada and the United States, on the one hand, and the rest of the Caribbean, on the other, exerts a strong pull. Whatever the reasons provided to the immigration authorities in the receiving countries, the economic factor is crucial, although other conditions do reinforce this factor.[9]

Of equal, if not greater, concern in the 1980s was the flight of capital, which is strongly related to a desire for safety and financial returns. Economic policies involving devaluations and inflation encouraged such flight. In such circumstances, schemes involving higher interest rates and political guarantees generally are not enough to persuade the return of savings for public use.[10] The fact that the flight of savings often took place through illegal channels tends to make the fear of punishment, particularly in situations where a government's credibility or integrity is in question, a serious disincentive to conditional repatriations.

In short, events in the 1980s indicate that the economic strategies pursued in the three decades following independence have not solved the economic and social problems facing the countries of the Commonwealth Caribbean. They continue to be extremely vulnerable. A few traditional products still dominate the export trade, and guaranteed markets and prices are, in certain cases, required for their survival. Production and export diversification has been an elusive goal. However, this record, in combination with changes in the international environment and the policies of the industrial countries, gradually forced Commonwealth Caribbean governments to rethink traditional approaches to development. The fact that states less endowed than those in this region

ducing repercussions that reinforced the economic vicissitudes associated with Caribbean economies. There was the illusion, too, that economic transformation entailed a simple formula, incorporating the creation of institutions and the investment of capital. Indeed, capital, mixed in a given proportion with labor, became the major tool of planners in projecting output growth.

This type of thinking was not confined to national governments. It formed the basis of aid programs and influenced regional and international development agencies. In a number of cases the physical infrastructure and social conditions did improve. However, production of nontraditional products on competitive terms was a major failure. With adverse price and marketing conditions for traditional products, substitute foreign exchange earners in the form of new products were limited. The prolonged and severe foreign exchange crisis of the 1980s and its continuation into the 1990s reflect downward production and price trends for major exports but also signaled a major turning point in the economic conditions of the Commonwealth Caribbean countries. It was not, in other words, a simple downward turn in the cycle: there were new and dynamic traders in the world economy. Technological and other marketing conditions influenced the bauxite market. Sugar prices were linked more to prices paid to European beet farmers than to the cost of production in the Caribbean. Oil prices fluctuated in response to factors completely outside regional control, and in the case of sugar and bananas, the intense political lobbying by Caribbean states evoked discouraging political responses.

The severity of the economic crisis of the 1980s shattered many early postindependence illusions. Reasonably good growth rates in the 1960s and early 1970s and the absence of severe foreign exchange problems had allowed a certain amount of autonomy in policy making and goal articulation. However, the need for IMF and World Bank assistance forced conformity to the ideology of these institutions. In Guyana, for example, the poor performance of state-owned enterprises in the context of persistent economic contraction and foreign exchange problems forced the government to sharply reduce the size of the state sector, which had grown in the 1970s to encompass every major area of the economy.[13] In order to create a more favorable atmosphere for private investment, the country's external relations were also revamped, with greater attention being paid to the United States and Britain, with whom relations had grown cool under former President Forbes Burnham. Unable to service its foreign debt, the country was effectively barred from raising new loans, particularly in the absence of an

were able, during the 1970s and 1980s, to significantly incı
manufactured exports points to the need for a critical apprais.
existing policies. In particular, it makes clear that the objective
which Caribbean countries aspired were inconsistent with th
increasing reliance on foreign savings, particularly when access
such savings required economic and political conduct likely ı
undermine longer-term goals.

For a long time, economic policies in the Caribbean were formulated on unproven presumptions drawn from other experiences
and on what was perceived to be an almost static international
environment. Policies were hardly ever reviewed even though goals
and objectives might fail to materialize. The economic idealism
articulated in the early postindependence years in the context of
unrealistic time frames and resource availability persisted despite
increasing evidence of its inability to move policy making in a
direction that could satisfy material needs. The attempts in
Guyana under Forbes Burnham to create a highly centralized economy and in Grenada under Maurice Bishop to do something of the
same, albeit for different purposes, were temporary aberrations
from the mixed-economy "industrialization by invitation" model,
which had become the regional norm. These experiments failed for
different reasons. In Guyana, the economic experiment foundered
on the politics of race and corruption, while in Grenada internal
dissension and external pressure contributed to the demise of the
Bishop regime.[11] Jamaica's flirtation with democratic socialism
under Michael Manley in the period 1972–80 was also a reaction to
the fact that this early postindependence strategy could not come
to terms with the social and economic problems of the country.[12]

With the private sector unable to respond adequately to the
varied government incentives, the state's role quickly expanded
from regulator to major actor, not only providing welfare services
but competing with the private sector. This was facilitated by a
perspective that saw development in purely economic terms. The
state became an instrument for achieving a wide range of nationalistic goals. Dependence on the state also increased gradually
over time, and its share in gross domestic product grew just as
steadily. Yet the role of the state in Commonwealth Caribbean
economies and societies has never been properly conceptualized.
Its various functions became intermixed, and it lost its focus in an
attempt to reform the colonial economy and society to satisfy
postindependence nationalistic aspirations and, later, to satisfy
the whims and fancies of politicians. In certain cases, it deteriorated into a major instrument of control and manipulation, pro-

agreement with the IMF (which suspended lending to Guyana in 1986). With funds raised by an external support group, outstanding debts to the IMF, the World Bank and the Caribbean Development Bank have lately been cleared, and lending has resumed against the background of an economic recovery program initiated by the Hoyte government in 1989 and closely monitored by the IMF. Privatization, devaluation, wage and salary guidelines, and the removal of various controls were major elements in this program, which was intended to reverse almost fifteen years of decline in an economy experiencing continuous flight of people and capital. The informal sector became more significant than the formal sector.

The picture is similar in other Commonwealth Caribbean states, notably Jamaica, where the Seaga government implemented no less than five IMF agreements during the 1980s. Even though Michael Manley returned to power in early 1989, his actions indicated that he was carrying on where Seaga left off, as far as relations with the Bretton Woods institutions are concerned. Jamaica's debt level and the need for external finance left him with little real choice. In Trinidad and Tobago, the National Alliance for Reconstruction government, which had strong aversions to seeking IMF assistance early in its life, entered into a second agreement with that institution, following a fourteen-month stand-by loan approved in January 1989.[14] It also successfully negotiated a structural adjustment loan with the World Bank. Finally, the deteriorating economic situation in Barbados was expected to lead to IMF involvement in that economy.

The adjustment process experienced during the 1980s thus indicates the strong influence of the IMF/World-Bank group, not only on macropolicies but on social policies, the role of the state, the role of the private sector, and the general orientation of the economy. Tax reforms and economic liberalization were intended to spur the private sector. The removal of price controls and subsidies and the dismantling of protective regimes, accompanied by adjustments in exchange rates, were designed to improve resource allocation and increase efficiency. The Caribbean, in short, was forced to accept a level of external intervention in the late 1980s that was inconceivable a few years earlier. The Bretton Woods institutions argue that adjustment is a long-term process, and results may not be immediately forthcoming. As the Jamaican and Trinidad and Tobago cases show, governments enter IMF/World-Bank-supported adjustment programs at great political peril. The longer it takes to reach the promised land, the greater the likelihood of social unrest, with all that implies for production, the attraction of tourists and private capital, and other features of the market model. There is another major side effect of adjustment, which may be felt in the long term: in the absence of adequate income or public assistance, nutritional deficiencies may occur, the result of which will be physical damage, with perhaps irreversible consequences. Social programs always tend to be afterthoughts rather than integrated parts of the adjustment process.

## CARIBBEAN DEVELOPMENT AND EXTERNAL FACTORS

The natural or structural openness of the small Commonwealth Caribbean economies makes them extremely vulnerable to external developments. Paradoxically, policies intended to reduce this vulnerability, particularly for the production base, have merely increased it. In response to nationalistic policies aimed at encouraging indigenous production and local ownership or at developing domestic expertise, the forms of external penetration have changed. External interests in the postindependence period, in fact, became more strongly tied to the survival of the economies themselves, even if the form was different. What is more, this foreign economic presence became increasingly acceptable, even though some of the new arrangements could stunt local initiatives and truly indigenous ventures. In the face of persisting unemployment and worsening economic conditions generally, policies geared to increasing economic independence tended to recede, as did the rhetoric of radicalism, which had been a reaction to the close ties with the imperial power. At the beginning of the 1990s, the populations of some countries had problems merely surviving day to day, underlining the narrowness of the available policy options. The need to obtain foreign resources in the absence of adequate domestic savings became intense. In such circumstances, succumbing to external dictates is easy. The goals may not need redefining, but the means clearly do.

Higher gross domestic product growth rates, increased employment, a more diversified economy in terms of output and exports, a more equitable distribution of income, and a generally higher standard of living are objectives that external aid donors and agencies have supported. Aid, however, can be provided for a variety of reasons and very often has little to do with development. In the case of the United States, for instance, which is the region's most important trading partner and aid donor, protecting or strengthening its own security is a major objective of aid, which, in turn, is often used to influence the behavior of states. Once the desired behavior is forthcoming, what happens to the aid itself is often immaterial. The poorer a country or the more critical its economic problems, the more likely it is it will accept the conditions attached to the aid. The United States also exerts influence through those institutions in which it is a major contributor, and assistance from these institutions is not always tailored to meet the needs of the recipients but often reflects the perceptions of the donors and serves their interests.[15] Developing countries have complained about the ideological bias of institutions like the IMF and the World Bank. Increasingly, structural adjustment programs that assume perfectly functioning markets and developed institutional structures have given rise to even more severe criticism in terms of their relevance and effectiveness.[16] Jamaica's continuing difficulties after more than a decade of IMF and World Bank involvement considerably fueled skepticism regarding their programs.

A similar reaction was generated with respect to the U.S. Caribbean Basin Initiative, which the Reagan administration launched with great fanfare in 1982 as an aid and trade package intended to help some twenty-two countries in Central America and the Caribbean. The structure of this program and the subsequent results prompted the question as to whether the United States was really interested in Caribbean development or was simply fashioning mechanisms of control through the carrot and the stick device.[17] The Caribbean Basin Initiative was to have lasted twelve years— which in itself seems at variance with serious private investment, which needs longer-term guarantees. In the early stages of the discussions, a 10 percent tax credit was proposed to push this objective, but this incentive was omitted in the final document. As a consequence, foreign private investment in the region declined. The impact of the new products said to be manufactured in the Commonwealth Caribbean as a result of this CBI arrangement is difficult to discern, but the limited number of offshore assembly plants initiated in recent years has made no noticeable impression on economic conditions. Nor have the US$10 billion of Section 936 funds, reportedly available for investment in the region, been translated into projects of any significance.[18]

Another major objective of the Caribbean Basin Initiative was to promote the export of nontraditional manufactures to the U.S. market, where the bulk of traditional goods already entered duty free or at preferential rates under the Generalized System of Preferences adopted in the 1970s. Yet, in deference to lobbyists, the agreement excluded a range of products—including textiles, luggage, leather, apparel, petroleum, and petroleum products—that

Caribbean states manufacture for export. In response to mounting criticism, the U.S. government took some limited action in 1986 with respect to the Caribbean garment industry by implementing a special regime allowing for reexport to the United States of garments assembled from fabrics made and cut in the United States. In bilateral treaties, Caribbean states were guaranteed specific export quantities of garments, with duty paid in the United States only on the value added by assembly, and were allowed to export agreed-upon quantities produced from fabrics made in other countries.

Despite the Caribbean Basin Initiative and subsequent changes, trade between the Caribbean and the United States did not grow to the degree initially envisaged or to a point where trade with the United States made a major impact on the foreign exchange position of these countries. The evidence in fact indicates that, in some ways, their trading positions may have worsened after the Caribbean Basin Initiative. Exports to the United States from twenty-two states declined from US$8.73 billion in 1983 to US$6.18 billion in 1988.[19] One U.S. official argued that this drop reflects the fall in oil prices in the period, whereas the reality is that production of goods such as chemicals, fruits and vegetables, and manufactured goods were increasing.[20] While there may be some truth to his argument, particularly using global figures, a specific examination of the Commonwealth Caribbean region shows that for most countries the impact of the initiative on the trade situation was extremely limited. Even where some growth in nontraditional products took place, as in Jamaica, it was highly concentrated in a few products. In itself, this is not surprising. The limit placed on the life of the Caribbean Basin Initiative, as indicated earlier, was a major constraint on investment. It was also felt that, because the initiative was not a negotiated agreement, it could be withdrawn unilaterally—and this, too, was not conducive to investment.

In general, then, U.S. policy with respect to products that the Caribbean was capable of exporting competitively raises questions about whether the United States was interested in promoting trade or merely in influencing policies in these states at minimal cost to itself. Sugar is another case in point: sugar and its by-products were still important products, both economically and socially, for several countries of the region, such as Jamaica, St. Kitts–Nevis, Guyana, and Trinidad and Tobago. Yet despite the pleadings of these states, the United States reduced sugar quotas in response to domestic lobbyists (see table 10.1). Also, the export of steel from Trinidad and Tobago, which forms an insignificant proportion of

*Table 10.1*   U.S. Sugar Import Quotas from the Caribbean, 1986–1989
(short tons)

| Country | 1986 | 1987 | 1988 | 1988 (revised) | 1989 |
|---|---|---|---|---|---|
| Barbados | 12,500 | 7,500 | 5,770 | 8,205 | 7,444 |
| Belize | 18,886 | 10,010 | 7,770 | 11,045 | 11,583 |
| Guyana | 20,952 | 10,920 | 8,400 | 12,050 | 7,258 |
| Jamaica | 18,886 | 10,010 | 7,770 | 11,045 | 11,583 |
| St. Kitts–Nevis | 12,500 | 7,500 | 5,770 | 8,000 | 7,258 |
| Trinidad and Tobago | 12,500 | 7,500 | 5,770 | 8,205 | 7,444 |
| Total Commonwealth Caribbean | 96,224 | 53,440 | 41,250 | 58,550 | 52,570 |

*Sources: Caribbean Insight*, various issues; CECON *Trade News*, various issues.

U.S. steel imports, was made subject to a voluntary export restraint.

The U.S. Congress later formalized the second Caribbean Basin Initiative after protracted discussions, but Caribbean states were not enthusiastic. Although tariffs on some products were reduced and the initiative has now been made indefinite, the lobbyists still won the day. Many of the suggestions put forward by Caribbean states were ignored. Incidentally, in 1986 Canada introduced a similar agreement, called CARIBCAN. It also had a life span of twelve years and also excluded a range of products of interest to the Caribbean, including footwear, clothing, textiles, luggage, handbags, leather goods, lubricating oils, and methanol. Since CARIBCAN suffered from the same kinds of deficiencies as the CBI, there were suggestions that the CBI and CARIBCAN should be merged and the Caribbean be guaranteed a part of the U.S. and Canadian market for a select range of products, such as sugar, textiles, and clothing. With respect to the latter, the fear in the United States is that producers from Southeast Asia would try to overcome U.S. quotas on their own exports by moving to the Caribbean and using the areas as a base for further penetration of the U.S. market. Although such arguments have been used to prohibit a range of imports from the region, they are particularly weak with respect to the garment industry, which has a long tradition as a skilled and organized trade and is perhaps one of the most indigenous sectors of the Caribbean economy. Caribbean countries thus found that, while they were being asked to liberalize their economies and become more competitive, restrictions by the rich countries continued. The pressure from international organizations on the Caribbean countries to remove trade barriers and produce on the basis of comparative advantage while not addressing the issue of trade restrictions in the rich countries only delays adjustment and worsens the already critical social situation, which has led to the flight of people from the region.

The United States, like other industrial countries, provided little support during the 1980s for international commodity agreements that could have brought some order to the market. Caribbean and Latin American countries complained that, while the United States put pressure on them to discourage the production of illegal drugs, it did little to help them remove the social and economic conditions that encouraged drug trafficking, and to them the two were linked. The development of service industries, like offshore banking, and the introduction of casino gambling to enhance tourism were to some extent a reaction to the difficulties in developing the goods sector. Regardless of their economic situation, countries perceived as not doing enough to discourage the drug trade could find themselves the subject of U.S. trade and aid sanctions.[21] Commonwealth Caribbean countries, particularly those like the Bahamas that became closely associated with the drug trade, had to continually publicize their efforts at discouraging drug trafficking. Gradually, the U.S. focus shifted to drug producing and transit countries.[22]

Since the early 1970s, the Commonwealth Caribbean enjoyed preferential access to the markets of the major industrial countries under the Generalized System of Preferences and the Lomé Conventions, and the CBI and CARIBCAN only enhanced these arrangements. Yet the economies of the region were not able to penetrate these markets with nontraditional products. There are, of course, problems on the supply side. But the nominal free access was offset by nontariff barriers and by bureaucratic arrangements of various kinds. The Commonwealth Caribbean's weakness in the area of trade promotion and marketing techniques did not help matters. They needed to develop effective marketing strategies and to understand the competitiveness of the market. The margin of preference traditionally enjoyed by Commonwealth Caribbean states in the European Community was eroded as a result of the EC's participation in the General Agreement on Tariffs and Trade discussions and the EC's concessions to other developing countries.

Commonwealth Caribbean countries traditionally gave an important role to foreign savings in their economic development, but following independence, they attempted to reduce foreign involvement in key sectors of their economies. One result of this policy

*Table 10.2*   U.S. Direct Investment Position in the Caribbean, 1980–1987

| Country | 1980 | 1985 | 1986 | 1987 |
|---|---|---|---|---|
| Bahamas | 2,712 | 3,795 | 2,762 | 2,566 |
| Bermuda | 11,045 | 13,116 | 14,765 | 18,229 |
| Jamaica | 429 | 122 | 107 | 90 |
| Netherlands Antilles | −4,336 | −20,499 | −15,817 | −13,208 |
| Trinidad and Tobago | 951 | 484 | 368 | 356 |
| U.K. [Caribbean] islands | 979 | 3,490 | 3,771 | 3,970 |

*Source:* U.S. Department of Commerce, *Survey of Current Business,* various issues.
*Note:* Bahamas, Bermuda, and Netherlands Antilles are tax havens.

was declining U.S. direct investment in some countries of the region (see table 10.2). Although there was some ambivalence toward private foreign capital during the 1980s, a role for foreign investment in some sectors of the economy was still envisaged, and incentives were offered to attract investors. However, the forms of direct investment changed over time,[23] as did the whole investment environment. Developments in transportation, communication, and technology influenced the pattern of private investment during the 1980s. Increasingly, the Caribbean had to compete with economies with better growth records, more liberal tax regimes, and a less regulated environment. There was also a flight of capital from the Caribbean, even from politically stable states like Barbados.[24] Nor were the various new measures put in place in Jamaica able to reverse the same trend in that country.[25]

With inadequate domestic savings, poorly performing local private sectors, and pressure from donors and agencies, the Commonwealth Caribbean made greater efforts during the 1980s to attract foreign private capital. These efforts were related to a commitment to reduce the role of the state in the economy and to encourage the private sector. Against the background of the nationalizations of the 1960s and 1970s, and given the depressed state of some of the economies in the region, the response of foreign private investment was far from satisfactory. Competition among regional states and from the larger world community put foreign investors in a position to dictate the terms of their involvement in a particular economy. The operational dimensions of sovereignty for small states have always been a subject of speculation but became increasingly so in view of their need to raise standards of living for populations exposed, through various media, to the consumption habits of the United States and other rich countries. This exposure

is continuous and has a more lasting effect on people's expectations than their occasional glimpses of life in poorer countries
such as Bangladesh, Ethiopia, and the Sudan.

To show their commitment to attracting private foreign enterprise, some Commonwealth Caribbean countries, such as Jamaica,
Guyana, Barbados, and Trinidad and Tobago, became members of
international agreements (e.g., the International Centre for the
Settlement of International Disputes associated with the World
Bank) or, as in the case of St. Lucia, signed bilateral treaties with
individual governments offering certain guarantees to their investors.[26] The Multilateral Guarantee Insurance Arrangement set up
by the World Bank is also intended to provide guarantees against
certain kinds of political risks. In the Lomé IV negotiations, the
European Community refused to make a multilateral guarantee
part of the convention but insisted instead that African, Caribbean, and Pacific states be encouraged to enter into bilateral agreements. The developed countries seemed to think that encouraging
private capital flows to developing countries mainly required protection against political risks, but there were also economic factors
involved. Frequent and significant changes in the exchange rates of
domestic currencies was one factor. Bureaucracy was also a major
factor. And the absence of a dynamic local private sector was seen
as an indication of poor economic performance, inefficient or costly labor, or an inadequate regulatory framework. The hope that
external actors would make the difference in the Commonwealth
Caribbean may have been misplaced: a whole range of social, political, and economic changes designed to increase the effectiveness
of human and other resources and to encourage creativity and
enterprise were prerequisites. In a similar way, educational policies lacked a developmental thrust, partly as a result of the view
that economic instruments by themselves would instigate change.

The emphasis on private investment can be also laid at the door
of the critical public debt situation of a number of countries in the
Commonwealth Caribbean. Of the many factors that contributed
to this debt situation, among the most important were the production and marketing of traditional exports. The lack of adequate
controls over borrowing and the financing of consumption with
borrowed funds also contributed, as did the undertaking of badly
conceived projects. The failure to raise soft loans led to borrowing
on hard terms from private sources. In the absence of satisfactory
export performances, further borrowing became necessary to service past loans, which exacerbated the debt position. Rescheduling
eases debt service but does not reduce the debt, which means that

countries that resorted to rescheduling found their debt growing as a result of new credits and capitalized interest payments.

The serious debt situation of the early 1990s could get worse. As small middle-income debtors, Commonwealth Caribbean countries are not likely to attract the assistance that large debtors, like Brazil and Mexico, attracted. Yet there were signs of the beginnings of an international political response incorporating the region. In March 1990 the Canadian government took a major initiative by forgiving Can$182 million of outstanding assistance owed by Commonwealth Caribbean countries to Canada. President Bush followed in June 1990 with a broader program encompassing both the Caribbean and Latin America. Termed the Enterprise for the Americas, the plan was built around three elements: (1) restructuring or reducing the debt owed by Latin America and the Caribbean to the U.S. government (about US$12 billion), (2) a US$100-million contribution to a new World-Bank-administered fund to help eliminate the red tape that hinders foreign investment in order to encourage market-oriented investment (Europe and Japan were asked to contribute matching funds), and (3) support in the Uruguay Round of GATT negotiations for tariff reductions on products of importance to Latin America and the Caribbean. The U.S. president clearly envisaged a hemispheric free-trade zone built upon both a U.S. arrangement with Canada and its negotiations with Mexico. To qualify, beneficiary countries must liberalize their trade and investment policies and have their adjustment programs approved by the IMF.

A reduction of the commercial debt owed by regional governments was not included in the U.S. proposal. It was not clear, either, whether U.S. exports would get reciprocal free-trade treatment or whether this would be done within a bilateral or multilateral framework. Whatever the merits of free trade, Commonwealth Caribbean governments certainly would be reluctant to enter into arrangements that could destroy their fledgling industrial sectors or threaten their regional integration movement, which began to receive renewed attention following the move toward a unified market in Western Europe. Past U.S. trade and aid initiatives in the region have not been spectacularly successful, and the Enterprise for the Americas may be merely an attempt to strengthen U.S. influence over hemispheric trade in reaction to the emergence of economic blocs in other parts of the world.

The critical question is, If political solutions of the debt problem do not work, can Commonwealth Caribbean countries significantly expand their export capacity? If they cannot—and are then

unable to service their debts—the likelihood of obtaining new
external aid becomes even more bleak. There are limits to rescheduling; the multilateral agencies do not, in any case, operate
in this way. This means that servicing these particular debts could
take such a high proportion of foreign earnings that there would be
little left over for consumption goods, raw materials, spare parts,
and capital goods. In such a situation, the economy could grind to a
halt. Guyana, which became a classic "basket case" during the
1980s, shows that this scenario is not an impossibility. Guyana did
settle its arrears with the regional and international financial organizations in 1990, and lending resumed with Guyana subject to an
IMF-monitored economic recovery program. However, the massive
devaluations of the 1980s did substantially reduce the gap between
Guyana's official exchange rate and its black market rate, indicating a serious lack of confidence in the management of the
economy—for which technical solutions alone were clearly not
sufficient. The resumed inflow of foreign resources without internal changes capable of inspiring the local population will not stop
the continuous downward slide of its economy.

Certain countries, such as Trinidad and Tobago, argued that, if
they did not borrow to finance development, there could be no
development program, given the scarcity of domestic resources. In
the absence of such a program, the standard of living would fall
even further in response to more severe adjustments. The question
here concerns the extent, and the length of time, that foreign borrowing can be used to prop up a given standard of living. One
argument was that the new circumstances facing the traditional
exports, which for so long carried Caribbean economies, warranted
a cut in the overall standard of living, given the failure of substitute
activities to emerge. Tourism cushioned some of the fall in certain
cases, but decline was inevitable in the absence of major growth
sectors that could galvanize economic performance. Some policy
makers hoped that traditional export sectors would recover, making a serious lack of confidence in the management of the
economy—for which technical solutions alone were clearly not
sufficient. The resumed inflow of foreign resources without internal changes capable of inspiring the local population will not stop
the continuous downward slide of its economy.

## CONSTRAINTS AND PROSPECTS IN THE 1990S

The Commonwealth Caribbean countries entered the 1990s uncertain about their economic prospects, to a degree perhaps ex-

ceeding that at the beginning of the three previous decades. Their economic strategies had failed to achieve the economic transformation they had envisaged, and the guidelines appropriate for new approaches or new models were far from clear, particularly in the light of the rapid political and economic changes taking place in the world system. The region's prospects for aid and trade will be affected by these developments. The attention of Western Europe and the United States, on whom the Commonwealth Caribbean has traditionally depended for finance and markets, is likely to be increasingly diverted to Eastern Europe and the Russian states, as these countries attempt to make the transition to market-oriented systems. The real per capita financial assistance granted by the European Community to the African, Caribbean, and Pacific (ACP) countries under Lomé IV (agreed to in 1990) was virtually the same as that granted under the previous convention, and this was no doubt influenced by what the EC perceived would be the need for a greater commitment toward its neighbors to the east. With the decreased likelihood of a communist threat in the Caribbean, there were indications (e.g., the reduction of aid to Grenada and Jamaica) that the United States had become indifferent to the financial needs of Caribbean countries. Private foreign investment in the region also fell, and increased opportunities in Europe and fast-growing eastern Asian states could not reverse this process.

The apparent failure of past economic strategies, the rapidly changing environment, and the external pressures to liberalize economic structures and adopt certain policies point overwhelmingly to the need for a new model of development in the Commonwealth Caribbean. Even in Barbados, which once was an example of good management, pragmatism, and sound policies, problems of growth, foreign exchange, and employment prompt questions about the adequacy of the existing approach. And even in countries with reasonably good growth in the economy, governments find themselves pressed for funds and unable to deal with unemployment. In reconstructing the framework for renewed growth, the experience of successful small economies such as Hong Kong's and Singapore's offers lessons.

No model, however, can completely satisfy all economic, social, and political criteria in the context of the Commonwealth Caribbean. No approach can safely ignore the views of the United States, as both Grenada under the People's Revolutionary Government of Maurice Bishop between 1979 and 1983 and Jamaica under Michael Manley in the period 1972–80 show. Economic decline and increased reliance on institutions like the International Monetary

Fund and the World Bank also influence the context of economic policy, which is forced to reflect the ideological biases of these organizations and the right-of-center cliques that dominate decision making in major aid-giving countries like the United States and Britain. Foreign policy positions have also been increasingly forced to come to terms with the reality of economic conditions. The scope for independence of action has shrunk, since countries can be punished for not toeing a particular line or moving in a particular direction. Not surprisingly, all current governments in the Commonwealth Caribbean are now center or right of center in ideology. In these circumstances, welfare state considerations tend to weigh less, even though the rhetoric of social concern is likely to continue to be strong in the region. An increase in welfare tends to be seen as a medium-to-long-term objective, with growth at the forefront of concerns.

The parameters within which Commonwealth Caribbean countries formulate their policies similarly changed: global commodity markets have been depressed for years and nontariff trade barriers became more entrenched in the industrial countries. Movements in international interest rates and exchange rates among major currencies also cannot be ignored. The economic performance of the industrial countries is closely monitored by the Caribbean, since this performance shapes their own trade and aid policies. The persistent domestic and external deficits of the United States are a real source of concern: almost all Caribbean countries have their currencies pegged to the U.S. dollar, and a large part of their foreign earnings come from exports of goods and services to the United States. A significant proportion of reserves are held in U.S. dollars, and about 75 percent of Latin American and Caribbean external debt is denominated in U.S. dollars. In addition, the rate of inflation in the United States affects prices in Caribbean countries, since the United States is a major source of imports. Caribbean countries also have economic ties with other industrial countries, and therefore the relationship between the U.S. dollar and other major currencies influences their decisions still further.

It is clear, then, that fashioning national economic systems that can meet the material needs of their peoples has proved to be a more difficult task for Commonwealth Caribbean governments than the struggle for political independence. In the face of increasing deprivation and suffering, rhetoric can no longer suffice. The reduction of the bauxite levy in Jamaica and the revision or drawing up of new foreign investment codes by Guyana and Trinidad and Tobago reflect the reversal of policies intended to foster independent development. Transnationals are openly courted, with assurances of fair treatment. Under pressure from international financial institutions and other major donors, Commonwealth Caribbean countries have generally reduced state ownership and made efforts to establish more market-oriented economic systems. Yet this transition is taking place in the context of serious social and economic problems.

The liberalization of the domestic economy is consistent with the move by the industrial countries to liberalize trade in services, which it is argued, on good Ricardian grounds, would enhance world income and welfare. With a services capacity in an even lower state of development than their goods capacity, the consequences of such policies for the Commonwealth Caribbean are not difficult to envision. The development of these sectors will require protection, but this has to be done within a rational framework. Even so, the capacity to export competitively does not ensure access to markets—countries that insist on free trade do not necessarily practice it. There are not many signs that the rich countries fully appreciate the link between effective market access and poor economic performance in the Caribbean countries or, for that matter, the link between the drug trade and unemployment.

The prospects are that, even if export earnings were to increase, an increasing share of these earnings is likely to be diverted to debt servicing in the case of the highly indebted countries of the region. The failure to articulate an international debt strategy that could significantly relieve debtor countries powerfully influences these countries. Servicing debt necessarily became a major preoccupation, as default could halt all current inflows. The U.S. initiatives, such as the Baker and Brady plans, failed to inspire private lenders to deal more effectively with the debt problem.[27] In addition, in the Lomé IV negotiations, the European Community declined to launch any major initiative of its own, although it agreed to take certain debt reduction action for the ACP states. The request to cancel existing ACP debt to the European Community was refused.

The road to self-sustaining growth apparently has to come through policy changes, with the Bretton Woods institutions assuming the role of chief architects. U.S. bilateral aid is being increasingly tied to IMF or World Bank programs that will eventually make these economies models of efficiency. By downplaying issues of equity and social considerations in a situation where safety nets are not well developed, the seeds have been sown for the creation of more unstable societies. Policy changes are necessary, but the pace of these changes and the substance of these policies cannot afford to ignore the local economy and society and the realities of the international environment.

The experience of the 1980s has shown that Caribbean economies are extremely vulnerable to external developments and also that progress in income, employment, nutrition, and health can be quickly reversed. The development process has to be constantly nurtured and encouraged and not be subject to the political whims of trade and aid partners. External packages have to be specifically tailored to meet the needs of Commonwealth Caribbean countries, which ought not always to be lumped with the rest of Latin America. Each bout of economic recession leads to the loss of skilled people who emigrate to the rich countries. The trends toward the removal of controls and various other policy reforms are not a panacea. A failure to reverse the trends in major social indicators could intensify discontent, resulting in increased instability, which, to say the least, will certainly not help the investment climate deemed so crucial to recovery and growth.

# 11   The Offshore Caribbean

*Anthony P. Maingot*

Many small Caribbean countries confronted with a lack of natural resources have adopted a three-pronged approach to development: export-driven manufacturing, offshore financial services, and tourism.[1] These three industries, it was thought, would serve these countries well in that they employ both blue-collar and white-collar labor, bring in hard currency, and use the countries' strategic geographical location. For very small countries, the financial services and tourism sectors were particularly attractive, since they could exist in productive symbiosis. The financial service industry is environmentally clean, and it coexists nicely with tourist-attracting natural resources.

There can be no doubt about the compelling logic in this development thrust, a logic made more evident by the question: What were the alternatives, not theoretical or ideological, but actual and practical? A kind of economic law of necessity increasingly exercised a strong influence on development thinking, especially in the insular Caribbean. Decades of excessively ideological and partisan attacks on any offshore activity, whether tourism, medical schools, free-trade zones, or even straightforward foreign investment, exhausted the tolerance toward virtually any criticism of offshore development.[2] This situation was especially lamentable in the Caribbean, where the offshore approach was fraught with potential pitfalls. There is a need to scrutinize this path, reveal how it performed elsewhere, and discern the danger signs.

The Caribbean region experienced a dramatic increase in a wide array of transnational, or offshore, activities at a time when its capacity for collective, regionwide responses was at a low point. Certainly, not all offshore activities are nefarious or detrimental. It is plausible, however, that activities detrimental to the well-being of these small societies tend to take advantage of the arrangements and the milieu created by benign offshore activities. The offshore activities described here—the illicit drug trade and offshore banking and tax havens—illustrate this point.

A first question relates to the issue of state capabilities vis-à-vis the size of the tasks involved. Capabilities have to include the capacity to discriminate the good from the bad—a task not even major societies seem capable of—and then both promote and defend healthy development initiatives. Since by definition transnational and offshore activities are largely beyond the authority of states or international agencies, policing such activities is not easy. It is even more intractable when geopolitical factors favor those who place a premium on secrecy and evasion. This was clearly the case in the Caribbean in the 1980s, when all three elements of transnational development were present: (1) a society with outside clients (tourists and drug users) and outside money, (2) a society with saleable geographical location and commodities (sun, sand, and relaxed banking and company laws), and (3) native elites with the will and the talent to exploit the first two elements.

The issue was not an absence of public opinion but the fragmentation of that opinion, typical of archipelagic areas. While region-wide agencies limited themselves to the technical or legal side of development, none concerned themselves with the creation of a climate of opinion or regional consciousness raising. Certainly by the early 1990s, no Caribbean leaders exercised regionwide moral influence or addressed these issues. The days of influential and broad-gauged models (the Puerto Rican, the Cuban, and the democratic socialist) vanished with surprising speed. What was evident in the area was a variety of responses to the threats created by many of these offshore activities, ranging from the draconian measures taken by Cuban authorities to the more relaxed approach of most of the others. Whatever the response, the reality was that no Caribbean state—not even puritanical Cuba—escaped the ravages of these offshore activities, the most dangerous of which is the illicit drug trade.

## THE ILLICIT DRUG TRADE

The Caribbean, although only a minor player in the production of illicit drugs, is not at all a small player in the total picture of the U.S. drug problem. Yet it has taken Caribbean societies far too long to become aware that drugs are not purely an American problem but one that affects them as well. Only two Caribbean countries are involved in any substantial drug production: Jamaica and Belize. U.S. State Department figures indicate that Jamaica reduced marijuana production from between 625–1,280 tons in 1980 to 300 tons in 1988. Its share of the U.S. marijuana market was a mere 1.7 percent in 1987. Belize's production of marijuana dropped from 645 tons in 1985 to 180 tons in 1988, supplying 1.6 percent of the U.S. market.[3]

There is no known significant production elsewhere in the islands of marijuana or of other illegal drugs. Rather, the importance of the Caribbean lies in two other assets it possesses that are vital to the drug business: (1) geographical location and (2) expertise in the culture, language, finances, and consumption preferences of the United States and Europe. The first factor led to the area's becoming a major route for the transport of drugs. Despite the rapid increase in the amount of drugs coming in through Mexico, 70 percent of the cocaine and marijuana entering the United States still moves through its Caribbean border. The second factor gives some Caribbean peoples a relative advantage in offshore banking, money-laundering schemes, and in organizing criminal gangs of extraordinary efficiency, not to mention brutality. The Jamaican *posses* (known in the United Kingdom as "yardies") are merely the best known of these.

Fortunately, indifference has given way to a long overdue consciousness about this problem. One indication of this involves Jamaica's most influential pollster, columnist, and public opinion shaper, Carl Stone. In April 1988, Stone was distressed that, in a year when Jamaicans were electing a new government, "we are spending as much time agonizing over petty U.S. gossip about supposed mafia-type links between local politics and drug dons."[4] He called for a discussion of the "real issues." Yet, exactly one year later, after the Jamaican electorate had democratically elected a new government without any serious discussion of the Jamaican drug problem, Stone changed his tune. His new words reflected the seriousness of the Jamaican situation. The drug dealers, he said, were "crippling Jamaica. . . . The very future and livelihood of this country and its people are at risk." He urged that "steps be taken 'in a hurry' to stop this trade, including any constitutional changes necessary."[5]

The Jamaican government's attitude has also changed. In July 1988, under U.S. pressure, the Seaga government was defensive. Minister of Labor J. A. G. Smith told reporters that "small, developing Third World countries can ill afford to divert more of their hard-earned or hard-bargained foreign currency to eradication of the drug trade." Not even the United States had been successful in combating it, he pointed out. He then interjected the subject of race, comparing mild U.S. treatment of "white" countries that grow drugs, such as Turkey, to its stern policy toward Jamaica.[6] The irony was that while the minister was engaging in this pernicious comparison—that Jamaica as producer was a victim of U.S. demand—the situation in Jamaica was getting desperate. By 1987, the major shipping lines serving the island's new transshipment port were warning that drug smuggling was harming their business. In early 1988, the largest shipping line, Evergreen, stopped shipping goods out of Jamaica, having already paid US$137 million in fines to U.S. customs. In early 1989, a second major shipper, Sea-Land Services, also embargoed Jamaican exports: it had paid US$85 million in fines. Likewise, free-zone manufacturers were said to be in a "tailspin" because of the use of the port by drug lords.

The situation was deteriorating so fast that, in January 1989, the government ordered a search of every container leaving the island, revealing the dilemma of open economies caught in the grip of the drug trade. The 280 members of the Jamaican Exporters Association, who had wanted the government to keep the ports open, were up in arms. Now there were not only massive delays in shipping but substantial additional costs for inspection. The inspection policy was soon changed to "selective checking" which meant, in effect, selective smuggling.

It was not surprising, therefore, that upon being elected in 1989, Michael Manley put the war against drugs directly under his control. This was indeed a new Manley. For the eight years of his previous administration (1972–80), Manley had made the construction of socialism his top priority; by 1989, he was declaring that his new focus was the war on drugs. "We are threatened," he told an audience in Toronto in April, "by an international criminal network in drug trafficking that has no precedent in history." Yet only days after his Toronto declaration, U.S. customs discovered 3,595 pounds of *ganja* (marijuana) on an Air Jamaica flight to Miami. This was not merely an embarrassment for Manley but a direct challenge to his government's authority. Manley's response was swift and drastic: a purge of Air Jamaica and customs personnel and the "militarization" of airports and ports.

Again the Catch-22 situation confronting economies such as Jamaica's soon revealed itself. Leaders of the tourist industry protested that the atmosphere for tourism was being ruined. Indeed, a Jamaican journalist calculated that, on any single day, Air Jamaica passengers were confronted by at least twenty-five soldiers and had their documents checked up to four times before boarding. The new minister of tourism agreed to remove guards armed with heavy weapons and to train a special security force more acceptable to travelers, but he refused to make further concessions, saying, "we have a real problem, which will smash up the tourist industry. We cannot pussyfoot over it."[7]

It was also becoming evident to Jamaicans that the drug threat was not purely economic. The discovery on 6 January 1989 of a container with US$8 million worth of arms illustrates the wider problem. Of West German manufacture, the munitions had been shipped from Portugal and were destined for an unspecified guerrilla group in Colombia. It took a joint effort of Jamaican, British, U.S., and Colombian authorities to break the Jamaican link in "an international network of drug traffickers and terrorists."[8]

But the threat to Jamaica by drug barons was not the only or even the worst case. In Antigua, the government of Vere Bird was shaken in mid-1990 by revelations that weapons purchased for the Antiguan armed forces (100 Galil rifles and 100 Uzi submachine guns) ended up on the farm of Gonzalo Rodriguez Gacha, one of Colombia's top drug barons. The regionwide and complex relationship among drug trafficking, arms trading, and government corruption was evident from the murky involvement of an Israeli "special envoy" appointed by the government of Antigua[9] and of an Israeli specialist in guerrilla warfare who had previously been sought in Colombia for training narcoterrorists; from the possible Panamanian links to the affair;[10] and from reports from Colombia that a training camp was to be financed by the Medellin cartel for Colombian and Sri Lankan Tamil terrorists.[11] The Tamils were supposed to help the Medellin cartel expand the drug trade in Asia and Europe. Such was the uproar in Antigua that the government appointed a one-man commission of inquiry, in the hope that by singling out individual culprits the nation would be saved from condemnation as a "terrorist state." As a strategy, it was only partly successful, given the depth and scope of the scandal.[12]

The Haitian case also illustrates the dangers of drug dealing. On that island, there appears to be no end to the murderous round of intramilitary and intraelite conflicts over control of the drug and contraband trade. This trade increased during the 1980s, as did Haitian criminal gangs in U.S. cities. The commissioner for the southeastern division of the U.S. Customs Service, George Heavey, testified before the U.S. Senate's Caucus on International Narcotics Control that 45 percent of the Haitian vessels and 60 percent of the vessel agents operating on the Miami River were allegedly involved in smuggling aliens and narcotics.[13]

Up to the time of the U.S. invasion (December 1989), Panama's case was perhaps the most akin to Haiti's. In both countries, it was not state authorities pitted against illicit groups but authorities against authorities, and the sums involved were huge.[14] Operation Pisces, a sting operation against only one of the estimated thirty groups involved in money laundering, illustrates this. In one day, the operation impounded US$5.6 million in cash from fifty-six bank accounts and US$21 million in assets. But as the Drug Enforcement Agency spokesman told the U.S. Senate, this was only "a snapshot of any weekly activity of one money-laundering operation in the U.S. pertaining to only one drug, cocaine."[15]

Fortunately, Caribbean governments have become aware that the corruption is deep rooted, not epiphenomenal, and that there are potentially very serious consequences to their political cultures. Examples abound: in the Dominican Republic, the trial for corruption of former President Jorge Blanco; in the Turks and Caicos Islands, the arrest in Miami on drug running charges of a sitting premier; in the Netherlands Antilles, the use of the free zone to tranship drugs.[16] The questions were hardly different in the Bahamas, where Bahamians have been asking for years about the luxurious life-style of their prime minister, Lynden Pindling. In the latter case, a certain degree of cynicism or, at a minimum, jadedness, pervaded the political culture.[17] Public tolerance of corruption increased—what the outer boundaries of this tolerance will be is hard to predict. In many ways, Suriname provides a chilling example. The civilian population, desperate to get the military off its back, gradually reconciled themselves to the criminal ways of its men in uniform. As Suriname fast became one of the biggest transshipment centers for the expanding European appetite for cocaine, it was clear that the elected civilian government would be unable to control the narcotics-military alliance.[18] The military coup d'état of 24 December 1990 removed any pretense that it could.

## OFFSHORE BANKING AND TAX HAVENS

Offshore banking is not a topic taught in Caribbean classes on banking and finance. And yet, grey market and black market money that seeks safe and anonymous financial havens caught the attention of "forensic" investigators as early as the 1970s. It is not, therefore, an unstudied topic: to Ingo Walters, for instance, the flow of monies to tax havens was of enormous qualitative and quantitative importance, and he lamented that there was so little hard evidence on the subject. According to Walters, the reason for this secrecy was that the offshore tax haven business was "of great value to some, yet positively bad for others." An additional obstacle was that the business thrives on schemes of "almost diabolical complexity" made possible by sophisticated technology.[19] As the chief executive officer of one of Canada's largest banks told a Canadian Senate committee, "I can hide money in the twinkle of an eye from all the bloodhounds that could be put on the case, and I would be so far ahead of them that there would never be a hope of unraveling the trail." The secret, he concluded, was electronics.[20]

The sources of the money are various and certainly not all illegal. For instance, an increasing number of specialized and legitimate investment advisers are available to recommend to companies which of an estimated forty-five tax havens they should use. This is not a new phenomenon, though the amounts involved have grown steadily. In fact, the tax haven is one of the fastest growing areas for U.S. investment abroad. In 1968, the total assets of U.S.-controlled corporations held in these havens stood at 12.1 percent of their worldwide assets; by 1976, this had grown to 17.6 percent. This growth was particularly rapid in tax havens in the Western Hemisphere, whose growth increased forty times over—to 108.1 investments per 100,000 population—between 1970 and 1979, compared to a growth rate of 2.0–2.11 per 100,000 population in areas that were not tax havens. In 1979, banks in tax havens held some US$385,000 billion.[21] The trend continued into the 1990s and for the same reasons. As Sara West of the *Financial Times* put it, "more investors are showing an interest in offshore asset management, either for fear of a change of government or because they want to minimize their tax bills by using offshore trusts."[22] Those who were planning national economies in the Caribbean consequently came to realize that offshore financial services were a growth industry and that they had the location, the communications infrastructure, and the educated work force to be competitive. They intended to get their share of this international river of money in the same fashion that Switzerland, Liechtenstein, Luxembourg, Monaco, and so many other financial centers have. In the Caribbean, however, there is an additional and major source of these offshore funds: laundered drug money. The link between the criminal drug trade flowing through the Caribbean and the presence of money-laundering facilities there is in part explained by R.

Thomas Naylor, who wrote, "the ultimate objective of the criminal is to enjoy his gains, perhaps in a tropical haven, more likely within the same geographic milieu in which his criminal enterprise operates."[23]

Despite the secret and largely inscrutable nature of offshore tax havens, we know some general facts about them and about those in the Caribbean in particular. Referring to the "staggering" amount of actual cash that has moved through the Caribbean, Ingo Walters outlined a typical laundering process:

Step 1: Money is transferred (occasionally wired) to a secret haven abroad.

Step 2: Lawyers there create a dummy corporation, using boilerplate documentation.

Step 3: Funds are deposited in the name of this dummy corporation in a cooperative local bank, usually an offshore bank authorized to conduct transactions only with non-residents.

Step 4: Money is then transferred to a larger international bank.

Step 5: The corporation then borrows money from this bank (secured by the deposits) for legitimate use in the original country.[24]

The growth of the offshore banking business was fueled by the phenomenal increase in cash from the U.S. drug trade as well as from capital flight. One estimate of the interest earned on drug profits stored in "safe" banks is US$3 million per hour.[25] These Caribbean financial centers are hardly unfamiliar with flight capital and laundered monies: the vast majority of the criminal cases identified in the criminal investigations of the Internal Revenue Service in the late 1970s and early 1980s occurred in the Caribbean. Between 1978 and 1983, there were 464 such cases, of which 45 percent represented illegal transactions with legal income. Of the other 55 percent, illegal income was involved (161 cases of which dealt with the drug trade). Of these, 29 percent involved the Cayman Islands, 22 percent the Bahamas, and 11 percent the Netherlands Antilles.[26] This movement of large amounts of cash throughout the Caribbean thus made a mockery of many of the official statistics on the nature of the regional economy.

The Caribbean islands, however, were not the only places where big money was moving in the area. It is critical to an understanding of the growth of Caribbean offshore centers to know that, in many ways, they are part of a larger financial region, which includes Florida. Indeed, by the late 1970s, Florida had become the banking center for the Caribbean and, perhaps, Latin America. The climate for banking in Florida was clearly propitious: in 1982, Florida banks held 33 percent of all commercial bank deposits and an extraordinary 51 percent of all savings and loan deposits in the southeastern part of the United States. One Florida banker (William H. Allen, Jr., chairman of Pan American Bank) calculated that Florida received some US$5–6 billion in 1982 in flight capital.[27] Another (J. S. Hudson, executive vice president of Flagship Bank) reckoned that roughly 20 percent of the total deposits of his own banks were from nonnationals.

However, the amounts involved in capital flight pale by comparison with those stemming from the illegal drug trade. A report from the Group of Seven calculates that in the late 1980s the retail proceeds of the drug trade were US$122 billion, US$85 billion of which was "available to be laundered through the banking system" every year.[28] With the drug traffic of the early 1980s amounting to some US$50 billion per year, US$7 billion of which was believed to have remained in Florida, it is clear that this trade represented by far the largest single financial link between Miami and the Caribbean. In 1983, Miami's Federal Reserve District bank showed a cash *surplus* of US$3–4 billion, while New York's Federal Reserve District showed a *deficit* of US$4 billion.[29] Miami's banks were taking in so much cash that they began to charge a fee to accept a deposit! U.S. Customs Commissioner William Von Raab provides an interesting calculation of deposits and trips abroad that only US$74 million in cash would require of anyone wishing to avoid the reporting requirements of U.S. banking law: 7,500 deposits (each under $10,000) in U.S. banks and 15,000 trips abroad (to avoid the $5,000 reporting limit). The commissioner made it clear that moving so much money required the active collaboration of banks both in the United States and offshore.[30] The Miami banking system was the crucial link between the financier, the seller, and the market.

By the mid-1980s, however, the social and political climate in the United States had changed. A war on drugs was declared and, with it, greater control and supervision of the banking system. New standards of "flagrant organizational indifference" and "collective knowledge" were exacted from the banks as part of the Anti-Drug Abuse Act of 1986. The traditional distinction between "deliberate intent to violate the law" and "indifference to legal requirements" was for all practical purposes abolished. It might well be, as one legal scholar put it, that the new provisions against money laundering placed an impossible burden on the banks and that Congress had "simply dropped the problem in the lap of the financial services industry and walked away."[31]

Whatever the legal arguments, the fact is that, despite the existence of antilaundering legislation since 1970, the mid-1980s were a watershed in terms of public and political concern about the link between drugs and "hot" money and about the role of banks in moving and hiding drug money. Not surprisingly, this was the period when the offshore centers really began to boom and proliferate. With the United States declaring war on drugs, there was an even more obvious role for offshore centers, not controlled by the United States, that could serve not only as tax havens but as launderers of dirty money. This money came out of the United States and often went back into the United States as legitimate real estate and business.

The money-laundering business became so lucrative that in the late 1980s Caribbean states were no longer content to simply interact with Miami but were determined to become world-class offshore banking centers in their own right. They did not all, of course, make it, but at one time or another, virtually every island in the Caribbean tried. St. Vincent published its own little book, calling itself "today's most desirable haven to protect your money and assets from inflation, from dollar devaluation, from the tax collector, from creditors, and even from your spouse in the event of divorce."[32] It really never took off. Little Anguilla, on the other hand, which had three banks in 1980, had ninety-six by 1983, only one of which even had a vault. In the Turks and Caicos Islands, things were going well until several senior government ministers were jailed for running drugs. It is now recovering as a haven for companies, especially U.S. credit life insurance companies. In early 1989 there were 6,729 companies registered on these minute islands.[33]

The activity was just as feverish in Montserrat, which was ranked by a known authority on establishing offshore banks as "a wise jurisdictional choice."[34] It contained the vital characteristics for the easy establishment of a bank: (1) good communications between the island and the rest of the world, (2) no taxes on any banking activity, (3) a very low license fee (US$7,600), (4) tight secrecy laws, (5) a very low requirement for paid-in capital (US$300,000), which could "sometimes be waived or postponed," and (6) no monetary ties with, or supervision by, the United States. Within a short time, the corruption surrounding the establishment of offshore banks had created a political and constitutional crisis, which led to constitutional "devolution," that is, recolonization. The British governor exercised colonial regulatory control over the Montserrat Ministry of Finance, imposed a moratorium on the granting of new bank licenses, and closed several suspicious banks.

The outrageous and regionwide nature of the problem is illustrated by the 1981 headline in a major business daily: "Con Men Are Raking in Millions by Setting up Own Caribbean Banks." The essence of the story was that many Caribbean islands (Montserrat, St. Vincent, Anguilla) had become "a spawning ground for dozens of small, shadowy private banks, whose main activity seems to be turning out phony financial documents that are used in this country as collateral for loans and other illegal purposes."[35] The story also cited an unpublished study of offshore banking, commissioned by the Ford Foundation, which concluded that the Caribbean had become "a playground for fraudulent and other criminal bank users." Not even much shame was left, as evidenced by the following exchange between a U.S. senator and the former president of the bank in Montserrat:

> *Senator Rudman.* Didn't it bother you travelling around the Caribbean with one-half million dollars in a suitcase?
> *Mr. Stocks.* Now that I have had more time to reflect on it, I guess it was a little bit ridiculous.[36]

Among the various factors contributing to such situations in some of the islands were the lack of a central bank, of trained personnel, of regulations, and of a willingness on the part of government officials to provide information on their dealings. "There is no question," concluded the *Wall Street Journal*, "that the buccaneer forays into banking . . . will continue. Once established on a Caribbean isle, the pirates are difficult to dislodge."[37]

Clearly much of the Caribbean continued in the 1990s to be involved in this offshore business. The fact that so much of it took place in former British colonial territories concerned the British Department of Trade and Industry, which commissioned a study of the offshore financial centers in the Caribbean. The report, by Rodney Gallagher of Coopers and Lybrand, indicates that there were many grounds for concern if for no other reason than the virtual absence of local inspection and investigation of financial activities. Most of the local effort and talent had gone instead into attracting and registering firms.[38] British concern was particularly acute over the patently illicit activities of banks in Anguilla and Montserrat. In the latter, two-thirds of the 350 local banks were closed down after a 1989 Scotland Yard investigation, and a moratorium on new banks was mandated in Anguilla in May 1990. By that time, this little island of 7,000 inhabitants had registered 3,500 companies—including forty-two banks.[39]

## THE BAHAMAS, THE CAYMAN ISLANDS, AND THE BRITISH VIRGIN ISLANDS

Three cases, which tower above the rest in the Caribbean, illustrate some of the benefits and many of the dangers and risks that accompanied the rush into the offshore business: the older centers of the Bahamas and the Cayman Islands and the new entrant, the British Virgin Islands (BVI).

The Bahamas is one of the oldest and best-established financial centers. This did not prevent it, however, from experiencing difficulties. It showed no growth in the late 1980s, in part because of the fierce competition from a plethora of new offshore centers in the Caribbean and the Atlantic. But another reason points to the double-edged sword of offshore business. Rachel Johnson explained that among the reasons for this decline were "publicity about alleged drug-trafficking, endemic corruption, bureaucratic delays and inefficiency, and growing drug-related crime and violence in Nassau."[40] Nevertheless, banking remains the second most important industry in the Bahamas after tourism. The initial expansion of the banking sector occurred while the Banks Act of 1909 was operational. This act was not brought up to date until 1966. By then, over six hundred companies were, in the words of an official publication, "transacting banking or trust business . . . including a number of 'so called' banks that created an unfavorable image."[41]

In analyzing the forces behind the rise of the Bahamas as an offshore banking and trust center in 1968–70, one is made aware of how little depended on Bahamian actions themselves. The three main causes were: (1) U.S. Federal Reserve Board restrictions on export of capital for foreign lending or investment, (2) the expansion of the pool of Eurodollars, and (3) the fact that the Federal Reserve permitted U.S. banks to set up foreign branches with little regulation. With these factors as impetus, the Bahamas opened the door even further, removing the requirements for either separate premises or a full-time staff or establishing corporation in the Bahamas.

The result was that by the late 1980s the country had some 380 banks, only 180 of which had more than a nameplate and a post office box.[42] There are those in the Bahamas who question the overall benefits—compared to the toll in corruption and bad reputation—derived from this offshore operation. They note that the banking sector provided 10 percent of gross domestic product in 1988 but directly employed only 3,000 people, or 2 percent of the labor force, plus another 2,000 indirectly provided jobs.[43] However, these criticisms came from a minority, and the offshore sector is politically well established, rooted both institutionally and socially. In other words, it is an integral part of Bahamians' conception of themselves as a nation.

Considerable efforts have been made to improve the image of the Bahamas as a financial center, to expand and facilitate the registration of international business companies, and to improve its ranking as an offshore ship registration (flag of convenience) center. (It ranks tenth in the World Shipping League.) Bahamian officials, like their counterparts in other offshore centers, hope that Hong Kong's problems and the standardization and stricter reporting in the European Community will send new monies their way.[44] Charges of corruption against Prime Minister Sir Lynden Pindling and various members of his cabinet and personal inner circle did not make a dent in their political fortunes. The high standard of living of the population (per capita gross national product of US$10,560) is certainly one reason for such tolerance. Another is the collective memory of black nationalism, which recalls the early contributions of Pindling and his Progressive Liberal Party. But, perhaps more important might be a resignation about national capabilities, an awareness that the Bahamas has tried to fight the drug trade but to no avail. Can anyone be expected to do better? There is much to be said in support of the Bahamian assertion that, on a per capita basis, the contribution to the antidrug effort "is unequalled anywhere else in the world."[45] This combination of reasons augured well for Pindling in respect to the 1992 elections.

But there are still dark clouds on the horizon. The fact is that increased U.S. pressure with respect to drug interdiction, combined with increased indebtedness and unemployment, have had the Pindling administration worried. A Central Bank economist admitted that "what we are seeing now is the real economy emerging." That real economy, said a journalist, "stripped of its drug-related froth, is in difficulties."[46] Certainly, the opposition has an attractive leader in Hubert Ingraham. He is untainted by any charges of corruption and nepotism and highly skeptical about too heavy a dependence on offshore activities. The modern political history of the Bahamas suggests, however, that honesty and good intentions are not enough to wrest power from the wily Sir

Lynden. Aged sixty-two in 1992, by Caribbean standards comparatively young, he still has another election or two left in him.

One archipelago with no dissenting voices on the issue of offshore activities is the Cayman Islands, one of the five remaining British colonies in the Caribbean. It is interesting that it is its colonial status that provides the Caymans with an edge over areas such as the Bahamas. This was the calculation behind the Caymans Legislative Assembly's petition to Britain in 1963 that it be allowed to break away from Jamaica and revert to Crown Colony status. If constitutional devolution was used in Montserrat to dismantle an offshore center gone awry, in the Caymans it was used to promote one. Three years after the return to Crown Colony government, the Caymans began its move toward becoming the number one tax haven in the world. By 1987 there were more than 18,000 companies on the register. Among these were 520 banks and trust companies with assets in excess of US$200 billion.[47]

The Cayman Islands, through the British connection, made efforts to maintain banking respectability. In 1984, a U.S.-U.K. Cayman Islands Narcotics Assistance Agreement was signed. But according to well-placed investigators, that agreement merely slowed the flow of illicit cash.[48] Although it has continually denied any role in laundering dirty money, the Cayman Islands has not been shy about admitting that it benefits from the travails of others. Note the language of its financial secretary, Tom Jefferson, in a 1984 interview:

> Look around us. The U.S. has $200 billion of debt and a loss in purchasing power, per dollar, of almost 50% in 15 years. Canada is in a similar position. Mexico has been having serious financial problems despite the vast oil reserves and, additionally, has to provide jobs for a massive labour force.
>
> The economies of El Salvador, Guatemala and Nicaragua are unfortunately depressed from falling production due to political turmoil. Costa Rica's inflation continues on an upward trend. Venezuela has imposed major exchange controls as a possible solution to its problems. Brazil is on the verge of a real currency crisis, and Argentina faces years of economic turmoil ahead. Haiti has the worst unemployment situation in the hemisphere, and the population continues to grow at about 3%. Jamaica is rebounding well in the face of adversity.
>
> As you can see, the economic stability of our region is questionable. Yet, in Cayman, in the midst of it, we enjoy a very stable economy and marginal inflation—a mere 5% per annum over the last two years.[49]

Indeed, as early as 1984, it was talking about capturing flight capital from Hong Kong, showing in the process some keen political insights: "We can now observe the waning of investor confidence in Hong Kong as the New Territories lease nears determination in 1997."[50] By the late 1980s, it was also benefiting from the turmoil in Panama and even picking up nervous money from the Bahamas. Again, the financial secretary showed the self-confidence characteristic of the Caymans when he noted that other competitors for the offshore business—the British Virgin Islands and the Turks and Caicos Islands—were "gaining ground," but none could come even close to the Cayman operation. (The British Virgin Islands, for example, did not send a mission to Hong Kong until July 1990.[51])

It is of course evident that much of what the Cayman Islands and the other offshore centers do is legitimate by any nation's laws, that other parts of their services are illegal elsewhere but legal in the offshore center, but that laundering monies is illegal by any country's laws. It does not appear, however, to be the business of offshore centers to figure out which is which. The financial secretary of the Caymans made this quite plain in a 1984 interview:

> *Question.* Cayman has been portrayed by some as a major component in drug trafficking, money laundering and tax evasion. Respond to that, please.
>
> *Answer.* As others have stated, "we are a tax haven, not a crime haven." That statement is irrefutable. Our drug laws are harsh and justice is swift for violators. As for money laundering, in any financial centre, New York City, Chicago, etc., you can find illegal dealings. Their financial screening of clients, etc., has not been perfect and they have been in the business for many more years than ourselves. Therefore, why is it that, whatever we do in Cayman, perfection is expected of us? Tax evasion is not a crime under our laws and we have no jurisdiction over U.S., Canada or any other country's tax matters.[52]

The attitude is not much different in the fastest growing offshore center in the Caribbean, the British Virgin Islands, which came on line in 1984. This was the year in which the favorable double taxation agreement between Britain and the United States was terminated. The BVI's response was an innovative international business company ordinance, which proved to be a boon. In 1988, there were 13,000 of these companies established on the island; a year later (in part reflecting the flight from Panama), there were 22,000. Other centers, most recently the Bahamas, began to adopt similar legislation. The BVI has not had similar success in the banking and financial institutions sector. By 1989 there were eight banks, with a mere US$269 million in deposits.

Despite the fact that the BVI adopted model legislation for drug trafficking offenses and does cooperate with U.S. authorities in narcotics-related investigations, they are as casual as are the Cayman Islanders about the provenance of the funds. "There is no such thing as a clean money market," says Robert Mathavious, the BVI's financial secretary. "There is no way to know whether the companies registered in the BVI represent drugs' profits."[53] Even lawyers profess to depending on "bigger legal firms in the U.S. and the U.K. to weed out the bad apples." And, as in the other centers of the Caribbean, both regulation and inspection, especially for trust companies, were found to be at a "bare minimum" by the Coopers and Lybrand investigator. Meanwhile, reports refer to a growing drug trade, local drug use, increasing crime, the importing of 55–70 percent of the work force, and growing inflation.[54] It sounds in many ways like the Bahamas a few years into its development as an offshore financial center. Is this, then, the fate that awaits these offshore centers in the Caribbean?

## CONCLUSION

There has been a certain resigned realism among those who have to administer offshore banking havens. "I wish I could put my hand on my heart and say we won't have any more trouble," said the governor of Anguilla after an official crackdown on illicit banking, "But the crook will always be one step ahead of law enforcement. And how much clean business is there out there?"[55]

The risk appears to be in the nature of the beast itself and not necessarily related to any particular Caribbean propensity to corruption. As Barry Riley noted about the British dependencies, the Channel Islands, being offshore is not the same as being onshore. "The regulations are not usually quite as tight, and there may be unregulated as well as regulated sectors." He further noted that "what goes in the shadowy offshore trust business in the Channel Islands is still largely unknown."[56] A new European consciousness about the dangers of this dirty money business, however, has developed, especially since national regulatory barriers were dropped after 1992. Because of the need for revised banking legislation in anticipation of 1992, there was a "search for respectability" among major offshore centers. If at first it was the absence of regulations that was the bait, later the appeal tended to be the opposite: security through tight (but understanding) supervision and regulation.

In April 1990, eight major banking centers, famous for their tight secrecy laws, joined the Group of Seven industrialized countries in proposing new banking regulations. Their target was specifically the laundering of dirty money. There were no Latin American or Caribbean countries at that meeting. This led some observers to speculate that such European measures would make the Caribbean secrecy havens even more attractive to the laundering business.[57] The Caribbean, though, was not long in responding to the new concern with banking ethics. In a meeting in Aruba in June 1990, representatives of twenty Caribbean islands discussed North American and European concerns and concluded by signing the forty-point anti-money laundering program agreed upon by the Group of Seven as well as a twenty-one point plan tailored to Caribbean circumstances. But as the business writer for the *Miami Herald* reported, the dominant tone in Aruba was, if you want us to give up our lucrative offshore banking business, you will have to pay for it.[58] It is, in short, a utility, not a moral, calculation. This leaves us with the empirical question: What are the risks and benefits of an offshore development strategy?

The independent states argue that the service provides employment and sources of capital for local development. Independence allows them the flexibility to pursue innovative strategies of development that maximize the linkages between offshore banking and other sectors. These claims are not upheld by those who have studied the issue independently. The small economic gains in white-collar employment and stamp and tax revenues do not outweigh the risks involved. The most serious of these are the corruption of state institutions and personnel and, deriving from this, the loss of credibility of the state and society.[59]

Colonies or dependencies have a different perspective. To them, colonialism represents a guarantee of political and social tranquility and a protection against prying U.S. authorities. Both ensure confidentiality, predictability, and secrecy, which are the hallmarks of a good offshore haven. In the climate of concern over dirty money, the colonial tie also provides a barrier to runaway corruption. It is doubtful, therefore, that the Cayman Islands, the British Virgin Islands, and the Turks and Caicos Islands will follow the corrupt ways of the Bahamas. British actions in both Montserrat and Anguilla illustrate this reality.

All this reveals the paradox and irony of modern Caribbean politics. Independence was meant to bring liberation from the evils of colonialism, and in many ways it did. But independence also resulted in a dangerous, because insidious, vulnerability: threats were built into certain routes to development because of the islands' geographic location, educational standards, and political systems. And if the pressure for strict and uniform banking regulations in the European Community after 1992 results in a detrimental situation for the dependencies, then they might also opt for independence. Should they remain colonial—and thus regulated from the metropolis—then much of the dirty money will seek havens in independent Caribbean islands. There will be plenty of candidates. As long as there is money to be made from the sale of drugs, there will be havens where the profits can be safely tucked away.

The mismatch between the instruments of the law and those of the criminals is only quantitatively larger in the islands than it is in industrial countries. In the final analysis, they all face a task chillingly described by R. Thomas Naylor: given present laws and technology, the task facing states trying to catch financial wrong-doers is "a little like trying to capture a laser-beam in a cardboard box."[60] The British representative to the task force on money laundering initiated by the Group of Seven asserted that money laundering "is an international problem which cannot be tackled by individual countries in isolation. The commitment by the major industrialized countries to strengthen international co-operation in the fight against money laundering is therefore all the more welcome."[61] The excolonial powers have a responsibility to help the newly independent countries sustain a civil and democratic independence.

# 12 U.S. Intervention, Regional Security, and Militarization in the Caribbean

*Paul Sutton*

The Caribbean is littered with sunken warships and crumbling fortifications. Its islands have long been fought over and exchanged, its sea-lanes carefully guarded and patrolled. Security has been a constant preoccupation for whoever has controlled the region, and the means to secure it have been remarkably consistent over time: military bases, protected sea lines of communication, and the ability to exclude, contain, or otherwise limit the challenges and depredations of hostile powers. This last point is critical.

Soon after its "discovery" by Columbus, the Caribbean became a theater for conflict and competition where the military capabilities of the then great powers could be probed and from which appropriate conclusions as to their resolve could be drawn. In struggles between these powers, the hegemony of Spain was lost to Britain or France according to the fortunes of war. Each briefly held the stage in the eighteenth century, with Britain finally emerging victorious in 1815. Thereafter, Britain "ruled the waves" and the majority of the islands until the Spanish-American War of 1898. The U.S. defeat of Spain and the U.S. occupation of the remaining Spanish colonies of Cuba and Puerto Rico brought European hegemony to an end and ushered in that of the United States.

The history of U.S. involvement in the Caribbean in the twentieth century has been the expansion and protection of that hegemony. It has not been uncontested, and it has had at its heart a belief that the national security of the continental United States is at stake in the Caribbean. In the interest of that security, presumed or real, the United States has intervened in the affairs of Caribbean states on numerous occasions and, in a number of instances, has invaded them with U.S. forces, twice in the 1980s (Grenada in 1983 and Panama in 1989). The distinguishing feature of U.S. policy toward the Caribbean basin (as compared to Latin America south of Panama) has thus lain in the readiness, willingness, and ability of the United States to intervene, directly or indirectly, in the affairs of the Caribbean and Central America in defense of its interests.

The policies of the Reagan administration very much drew on, and added to, this historical record. In the presidential campaign of 1980 the Caribbean basin was projected as a "region in turmoil." Insurgencies in El Salvador and Guatemala, the victory the previous year of left-wing revolutions in Grenada and Nicaragua, as well as the "rediscovery" of a Soviet "combat" brigade in Cuba, were seen as symptomatic of a dangerous decline in U.S. hegemony directly threatening to U.S. security. These changes were also seen (albeit without much real evidence) as being orchestrated by the Soviet Union.

The Reagan administration sought to reverse this situation and to restore U.S. power in the region. This chapter examines how it went about doing so and assesses the results of its policies. These were, in the security field, to assert a new framework for intervention, effect a new or renewed militarization of selected states in the Caribbean basin, and ultimately provide a new security agenda for the region. In keeping with the focus of the other chapters, only the Caribbean is considered, although the United States frequently links its security policy in the Caribbean with that toward Central America, Panama, and on occasion, Mexico, Venezuela, and Colombia.

## THE TRADITIONAL FRAMEWORK FOR INTERVENTION

U.S. policy toward the Caribbean basin has traditionally served two crucial strategic functions: (1) preventing extrahemispheric powers from posing threats to the U.S. mainland through acquiring military bases or a significant geopolitical presence in the area, and (2) enhancing U.S. capabilities as a global power by ensuring that it can draw resources from the region and use it to demonstrate U.S. resolve. These aims are interconnected and constitute a framework for intervention that has led, over the years, to a definition of the region as "vital" to U.S. interests. The Reagan administration shared this view and, indeed, used it to assert the primacy of the Caribbean basin in U.S. policy toward Latin America as a whole.

It did so, first of all, through the reassertion of traditional interests in strategic access. U.S. bases, strategic raw materials, and secure sea lines of communication were the bedrock of this concern.[1] In his first year in office, Reagan demonstrated the significance of all three functions when he upgraded the Caribbean Joint Task Force in Key West, Florida, to one of three Atlantic NATO commands; requested the purchase of 1.6 million tons of Jamaican bauxite for the U.S. national defense stockpile of strategic materials; and authorized Ocean Venture 81, a major military exercise that took place off Puerto Rico and involved over 120,000 troops, 250 warships, and 1,000 aircraft. This was followed by action that confirmed the importance of maintaining U.S. bases and installations in Antigua, the Bahamas, Cuba, and Puerto Rico and further established as routine massive annual military exercises in the region.

The concerns motivating this high level of interest were many, but above all they were related to the Caribbean as the area of greatest concentration of maritime routes regarded as essential to U.S. commerce and defense. Anything up to two-thirds of foreign trade and a half of petroleum imports were said to pass through sea-lanes focused on the Panama Canal, the Mona and Windward passages, and the Florida Straits. These routes were also deemed essential to NATO. In the case of conflict in Europe, more than 50 percent of the planned reinforcement of men and materials was expected to transit the Caribbean, raising important questions as to their security in time of war. Although, in retrospect, the Reagan administration exaggerated the vulnerability of these sea-lanes to attack, the threat of interdiction of them by Cuba and the Soviet Union was nevertheless a real enough possibility for military planners to take it fully into account.[2] In particular, it provided a rationale for expanding the U.S. military presence in the Caribbean and justification, if any more were needed, for the continued close monitoring by the United States of developments in the region.

The perception of a Soviet threat also confirmed the importance of strategic denial. This has been an axiom of U.S. policy in the Western Hemisphere ever since it was first enunciated by President Monroe in 1823. In the modern Caribbean, it has sought to prevent both the establishment of Soviet and Cuban bases in the region and the emergence and the consolidation of regimes supportive of Soviet and Cuban foreign policy goals. The compelling importance attached to these aims by the Reagan administration was shown by its policy toward Grenada under the People's Revolutionary Government. Whereas the Carter administration expressed displeasure with the PRG over the development of links with Cuba and alarm at the construction with Cuban assistance of a major international airport with the perceived potential of acting as a forward Soviet-Cuban base, the Reagan administration raised both concerns to the status of major threats.

Accordingly, an escalating policy of weakening and containing the Grenada revolution was set in train, with the country subject to an intense propaganda war, a crippling policy of economic sanctions, and massive military intimidation, culminating in invasion in October 1983. The fact that Grenada was a small, poor country, one of whose principal exports was nutmeg, was judged immaterial. Or as Reagan put it in a widely circulated speech in March 1983, "the so-called experts [and others who] had argued that we shouldn't worry about Castroite control over the island of Grenada . . . haven't taken a good look at a map lately or followed the extraordinary buildup of Soviet and Cuban military power in the region. . . . It isn't nutmeg that is at stake in the Caribbean and Central America; it is the United States national security."[3] In other words, the Monroe Doctrine was being challenged at the same time as geographic proximity demanded decisive action. The invasion of Grenada removed these worries at one stroke and demonstrated the Reagan administration's resolve not to permit a second Cuba in the Caribbean.[4]

In reality, this has been the nub of U.S. policy in the Caribbean basin. The region is seen as a backyard, over which the United States must exercise hegemony if it is to sustain its claim to global power. Weakness here is seen as limiting its ability to act elsewhere. The National Bipartisan Commission on Central America (the Kissinger Commission), established by Reagan in 1984, argued this explicitly: "Beyond the issue of U.S. security interests in the Central America–Caribbean region, our credibility worldwide is engaged. The triumph of hostile forces in what the Soviets call the 'strategic rear' of the United States would be seen as a sign of U.S. impotence."[5]

Reagan himself also subscribed to this view, declaring in a speech to the Joint Session of Congress in 1983, "I say to you that tonight there can be no question: the national security of all the Americas is at stake in Central America. If we cannot defend ourselves there we cannot expect to prevail elsewhere. Our credibility would collapse, our alliances would crumble and the safety of the homeland would be put in jeopardy."[6] Exactly so. Irrespective of a calculus of interest, economic or strategic, the Caribbean basin matters as a place in which to demonstrate U.S. power and global credibility. In Reagan's bid to reassert U.S. supremacy vis-à-vis the

Soviet Union, the Caribbean was not incidental to such considerations but absolutely central to them.

## THE NEW FRAMEWORK FOR INTERVENTION

The main impact of these traditional concerns with security in the
Caribbean was the elaboration by the Reagan administration of a
new framework for intervention, which coupled security with development and increased militarization. The concerns of development were advanced through the Caribbean Basin Initiative (CBI),
the concerns of militarization through an increased emphasis on
military assistance to the region.

The CBI was Reagan's major foreign policy proposal toward Latin America in his first term in office. It was unveiled in February
1982 in an address before the Organization of American States and
proposed one-way duty-free access to the U.S. market for twelve
years for a number of products from the countries of Central America and the Caribbean. It also proposed supplemental assistance
and several other "growth-generating" concessions. The economic
impact of the CBI has been examined elsewhere. It is important to
recognize, however, that its origins lay in a preoccupation with
security, not development.

The initial distribution of economic assistance, the designation
of beneficiary countries according to political criteria, and the emphasis on bilateral agreements all indicate that security interests
were uppermost in—and correspondent with—established U.S.
unilateral determination of policy toward the region.[7] So also was
the thinking behind the policy that, like the Alliance for Progress
of the Kennedy administration, associated poverty with instability, potential turmoil, and consequently, insecurity in the
Caribbean. What was new was the mechanism by which it was to
be tackled—vigorous promotion of the private sector through preferential regionalism. As Kenneth Dam, Deputy Secretary of State,
put it: "the CBI marks the first time that the United States has
granted preferential economic treatment to an entire geographic
region. And it does so not on the basis of traditional bilateral aid
but by providing long-term incentives to private enterprise."[8]

In support of this policy, the Reagan administration mobilized
the private sector in the United States. Caribbean/Central American Action (C/CAA), an organization of U.S. companies with interests in the Caribbean, was given the encouragement and the
resources to promote business in the region and to lobby for the

Caribbean Basin Initiative in Washington. The C/CAA also established close links with the Caribbean Association of Industry and
Commerce (CAIC), which was restructured and revitalized to provide a comprehensive service to local businesses, particularly in
respect to export opportunities in the U.S. market. Allied to this
was the provision of political support to like-minded leaders in the
region. The prime minister of Jamaica, Edward Seaga, was especially favored and was instrumental in founding the political counterpart to the C/CAA-CAIC nexus, the Caribbean Democratic
Union, an alliance of eight conservative political parties in the
English-speaking Caribbean closely linked to the Republican Party
and funded through the Reagan-inspired National Endowment for
Democracy. In short, a network of complementary and reciprocal
relations was promoted among key businessmen and policy influ-
entials in the expectation of developing a new and expanding basis
of association and identification by Caribbean elites with U.S.
interests.

Not everything, however, could be left to political and economic
initiatives: a supportive military program was also thought necessary. The case for this program was made in a study completed in
October 1981 by the Strategic Studies Institute of the U.S. Army
War College, which recommended (1) a policy of "indirect confrontation" with Cuba, which could include military measures in
those countries where there was a Cuban presence; (2) an increase
in the direct military presence of the United States in the region,
including the unification of commands to reflect the fact that
Central America and the Caribbean are a "single strategic entity";
and (3) policies to increase the military capabilities, including intelligence activities, of the armies and police forces of the region.[9]

This last recommendation was seen as critical in developing
regional support for an increasing U.S. role. The local military
forces in the Caribbean (including the police, the constabulary, and
coastguard forces in the Commonwealth Caribbean) were accordingly to be the beneficiaries of an enhanced U.S. military assistance program, with provision for training, equipment, and personnel. By these means, as the report made clear, the United States
would "establish a network of military-to-military relationships
which can: (1) gain for the United States an understanding of the
current position and future direction of the various Caribbean mil-
itaries and leadership elites; (2) foster increased access to decision-
al elites in order to enhance United States influence; and (3) serve
as a bridge between regional military elites in order to encourage
intraregional cooperation and the peaceful solution of conflicting

interest."[10] Again, the aim was to win friends and allies in support of specific U.S. interests.

This emphasis on a presumed identity of interest between Caribbean elites and U.S. policy was the essence of the Reagan initiatives toward the Caribbean. Determination of policy continued to lie wholly with the United States, and thus the traditional emphasis on unilateral initiative remained. Later, it was realized that the effective implementation of policy required the cultivation of regional support, which meant that hegemony, once restored, could be best furthered if shared, albeit on U.S. terms.[11] This goal was never to be fully realized, although it was promoted more effectively than ever before. U.S. interests in the Caribbean (including geopolitical interests) thus won sufficient support for the Reagan administration to feel more confident about security in the region, particularly after the invasion of Grenada.

THE THREAT OF MILITARIZATION

The invasion of Grenada by six thousand U.S. troops took place on 25 October 1983. It was justified by Reagan on three grounds: "to protect innocent lives, including up to 1,000 Americans (then on the island) . . . to forestall further chaos, and to assist in the restoration of conditions of law and order and governmental institutions."[12] None of these reasons were necessarily invalid, but neither were they, singly or collectively, wholly persuasive. American lives were not in immediate danger, the Revolutionary Military Council, which had taken power in Grenada, was a de facto (if deeply feared) government, and the question of assistance to restore order was based, at best, on questionable legal grounds.[13]

What was important, in fact, was not the immediate context but the opportunity the confusing situation in Grenada provided to advance broader U.S. interests in the region. Up until then, not much had been achieved in real terms (as opposed to rhetoric) in this area. In El Salvador the insurgency had not been defeated, nor in Nicaragua had the revolution been halted. In consequence, U.S. policy in Central America was increasingly coming under searching criticism by the Congress. The U.S. confrontation of Cuba had equally failed to yield the intended results: indeed, the reverse was the case. Instead of becoming more amenable to U.S. interests, Cuba had become more defiant and had set about strengthening its armed forces.

The Reagan administration's objective position in the Caribbean basin in 1983 was thus not much more advanced than it was in 1981. Grenada became the unexpected means to correct this and to demonstrate U.S. resolve. The invasion was carried out on very short notice and with minimal political consultation, both within the administration and among allies. Fortuitously for an ill-prepared U.S. military, it met with only light resistance, so that U.S. casualties were relatively few. This, plus the decisiveness of the action, meant that the invasion quickly won domestic approval in the United States. It was also welcomed by the vast majority of Grenadians and was backed by the majority of Commonwealth Caribbean countries, seven of which provided token military assistance. The international reaction to the invasion, although initially hostile, was comparatively short-lived, at least compared with analogous action by the Soviet Union. In other words, as far as the Reagan administration was concerned, the invasion was an unqualified political and military victory, won at little cost. In one fell swoop, it restored U.S. fortunes in the Caribbean and underlined the U.S. will to maintain and advance its hegemony in the region.

As such, the Grenada invasion is widely regarded as a turning point in U.S.-Caribbean relations. Until the invasion of Grenada, the involvement of the United States in security provision in the Commonwealth Caribbean, Jamaica excepted, was relatively small. Security, particularly in the Eastern Caribbean and Belize, was left to Britain. In the relatively threat-free environment of the 1970s, this meant that security was regarded as of only minor concern, and several of the countries became independent without establishing regular armed forces. The seizure of power in Grenada by the New Jewel Movement in 1979 altered this perception among a number of these countries. In 1982, Antigua, Barbados, Dominica, St. Lucia, and St. Vincent signed a Memorandum of Understanding Relating to Security and Military Cooperation, agreeing to provide "mutual assistance on request" for a range of contingencies, including "threats to national security."[14]

The United States was not directly involved in the creation of the Regional Security System (RSS); it did, however, from 1981 onward, provide modest funds for training and military equipment in the Eastern Caribbean. In August 1983, the United States was asked to contribute substantially to the development of the para-military special service units, which, along with the small Barbados Defence Force and the coastguard units planned for each island, were to be the foundation of the RSS.

At the invasion of Grenada, this embryonic U.S. involvement was immediately escalated. The RSS had facilitated the invasion, and token forces from Jamaica, Barbados, Antigua, Dominica, St. Lucia, St. Vincent, and St. Kitts–Nevis participated as a separately constituted Caribbean peacekeeping force. Requests for increased U.S. assistance were made to, and sympathetically received by, a delegation of U.S. congressmen visiting the region to report on the invasion and, more important, were put to U.S. Secretary of State George Schultz on his visit to Barbados in February 1984. By this time these requests had developed into plans for a force of 1,800 men, 700 of them infantry and the remainder in the coastguard and support force. The headquarters was to be in Barbados, with smaller garrisons of 50 to 90 men on the other islands. The projected cost was around US$100 million.

The U.S. reaction to this latter proposal was unfavorable from the outset, in part because of the expense. However, other objections soon began to surface, focusing on the consequences of a needless militarization of the region when there were many other pressing problems to resolve. James Mitchell, elected as prime minister of St. Vincent in June 1984, expressed this view: "the sores of poverty in our region cannot be cured by military therapy. . . . The more arms we have available in the country the greater will be the temptation to solve our problems with a coup."[15] Other Eastern Caribbean leaders, worried by the age-old problem of "who will guard the guards," joined him, and by the end of 1984 a consensus had been reached among these leaders and with the United States that such a force was not appropriate to their needs.[16] The idea was therefore shelved and, with the death in office shortly afterward of Tom Adams, the prime minister of Barbados and the principal advocate of the scheme, it was finally buried.

A measure of militarization of the region had, nevertheless, been accomplished.[17] Special service units trained by U.S. and British military personnel were in place in Dominica, Grenada, St. Kitts–Nevis, St. Lucia, and St. Vincent. Antigua and Barbados had small defense forces, and a coastguard on each island was being developed, with British, Canadian, and U.S. assistance. Their combined force levels in 1984 were probably in excess of a thousand men. Direct military assistance to the Eastern Caribbean also rose precipitately from less than US$100,000 a year in 1981 and 1982 to more than US$5.6 million a year in 1985–87.

The Eastern Caribbean was also being drawn into the framework of U.S. strategic planning through regular participation in military exercises with U.S. forces (including an annual exercise expressly designed to test the capabilities of the RSS) and through the redesignation and upgrading of the U.S. base in Antigua. Finally, Jamaica and, to a lesser extent, Trinidad and Tobago were affected by the heightened military profile of the United States in the Caribbean in the mid-1980s. Direct U.S. military assistance to the former expanded to more than US$5 million a year on average in 1984–87, further opening the Jamaican Defence Force to penetration by U.S. military doctrine and increasing its dependence on the United States for military supplies.[18] It also became a regular participant in U.S. military exercises (and provided the principal element of the Caribbean peacekeeping force, maintaining more than 300 soldiers in Grenada for more than two years after October 1983). Developments in Trinidad, which for many years had been reluctant to develop its military capability, now complemented those in Jamaica. In short, by the end of 1987 the Commonwealth Caribbean looked decidedly different in security terms than it had in 1981, when it saw ideological pluralism as the basis for international relations, including recognition of both socialist and capitalist states. The Commonwealth Caribbean saw itself then as a possible "zone of peace."[19] None of these features were any longer true in discussions of security; instead, the agenda deferred to the inevitability of U.S. domination of the region.

## The Expanded U.S. Presence

In November 1981 the U.S. Defense Department reorganized its Caribbean network under a single umbrella: the U.S. Forces Caribbean Command (USFCC), comprising the Caribbean Joint Task Force at Key West, the Antilles Defense Command in Puerto Rico, a naval force, and air force, army, and marine units. The command had its headquarters in Key West and was charged with the coordination of joint and combined exercises in the Caribbean and the implementation of security assistance programs for designated countries in the region. Since the USFCC was a subcommand of U.S. Atlantic Command, naval forces predominated, averaging 80 percent of 7,000–8,000 personnel throughout the Reagan years. The other U.S. command with an interest in the Caribbean, insofar as the region was frequently considered one strategic entity with Central America, was the U.S. Southern Command (SOUTHCOM), with headquarters in Panama. Its particular responsibility was defense of the Panama Canal and the coordination of military assistance in South and Central America. Forces assigned to it were principally drawn from the army and numbered around 10,000.[20]

The Reagan administration thus maintained the traditional

configuration of U.S. forces in the region. Indeed, it enhanced the U.S. position in several ways, for example, increasing the range of activities carried out at the base in Guantanamo in Cuba, turning the U.S. base in Antigua into a regional training center for the Eastern Caribbean, and concluding an agreement with the Bahamas for the lease of facilities vital to U.S. antisubmarine warfare capability.[21]

It was in Puerto Rico, however, that the new policies were most pronounced, which led to a reactivation of bases in that country and an expansion of the role of the military forces stationed there to include cooperation with other Caribbean forces. Important to both developments was the Roosevelt Roads Naval Station, the main U.S. base in Puerto Rico (and in the Caribbean). It is assigned roles in both nuclear and conventional warfare, with the latter having an important regional dimension (under the Reagan administration, forces from the station facilitated the invasion of Grenada). It has also—and less publicly—hosted a school for training police drawn from the Caribbean basin, complementing the role played by the Puerto Rican National Guard, which has military cooperation agreements with a number of Caribbean countries and regularly participates in maneuvers and training with military personnel from them.

The sum effect of these and other military activities was to revise the security relationship that Puerto Rico had previously maintained with the region. For most of the 1960s and 1970s this relationship was one of relative isolation. This ended in the 1980s, as Puerto Rico became host to numerous military exercises, many involving other Caribbean countries and two of which, Operation Amber in 1981 and Universal Trek in 1983, were rehearsals for the invasion of Grenada. Real fears were therefore expressed of a remilitarization of Puerto Rican society and the consequent emergence of the country as a bastion state, with a role equivalent to that of Hawaii in the Pacific.[22] Even though the process did not go that far, by the late 1980s Puerto Rico had contributed directly to accelerating the militarization of countries in the region. It also contributed to security by promoting the Caribbean Basin Initiative and by developing links with Caribbean businessmen through joint ventures. In short, Puerto Rico emerged as an important element, perhaps the central element, in the Caribbean security framework developed by the Reagan administration in its early years.

## THE NEW SECURITY AGENDA

Although the new security framework was important for the reassertion of U.S. hegemony in the Caribbean, new threats were emerging. One of these had occupied policy makers earlier—that of a massive and increasing flow of immigrants from the Caribbean. Two other threats, however, were new; these were drug trafficking and the associated business of money laundering.

Large-scale migration from the Caribbean to the United States was evident since the 1950s. However, it did not arouse much controversy until 1980, when in the space of a few months over 120,000 refugees from Cuba and nearly 25,000 from Haiti arrived in southern Florida. U.S. officials were apparently powerless to stop the flow. The idea (and fear) of the United States losing control of its borders quickly took hold, and immigration became an issue in the 1980 election campaign. On taking office, the Reagan administration sought to meet the problem by stemming the flow of illegal immigrants, estimated at more than one million from the Caribbean. But at the same time the administration sought to satisfy demand for continuing access to the United States by a politically active lobby of Caribbean-origin immigrants legally resident in the United States, 1.5 million of whom had settled in the period 1960–80.[23]

The Immigration Reform and Control Act of 1986 eventually emerged as the main response to the situation. It sought to close the backdoor to illegal migration in the short term by providing illegal workers the opportunity to apply for resident status, while in the long term a policy of sanctions against employers who hired undocumented aliens was expected to reduce their numbers. At the same time, the act did not seek to close the legal front door to immigrants from the Caribbean or elsewhere (approximately the same number entered the United States from the Caribbean in the second half of the 1980s as in the first half, to total a million in all). The act did, however, reaffirm the importance of strict procedures, particularly in the granting of nonimmigrant visas and, more generally, strengthening border controls. The question of enforcement (including sweeps to apprehend and deport illegal immigrants) was thus given greater prominence than hitherto had been the case.

Although no military personnel were assigned to these functions, the relevance of them to security in the United States was not lost on defense analysts. Toward the end of the 1980s, serious consideration was thus being given to revising the traditional arm's-length security posture of the United States military toward its southern borders on the grounds that continuing immigration from the Caribbean basin was potentially damaging to the social integrity of the United States.[24]

This question of a new approach was, of course, most vividly expressed in the growing problem of the illicit drug trade. In 1986 President Reagan determined that drugs were a national security threat; and in that year the Anti-Drug Abuse Act promised a comprehensive effort to lower the domestic demand for drugs and reduce the supply from the Third World.[25] The Caribbean featured largely, though not exclusively, in the latter dimension. It was, for most of the 1980s, an important source for marijuana; and it was— and continues to be—a region through which up to 70 percent of the cocaine entering the United States is believed to transit. The Caribbean has therefore received considerable attention by programs to eradicate drugs at the source and programs to interdict drug traffickers outside or at U.S. borders.

The U.S. military became increasingly involved in the pursuit of these objectives. In Belize and Jamaica (the only Caribbean producers and exporters of marijuana), U.S. military assistance programs were directed at crop destruction, with the result that by 1988 production was severely curtailed and represented only 4 percent of total marijuana production from the main source countries (Mexico, Colombia, and the United States).[26] U.S. efforts at maritime interdiction, by contrast, were not as successful. Between 1981 and 1987, the U.S. Navy assisted the Coast Guard in impounding ninety-five vessels, resulting in 480 arrests and the seizure of 1.6 million pounds of marijuana and 2,376 pounds of cocaine.[27]

At best, however, this was but a small part of the total (less than 20 percent), and although increased equipment and manpower were made available, the record did not dramatically improve. Nevertheless, policy pronouncements of the Reagan and Bush administrations continued to emphasize a law-and-order approach, in which the military were given a high profile. The militarization of the war on drugs thus targeted the Caribbean basin as a priority area in its counternarcotics operations.[28] The practice, which began under the second Reagan administration, of routine joint military training exercises by U.S. personnel with their Caribbean military and paramilitary equivalents, the objectives of which were nearly always drug interdiction, thus continues and will most likely expand.

Finally, U.S. security interests in the Caribbean increasingly engaged the question of financial surveillance of the Caribbean's many offshore financial centers. These are now to be found in Anguilla, Aruba, Antigua, the Bahamas, Barbados, Belize, the Cayman Islands, Montserrat, the Netherlands Antilles, St. Vincent, and the Turks and Caicos Islands in the form of banks, casinos, tax havens, and company and shipping registers. Their number and success attracted the attention of the U.S. Inland Revenue Service and the U.S. Drug Enforcement Agency, which attempt to defeat tax evasion and combat drug trafficking. The latter, in particular, became a major objective, since it is clear that such facilities provide opportunities for the laundering of billions of U.S. dollars each year.[29]

The United States sought to counter these ventures in various ways, ranging from disclosure treaties and exchange of information agreements with the governments in the region to sophisticated "sting" operations, in which agents infiltrate and close down money-laundering schemes. As with drug interdiction, however, success in one place may merely mean the displacement of the operation. The question, therefore, has wider international implications. This was recognized in the proposals for new banking regulations put forward by the major industrial countries in April 1990 and accepted later that year at a regional conference involving all Caribbean offshore centers. However, the point was made at that meeting that measures to improve border controls, monitor banks and financial institutions, and investigate money-laundering conspiracies were beyond the capacities (and sometimes contrary to the interests) of the small states.[30]

The new security agenda that emerged in the late 1980s slowly redefined the concept of U.S. security in the Caribbean. It now involved not only a concern about military hegemony but also a new interest in law enforcement. The distinction between the military and the police functions that holds in the United States became blurred in the Caribbean, as the Department of Defense, the FBI, the Drug Enforcement Agency, the CIA, and a host of other U.S. agencies sought to meet the threats from drug trafficking, money laundering, and illegal immigration. Borders also were breaking down. The right to hot pursuit of drug traffickers in Bahamian waters by U.S. forces was conceded, and U.S. law now provides for indictment in U.S. courts of foreigners who allegedly conspired to import drugs into the U.S. mainland.

The emergence of Miami as the crime center of the Caribbean is a counterpart to this development. Its attraction to immigrants from the Caribbean and its involvement in the illicit drug trade is well documented.[31] The city has an important part to play in the

U.S. security network in the Caribbean, whether as a base for intelligence operations or, more indirectly, as host to the annual conference on the Caribbean, which has emerged as the principal means to promote the Caribbean Basin Initiative. Its future, and that of the Caribbean, are thus increasingly intertwined. They are not, however, interdependent. The distinction is important and is illustrative of wider U.S. policy.

Notwithstanding the growing commonality of interest in security matters between Caribbean governments and the United States, which the new agenda implies, the United States maintains the initiative and sets the parameters by which Caribbean governments must abide. It continues to favor bilateral rather than regional solutions to security problems and retains the right to unilateral intervention. The U.S. invasion of Panama in December 1989 is witness to this and to the new security agenda. To the familiar litany of intervention motives—safeguarding the lives of U.S. citizens, defending democracy, and maintaining U.S. strategic interests (in this instance, the integrity of the Panama Canal treaties)—was added the imperative to combat drug trafficking.[32] Although it is too early to see this as evidence of a full-fledged new national security doctrine defining U.S.—Latin American relations in total,[33] its importance for the Caribbean cannot be underestimated, particularly as the traditional threat to hegemony in the region posed by the Soviet Union (and to a lesser extent Cuba) has receded.

## CONTINUITY AND CHANGE IN SECURITY POLICY

The 1980s were, by any measure, an important decade in the evolution of U.S. security policy in the Caribbean. In historical perspective the decade ranks with the first half of the 1960s and the first thirty years of the century as high points of U.S. intervention in the affairs of the region. To justify hegemony, the United States asserted, as before, the imperatives of strategic access and strategic denial; while to confirm hegemony, it once again committed U.S. forces to invasion in overwhelming number with little regard for either the views of other Western Hemisphere states or the principles of international law. In other words, the United States acted unilaterally in the belief that the Caribbean constituted a sphere of influence, the unqualified domination of which was essential to the U.S. ability to act as a world power. Security was defined in essentially traditional terms and carried out by essentially traditional means.

At the same time, however, the 1980s were different from earlier decades. The priorities were no longer simply those of defending key facilities and lines of communication but also, as General Gorman, the commander of SOUTHCOM from 1983 to 1985, put it, ones of "support for democracy, economic recovery, stemming the migrant flow and controlling international narcotic trafficking."[34] The definition of U.S. security interests, therefore, broadened to include social and economic dimensions as well as favored political arrangements. The promotion of the Caribbean Basin Initiative and political support for regional allies bears witness to this, as did the U.S. condemnation and isolation of countries purportedly violating these interests. The inclusion of the Commonwealth Caribbean in this policy also demonstrates a geographical widening of U.S. security interests. The invasion of Grenada pointed in this direction and to the unambiguous inclusion of the Commonwealth Caribbean as a subregion to which a distinctive, but nevertheless common, security policy was to apply. The sense of this was accurately caught by Tom Adams in London shortly afterward, when he claimed that 1983 marked "the watershed year in which the influence of the United States, willy-nilly, came observably to replace that of Great Britain" in the Eastern Caribbean.[35]

The 1980s therefore saw new forms of U.S. engagement in the region. The military option continued and in some respects, as in Puerto Rico and in regard to the Regional Security System, was strengthened. But so also was general enforcement capability. Its adoption is to some extent a return to the policing function assumed by the United States in the Caribbean at the turn of the century, but it is qualitatively different in that it directly addresses U.S. domestic issues as well as foreign policy concerns. In the era of the Good Neighbor policy, the United States did not have to occupy Caribbean basin countries but secured its interests by military and diplomatic means. It is no longer able to do so as easily, as witness its disengagement from Panama in the early 1980s and its return a few years later via sanctions and, ultimately, invasion.

The lesson is that the new U.S. security agenda is not as open to easy victories as was the traditional agenda. It also complicates policy, dissolving the distinction between U.S. domestic and foreign policy interests. Security for Caribbean states as well as for the United States in the region has become a seamless web, in which all interests are engaged. The United States in consequence—and by myriad threads—is drawn ever more into the affairs of the region.

In conclusion, the U.S. administrations of the 1980s and early 1990s presided over a transformation of the Caribbean as a strategic zone. It became not the U.S. backyard but its front porch, across which there was increasing passage into the U.S. living room. This transformation is by no means complete, and so the traditional way of defending U.S. interests in the region remains in place. Nevertheless, the new security agenda suggests that it is but a matter of time before it supplants traditional concerns. Both the United States and the Caribbean states need to consider the implications of this new agenda for their own security and sovereignty.

## Appendix: Statistical Data on the Countries of the Caribbean

| Country | Area (square km.) | Population | Life Expectancy | Gross Domestic Product per Capita (US$) | Foreign Debt per Capita (US$) | Political Status | Year of Last Election (up to 31 Dec. 1990) |
|---|---|---|---|---|---|---|---|
| Anguilla | 96 | 7,200 | 70 | 3,562 | 333 | British colony | 1989 |
| Antigua-Barbuda | 442 | 81,100 | 72 | 3,399 | 3,205 | Independent (1981) | 1989 |
| Aruba | 193 | 62,000 | 76 | 13,145 | n.a. | Part of Kingdom of the Netherlands | 1989 |
| Bahamas | 13,935 | 234,000 | 71 | 11,317 | 866 | Independent (1973) | 1987 |
| Barbados | 430 | 254,000 | 73 | 4,233 | 1,608 | Independent (1966) | 1986 |
| Belize | 22,963 | 185,000 | 69 | 1,149 | 611 | Independent (1981) | 1989 |
| British Virgin Islands | 153 | 14,500 | 70 | 10,345 | 2,690 | British colony | 1986 |
| Cayman Islands | 259 | 25,800 | 75 | 20,160 | 227 | British colony | 1988 |
| Cuba | 114,524 | 10,360,000 | 75 | 1,590 (1983) | 623 | Independent (1902) | 1985/86[a] |
| Dominica | 751 | 81,200 | 66 | 1,550 | 813 | Independent (1978) | 1990 |
| Dominican Republic | 48,422 | 7,000,000 | 66 | 957 | 690 | Independent (1844) | 1990 |
| French Guiana | 91,000 | 91,640 | n.a. | 3,240 (1981) | n.a. | DOM | 1988 |
| Grenada | 344 | 103,400 | 67 | 1,346 | 546 | Independent (1974) | 1990 |

| Country | | | | | | Status | Year |
|---|---|---|---|---|---|---|---|
| Guadeloupe | 1,705 | 386,000 | 73 | 3,600 | 157 | DOM | 1988 |
| Guyana | 214,970 | 765,796 | 70 | 680 | n.a. | Independent (1966) | 1985 |
| Haiti | 27,749 | 6,300,000 | 55 | 319 | 121 | Independent (1804) | 1990 |
| Jamaica | 10,991 | 2,400,000 | 70 | 1,843 | 1,875 | Independent (1962) | 1989 |
| Martinique | 1,100 | 359,800 | 74 | 4,761 | 83 | DOM | 1988 |
| Montserrat | 102 | 11,900 | 68 | 4,000 | 176 | British colony | 1987 |
| Netherlands Antilles | 800 | 194,700 | 77 | 6,110 | 5,338 | Part of Kingdom of the Netherlands | 1990 |
| Puerto Rico | 8,959 | 3,300,000 | 75 | 6,171 | 3,673 | Commonwealth assoc. with U.S. | 1988 |
| St. Kitts–Nevis | 269 | 46,500 | 65 | 2,119 | 473 | Independent (1983) | 1989 |
| St. Lucia | 616 | 142,400 | 71 | 1,400 | 79 | Independent (1979) | 1987 |
| St. Vincent | 389 | 112,600 | 71 | 1,148 | 507 | Independent (1979) | 1989 |
| Suriname | 163,270 | 394,999 | 68 | 2,290 | n.a. | Independent (1975) | 1987 |
| Trinidad and Tobago | 5,128 | 1,290,000 | 70 | 5,510 | 1,610 | Independent (1962) | 1986 |
| Turks and Caicos Islands | 430 | 13,000 | 70 | 5,215 | 207 | British colony | 1988 |
| U.S. Virgin Islands | 355 | 110,000 | 68 | 12,264 | n.a. | U.S. possession | 1988 |

Sources: Figures are from Phil Gunson, Greg Chamberlain, and Andrew Thompson, *The Dictionary of Contemporary Politics of Central America and the Caribbean* (London: Routledge, 1991), except for French Guiana, Guyana, and Suriname, which are from Central Intelligence Agency, *World Fact Book, 1988* (Washington, D.C.: U.S. Government Printing Office, n.d.).

Note: Figures are for the mid- or late 1980s unless otherwise indicated. The figure for life expectancy is from birth.

[a]Dates of Communist Party Congress, not election.

# Notes

## Introduction: The Contours of Modern Caribbean Politics

1. For basic data on the various territories of the Caribbean, see the appendix to this book.

2. Malcolm Cross, *Urbanization and Urban Growth in the Caribbean* (Cambridge: Cambridge University Press, 1979), 5.

3. Excerpt from the Puerto Rican constitution of March 1952.

4. Gordon K. Lewis, "The Contemporary Caribbean: A General Overview," in Sidney W. Mintz and Sally Price, eds., *Caribbean Contours* (Baltimore: Johns Hopkins University Press, 1985), 225.

5. See C. L. R. James, *The Black Jacobins*, 2nd rev. (New York: Vintage, 1963); Eric Williams, *From Columbus to Castro: The History of the Caribbean 1492–1969* (London: André Deutsch, 1970); and Juan Bosch, *De Cristóbal Colón a Fidel Castro* (Madrid: Alfaguara, 1970).

6. The phrase was coined by the group of New World economists formed during the 1960s at the University of the West Indies. See Norman Girvan and Owen Jefferson, eds., *Readings in the Political Economy of the Caribbean* (Kingston: Institute of Social and Economic Research, University of the West Indies, 1971), 1.

7. Commonwealth Caribbean Regional Secretariat, *From CARIFTA to Caribbean Community* (Georgetown: Commonwealth Caribbean Regional Secretariat, 1972), 14.

8. Cited in Don Mills, "Jamaica's International Relations in Independence," in Rex Nettleford, ed., *Jamaica in Independence: Essays on the Early Years* (London: James Currey; and Kingston: Heinemann Caribbean, 1989), 133.

9. *Trinidad Guardian* (Port of Spain), 1 November 1972.

10. Anthony Payne and Paul Sutton, eds., *Dependency under Challenge: The Political Economy of the Commonwealth Caribbean* (Manchester: Manchester University Press, 1984).

11. Michael Manley, *Jamaica: Struggle in the Periphery* (London: Third World Media, 1982), 38.

12. Paul Sutton, "Living with Dependency in the Commonwealth Caribbean," in Payne and Sutton, *Dependency under Challenge*, 281.

13. C. W. Kegley, Jr., and E. R. Wittkopf, "The Reagan Administration's World View," *Orbis* 26, no. 1 (1982): 225–31.

14. U.S. Department of State, *Democracy in Latin America and the Caribbean: The Promise and the Challenge*, Special Report 158 (Washington, D.C.: U.S. Department of State, 1987), 13.

15. Elliott Abrams, *Caribbean Basin: Accomplishments and Challenges*, Current Policy 1137 (Washington, D.C.: U.S. Department of State, 1989), 1.

16. *Business Week*, 11 July 1983, p. 28.

17. *The Nassau Understanding*, a declaration issued by the heads of government of Caribbean Community countries, Nassau, 1984.

18. Carmen Diana Deere et al., *In the Shadows of the Sun: Caribbean Development Alternatives and U.S. Policy* (Boulder: Westview, for Policy Alternatives for the Caribbean and Central America, 1990), 46.

19. President Reagan's speech to the National Association of Manufacturers, cited in *Caribbean Contact* (Bridgetown), April 1983.

20. A. N. R. Robinson, "The West Indies beyond 1992," paper prepared for the CARICOM Heads of Government Conference, Grand Anse, Grenada, July 1989.

## Chapter 1: Liberal Economics versus Electoral Politics in Jamaica

1. For discussions of Jamaican economic development in this period, see Norman Girvan, *Foreign Capital and Economic Underdevelopment in Jamaica* (Kingston: Institute of Social and Economic Research, University of the West Indies, 1971); and Owen Jefferson, *The Post-War Economic Development of Jamaica* (Kingston: Institute of Social and Economic Research, University of the West Indies, 1972).

2. For discussions of the Manley government, see, among a vast literature, Michael Kaufman, *Jamaica under Manley: Dilemmas of Socialism and Democracy* (London: Zed Books, 1985); Anthony Payne, *Politics in Jamaica* (London: Christopher Hurst; and New York: St. Martin's 1988); and Evelyne Huber Stephens and John D. Stephens, *Democratic Socialism in Jamaica: The Political Movement and Social Transformation in Dependent Capitalism* (London: Macmillan, 1986).

3. E. A. Brett, *The World Economy since the War: The Politics of Uneven Development* (London: Macmillan, 1985), 219.

4. "The Arusha Initiative," *Development Dialogue* 2 (1982): 14–16.

5. Manuel Guitian, "Economic Management and IMF Conditionality," in Tony Killick, ed., *Adjustment and Financing in the Developing World* (Washington, D.C.: International Monetary Fund, in cooperation with the Overseas Development Institute, 1982), 88.

6. Brett, *World Economy*, 223.

7. Guitian, "Economic Management," 88.

8. See the Jamaica Labour Party manifesto for the 1980 election, *Change without Chaos: A National Programme for Reconstruction* (Kingston: JLP, 1980).

9. For further discussion, see Payne, *Politics in Jamaica*, 83–91.

10. For the details, see *Government Ministry Paper*, 9, (Kingston: Government Printing Office, 1981).

11. See Timothy Ashby, *Missed Opportunities: The Rise and Fall of Jamaica's Edward Seaga* (Indianapolis: Hudson Institute, 1989), 12. Ashby, in fact, suggests that the agreement also stipulated a reduction of six thousand persons in the government work force, but no other source confirms this.

12. This judgment is confirmed by Jennifer Sharpley, "Jamaica 1972–80" in Tony Killick, ed., *The IMF and Stabilisation: Developing Country Experiences* (London: Heinemann; and New York: St. Martin's, 1984), 115–17.

13. *Daily Gleaner* (Kingston), 1 June 1981.

14. Ibid.

15. National Planning Agency, *Economic and Social Survey—Jamaica 1982* (Kingston: NPA, 1983), 9.3–9.5.

16. Ibid., 8.1.

17. Stephens and Stephens, *Democratic Socialism in Jamaica*, 255.

18. National Planning Agency, *Economic and Social Survey*, 8.1.

19. For the details of the system's operation, see Michael Witter, "Exchange Rate Policy in Jamaica: A Critical Assessment," *Social and Economic Studies* 32, no. 4 (1983): 27–29.

20. See Derick Boyd and Everton Pryce, "Jamaica's Devaluation Spree," *Caribbean Contact* (Bridgetown), October 1984.

21. For further discussion, see Colin Bullock, "IMF Conditionality and Jamaica's Economic Policy in the 1980s," *Social and Economic Studies* 35, no. 4 (1986): 146.

22. See Carl Stone, *The Political Opinions of the Jamaican People* (Kingston: Jamaica Publishing House, 1982).

23. Anthony Payne, Paul Sutton, and Tony Thorndike, *Grenada: Revolution and Invasion* (London: Croom Helm; and New York: St. Martin's, 1984), 211.

24. For further discussion, see Payne, *Politics in Jamaica*, 92–102.

25. *Caribbean Insight* (London), April 1984.

26. IMF press release, Washington D.C., June 1984.

27. *Caribbean Insight* (London), August 1984.

28. For further discussion, see Payne, *Politics in Jamaica*, 103–10.

29. See Evelyne Huber Stephens and John D. Stephens, "The Political Economy of Jamaican Development: From Manley to Seaga to Manley," paper prepared for the Latin American Studies Association, Miami, December 1989.

30. *Caribbean Insight* (London), November 1985.

31. *Jamaica: A Medium-Term Assessment, Report of the Tripartite Mission* (Washington D.C.: IMF, 1986), 32, cited in Ashby, *Missed Opportunities*, 14.

32. *Caribbean Insight* (London), May 1986.

33. See ibid., August 1986.

34. See Ashby, *Missed Opportunities*, 35.

35. Edward Seaga, "Statement to Parliament on the International Monetary Fund Agreement, January 13, 1987," press release, Kingston, 1987, 7–8.

36. Ibid., 11.

37. For further details, see Tony Thorndike, "Trade, Finance and Politics: The Political Economy of Jamaica," paper prepared for the Caribbean Studies Association, Belize City, May 1987.

38. See *Caribbean Insight* (London), May 1988.

39. A 9 percent swing to the JLP took place between the poll taken by Stone at the beginning of September and his poll at the end of September, although the PNP remained in the lead by 2 percent even in the immediate post-Gilbert poll. See Carl Stone, "'Gilbert' Swings Public Opinion towards Seaga," *Jamaica Weekly Gleaner* (London), 25 October 1988.

40. For an analysis of the 1989 election, see Carl Stone, *Politics versus Economics: The 1989 Elections in Jamaica* (Kingston: Heinemann Caribbean, 1989).

41. George Beckford and Michael Witter, *Small Garden . . . Bitter Weed: The Political Economy of Struggle and Change in Jamaica* (Morant Bay: Maroon Publishing, 1980), 99.

42. See Rex M. Nettleford, *Mirror Mirror: Identity, Race and Protest in Jamaica* (Kingston: William Collins and Sangster, 1970), 131.

43. Ashby, *Missed Opportunities*, 25.

44. Stephens and Stephens, "The Political Economy of Jamaican Development," 14.

45. Carl Stone, "Mr Seaga's Correct Priorities," in Carl Stone, *On Jamaican Politics, Economics and Society* (columns from the *Gleaner* 1987–88) (Kingston: Gleaner, 1989), 12.

**Chapter 2: Democracy and Disillusionment in the Dominican Republic**

1. There is a large body of literature on this intervention. See, in particular, Jerome Slater, *Intervention and Negotiation: The United States and the Dominican Republic* (New York: Harper and Row, 1970); and Abraham Lowenthal, *The Dominican Intervention* (Cambridge: Harvard University Press, 1972).

2. G. Pope Atkins, *Arms and Politics in the Dominican Republic* (Boulder: Westview, 1981), 104–7.

3. Ibid., 125–55.

4. Guido D'Alessandro, who as minister of mining and commerce in 1975–76 had tightened national controls over the partially U.S.-owned

gold mining company Rosario Dominicano S.A., believes that the Guzmán government paid private shareholders far more than the mine was worth because Guzmán's daughter had invested in the company. Interviews, Santo Domingo, 4 and 13 January 1985.

5. The trade deficit in the early 1980s was hovering around US$100 million, and the foreign debt was climbing toward US$3 billion. See Rubén Berríos Martinez, "Dependent Capitalism and the Prospects for Democracy in Puerto Rico and the Dominican Republic," in Paget Henry and Carl Stone, eds., *The Newer Caribbean: Decolonisation, Democracy and Development* (Philadelphia: Institute for the Study of Human Issues, 1983), 327–39.

6. Marion Ford, agricultural officer, U.S. Agency for International Development, was one of several sources offering this assessment. Interview, Santo Domingo, 8 January 1985.

7. See Jan Knippers Black, *The Dominican Republic: Politics and Development in an Unsovereign State* (Boston: Allen & Unwin, 1986), chap. 8.

8. Sources include Colonel Wayne Wheeler, U.S. military attaché, Lt. Bob Brown, Staff Attaché Office, and Richard Hines, political counsellor, all from the U.S. Embassy, Santo Domingo. Interviews, Santo Domingo, 8 January 1985, 9 January 1985, and 3 January 1985, respectively.

9. The government acknowledged only 55 casualties; human rights organizations, however, documented 101 protesters killed by security forces.

10. Michael Kryzanek and Howard J. Wiarda, *The Politics of External Influence in the Dominican Republic* (New York: Praeger, 1988), 58.

11. The charges against Jorge Blanco ranged from the massive allocation to friends and political cronies of tax exemptions for the importation of cars and industrial products to conspiracy in currency exchange and drug-trafficking deals. Moreover, it was widely rumored that several million U.S. dollars allotted annually to "national security" simply disappeared.

12. Jean Ribaldi, PRD leader (Majluta faction) and governor of La Romana province under the presidency of Jorge Blanco. Interview, La Romana, 9 December 1989.

13. Ibid.

14. The Christian Democrats, known in the Dominican Republic as the Social Christian Revolutionary Party, had a promising beginning in the 1960s, when they were usually allied with the PRD. They declined, however, in the 1970s, finishing a poor fourth in the elections of 1978. Their strength was precisely in the areas where Balaguer's Reformist Party was weakest: solid ideological grounding, well-developed programs, and well-trained and respected leaders. What they lacked—and hoped to gain through the merger—was a political space, or unclaimed constituency, in the political spectrum.

15. Doña Luisa Isaura de Liuberes, governor of the province of La Romana. Interview, La Romana, 10 December 1989. Doña Luisa was a house-

wife without previous political experience when she became involved in the presidential campaign of 1986. She said that her allegiance was to Balaguer personally, not necessarily to the PRSC.

16. Former President Juan Bosch. Interview, Santo Domingo, 12 January 1988.

17. Dr. Joaquín Salazar, professor of psychology (UCA and UNFO), personnel manager, Caribbean Data, Inc., and grandnephew of Trujillo. Interview, Altos De Chavon, 8 December 1989.

18. Tulio Navarrete, "JCE reitera que mantendrá boleta integrada sin arrastre," *Listín Diario* (Santo Domingo), 6 December 1989.

19. Ribaldi interview.

20. Salazar interview.

21. Ibid.

22. *El Nuevo Herald* (Miami), 27 April 1990. The poll covered 2,509 adults, 1,931 of whom were registered voters.

23. *New York Times* (International), 13 June 1990.

**Chapter 3: The Duvalier Dictatorship and Its Legacy of Crisis in Haiti**

1. UN Economic Commission for Latin America and the Caribbean, *Statistical Year-book for Latin America and the Caribbean 1989* (Santiago de Chile: ECLAC, 1990), 182–83.

2. Centre Haitien de Recherches pour le Développement, *Haiti, pays écorcé* (Port-au-Prince: CHRD, 1989), 42. For a survey of social conditions in the mid-1980s, see Rod Prince, *Haiti: Family Business* (London: Latin America Bureau, 1985).

3. The establishment and role of the Tonton Macoute militia are described in Bernard Diederich and Al Burt, *Papa Doc: Haiti and Its Dictator* (London: Bodley Head, 1970). See also Robert Rotberg, *Haiti: The Politics of Squalor* (Boston: Houghton-Mifflin, 1971).

4. For a full discussion of the role of race and color in Haitian political history, see David Nicholls, *From Dessalines to Duvalier: Race, Colour and National Independence in Haiti* (London: Macmillan, 1988).

5. Tom Barry, Beth Wood, and Deb Preusch, *The Other Side of Paradise: Foreign Control in the Caribbean* (New York: Grove, 1984), 161.

6. Prince, *Haiti*, 50.

7. Barry, Wood, and Preusch, *The Other Side of Paradise*, 339.

8. *Haiti Insight* (New York), January 1990.

9. A fuller account of the anti-Duvalier rebellion is to be found in James Ferguson, *Papa Doc, Baby Doc: Haiti and the Duvaliers* (Oxford: Basil Blackwell, 1987), 90–118.

10. Kern Delince, *Armée et politique en Haiti* (Paris: L'Harmattan, 1979), 100–116.

11. For accounts of the agreement reached between Duvalier, the army, and U.S. authorities, see Amy Wilentz, *The Rainy Season: Haiti since*

*Duvalier* (London: Jonathan Cape, 1989), 129; and Mark Danner, "Beyond the Mountains", *New Yorker*, 27 November 1989.

12. *Caribbean Contact* (Bridgetown), June 1986.

13. Wilentz, *Rainy Season*, 269.

14. Josh de Wind and David Kinley, *Aiding Migration: The Impact of International Development Assistance on Haiti* (New York: Columbia University Center for the Social Sciences, 1986).

15. *Caribbean Insight* (London), September 1987.

16. Council on Hemispheric Affairs, *Washington Report on the Hemisphere* (Washington, D.C.), 22 July 1987.

17. James Ferguson, "Duvalierism Is Alive and Kicking", *Guardian* (London), 29 August 1987.

18. Americas Watch, *Haiti: Terror and the 1987 Elections* (New York: Americas Watch, 1987).

19. *Caribbean Insight* (London), November 1987.

20. "Haiti: plus ça change," *NACLA Report on the Hemisphere* (May–June 1987): 33.

21. Council on Hemispheric Affairs, *Washington Report on the Hemisphere* (Washington, D.C.), 20 January 1988.

22. Wilentz, *Rainy Season*, 334–35.

23. "After the Fall," *Caribbean Review* (Miami), Winter 1988.

24. Americas Watch, *The More Things Change . . . Human Rights in Haiti* (New York: Americas Watch, 1989).

25. *Caribbean Insight* (London), October 1988.

26. *Haiti Insight* (New York), July 1989.

27. Americas Watch, *The More Things Change*, 46–63. See also *Amnesty International Report 1989* (London: Amnesty International, 1989).

28. *Caribbean Insight* (London), May 1989.

29. *Haiti Insight* (New York), July 1989.

30. Ferguson, *Papa Doc, Baby Doc*, 187.

31. Wilentz, *Rainy Season*, 401. See also *Latinamerica Press* (Lima), 30 November 1989.

32. Claudette Werleigh, *Working for Change in Haiti* (London: Catholic Institute of International Relations, 1989), 14–15.

## Chapter 4: Race, Politics, and Succession in Trinidad and Guyana

I would like to thank my doctoral student, Bishnu Ragoonath, for assisting me in putting some finishing touches to the Trinidad portion of this chapter. I would also like to clarify certain usages in this chapter. Instead of using Trinidad and Tobago, I use only Trinidad, meaning the same thing. In Trinidad, persons of African descent are called Creoles, but in Guyana they are referred to as Africans or Afro-Guyanese.

1. For the impact of Indians in Trinidad, see John La Guerre, ed., *From Calcutta to Caroni* (London: Longmans, 1974).

2. For Trinidad's ethnically polarized politics, see Selwyn D. Ryan, *Race and Nationalism in Trinidad and Tobago: A Study of Decolonization in a Multiracial Society* (Toronto: University of Toronto Press, 1972); and for the role of integrative forces in forming a new national identity in British Guiana, see Raymond Smith, *British Guiana* (London: Oxford University Press, 1962).

3. See Paul Sutton, "Black Power in Trinidad and Tobago: The Crisis of 1970," *Journal of Commonwealth and Comparative Politics* 21, no. 2 (July 1983): 116–31.

4. See José M. Sandoval, "State Capitalism in a Petroleum-Based Economy: The Case of Trinidad and Tobago," in F. Ambursley and R. Cohen, eds., *Crisis in the Caribbean* (London: Heinemann, 1983), 147–269; see also Paul Sutton, "Trinidad and Tobago: Oil Capitalism and the 'Presidential Power' of Eric Williams," in Anthony Payne and Paul Sutton, eds., *Dependency under Challenge: The Political Economy of the Commonwealth Caribbean* (Manchester: Manchester University Press, 1984), 43–76.

5. See Dennis A. Pantin, "Whither Pt. Lisas: Lessons for the Future," in S. Ryan, ed., *The Independence Experience 1962–87* (St. Augustine: Institute of Social and Economic Research, 1988), 27–46.

6. See I. Oxaal, *Black Intellectuals Come to Power* (Cambridge: Schenkman, 1968), 137–58.

7. See Percy Hintzen, *The Costs of Regime Survival: Racial Mobilization, Ethnic Domination, and Control of the State in Guyana and Trinidad* (Cambridge: Cambridge University Press, 1989).

8. See Scott B. MacDonald, *Trinidad and Tobago: Democracy and Development in the Caribbean* (New York: Praeger, 1986), 177–79.

9. See Selwyn D. Ryan, "New Directions in Trinidad and Tobago," *Caribbean Affairs* 1, no. 1 (January–March 1988): 132–35; see also Selwyn D. Ryan, "One Love Revisited," *Caribbean Affairs* 1, no. 2 (April–June 1988): 67–127.

10. See Ryan, "One Love Revisited," 74, 75.

11. Ibid., 69.

12. Ibid.

13. *Sunday Express* (Port of Spain), 13 December 1987.

14. A. Johnson, "Public Service 29% Indians," *Express* (Port of Spain), 4 December 1989.

15. A. Johnson, "No Room for Racism in T and T," *Express* (Port of Spain), 4 December 1989.

16. See Ralph R. Premdas, "Fiji: The Anatomy of the Revolution," *Pacifica* 1, no. 1 (1988); also Ralph R. Premdas, "The Relevance of the Fiji Coup to the Caribbean," *Caribbean Issues* (in press).

17. Most of the statistical data cited on Guyana's demography and representation in the public service can be found in *Report of the British Guiana Commission of Enquiry on Racial Problems in the Public Service* (Geneva: International Commission of Jurists, 1965).

18. See Ralph R. Premdas, "The Rise of the First Mass-Based Multi-

Racial Party in Guyana," *Caribbean Quarterly* 20, no. 3–4 (September–December 1974): 5–20.

19. Ibid.

20. See *Report of a Commission of Inquiry into Disturbances in British Guiana in February 1962* (London: HMSO 2849, 1965); Peter Newman, *British Guiana* (London: Oxford University Press, 1964); and Ralph Premdas, "Elections and Campaigns in a Racially Bifurcated State," *Journal of Interamerican Studies and World Affairs* 14, no. 3 (August 1972): 271–96.

21. See R. S. Milne, *Politics in Ethnically Bipolar States* (Vancouver: University of British Colombia Press, 1982).

22. See C. Thomas, "Bread and Justice: The Struggle for Socialism in Guyana," *Monthly Review* 28 (September 1976): 23–35; also R. Premdas, "Guyana: Socialist Reconstruction or Political Opportunism?," *Journal of Interamerican Studies and World Affairs* 20, no. 2 (May 1978): 133–63; and L. F. S. Burnham, *Birth of the Cooperative Republic in Guyana* (Georgetown: Ministry of Information, 1970).

23. See Ralph R. Premdas and P. Hintzen, "Guyana: Coercion and Control in Political Change," *Journal of Interamerican Studies and World Affairs* 24, no. 3 (August 1982): 337–54.

24. See Latin America Bureau, *Guyana: Fraudulent Revolution* (London: LAB, 1984).

25. Jay Mandle, "Continuity and Change in Guyanese Underdevelopment," *Monthly Review* 21, no. 2 (September 1976): 48–50.

26. See G. K. Danns, "Militarisation and Development: An Experiment in Nation Building in Guyana," *Transition* (Guyana), 1, no. 1 (1978): 23–44.

27. See Ralph R. Premdas, "Guyana: Changes in Ideology and Foreign Policy," *World Affairs* 145, no. 2 (Fall 1982): 177–202.

28. See David de Caires, "Guyana after Burnham," *Caribbean Affairs* 1, no. 1 (January–March 1988): 183–98.

## Chapter 5: The March of Militarization in Suriname

1. For Surinamese politics during World War II, see C. D. Ooft, *Ontwikkeling van het constitutionele recht van Suriname* (Assen: Van Gorcum, 1972), 113–40; J. van de Walle, *Een oog boven Paramaribo* (Amsterdam: Arbeiderspers, 1975), 22–28, 59–66, 75–83, 104–29; J. van de Walle, "Suriname in oorlogstijd," in Glenn Willemsen, ed., *Suriname: de schele onafhankelijkheid* (Amsterdam: Arbeiderspers, 1983); Edward Dew, *The Difficult Flowering of Surinam: Ethnicity and Politics in a Plural Society* (The Hague: Martinus Nijhoff, 1978), 42–59; Ben Scholtens, *Suriname tijdens de Tweede Wereldoorlog* (Paramaribo: Anton de Kom Universiteit van Suriname, 1985), 47–79.

2. The Charter for the Kingdom of the Netherlands is discussed most extensively in W. H. van Helsdingen, *Het Statuut voor het Koninkrijk der*

*Nederlanden: Wordingsgeschiedenis, commentaar en praktijk* (The Hague: Staatsdrukkerij, 1957); F. E. M. Mitrasing, *Tien jaar Suriname: Van afhankelijkheid tot gelijkberechtigdheid* (Leiden: Luctor et Emergo, 1959); Albert L. Gastmann, *The Politics of Suriname and the Netherlands Antilles* (Río Piedras: University of Puerto Rico, 1968); and Ooft, *Ontwikkeling van het constitutionele recht van Suriname,* 138–202.

3. The road to Surinamese independence is examined in Benny Ch. Ooft, *Het laatste hoofdstuk: Een analytisch verslag van het overleg en de ontwikkelingen rond de onafhankelijkheid van Suriname in 1974 en 1975* (Utrecht: Stichting Landelijke Federatie van Welzijnsstichtingen van Surinamers, 1976); Dew, *Difficult Flowering of Surinam,* 175–96; and H. K. Fernandes Mendes, *Onafhankelijkheid en parlementair stelsel in Suriname: Hoofdlijnen van een nieuw en democratish staatsbestel* (Zwolle: Tjeenk Willink, 1989), 81–167.

4. The 1975–80 period is described in Henk Boom, *Staatsgreep in Suriname* (Utrecht and Amsterdam: Veen, 1982), 11–43; Benny Ch. Ooft, *Suriname 10 jaar republiek* (Nieuwegein: Stichting Basispers, 1985), 41–79; and Anna Maria Janssen, *Suriname ontwikkelingsland in het Caraibisch gebied* (Amsterdam: SUA, 1986), 94–98.

5. H. K. Fernandes Mendes, "Suriname: Military Threat and the Restoration of Democracy," *Internationale Spectator* 43, no. 11 (1989): 664–65. See also Boom, *Staatsgreep in Suriname,* 45–112; and Ooft, *Suriname 10 jaar republiek,* 83–96.

6. See also Gary Brana-Shute, "Back to the Barracks? Five Years 'Revo' in Suriname," *Journal of Interamerican Studies and World Affairs* 28, no. 1 (1986): 103–4; and Jozef Slagveer, *Denacht van de revolutie* (Paramaribo: Kersten, 1980), 82–105.

7. Boom, *Staatsgreep in Suriname,* 179–83.

8. H. E. Chin and Hans Buddingh', *Surinam: Politics, Economics and Society* (London: Frances Pinter, 1987), 44-46; André Haakmat, *De revolutie uitgegleden: Politieke herinnerigen* (Amsterdam: Jan Mets, 1987), 78–80.

9. Gerard van Westerloo, "Suriname acht jaar onafhankelijk," in Willemsen, *Suriname,* 255–57.

10. The involvement of the Dutch military mission in the coup d'état of 25 February 1980 has been investigated thoroughly by Elma Verhey and Gerard van Westerloo, *Het legergroene Suriname* (Amsterdam: Weekbladpers, 1983), 30–48, 60–62, 123–65.

11. Mendes, *Onafhankelijkheid en parlementair stelsel in Suriname,* 221–24; Osvaldo Cardénas, *De revolutie van sergeanten: Getuigenis van mijn werk als residerend ambassadeur van Cuba* (Nijmegen: Studiecentrum voor Vredesvraagstukken KUN, 1988), 25–26.

12. Haakmat, *De revolutie uitgegleden,* 156–57.

13. Van Westerloo, "Suriname acht jaar onafhankelijk," 241–44; *Gevangenen van Suriname* (Rotterdam: Makmur, 1984), 60–81; and Haakmat, *De revolutie uitgegleden,* 150–52.

14. Van Westerloo, "Suriname acht jaar onafhankelijk," 244–54; Jan

Sariman, *De decembermoorden in Suriname: Verslag van een ooggetuige* (Bussum: Het Wereldvenster, 1983); Ooft, *Suriname 10 jaar republiek*, 110–15; Willem Oltmans, *Willem Oltmans in gesprek met Desi Bouterse* (Amsterdam: Jan Mets, 1984), 42–46; Haakmat, *De revolutie uitgegleden*, 159–88, 195–200; Chin and Buddingh', *Surinam*, 52–58; Rudi F. Kross, *Anders maakt het leven je dood: De dreigende verdwijning van de staat Suriname* (Groningen: Muuses, 1987), 56–67; Cardénas, *De revolutie van sergeanten*, 36–51.

15. Chin and Buddingh', *Surinam*, 42, 45, 48–49, 60–62, 175–80; Cardénas, *De revolutie van sergeanten*, 33–36, 55–77, 82.

16. I was led to this characterization having read van Westerloo, "Suriname acht jaar onafhankelijk," 230; and Brana-Shute, "Back to the Barracks?" 110–11.

17. The best introduction to the Brunswijk guerrilla is H. U. E. Thoden van Velzen, "De Brunswijk-opstand: Antropologische kanttekeningen bij de Surinaamse burgeroorlog," *Sociologische Gids* 35, no. 3 (1988): 212–36.

18. A lively picture of the November 1987 elections is presented in Gary Brana-Shute, "Politics and Militarism in Suriname," *Hemisphere* 1, no. 2 (1989): 32–35.

19. This paragraph is largely based on fieldwork I did in Suriname in the autumn of 1988.

## Chapter 6: Revolution, Democracy, and Regional Integration in the Eastern Caribbean

1. *Caribbean Insight* (London), April 1990.

2. *Latin American Regional Report: Caribbean* (London), 21 June 1990.

3. Louis Blom-Cooper, *Guns for Antigua* (London: Duckworths, 1990), 188–89.

4. For a fuller discussion of these themes, see Tony Thorndike, *Grenada: Politics, Economics and Society* (London: Frances Pinter; and Boulder: Lynne Rienner, 1985).

5. Anthony J. Payne, "Westminster Adapted: The Political Order of the Commonwealth Caribbean," in Jorge I. Domínguez, Robert A. Pastor, and R. DeLisle Worrell, eds., *Democracy in the Caribbean: Political, Economic, and Social Perspectives* (Baltimore: Johns Hopkins University Press, forthcoming).

6. The impact of smallness on political institutions and political behavior is discussed by Paul Sutton, "Political Aspects," in Colin Clarke and Tony Payne, eds., *Politics, Security and Development in Small States* (London: Allen and Unwin, 1987), 8–19.

7. *New Chronicle* (Dominica), 5 May 1986.

8. International Monetary Fund, *IMF Survey 17 June 1989* (Washington D.C.: IMF, 1989), 188.

9. *The Independent* (London), 2 April 1990.

10. For a discussion of the emergence of these associations, see Morley

Ayearst, *The British West Indies: The Search for Self-Government* (New York: New York University Press, 1960).

11. See, for example, the experience of Samuel Smith, in Keithley B. Smith and Fernando C. Smith, *To Shoot Hard Labour: The Life and Times of Samuel Smith—an Antiguan Workingman 1877–1982* (Scarborough, Ont.: Edan's, 1986), 76–78.

12. See K. Bahadoorsingh, "The Eastern Caribbean Federation Attempt," in Roy Preiswerk, eds., *Regionalism and the Commonwealth Caribbean* (St. Augustine: Institute of International Relations, University of West Indies, 1969), 157–69.

13. F. A. Hoyos, *Barbados: A History from the Amerindians to Independence* (London: Macmillan, 1979), 168.

14. F. A. Hoyos, *Grantley Adams and the Social Revolution* (London: Macmillan, 1974), 232.

15. Richard Hart, introduction to Chris Searle, ed., *In Nobody's Backyard: Maurice Bishop's Speeches 1979–83* (London: Zed Books, 1984), xi.

16. A. W. Singham, *The Hero and the Crowd in a Colonial Polity* (New Haven: Yale University Press, 1968), 132–59.

17. Government of Barbados, *The House of Assembly Debates, Official Report*, 2d sess. 15 November 1983 (Bridgetown).

18. I. Andreyev, *The Non-Capitalist Way* (Moscow: Progress Publishers, 1974); V. G. Solodivonikov and V. Bogoslovsky, *Non-Capitalist Development: An Historical Outline* (Moscow: Progress Publishers, 1975); and R. A. Ulyanovsky, *Socialism and the Newly Independent Nations* (Moscow: Progress Publishers, 1974).

19. See Patrick Emmanuel, "Revolutionary Theory and Political Reality in the Eastern Caribbean," *Journal of Interamerican Studies and World Affairs* 25, no. 2 (1983): 204.

20. "Interview with Maurice Bishop," *Caribbean Monthly Bulletin* (Puerto Rico) 8, no. 3 (March 1974): 31.

21. Tony Thorndike, "People's Power in Theory and Practice," in Jorge Heine, ed., *A Revolution Aborted: The Lessons of Grenada* (Pittsburgh: University of Pittsburgh Press, 1990), 38–45.

22. Thorndike, *Grenada*, 79.

23. Ibid., 72–73.

24. Anthony Payne, "The Foreign Policy of the People's Revolutionary Government" in Heine, *Revolution Aborted*, 131–33.

25. This argument is extensively discussed in Thorndike, *Grenada*, 176–91.

26. *Foreign Affairs Bulletin* (Berlin) 22, no. 9–10 (October 1982).

27. Central Committee of the New Jewel Movement, "Minutes, 28 September 1983" (St. George's), 3.

28. Extraordinary Meeting of the Central Committee of the New Jewel Movement, "Minutes, 14–16 September 1983" (St. George's), 18–19.

29. Full accounts are given in Anthony Payne, Paul Sutton, and Tony Thorndike, *Grenada: Revolution and Invasion* (London: Croom Helm;

and New York: St. Martin's, 1984); and Hugh O' Shaughnessy, *Grenada: Revolution, Invasion and Aftermath* (London: Hamish Hamilton, 1984).

30. Tony Thorndike, "Grenada," in J. Hopkins, ed., *Latin America and Caribbean Contemporary Record, 1983–84* (New York: Holmes and Meier, 1985), 801.

31. *Caribbean Contact* (Bridgetown), April 1984.

32. See James Ferguson, *Grenada: Revolution in Reverse* (London: Latin America Bureau, 1990).

33. For an alternative discussion of these issues, see Arend Lijphart, "Size, Pluralism and the Westminster Model of Democracy: Implications for the Eastern Caribbean," in Heine, *Revolution Aborted.*

34. *Caribbean Insight* (London), August 1987.

35. Ibid.

36. Ron Sanders, "Disunity in the OECS," *Caribbean Affairs* 2, no. 2 (1989): 124.

37. *Trinidad Guardian* (Port of Spain), 12 August 1990.

38. *Caribbean Insight* (London), December 1990.

39. *Caribbean Contact* (Bridgetown), November–December 1990.

## Chapter 7: The Grenadian Revolution in Retrospect

This chapter is based on Courtney Smith, "The Development Strategy of the People's Revolutionary Government: The Political Economy of Economic Transformation in Grenada, 1979–1983," Ph.D. thesis, University of Hull, 1988.

1. United Nations, *Agricultural Statistics,* vols. 4, 5 (Port of Spain: Economic Commission for Latin America and the Caribbean, 1982). See also George Brizan, *Grenada: Island of Conflict: From Amerindians to People's Revolution 1498–1979* (London: Zed Books, 1984), chap. 16.

2. For a detailed study of the structure of Grenada's peasant agricultural sector, see John Brierley, *Small Farming in Grenada* (Winnipeg: University of Manitoba, 1974).

3. Cited in Theodore Ferguson, "Potential for Increasing Agricultural Production in Grenada," in Institute of International Relations, *Independence for Grenada: Myth or Reality?* (St. Augustine: Institute of International Relations, University of the West Indies, 1974), 97.

4. Embassy of Grenada, "Proceedings of Aid Donor's Meeting held in Brussels at ACP House on 14–15 April 1981," 5.

5. Smith, "The Development Strategy of the People's Revolutionary Government," 86.

6. Government of Grenada, "Industry," (St. George's: Ministry of Finance, n.d.), 2.

7. Fitzroy Ambursley, "Grenada: The New Jewel Revolution," in Fitzroy Ambursley and Robin Cohen, eds., *Crisis in the Caribbean* (London: Heinemann, 1983), 200.

8. Central Statistical Office, St. George's.

9. Cited in W. Richard Jacobs and Ian Jacobs, *Grenada: The Route to Revolution* (Havana: Casa de las Americas, 1980), 47.

10. World Bank, "Economic Memorandum on Grenada, 1984" (Washington D.C., 1984), 8.

11. See Jacobs and Jacobs, *Grenada*, for a comprehensive account of the emergence of the New Jewel Movement party and further discussion of the conditions that gave rise to the Grenada revolution.

12. New Jewel Movement, "Manifesto of the New Jewel Movement, 1973," in Institute of International Relations, *Independence for Grenada*, 143–56.

13. See Smith, "The Development Strategy of the People's Revolutionary Government," chap. 4, for a critical assessment of the economic thought of the New World Group.

14. Maurice Bishop, "Imperialism Is the Real Problem," in Maurice Bishop, *Selected Speeches 1979–1981* (Havana: Casa de las Americas, 1982), 190.

15. Clive Thomas, *Dependence and Transformation: The Economics of the Transition to Socialism* (New York: Monthly Review Press, 1974).

16. New Jewel Movement, "Manifesto of the New Jewel Movement," 153.

17. Jacobs and Jacobs, *Grenada*, 78.

18. Cited in Maurice Bishop, *Forward Ever! Three Years of the Grenadian Revolution* (Sydney: Pathfinder Press, 1982), 15–16.

19. Maurice Bishop, "We'll Always Choose to Stand Up," interview by Grace Dana, *Granma Weekly Review* (Havana), July 1981.

20. Fitzroy Ambursley, "Grenada: The New Jewel Revolution," in Ambursley and Cohen, *Crisis in the Caribbean*; and Hilbourne Watson, "Grenada: Non-capitalist Path and the Derailment of a Populist Revolution," paper prepared for the Caribbean Studies Association, St. Kitts, 29 May–2 June 1985. Referring to the PRG's Investment Code, Watson argues that "it had taken a revolutionary democratic regime to bring Grenada to the Puerto Rican model," 20.

21. Maurice Bishop, "Line of March for the Party," address to the General Meeting of the Party on 13 September 1982, in U.S. State Department and Department of Defense, *Grenada Documents: An Overview and Selection* (Washington D.C.: U.S. State and Defense Depts., 1984), 20.

22. Ibid., 23.

23. Bernard Coard, *Report on the National Economy for 1981 and the Prospects for 1982* (St. George's: Government Printing Office, 1982), 44.

24. Cited in Jay Mandle, *Big Revolution, Small Country: The Rise and Fall of the Grenada Revolution* (Lanham: North-South, 1985), 25.

25. The main features of the "old tourism" were articulated in the party's 1973 manifesto and reiterated in an address made by Maurice Bishop in December 1979, "The New Tourism," in Bishop, *Selected Speeches 1979–1981*, 68.

26. For insights into the structure and functioning of the handicraft

sector before 1979 and the main initiatives introduced by the PRG in this regard, see Barrington Brown, "Report on the Handicraft Development Project for the Period 15th May–15th December 1982" (St. George's, 1982).

27. Caribbean Tourism and Research Centre, *Grenada, Visitor Survey*, vol. 1 (Bridgetown: CTRC, 1982), 5.

28. The government's efforts in this sector were acknowledged and applauded by the Grenada Hotel Association. See Grenada Hotel Association, "Report of the President to the Twenty First Annual General Meeting" (St. George's, November 1982), 4.

29. Grenada Department of Tourism, "Annual Statistical Overview" (St. George's, various years).

30. Bernard Coard, "National Reconstruction and Development in the Grenadian Revolutionary Process," in People's Revolutionary Government, *Grenada Is Not Alone* (St. George's: Fedon Publishers, 1982), 45.

31. For a discussion of the role assigned to this sector, see George Louison, "The Role of Agriculture in the Revolution," in People's Revolutionary Government, *Grenada Is Not Alone*, 95.

32. For a discussion of the significance of emulation in the context of the Grenada revolution, see Maurice Bishop, "Emulation Is the Seed that Brings the Fruit of Excellence" (St. George's, 1981).

33. See People's Revolutionary Government, *Agricultural Census— Final Report on Grenada Agricultural Census* (St. George's: PRG, 1982).

34. Figures from Central Statistical Office, Ministry of Finance, St. George's.

35. See Jiri Cerhonek, "A Project for Grenada's Economic Development in the Period 1983–1985" (St. George's: Grenada Documentation and Information Centre, July 1982). See also Anthony Boatswain, "The Development of the Manufacturing Sector in Grenada, 1980–2000: Problems and Prospects" (St. George's, 1984), for further discussion of the PRG's industrial strategy.

36. See People's Revolutionary Government, "The Grenada Investment Code (Draft)" (St. George's, June 1981). The final document was published by the Overseas Private Investment Corporation as the *Grenada Investment Guide* (St. George's: OPIC, 1983); the title was designed to avoid the legal connotation of the term *code*.

37. For a discussion of Lewis's thesis, see the special issue of *Social and Economic Studies* 29, no. 4 (1980). See, also, Richard Bernal et al., "Caribbean Economic Thought: the Critical Tradition," *Social and Economic Studies* 33, no. 2 (1984): 5–96.

38. United Nations Centre on Transnational Corporations, "Some Preliminary Comments on the Grenada Investment Code" (New York, 1982).

39. World Bank, "Economic Memorandum on Grenada, 1982," Report 3825-GRD (Washington D.C., April 1982), 20–21.

40. For a lengthy discussion of the relationship between the PRG and the private sector, see Smith, "The Development Strategy of the People's Revolutionary Government," chap. 7. See also Claremont Kirton, "Public

Policy and Private Capital in the Transition to Socialism: Grenada 1979–1983," n.p., n.d.

41. See People's Revolutionary Government, *Report on the National Economy for 1982* (St. George's: PRG, 1983).

42. International Monetary Fund, *Grenada: Recent Economic Developments* (Washington D.C.: IMF, 1984), 2.

43. Ibid., 1.

44. Central Statistical Office, St. George's, March 1987.

45. People's Revolutionary Government, "Revised Economic Memorandum on Grenada" (St. George's, June 1982), 12.

46. According to the 1984 World Bank Report, no private capital was attracted to Grenada during this period, a situation reminiscent of the immediate prerevolutionary period. See World Bank, "Economic Memorandum on Grenada, 1984," 23.

47. People's Revolutionary Government, *Report on the National Economy for 1982*, 73.

48. Ibid., 31.

49. Grenada Chamber of Industry and Commerce, "Brief History of the Private Sector" (St. George's, n.d.), 20.

50. Ibid., 2–4.

51. World Bank, "Economic Memorandum on Grenada, 1984," 42.

52. For example, in 1982 public sector investment accounted for 32 percent of gross domestic product, but only 5 percent in 1978. See IMF, *Grenada: Recent Economic Developments*, 31.

53. See People's Revolutionary Government, *Report on the National Economy for 1982*, 9.

54. As the World Bank notes, "the available data on the Grenadian labour force is inadequate for analysing trends in employment and unemployment over the period 1975 through 1982." See "Economic Memorandum on Grenada, 1984," 17. In a similar vein, the IMF notes that "no comprehensive labour survey has been undertaken to back this estimate." See IMF, *Grenada: Recent Economic Developments*, 19.

55. See "Extraordinary Meeting of the Central Committee of the New Jewel Movement, 14–16 September 1983," in U.S. State Department and Department of Defense, *Grenada Documents*, 5.

56. For a detailed discussion of the 1983 IMF program, see Claremont Kirton, "Grenada and the IMF: The People's Revolutionary Government's EFF Programme, 1983" n.p., n.d. The data in this section are drawn from Kirton's paper.

57. Ibid., 2.

58. Cited in U.S. State Department and Department of Defense, *Grenada Documents*, 3.

59. "Central Committee Report on First Plenary Session, 13–19 July 1983," in ibid., 4.

60. "Extraordinary Meeting of the Central Committee, 14–16 September 1983," in ibid. The following quotations are from ibid., 4, 6–8, 11–13.

61. Gordon Lewis, *Grenada: The Jewel Despoiled* (Baltimore: Johns Hopkins University Press, 1987), 44, 42–43.

62. World Bank, "Economic Memorandum on Grenada, 1982," 17–18.

63. For an insightful discussion of the performance of the PRG compared to the Grenada National Party during the postinvasion period, see James Ferguson, *Grenada: Revolution in Reverse* (London: Latin America Bureau, 1990).

64. Ivar Oxaal, *Black Intellectuals and the Dilemma of Race and Class in Trinidad* (Cambridge: Schenkman, 1982), xiv.

## Chapter 8: Political Economy and Foreign Policy in Puerto Rico

1. Remarks offered at the closing plenary session of the Caribbean Studies Association, San Juan, Puerto Rico, 31 May 1985.

2. For these and other data about the 1985–89 economic performance of Puerto Rico, see Rafael Hernández Colón, *Mensaje sobre el estado de situación del país a la Asamblea Legislativa en su Primera Sesión Ordinaria* (San Juan: Government Printing Office, 1989).

3. For a survey of the 1988 campaign, see Jorge Heine, "Puerto Rico in the Caribbean," in Jeremy Taylor, ed., *The Caribbean Handbook 1989* (St. John's: FT Caribbean, 1989), 26–27.

4. For an earlier assessment of this strategy, see Juan M. García-Passalacqua, "The Internationalization of Puerto Rico," paper prepared for the conference La política exterior de Puerto Rico, Universidad Metropolitana, San Juan, 10 April 1986. See also Jorge Heine, "Cruising Uncharted Waters: Puerto Rico's Foreign Policy 1986–87," in Abraham F. Lowenthal, *Latin America and Caribbean Contemporary Record IV* (New York: Holmes and Meier, 1989), 131–43, from which this chapter draws in part.

5. For an evaluation of the Caribbean Basin Initiative three years after it became law, see U.S. House of Representatives, Subcommittee on Oversight of the Committee on Ways and Means, *Report on the Committee Delegation to the Caribbean Basin and Recommendations to Improve the Effectiveness of the Caribbean Basin Initiative* (Washington D.C.: Government Printing Office, 1987).

6. For an analysis of the reality and potential of Puerto Rico's role in the Caribbean Basin Initiative, see Sara Grusky and Richard Ruth, "Puerto Rico and the Caribbean Basin Initiative: The Complexities of Interdependence" (Washington D.C.: Puerto Rico Research Institute, 1986).

7. For an excellent analysis of these changes with reference to the interaction between Puerto Rico and the Caribbean, see David Lewis, "The United States, the Caribbean and Puerto Rico: The Political Economy of Decolonization and Regional Interdependence," paper prepared for the Latin American Studies Association, Boston, 23–25 October 1986.

8. For a useful collection of essays discussing Puerto Rico's relations

with the Caribbean up to 1984, see Carmen Gautier et al., eds., *Puerto Rico y el Caribe Hoy* (Buenos Aires: CLACSO, 1987).

Although in absolute terms, trade between Puerto Rico and the Caribbean and Latin America increased considerably between 1970 and 1990, it continued to be a very small part of Puerto Rico's external trade. In 1987, 88.9 percent of all exports went to the United States, only 4.7 percent to the Caribbean. For an assessment of economic trends, see Juan A. Castaner and Angel Calderón Cruz, "Puerto Rico's Trade Linkages with the Rest of the Caribbean," *Caribbean Affairs* 2, no. 4 (October-December 1989): 123–40.

Puerto Rico's Education Department uses the Spanish language translations of U.S. textbooks for teaching cultural subjects. The expansion of the Puerto Rican University system, which led to a student population of 150,000 (5 percent of the population), was accompanied by a *reduction* in the number of foreign students (mostly Caribbeans and Latin Americans). UPR—Mayaguez, for example, which traditionally attracted many foreign students because of its engineering and agricultural schools, witnessed a 50 percent reduction in the number of foreign students between 1974 and 1984, from 418 to 221 students (of a total 9,500).

9. See "Berríos: los soberanos sí, las colonias No," *El Nuevo Día* (San Juan), 7 May 1985. For an elaboration of the ideas of PIP president Rubén Berríos on the subject, see his book *La independencia de Puerto Rico: razón y lucha* (Mexico City: Editorial Linea, 1983), chap. 8.

10. For an analysis of these possibilities, see Michael Reisman, *Puerto Rico and the International Process: New Roles in Association*, American Society of International Law, Studies in Transnational Legal Policy 6 (St. Paul: West, 1975). For a comparison of the Micronesian and the Puerto Rican cases, see Sara Grusky-Fajardo and Richard Ruth, "Puerto Rico and Micronesia: Reframing US Strategic Influence," paper prepared for the Caribbean Studies Association, Fort-de-France, 25–28 May 1988.

11. Angel Calderón Cruz, "Las relaciones del Estado Libre Asociado," in Angel Calderón Cruz, ed., *Problemas del Caribe Contemporaneo* (Río Piedras: Instituto de Estudios del Caribe, UPR, 1979).

12. Luis A. Passalacqua Christian, "Puerto Rico y el Caribe: cinco etapas de una relación," in ibid.

13. See Charles D. Ameringer, *The Democratic Left in Exile: The Antidictatorial Struggle in the Caribbean 1945–1959* (Miami: University of Miami Press, 1974).

14. Between 1953 and 1959, 6,500 technicians from 118 countries received training in Puerto Rico; 1,400 civic leaders visited the island during the same period to familiarize themselves with Puerto Rico's economic and social change. In addition, 2,200 visitors came for a program of international conferences. See Arturo Morales Carrión, *Puerto Rico: A Political and Cultural History* (New York: Norton, 1983), 292.

15. Ibid., 291.

16. Passalacqua, "Puerto Rico y el Caribe," 69.

17. Ibid., 72–73.

18. Carlos Romero Barceló, "Puerto Rico's Role in the Caribbean Basin Initiative" (San Juan, 17 December 1981), 6. This document was sent to U.S. Special Trade Representative William Brock.

19. Cited in *Caribbean Business* (San Juan), 17 April 1985.

20. See, for example, Harold Lidin, "Policy Paradox," *San Juan Star*, 10 May 1985.

21. As a candidate, Rafael Hernández Colón announced his full support for President Reagan's policies in the Caribbean and Central America in a speech given to the San Juan Rotary Club in October 1984. For his endorsement of the Nicaraguan embargo, see *El Nuevo Día* (San Juan), 4 May 1985.

## Chapter 9: The Odyssey of Revolution in Cuba

1. For examples of analyses of the Cuban revolution in which considerable attention is given to the themes of decay and decline, see Michael J. Mazarr, "Prospects for Revolution in Post-Castro Cuba," *Journal of Interamerican Studies and World Affairs* 31, no. 4 (Winter 1989): 61–90; Anthony Bryan, "A Tropical Perestroika?" *Caribbean Affairs* 2, no. 2 (April-June 1989): 92–103; and Irving L. Horowitz, ed., *Cuban Communism*, 7th ed. (New Brunswick: Transaction, 1989).

2. One example is Douglas Bravo, a Venezuelan Communist who was expelled from the party in 1967 in a dispute over strategy, with Bravo insisting on the primacy of armed struggle. The Cubans, who at that time were also promoting armed struggle as the only viable means for Latin revolutionaries to seize power, strongly supported Bravo's stance against the orthodox, pro-Moscow Venezuelan Communist Party, and a period of close cooperation ensued. Subsequently, however, Havana lowered its radical profile, concentrating instead on reconciliation with Moscow and on addressing its own domestic economic problems. Feeling betrayed, Bravo publicly denounced the Fidelistas. For details on the complex ideological dynamics of Cuba's foreign policy during this period, see K. S. Karol, *Guerrillas in Power* (New York: Hill and Wang, 1970). A discussion of Bravo's disenchantment can be found in ibid., 536.

3. For additional information on these and other incidents, see Richard Gott, *Guerrilla Movements in Latin America* (Garden City: Doubleday, 1972), 13–16.

4. See Robert D. Tomasek, "Caribbean Exile Invasions: A Special Regional Type of Conflict," *Orbis* 17 (Winter 1974): 1354–82, for discussion of foreign supported exile invasions as a well-established practice in Caribbean intra-regional politics. For a history of the Caribbean Legion, see Charles D. Ameringer, *The Democratic Left in Exile* (Miami: University of Miami Press, 1974), 59–110.

5. The entire Second Declaration can be found in Martin Fenner and James Petras, eds., *Fidel Castro Speaks* (New York: Grove, 1969), 85–106. The quotations are from 104–6.

6. W. Raymond Duncan, "Cuba," in Harold E. Davis and Larman C.

Wilson, eds., *Latin American Foreign Policies: An Analysis* (Baltimore: Johns Hopkins University Press, 1975), 166–69, divides this ebb and flow into three main segments: (1) 1962 to late 1963, during which Cuba stressed the need for armed insurrection as the basic path to revolutionary change in Latin America; (2) late 1963 to January 1966, which saw Havana moderate its position by saying that, even though it still placed primary emphasis on armed struggle, it was willing to recognize that there were other options, including assuming power nonviolently through elections; and (3) January 1966 to August 1968, during which Cuba returned to its hard line: that violent revolution was the only realistic means for hemispheric radicals to achieve power.

7. This publicity blitz included devoting the entire 22 July 1979 edition of the *Granma Weekly Review (GWR)* (Havana) to Carifesta. This is not standard procedure; when the *GWR* wants to give a topic special coverage, it normally does so by means of separate inserts. This was the first time in my experience that the *GWR* jettisoned all its normal features and turned a whole issue over to a single subject. The common economic and political heritage of the region's peoples and the need to break down the barriers separating the Spanish-speaking and English-speaking Caribbean were emphasized. Among the *GWR* articles in this vein were "The Rich and Legendary History of the 'Black Gladiators,'" "The Caribbean: 400 Years of Economic Exploitation," and "Antonio Maceo's Caribbean Odyssey, 1878–1895."

8. Other moderate-conservative candidates who prevailed in the late 1970s or early 1980s were Milton Cato in St. Vincent (December 1979), Kennedy Simmonds in St. Kitts–Nevis (February 1980), Vere Bird in Antigua (April 1980), Eugenia Charles in Dominica (July 1980), George Chambers in Trinidad and Tobago (November 1981), John Compton in St. Lucia (May 1982), and Lynden Pindling in the Bahamas (June 1982).

9. For details on the Cuban measurements of productivity, see Claes Brundenius, *Revolutionary Cuba: The Challenge of Growth with Equity* (Boulder: Westview, 1984), chap. 2; and James D. Rudolph, ed., *Cuba: A Country Study*, 3d ed. (Washington, D.C.: Department of the Army, 1985), 113.

10. Among the representative works of these two schools are Brundenius, *Revolutionary Cuba;* Claes Brundenius and Andrew Zimbalist, *Essays on the Cuban Economy: Structure and Performance* (forthcoming); Carmelo Mesa-Lago, *The Economy of Socialist Cuba: A Two-Decade Appraisal* (Albuquerque: University of New Mexico Press, 1981); and Jorge F. Perez-Lopez, *Measuring Cuban Economic Performance* (Austin: University of Texas Press, 1987).

11. The specific figures are in Max Azicri, *Cuba: Politics, Economics and Society* (London: Frances Pinter, 1988), 140; and Juan del Aguila, *Cuba: Dilemmas of a Revolution,* rev. ed. (Boulder: Westview, 1988), 107.

12. Information from "Economic Integration Imperative For Latin America," *Granma Weekly Review* (12 February 1984), 9. The article in

turn relies on figures released by the Economic Commission for Latin America (ECLA).

13. For additional information, see del Aguila, *Cuba*, 148.

14. Specific figures for the 1980–84 period can be found in ibid., 108; and the "Introduction" to Andrew Zimbalist, ed., *Cuban Political Economy: Controversies in Cubanology* (Boulder: Westview, 1988), 2.

15. Brundenius, *Revolutionary Cuba*, 62–64, provides an excellent summary of the different viewpoints regarding Cuba's trade dependency and concludes that it was no worse under Castro than in prerevolutionary Cuba and probably improved somewhat, since there was more diversity in the island's export profile.

16. Figures from del Aguila, *Cuba*, 203.

17. Azicri, *Cuba*, 145–46.

18. Some illustrative unemployment percentages are provided by Brundenius, *Revolutionary Cuba*, 73 and 113, as follows: 1953, 13.6; 1960, 11.8; 1970, 1.3; and 1980, 4.1.

19. The 5–6 percent range is mentioned in Mazarr, "Prospects for Revolution in Post-Castro Cuba," 64. While not mentioning any specific figures, Castro indicated in several speeches in the late 1980s that unemployment was indeed a problem and implied that the rate was rising.

20. Brundenius, *Revolutionary Cuba*, 110.

21. For more details regarding the PQLI, see Morris D. Morris, *Measuring Conditions of the World's Poor: The Physical Quality of Life Index* (New York: Pergamon, 1979). Criticisms of the PQLI were voiced almost immediately following the publication of this book. See for example David A. Larson and Walton T. Wilford, "The Physical Quality Of Life Index: A Useful Indicator?" *World Development*, no. 6 (1979): 581–84.

22. The 1984 rating, typical of Cuba's PQLI scores during the 1970s and 1980s, was published in Charles W. Kegley, Jr., and Eugene R. Wittkopf, *World Politics: Trends and Transformations*, 3d ed. (New York: St. Martin's, 1989), 112.

23. Del Aguila, *Cuba*, 176.

24. General Arnaldo Ochoa was one of the revolution's most famous and decorated military heroes, having served with great distinction as commander of Cuba's troops in Angola (1987–88) and as head of Havana's military advisory mission to Nicaragua (1985–86). Indeed, there was some speculation that his popularity (especially within the armed forces) made him a potential candidate to succeed Fidel. In 1989, however, Ochoa was implicated in international illegal drug trafficking. Havana had previously ignored suggestions that some high Cuban officials were active in the drug trade, particularly accusations originating in the United States and often seemingly politically motivated. However, as the evidence against Ochoa and others mounted, they were arrested, swiftly tried, and convicted. Ochoa and three others were immediately executed. For details regarding this incident, see "Reading the Coca Leaves," *Time*, 10 July 1989; and the following issues of the *Granma Weekly Review*: 2 July 1989; 9 July 1989; 16 July 1989; and 23 July 1989.

25. Information regarding the Third World vote comes from *Facts on File* 40, no. 2045 (18 January 1980): 25.

26. The surrogate thesis was firmly embraced by the Reagan administration, with the president one of its most enthusiastic exponents. Other Reagan officials who were among its strongest promoters were Jeanne Kirkpatrick, Alexander Haig, Elliot Abrams, and Roger Fontaine. Academics were not generally inclined to subscribe to the thesis in the stark terms deployed by the U.S. government. Nevertheless, it sometimes did exert an impact on their analyses, a few examples being Robert A. Packenham, "Cuba and the USSR Since 1959: What Kind of Dependency?" in Irving L. Horowitz, ed., *Cuban Communism*, 7th ed. (New Brunswick: Transaction, 1989); Jiri Valenta and Virginia Valenta, "Soviet Strategies and Policies in the Caribbean Basin," in Howard J. Wiarda and Mark Falcoff, eds., *The Communist Challenge in the Caribbean and Central America* (Washington, D.C.: American Enterprise Institute, 1987); Leon Goure and Morris Rothenburg, *Soviet Penetration of Latin America* (Miami: Center for Advanced International Studies, University of Miami, 1975); and James D. Theberge, *The Soviet Presence In Latin America* (New York: Crane, Russak, 1974).

27. Discussions of Cuban-Grenadian relations can be found in Jiri Valenta and Herbert Ellison, eds., *Grenada and Soviet/Cuban Policy: Internal Crisis and U.S./OECS Intervention* (Boulder: Westview, 1986); Anthony Payne, Paul Sutton, and Tony Thorndike, *Grenada: Revolution and Invasion* (London: Croom Helm; and New York: St. Martin's, 1984); and Hugh O'Shaughnessy, *Grenada: Revolution, Invasion, and Aftermath* (London: Hamish Hamilton, 1984).

28. There may be more flexibility in the Cuban stance than appears at first glance. In April 1990 a high Cuban official reportedly told a U.S. delegation that Havana recognized the wisdom of U.S. private investment and would accept increased U.S. influence in the island's affairs as a trade-off (Cable News Network report, 9 April 1990). This incident, which in Cuban terms represents thinking the unthinkable, suggests that there was sympathy for the Gorbachev line among some elements of the country's inner circle. Whether Castro embraced this position is not known.

29. The details concerning the expansion of Cuban-Argentine trade come from Jorge Domínguez, *To Make a World Safe for Revolution: Cuba's Foreign Policy* (Cambridge: Harvard University Press, 1989), 237–38.

30. This section on Cuba's debt policy is taken from H. Michael Erisman, "Cuban Foreign Policy and the Latin American Debt Crisis," *Cuban Studies 18* (Pittsburgh: University of Pittsburgh Press, 1988), 3–18.

31. This theme is developed much more extensively in H. Michael Erisman, *Cuba's International Relations: The Anatomy Of a Nationalistic Foreign Policy* (Boulder: Westview, 1985).

## Chapter 10: Domestic Policy, the External Environment, and the Economic Crisis in the Caribbean

1. For a more detailed discussion of these problems, see Ramesh F. Ramsaran, *The Commonwealth Caribbean in the World Economy* (London: Macmillan, 1989).

2. This view is shared by a number of regional institutions, including the Inter-American Development Bank. See the latter's *Annual Report 1989* (Washington, D.C.: IADB, 1990).

3. These figures are derived from official publications and the World Bank *Atlas* (Washington, D.C.: World Bank, various years).

4. Ibid.

5. Official estimates of the Barbados government.

6. Information on the debt question comes from official publications and publications of the World Bank and the IMF.

7. Multilateral institutions like the IMF and World Bank do not permit rescheduling of loans owed to them.

8. These are official rates and movements. Trading in the black market or parallel market is done at a more highly depreciated rate. For example, the black market rate for the Guyana dollar can be as high as twice the official rate. Data on official exchange rates come from the IMF's *International Financial Statistics* (Washington, D.C.: various years).

9. In recent years, some Trinidad and Tobago citizens seeking resident status in Canada have done so on the grounds that they are economic refugees.

10. See, for example, Robert A. Pastor, "Migration and Development," *Studies in Comparative International Development* 24 (Winter 1989–90): 46 64.

11. For a more detailed analysis of the Grenadian experiment, see Tony Thorndike, *Grenada: Politics, Economics and Society* (London: Frances Pinter; and Boulder: Lynne Rienner, 1985).

12. For an excellent discussion of Jamaica under Michael Manley in the period 1972 80, see E. H. Stephens and J. D. Stephens, *Democratic Socialism in Jamaica: The Political Movement and Social Transformation in Dependent Capitalism* (London: Macmillan, 1986).

13. Under the new policy, foreign corporations became involved in sugar, bauxite, and telecommunications in various capacities.

14. This country also sought access to the fund's Compensatory and Contingency Financing Facility.

15. For a more detailed reading on the kinds of conflict that arise, see Michael Manley, *Up the Down Escalator: Development and the International Economy; a Jamaican Case Study* (London: André Deutsch, 1987). For evidence with respect to the African experience, see Bade Onimode, ed., *The IMF, The World Bank and the African Debt*, vols. 1 and 2 (London: Zed Books, 1989).

16. See G. A. Cornia et al., eds., *Adjustment with a Human Face: A Study by UNICEF* (Oxford: Clarendon, 1988).

17. For a discussion of this theme in relation to the CBI, see Ramesh F. Ramsaran, "Issues in Commonwealth Caribbean—United States Relations," in Anthony Payne and Paul Sutton, eds., *Dependency under Challenge: The Political Economy of the Commonwealth Caribbean* (Manchester: Manchester University Press, 1984).

18. Section 936 refers to a part of the U.S. International Revenue Code that exempts the profits of subsidiaries of U.S. firms located in Puerto Rico from federal taxes. To receive the concession, firms must leave the money in Puerto Rico instead of sending it back to the mainland. Although Puerto Rico, with the encouragement of the Reagan administration, agreed that Section 936 funds should be used to push the objectives of the CBI, red tape and bureaucracy did not allow the use of these resources to the extent envisaged. The persistence of the U.S. budget deficit encouraged some members of the U.S. Congress to question the usefulness of this arrangement. In addition, in order to gain access to Section 936 funds, CBI countries are required to have a tax information exchange agreement with the United States. Trinidad and Tobago, Barbados, Dominica, Grenada, and Jamaica have such agreements.

19. Figures quoted by Canute James in the *Trinidad and Tobago Express* (Port of Spain), 24 April 1990, from the data supplied by the U.S. International Trade Commission. Figures quoted by the same author in the same article from the same source indicate that trade between the United States and CBI-listed countries in 1988 was US$1.3 billion in favor of the United States.

20. See ibid.; see also Peter D. Whitney, director of economic policy for Latin America and the Caribbean, paper prepared for the Conference on the Caribbean, Miami, November 1989, and quoted in the *Trinidad and Tobago Guardian* (Port of Spain), 11 April 1990.

21. In the case of the CBI, for instance, the U.S. president decides which countries qualify, and beneficiary status can be conferred or withdrawn on the basis of whether he believes the country is conforming to the rules.

22. See Howard J. Wiarda, "United States Policy in Latin America," *Current History*, no. 89 (January 1990).

23. See the OECD, *International Investment and Multinational Enterprises: Recent International Direct Investment Trends* (Paris: OECD, 1981).

24. See R. Ramsaran, "Capital Movement—The Experience of Commonwealth Caribbean Countries, 1970–84," in DeLisle Worrell and Compton Bourne, eds., *Economic Adjustment Policies for Small Nations* (New York: Praeger, 1989).

25. For example, Jamaicans were allowed to repatriate funds without any questions being asked about the origin of those funds.

26. ICSID was set up with the aim of arbitrating between host governments and foreign investors in the event of a dispute.

27. See Jeffrey Sachs, "Making the Brady Plan Work," *Foreign Affairs*, no. 68 (Summer 1989): 87–104.

## Chapter 11: The Offshore Caribbean

1. Robert C. Efros, ed., *Emerging Financial Centres* (Washington, D.C.: International Monetary Fund, 1982).

2. Perhaps typical of the overideologized objection to any type of foreign presence in the Caribbean is Tom Barry, Beth Wood, and Deb Preusch, *The Other Side of Paradise: Foreign Control in the Caribbean* (New York: Grove, 1984). This point of view was also (in the 1970s and 1980s) that of the bimonthly *NACLA Report on the Americas* and its Canadian twin, *Latin American Working Group Letter.* In the Caribbean, the journal of the Caribbean Conference of Churches, *Caribbean Contact* (Bridgetown), was generally critical of the tourist and assembly industries. In the United Kingdom, the publications of the Latin America Bureau have been systematically critical of foreign investment, from oil to bananas.

3. William Roy Surret, "The International Narcotics Trade: An Overview of Its Dimensions, Production Sources, and Organizations" (Washington, D.C.: Congressional Research Service, 1988).

4. *Jamaican Weekly Gleaner* (London), 18 April 1988.

5. Ibid., 17 April 1989.

6. Ibid., 18 July 1988.

7. Ibid.

8. Ibid., 16 January 1989.

9. The *Nation* (Antigua), 18 and 25 May 1990, reprinted several confidential Antiguan government documents on the affair.

10. *Miami Herald*, 18 May 1990.

11. *El Tiempo* (Bogota), 19 July 1990.

12. See Louis Blom-Cooper, *Guns for Antigua* (London: Duckworths, 1990). The book is the report of the Commission of Enquiry into the circumstances surrounding the shipment of arms from Israel to Antigua and transshipment on 24 April 1989 en route to Colombia.

13. Committee on Banking, Housing, and Urban Affairs, *Banks and Narcotics Flow in South Florida*, 95th Cong. 1st sess. (Washington D.C.: Government Printing Office, 1988). For more on the drug trade out of Haiti, see Committee on Foreign Relations, U.S. Senate, *Drugs, Law Enforcement and Foreign Policy: The Cartel, Haiti and Central America*, 100th Cong. 2d sess., pt. 4 (11 July 1988). See also Maureen Taft-Morales, "Haiti: Political Developments and U.S. Policy Concerns," Issue Brief, 14 March (Washington, D.C.: Congressional Research Service, 1989).

14. Frederick Kempe, *Divorcing the Dictator: America's Bungled Affair with Noriega* (New York: Putnam, 1990); and John Dinges, *Our Man in Panama: How General Noriega Used the United States and Made Millions in Drugs and Arms* (New York: Random House, 1990).

15. Committee on Banking, Housing, and Urban Affairs, *Banks and Narcotics Flow in South Florida*, 11.

16. U.S. House Committee on Foreign Affairs, *U.S. Narcotics Control Efforts in the Caribbean*, 100th Cong. 1st sess. (Washington, D.C.: Government Printing Office, 1987).

17. This assessment is based on a review of two commissions of inquiry in nearly two decades: Government of Bahamas, *Inquiry into the Illegal Use of the Bahamas for the Transshipment of Dangerous Drugs Destined for the United States of America*, 2 vols. (Nassau: Government Printing Office, 1984); and Government of Bahamas, *Report of the Commission of Inquiry into the Operation of the Business of Casinos in Freeport and in Nassau* (Nassau: Government Printing Office, 1967). On constant rumors about the Pindling government's corruption, see also stories in the *Sunday Times* (London), 26 April and 3 May 1987.

18. Note the rhetorical nature of Gary Brana-Shute's questions in a recent essay on Suriname dictator, Colonel Desi Bouterse: "What exactly is the agenda of the military? Would they again call upon Libyan assistance or strike financial deals with drug cartels? Clearly they have abandoned ideology and now maintain power through pragmatic thuggery." See "Suriname: Years of Living Dangerously," the *Times of the Americas*, 28 November 1990. For an essay on the Dutch pandering to Bouterse's corruption, see Peter Meel, "Money Talks, Morals Vex," *European Review of Latin American and Caribbean Studies* (June 1990): 75–98.

19. Ingo Walters, *Secret Money: The World of International Financial Secrecy* (Lexington: Lexington Books, 1985), 22.

20. Canadian Senate Standing Committee on Banking, Trade and Commerce, *Proceedings*, 2 October 1985 (Ottawa, 1985), 24.

21. The figures are taken from R. Gordon, *Tax Havens and Their Use by United States Taxpayers* (Washington, D.C.: Internal Revenue Service, 1981).

22. *Financial Times* (London), 30 June and 1 July 1990.

23. R. Thomas Naylor, "Drug Money, Hot Money, and Debt," *European Journal of International Affairs* 2, no. 3 (Winter 1989): 62.

24. Walters, *Secret Money*, 81–82.

25. Naylor, "Drug Money, Hot Money, and Debt," 58.

26. U.S. Treasury, *Tax Havens in the Caribbean Basin* (Washington, D.C.: Government Printing Office, 1984), 34.

27. *Miami Herald*, 3 January 1983.

28. *Financial Times* (London), 20 April 1990.

29. J. Schneider, testimony before the Permanent Subcommittee on Investigations of the Senate Committee on Government Affairs, 98th Cong. 1st sess., *Crime and Secrecy: The Use of Offshore Banks and Companies* (Washington D.C.: Government Printing Office, 1983), 66.

30. William Von Raab, testimony in ibid., 60.

31. John K. Villa, "A Critical View of Bank Secrecy Act Enforcement and the Money Laundering Statutes," *Catholic University Law Review* 37, no. 465 (1988): 502.

32. Jerome Schneider, *How to Profit and Avoid Taxes by Organizing Your Own Private International Bank in St. Vincent*, rev. 2d ed. (Los Angeles: WFI, 1979), 1.

33. *Financial Times* (London), 27 November 1989.

34. Jerome Schneider, *Using an Offshore Bank for Profit, Privacy and Tax Protection* (Los Angeles: WFI, 1985), 129.

35. "Con Men Are Raking in Millions by Setting up Own Caribbean Banks," *Wall Street Journal,* 1981.

36. Schneider, *Crime and Secrecy,* 36.

37. "Con Men Are Raking in Millions"; also Walters, *Secret Money.*

38. *Financial Times* (London), 29 June 1990.

39. *Observer* (London), 27 May 1990.

40. *Financial Times* (London), 10 July 1990.

41. *150 years of Banking in the Bahamas, 1936–1986* (Nassau: TCA, 1986), 35.

42. James H. Smith, governor of the Central Bank of the Bahamas, interview, *Business Monday,* 24 October 1988, 21.

43. Interviews in the Bahamas, June 1989.

44. James H. Smith, governor of the Central Bank of the Bahamas, interview, *Financial Times* (London), 10 July 1990.

45. Bahamian high commissioner to Britain, letter in the *Financial Times* (London), 14–15 July 1990.

46. Tim Coone, *Financial Times* (London), 10 July 1990.

47. Cayman Islands Bankers Association *Newsletter,* issue 2 (Summer 1988).

48. National Narcotics Intelligence, Consumers Committee Report, April 1988, cited in *American Banker,* 24 July 1989, 23.

49. *Cayman Horizons* 1, no. 4 (January-February 1984): 36.

50. Martin Connolly, "Property Investment in the Cayman Islands," *Cayman Horizons* 1 (January-February 1984): 65.

51. Cayman Islands Bankers Association *Newsletter,* 2.

52. *Cayman Horizons* 1 (January-February 1984): 37.

53. *Financial Times* (London), 29 June 1990.

54. Rachel Johnson, *Financial Times* (London), 29 June 1990.

55. *Observer* (London), 16 May 1990.

56. *Financial Times* (London), 19 December 1990.

57. *New York Times,* 20 April 1990.

58. *Miami Herald,* 10 June 1990.

59. On this, see the thorough analysis by Ramesh F. Ramsaran, *The Commonwealth Caribbean in the World Economy* (London: Macmillan, 1989), 95–114.

60. Naylor, "Drug Money, Hot Money, and Debt," 69.

61. *Financial Times* (London), 20 April 1990.

## Chapter 12: U.S. Intervention, Regional Security, and Militarization in the Caribbean

1. These concerns are set out in detail in Lars Schoultz, *National Security and United States Policy toward Latin America* (Princeton: Princeton University Press, 1987), chaps. 4–6.

2. Two useful and contrasting commentaries on this question are Joseph Cirincione and Leslie C. Hunter, "Military Threats, Actual and Potential," in R. S. Leiken, ed., *Central America: Anatomy of Conflict* (New York: Pergamon, 1984); and Michael C. Desch, "Turning the Caribbean Flank: Sea-Lane Vulnerability during a European War," *Survival* (November-December 1987): 528–51.

3. "Central America and El Salvador, March 10, 1983," *Weekly Compilation of Presidential Documents* 19, no. 10 (14 March 1983), 377. One of the experts referred to was Sally Shelton, who was Deputy Assistant Secretary of State for Latin America and the Caribbean in 1977–79 and ambassador to the Eastern Caribbean in 1979–81, during the Carter administration.

4. The motive behind the U.S. intervention in the Dominican Republic in 1965 was the belief of President Johnson that "a second Cuba" was in the making. The best study of this action continues to be Abraham Lowenthal, *The Dominican Intervention* (Cambridge: Harvard University Press, 1972).

5. U.S. National Bipartisan Commission on Central America, *Report of the National Bipartisan Commission on Central America* (Washington, D.C.: Government Printing Office, 1984), 93.

6. "Address to the Joint Session of Congress," *Vital Speeches of the Day* 49, no. 15 (15 May 1983).

7. Timothy Ashby, director of the Office of Mexico and the Caribbean basin at the U.S. Department of Commerce during the Reagan years, argues that the CBI was "the Reagan administration's corollary to the Monroe Doctrine." See his article "The Reagan Years," in S. MacDonald, H. Sandstrom, and P. Goodwin, eds., *The Caribbean after Grenada: Revolution, Conflict and Democracy* (New York: Praeger, 1988), 272.

8. "Address to International Trade Mart, 29 November 1983," cited in Kari Polanyi-Levitt, "The Origins and Implications of the Caribbean Basin Initiative: Mortgaging Sovereignty?" *International Journal* 40, no. 2 (1985): 236.

9. See Jorge Rodríguez Beruff, *Política Militar y Dominación: Puerto Rico en el Contexto Latinoamericano* (San Juan: Ediciones Huracán, 1988), 223–24.

10. *The Role of the U.S. Military: Caribbean Basin*, cited in ibid., 120–21.

11. The idea of collective hegemony as a means to assert U.S. primacy is argued in detail in a study undertaken for the U.S. Air Force by the Rand Corporation. See David Ronfeldt, *Geopolitics, Security and U.S. Strategy in the Caribbean Basin* (Santa Monica: Rand, 1983), particularly sect. 5.

12. Statement by President Reagan on U.S. involvement in Grenada, 25 October 1983 (Washington, D.C.: U.S. Information Service).

13. See Anthony Payne, Paul Sutton, and Tony Thorndike, *Grenada: Revolution and Invasion* (London: Croom Helm; and New York: St. Martin's, 1984), esp. chap. 7.

14. The purpose of the RSS is set out in detail in Headquarters Staff, Regional Security System, "The Roles of the Regional Security System in the East Caribbean," *Bulletin of Eastern Caribbean Affairs* 11, no. 6 (1986): 5–7.

15. Interview with Gary Brana-Shute, "An Eastern Caribbean Centrist," *Caribbean Review* 4, no. 4 (1985): 28.

16. This was reported in U.S. House of Representatives, Committee on Foreign Affairs, Subcommittee on Western Hemisphere Affairs, *The English-Speaking Caribbean: Current Conditions and Implications for U.S. Policy*, 99th Cong. 1st sess. 13 September 1985.

17. See, in particular, the study by Humberto García Muñiz, *Boots, Boots, Boots: Intervention, Regional Security and Militarization in the Caribbean, 1979–1986* (Río Piedras: Caribbean Project for Justice and Peace, 1986).

18. See Humberto García Muñiz, "Defense Policy and Planning in the Caribbean: An Assessment of Jamaica on its 25th Independence Anniversary," *Journal of Commonwealth and Comparative Politics* 27, no. 1 (1988): 74–102.

19. These issues are set out in Anthony Payne, *The International Crisis in the Caribbean* (Baltimore: Johns Hopkins University Press, 1984), chap. 7; and Andrés Serbin, *¿El Caribe: Zona de Paz?* (Caracas: Comisión Sudamericana de Paz/Editorial Nueva Sociedad, 1989).

20. The foregoing figures are from Humberto García Muñiz, *La Estrategia de Estados Unidos y la Militarización del Caribe*, Monograph 16 (San Juan: Instituto de Estudios del Caribe, Universidad de Puerto Rico, 1988), chap. 8.

21. Humberto García-Muñiz, *Decolonization, Demilitarization and Denuclearization in the Caribbean*, Occasional Paper, Dialogue 131 (Miami: Latin American and Caribbean Center, Florida International University, 1989).

22. Rodríguez Beruff, *Política Militar y Dominación*, 240.

23. All figures are drawn from Robert Pastor, "Caribbean Emigration and U.S. Immigration Policy," in Jorge Heine and Leslie Manigat, eds., *The Caribbean and World Politics: Cross Currents and Cleavages* (New York: Holmes & Meier, 1988); and Christopher Mitchell, "From Policy Frontier to Policy Dilemmas: The United States and Caribbean Migration, 1960–1990," paper prepared for the Conference on Alternatives for the 1990s Caribbean, University of London, January 1991.

24. See, for example, the arguments in Georges Fauriol, "Social and Economic Challenges to Hemispheric Security," in Georges Fauriol, ed., *Security in the Americas* (Washington D.C.: National Defense University Press, 1989).

25. A useful review of U.S. policy at the time is Bruce M. Bagley, "The New Hundred Years War? U.S. National Security and the War on Drugs in Latin America," *Journal of Interamerican Studies and World Affairs* 30, no. 1 (1988): 161–82.

26. The figures are from Ann B. Wrobleski, "Global Narcotics Cooperation and Presidential Certification," *Current Policy*, no. 1165 (Washington, D.C.: Bureau of Public Affairs, U.S. Department of State, 1989).

27. See James E. Meason, "War at Sea: Drug Interdiction in the Caribbean," *Journal of Defense and Diplomacy* (June 1988): 7–13.

28. The argument has been put forward by Raphael Perl, an expert on the illicit drug trade and a senior employee of the Congressional Research Service, in his "United States Drug Policy: Recent Developments and Issues," *Journal of Interamerican Studies and World Affairs* 32, no. 4 (1990): 123–35.

29. The Presidential Commission on Organized Crime estimates that some US$5–15 billion in illegal drug money passed each year through the offshore banking centers in the Caribbean in the early 1980s.

30. *Caribbean Insight* (London), September 1990.

31. See, in particular, Anthony Maingot, "The State of Florida and the Caribbean," in Heine and Manigat, *The Caribbean and World Politics*; and Anthony Maingot, "Laundering the Gains of the Drug Trade: Miami and Caribbean Tax Havens," *Journal of Interamerican Studies and World Affairs* 30, no. 2–3 (1988): 166–87.

32. John Weeks and Phil Gunson, *Panama: Made in the USA* (London: Latin America Bureau, 1991).

33. W. Queiser Morales, "The War on Drugs: A New National Security Doctrine?" *Third World Quarterly* 11, no. 3 (1989): 147–69.

34. Paul F. Gorman, "Defining a Long-Term US Strategy for the Caribbean Region," in Fauriol, *Security in the Americas*.

35. Speech before the Royal Commonwealth Society, London, 9 December 1983.

# Select Bibliography

Ambursley, F., and R. Cohen, eds. *Crisis in the Caribbean.* London: Heinemann, 1983.

Anderson, T., *Geopolitics of the Caribbean: Ministates in a Wider World.* New York: Praeger, 1984.

Azicri, M. *Cuba: Politics, Economics and Society.* London: Frances Pinter, 1988.

Baber, C., and H. B. Jeffrey. *Guyana: Politics, Economics and Society.* London: Frances Pinter, 1986.

Barry, T., B. Wood, and D. Preusch. *The Other Side of Paradise: Foreign Control in the Caribbean.* New York: Grove, 1984.

Beckford, G. L., ed. *Caribbean Economy: Dependence and Backwardness.* Kingston: Institute of Social and Economic Research, University of the West Indies, 1975.

Black, J. K. *The Dominican Republic: Politics and Development in an Unsovereign State.* Boston: Allen & Unwin, 1986.

Braveboy-Wagner, J. A. *The Caribbean in World Affairs: The Foreign Policies of the English-Speaking States.* Boulder: Westview, 1988.

Brundenius, C. *Revolutionary Cuba: The Challenge of Growth with Equity.* Boulder: Westview, 1984.

Bryan, A., J. E. Greene, and T. M. Shaw, eds. *Peace, Development and Security in the Caribbean.* London: Macmillan, 1990.

Calvert, P., ed. *The Central American Security System: North-South or East-West?* Cambridge: Cambridge University Press, 1988.

Carr, R. *Puerto Rico: A Colonial Experiment.* New York: New York University Press, 1984.

Chin, H. E., and H. Buddingh'. *Surinam: Politics, Economics and Society.* London: Frances Pinter, 1987.

Deere, C. D., et. al. *In the Shadows of the Sun: Caribbean Development Alternatives and U.S. Policy.* Boulder: Westview, 1990.

Domínguez, J. I. *To Make a World Safe for Revolution: Cuba's Foreign Policy.* Cambridge: Harvard University Press, 1989.

————, ed. *Cuba: Internal and International Affairs*. Beverly Hills: Sage, 1982.

Domínguez, J. I., and R. Hernández, eds. *U.S.-Cuban Relations in the 1990s*. Boulder: Westview, 1989.

Dupuy, A. *Haiti in the World Economy: Class, Race, and Underdevelopment since 1700*. Boulder: Westview, 1989.

Erisman, H. M., ed. *The Caribbean Challenge: US Policy in a Volatile Region*. Boulder: Westview, 1984.

————. *Cuba's International Relations: The Anatomy of a Nationalistic Foreign Policy*. Boulder: Westview, 1985.

Ferguson, J. *Papa Doc, Baby Doc: Haiti and the Duvaliers*. Oxford: Basil Blackwell, 1987.

————. *Grenada: Revolution in Reverse*. London: Latin America Bureau, 1990.

García-Muñiz, H. *Boots, Boots, Boots: Intervention, Regional Security and Militarisation in the Caribbean 1979–86*. Río Piedras: Caribbean Project for Justice and Peace, 1986.

Gunson, P., G. Chamberlain, and A. Thompson. *The Dictionary of Contemporary Politics of Central America and the Caribbean*. London: Routledge, 1991.

Heine, J., ed. *A Revolution Aborted: The Lessons of Grenada*. Pittsburgh: University of Pittsburgh Press, 1990.

Heine, J., and L. Manigat, eds. *The Caribbean and World Politics: Cross Currents and Cleavages*. New York: Holmes & Meier, 1988.

Henry, P., and C. Stone, eds. *The Newer Caribbean: Decolonisation, Democracy and Development*. Philadelphia: Institute for the Study of Human Issues, 1983.

Hintzen, P. *The Costs of Regime Survival: Racial Mobilization, Ethnic Domination, and Control of the State in Guyana and Trinidad*. Cambridge: Cambridge University Press, 1989.

Kaufman, M. *Jamaica under Manley: Dilemmas of Socialism and Democracy*. London: Zed Books, 1985.

Knight, F. W., and C. A. Palmer, *The Modern Caribbean*. Chapel Hill: University of North Carolina Press, 1989.

Langley, L. *The United States and the Caribbean in the Twentieth Century*. Athens: University of Georgia Press, 1980.

Levine, B., ed. *The New Cuban Presence in the Caribbean*. Boulder: Westview, 1983.

Lewis, G. K. *The Growth of the Modern West Indies*. New York: Monthly Review Press, 1963.

————. *Grenada: The Jewel Despoiled*. Baltimore: Johns Hopkins University Press, 1987.

Mandle, J. *Patterns of Caribbean Development: An Interpretative Essay on Economic Change*. New York: Gordon & Breach, 1982.

————. *Big Revolution, Small Country: The Rise and Fall of the Grenada Revolution*. Lanham: North-South, 1985.

Manley, M. *Jamaica: Struggle in the Periphery*. London: Third World Media, 1982.

Martin, J. B. *United States Policy in the Caribbean*. Boulder: Westview, 1982.

Mintz, S. W., and S. Price, eds. *Caribbean Contours*. Baltimore: Johns Hopkins University Press, 1985.

Nicholls, D. *From Dessalines to Duvalier: Race, Colour and National Independence in Haiti*. London: Macmillan, 1988.

Pastor, R. A., ed. *Migration and Development in the Caribbean: The Unexplored Connection*. Boulder: Westview, 1985.

Payne, A. J. *The Politics of the Caribbean Community 1961–79: Regional Integration amongst New States*. Manchester: Manchester University Press, 1980.

——. *The International Crisis in the Caribbean*. Baltimore: Johns Hopkins University Press, 1984.

——. *Politics in Jamaica*. London: Christopher Hurst; and New York: St. Martin's, 1988.

Payne, A. J., and P. K. Sutton, eds. *Dependency under Challenge: The Political Economy of the Commonwealth Caribbean*. Manchester: Manchester University Press, 1984.

Payne, A. J., P. K. Sutton, and T. Thorndike. *Grenada: Revolution and Invasion*. London: Croom Helm; and New York: St. Martin's, 1984.

Pearce, J. *Under the Eagle: US Intervention in Central America and the Caribbean*. London: Latin America Bureau, 1981.

Ramsaran, R. *The Commonwealth Caribbean in the World Economy*. London: Macmillan, 1989.

Ronfeldt, D. *Geopolitics, Security and U.S. Strategy in the Caribbean Basin*. Santa Monica: Rand, 1983.

Ryan, S. D., ed. *Trinidad and Tobago: The Independence Experience 1962–87*. St. Augustine: Institute of Social and Economic Research, University of the West Indies, 1988.

Schoultz, L. *National Security and United States Policy toward Latin America*. Princeton: Princeton University Press, 1987.

Searle, C., ed. *In Nobody's Backyard: Maurice Bishop's Speeches 1979–83*. London: Zed Books, 1984.

Serbin, A. *Caribbean Geopolitics: Toward Security through Peace*. Boulder: Lynne Rienner, 1990.

Shearman, P. *The Soviet Union and Cuba*. London: Routledge and Kegan Paul for the Royal Institute of International Affairs, 1987.

Stephens, E. H., and J. D. Stephens, *Democratic Socialism in Jamaica: The Political Movement and Social Transformation in Dependent Capitalism*. London: Macmillan, 1986.

Stone, C. *Democracy and Clientelism in Jamaica*. New Brunswick: Transaction, 1980.

——. *Power in the Caribbean Basin: A Comparative Study of Political Economy*. Philadelphia: Institute for the Study of Human Issues, 1986.

Sunshine, C. A. *The Caribbean: Survival, Struggle and Sovereignty.* Washington D.C.: EPICA, 1985.

Sutton, P. K., ed., *Forged from the Love of Liberty: Selected Speeches of Dr Eric Williams.* Port of Spain: Longmans, 1981.

——. *Dual Legacies in the Contemporary Caribbean: Continuing Aspects of British and French Dominion.* London: Frank Cass, 1986.

——. *Europe in the Caribbean.* London: Macmillan, 1991.

Thomas, C. Y. *The Poor and the Powerless: Economic Policy and Change in the Caribbean.* London: Latin America Bureau, 1988.

Thompson, R. *Green Gold: Bananas and Dependency in the Eastern Caribbean.* London: Latin America Bureau, 1987.

Thorndike, T. *Grenada: Politics, Economics and Society.* London: Frances Pinter; and Boulder: Lynne Rienner, 1985.

Wilentz, A. *The Rainy Season: Haiti since Duvalier.* London: Jonathan Cape, 1989.

Williams, E. *From Columbus to Castro: The History of the Caribbean 1492–1969.* London: André Deutsch, 1970.

Worrell, D. *Small Island Economies: Structures and Performance in the English-speaking Caribbean since 1970.* London: Praeger, 1988.

Young, A., and D. E. Phillips, eds. *Militarization in the Non-Hispanic Caribbean.* Boulder: Lynne Rienner, 1986.

Zimbalist, A., ed. *Cuban Political Economy: Controversies in Cubanology.* Boulder: Westview, 1988.

# Contributors

ANTHONY PAYNE is Senior Lecturer in Politics and Director of the Graduate Programme in International Studies at the University of Sheffield in England. He has also been a Research Associate of the International Institute of Strategic Studies in London. He has written several books on the politics, political economy, and international relations of the Caribbean, most recently *Politics in Jamaica* (1988). He has served as a specialist adviser to the Foreign Affairs Committee of the British House of Commons and acted as a consultant to the West Indian Commission.

PAUL SUTTON is Senior Lecturer in Politics at the University of Hull in England. He was also formerly the Director of the Centre of Developing Area Studies at Hull and a Research Associate of the International Institute of Strategic Studies in London. His main research interests are in the politics and international relations of the Caribbean, and he has acted as a consultant to several organizations, including the West Indian Commission. He has published a number of books on the area, most recently *Europe and the Caribbean* (1991).

JAN KNIPPERS BLACK is Professor of International Policy Studies at the Monterey Institute of International Studies. She has published widely on Latin American and Caribbean affairs and has had for many years a particular interest in the development of the Dominican Republic.

JAMES FERGUSON is a writer and researcher with the Latin America Bureau in London. He was formerly a research fellow at St. Edmund Hall, Oxford. He is a specialist on Haitian affairs and has published a substantial work on the politics of that country.

RALPH R. PREMDAS is Senior Lecturer in Government at the University of the West Indies in Trinidad. He is the author of a number of studies of

Guyana and is a specialist in the political problems of ethnically divided states in the Caribbean and the South Pacific.

PETER MEEL is Lecturer in Caribbean Studies at the Royal Institute of Linguistics and Anthropology in Leiden in the Netherlands. His research has focused upon Suriname, on which he has published several important articles and papers.

TONY THORNDIKE is Professor of International Relations at Staffordshire Polytechnic in England. He has published extensively on the politics and international relations of the Eastern Caribbean and has written the standard work on the modern politics of Grenada.

COURTNEY SMITH is a graduate of the University of the West Indies in Jamaica and the University of Hull in England. He has written a major study of the Grenada revolution and is now employed as a research officer with the British government.

JORGE HEINE is Senior Research Fellow at the Centro Latinoamericano de Economía y Política Internacional (CLEPI) in Santiago, Chile. He has authored, separately and with Juan M. García-Passalacqua, a number of studies on Puerto Rico and other parts of the Caribbean.

JUAN M. GARCÍA-PASSALACQUA is President of Analysis Inc. in San Juan, Puerto Rico. He has authored, separately and with Jorge Heine, a number of studies on Puerto Rico and other parts of the Caribbean.

H. MICHAEL ERISMAN is Chairman of the Department of Political Science at Indiana State University. He has published a major study of Cuban foreign policy and is the author of a number of works dealing with the international relations of the Caribbean basin.

RAMESH F. RAMSARAN is Senior Lecturer in the Institute of International Relations, University of the West Indies, Trinidad. He has published several studies on the economics of the Caribbean and has served as a consultant to the ACP Secretariat in Brussels and the World Bank.

ANTHONY P. MAINGOT is Professor of Sociology at the Florida International University in Miami and the editor of the magazine *Hemisphere*. He has written widely on the political sociology of the Caribbean and is a former President of the Caribbean Studies Association.